Soviet and East European Studies

THE PREDICTION OF COMMUNIST
ECONOMIC PERFORMANCE

Soviet and East European Studies

EDITORIAL BOARD

The National Association for Soviet and East European Studies exists for the purpose of promoting study and research on the social sciences as they relate to the Soviet Union and the countries of Eastern Europe. The Monograph Series is intended to promote the publication of works presenting substantial and original research in the economics, politics, sociology and modern history of the USSR and Eastern Europe.

FIRST BOOKS IN THE SERIES

A. Boltho, *Foreign Trade Criteria in Socialist Economies*
Sheila Fitzpatrick, *The Commissariat of Enlightenment*
Donald Male, *Russian Peasant Organisation before Collectivisation*
P. Wiles, ed., *The Prediction of Communist Economic Performance*

THE PREDICTION OF COMMUNIST ECONOMIC PERFORMANCE

Edited by

P. J. D. WILES

Professor of Russian
Social and Economic Studies
at London University

CAMBRIDGE

AT THE UNIVERSITY PRESS

1971

Published by the Syndics of the Cambridge University Press
Bentley House, 200 Euston Road, London N.W.1
American Branch: 32 East 57th Street, New York, N.Y.10022

© This collection Cambridge University Press 1971

Library of Congress Catalogue Card Number: 75-123677

ISBN: 0 521 07885 7

Printed in Great Britain
at the University Press, Aberdeen

CONTENTS

PREFACE

This project owes its birth to the imaginative encouragement of Bertrand de Jouvenel, who published the pieces dated '1967' in the table of contents in French in *Analyse et Prévision*, November 1967. There was also a too-little-bought special English edition. I am grateful to *Analyse et Prévision* for permission to reprint these early pieces, and to the contributors for their patience throughout the many delays which have dogged the publication of the completed volume. The nature of this volume is described in section 1 of the Introduction.

PETER WILES

March 1970

... when the number of exogenous variables in a forecast exceeds a certain limit, then the results are more dependent on the character and heroism of the forecaster than an objective presentation of determinants of future development.

ZDENÉK VERGNER

CONTRIBUTORS

ALAN A. BROWN
Visiting Professor of Economics, Indiana University

MICHAEL GAMARNIKOW
Senior Research Fellow at the Research Institute for Communist Affairs, Columbia University, New York

EVERETT M. JACOBS
Lecturer in Economic History, University of Sheffield

MICHAEL KASER
Fellow of St Antony's College, and Faculty Lecturer in Soviet Economics, in the University of Oxford

W. KLATT, O.B.E.
Fellow of St Antony's College, Oxford

GERT LEPTIN
Professor, Free University of Berlin

BOGDAN MIECZKOWSKI
Professor of Economics, Ithaca College, New York

HARUKI NIWA
Associate Professor, Kwansei Gakuin University, Hyogo-Ken, Japan

BORIS PESEK
Professor of Economics, University of Wisconsin-Milwaukee

R. D. PORTES
Assistant Professor of Economics and International Affairs, Princeton University

HORST SEIDLER
Head of Department, Deutsches Institut für Wirtschaftsforschung, Berlin

FRANCIS SETON
Fellow of Nuffield College and Lecturer in Economics in the University of Oxford

ix

PETER J. D. WILES
Professor of Russian Social and Economic Studies, London University

ALEXEJ WYNNYCZUK
Professor of Economics, Rensselaer Polytechnic Institute, Troy, New York

1

INTRODUCTION

(updated to 1970)

PETER WILES

(1) The general belief of the contributors to this symposium is that Sovietological economics has come of age, or that at least we can help it to do so. From the stage of craftsmanship and chronicling it must dare to become a science, i.e. to predict. There will of course be gross errors, but perhaps no grosser than in other social sciences; and it is better to make, and later to analyse, these errors than to do nothing. Such predictions will cover the manner in which the economy functions as well as the performance it attains. The essence of a good prophet is to recognize his own fallibility and to improve his own methods; for this reason our intention was to exercise *samokritika*, each on his own effort. This we have done here, though at a longer interval of time than we intended. Also the original articles are reprinted, and guest critics have contributed as well.

A hasty reader might complain of the inclusion of apparently obsolete pieces: this is 1970, yet here are pieces, written in 1967, incorrectly predicting 1970. Could they not have been updated, nay scrapped? The answer is that prediction is in its infancy: this volume is essentially methodological, and all other information is a mere by-product. To improve prediction we must study predictions, and that means ploughing through a lot of obsolete material. To permit one's past errors to be reprinted without change is an act of courage, for which the original contributors must be thanked. Everything dated '1967' is unchanged except for misprints and errors irrelevant to the predictions then made.

(2) In what follows, however, the editor speaks for himself alone. It has been my policy to 'let 100 schools of thought contend'. The most successful methods will emerge when the results are in; but the trend towards more sophisticated methods is probably inevitable, with whatever success they are attended.

2 PETER WILES

It shocks me that my own attempt should be the second most technically sophisticated, but it is reassuring that the attempt should be so thoroughly inconclusive.

I have, however, tried to extract predictions in a set of common minimum categories from each participant: this Procrustean table will be found at the end of the book. Meanwhile we concentrate on the Communist economies which make the most statistics available. Such economies present different and perhaps fewer problems of prediction than others. The Western econometric model has at least two advantages: it can assume constant institutions and base itself on a larger ration of crucial statistics, notably those of the balance of payments. But if the model is used at all for predictions they are essentially and inevitably based on an impossible *ceteris paribus* clause: this is what will happen if government policies and parameters remain as they are. Now of course this assumption is false. The mere publication of the prediction may well change the government's behaviour, but in any case it is subject to other, very unpredictable, influences. Will it be over- or under-sensitive to the next balance of payments crisis? will it dare to tax as much as it should? or 95% as much? History shows very few regularities indeed in this area, and still fewer in the wholly exogenous factors such as diplomatic crises and changes of the party in power.

It is therefore no reproach to the Western econometrician that his model cannot predict; its function is to enable the government to *falsify* its predictions in the most desirable and economical way. The essential missing element in Western prediction belongs to political economy, not econometrics: how will the Cabinet react to the predictions it receives, and to the crises, economic and non-economic, that will inevitably crop up? How indeed will the government itself change?

We too have to say what the Cabinet, or rather Politburo, will do. But in our case the government *is* the economy;[1] its behaviour must be definitively predicted; there is here no such thing as a self-generating, *ceteris paribus* model. However the

[1] Except in Yugoslavia, and possibly soon in Czechoslovakia. If the professions of some of its leaders are to be taken seriously (1967), Czechoslovakia will become a Yugoslavia without workers' councils, and we shall here too have to deal with a separate government presiding over enterprises whose autonomous interactions with each other can be described by a Western model.

government itself is rather more stable, and so are its policies. This statement is of course to be understood *mutatis mutandis*; for 'general election' read 'fall of Khrushchev', etc. Moreover we have one precious new source of information: the *binding medium-range plan.*

(3) The medium-range plan is by far the most important basis of Sovietological prediction, since it is binding not merely on the enterprise but even largely on the government. But surprisingly often there is something wrong with it: it is unpublished (the DDR); it is published only on broad lines (Rumania); it is not officially confirmed (USSR); it has been thrown into doubt by subsequent events (Czechoslovakia); it probably doesn't exist (China). But granted its existence, availability and legal confirmation we still face two main questions: is it realistic, and will it be changed?

On the question of the plan's realism there is need of something approaching Western econometrical work. There is, to be sure, no multiplier or accelerator; adequate demand is more or less guaranteed, and inflation though often present has little effect on production.

Mr Niwa, who however is not engaged in testing the plan's realism, has no demand or monetary equations. At macro-level he is surely right. Increasing use of market research at micro-level does not affect this. Only in the very decentralized Hungarian economy can we begin to speak of uncontrolled movements in macro-demand, as Mr Portes shows. Much as in, say, Britain these are preponderantly of a curious character: enterprises speculate on what the government is about to do. East and West, this is an element deserving much more attention from econometricians.

But many of the same economic laws continue to govern supply. Returns diminish in agriculture and mining, the terms of trade behave in the normal way, the potential labour force is demographically determined, resources remain scarce and products have opportunity costs. Above all the harvest, and harvest-related manufacturing output, remain as great a cloud in the crystal ball as ever.

Much of the work here presented is, then, a check on the physical feasibility of medium-term plans. But will not these medium term plans be altered? I assume for a start that fifteen-year or perspective plans are hardly worth the paper they are written on. Or, as M. Fraisse puts it so delicately:[1] 'It is difficult to decide in what degree this first twenty-year plan was an effective framework for the five-year plans, if only because the credit it enjoyed with the Soviet government was so transitory.' Published in 1961, this particular long-term plan was intimately connected with Khrushchev's new Party Programme. Both documents fell with their patron. If five-year plans (FYPs) are said to be deduced from them this is a mere pretence; they are too vague and too often changed univocally to determine a FYP. It is upon the stability of the FYP itself that everything depends.

At the very worst the useful tautology holds that a FYP is binding until altered. Therefore if it is coherent and feasible it will be fulfilled if it is not altered; and if we find that it is not we automatically predict that it will be altered. However it may also be altered in any case, for some exogenous cause such as a new government or a diplomatic crisis.

These exogenous causes are of course no easier to predict than in any other case, and we are on a par with all other specialists in being forced explicitly to assume them away. But we should perhaps be willing to predict the government's reaction to 'endogenous' troubles: those due to excessive ambition in the plan, to adverse movements in the terms of trade brought about by the plan, etc. In the absence of speculation and hot money flows the mere size, if not the number, of such crises is much smaller than under capitalism, and the government's reaction has hitherto been fairly standardized: e.g. cut collective consumption expenditure, raise work norms and compulsory farm deliveries.

(4) As to the technique of checking a FYP's consistency, one is ideally building up an input/output table for the end year and seeing if it coheres. I had hoped to present, in 1968, such a table for USSR. But unfortunately its compiler continues to hit snags. It is an honour, instead, to present Mr Niwa's much more Western type of econometrics. Since, however, he mainly concerns himself with Cobb–Douglas functions and with labour flows, he may be said to be virtually constructing an input/output matrix, albeit with extremely few rows and columns, and rectangular not square.

[1] *Analyse et Prévision* 4/1968, p. 275.

I present also my own perplexities on the appropriate values of Cobb–Douglas exponents in countries with a surplus agricultural labour force. But these are not the only perplexities in regard to these exponents.

For instance Mr Niwa tells me that during the evolution of his model he has switched in the course of time from a linear to a non-linear function for agricultural output (cf. p. 346), in view of the failure of agriculture to grow in the 'sixties. This switch is a most severe implicit self-criticism. Econometrics is nothing but more or less sophisticated extrapolation; it is helpless before the possibility that the future will not resemble the past. Mr Niwa had no other reason than this non-resemblance for making his switch. My own assumption merely appears to be more sophisticated: the Cobb–Douglas residual of past years in agriculture is a guide to the residual of future years. It is also regrettable that Mr Niwa has no separate series in his equation 19 for the vastly important current inputs of industry into agriculture, like petrol and mineral fertilizers. Too often in this type of work we either omit these inputs altogether – though they are of vast importance, reaching in many countries 50% of gross agricultural output – or assimilate them, falsely, to capital. It is incorrect, too, simply to subtract them from gross output to obtain a net figure, and relate such a net output to capital, land and labour. For these inputs have a marginal productivity of their own, which must be judged like any other, by the same statistical techniques.

Mr Niwa's industrial function, by the way, has extremely different exponents from those of the Soviet authors I quote (chap. 26): about 0·3 for capital instead of about 0·9. It will be observed that his industrial residual (equation 5) is negative; it would have been much more negative had he used Soviet weights. Although his weights differ extremely from mine, he also gets a negative agricultural residual, in his equation 6.

(5) But setting ideal methodologies aside, it is much more important, in the present state of our knowledge, to know *the essential points at which the plan works badly in practice*. It seems, according to the experience of many but not all countries, that:

(i) The agricultural exodus is under-estimated. For the planners cannot screw themselves up to spending so much money on urban housing; and labour turnover is greater than it should be by Marxist criteria; and there is not enough capital to provide urban work for everyone who asks for it.

(ii) So the growth of agricultural productivity is under-estimated, and that of urban, especially industrial, productivity over-estimated.

(iii) These two points do not only concern countries that ought to have agricultural exoduses. Such advanced countries as Czechoslovakia and the DDR continue to have, and to under-estimate, such exoduses; with consequent aging and labour shortage in agriculture. Hungary is entering this condition, though her current plan seems to have been correctly estimated (see Mr Portes's contribution below).

(iv) The actual completions of investment projects, especially in the domain of construction, are over-estimated in both number and punctuality. This is indeed an issue of enormous significance for Communism. 'Investment scatter' and 'funds frozen in half-finished projects' have indeed their parallels under capitalism, but are far less important.

(v) Exports, especially those to advanced capitalist countries, are over-estimated; so imports have to be cut.

(vi) On a somewhat different plane, Mr Kyril Fitzlyon[1] has shown that plans for large aggregates like the national income or industrial production are better fulfilled than plans for small aggregates like tractor output. This is one of those extremely valuable and practical propositions that turn out to be tauto-logies. But they are none the worse for that. The intuitively obvious can be rigorously demonstrated, even without algebra, as follows. We restate the proposition thus: *bad predictions are commoner among small categories than among the large ones of which they are parts, provided that the parts are exhaustively enumerated.* Then the error of the prediction of the large category is simply the weighted average of the errors of the predictions of its sub-categories. But for the first error to be equal to the largest of the other errors it would be necessary that all the other errors be of equal magnitude and sign. This is the limiting case: in all others at least one sub-category has a greater error than the total, and in most cases more than one. So bad predictions are commoner among sub-categories.[2]

---

[1] In *Soviet Studies*, October 1969. [2] See footnote opposite page.

(vii) A plan can be changed once confirmed, and this may even happen secretly.[1] It is certainly part of our job to detect such changes, though we can hardly be expected to predict the plans themselves!

In all this discussion of non-fulfilment and unpredictability I have avoided the suggestion that any Soviet-type fluctuations are *cyclical*. Not all contributors are quite so hostile to this notion as this. I understand by cyclical something endogenous, arising directly from the interactions of the economy; and agree that under central planning the normal behaviour of the government must be included in the endogenous interactions. I am simply unable to observe any repetitive pattern in any Communist country at any time, that might have resulted from such interactions.

(6) It will be noted that some contributors have used official Communist statistics where they are most easily challenged: the gross or global[2] output indices of agriculture and industry. There can be little harm in this over short periods: in a settled Communist economy net and global growth do not greatly differ. But where net figures are available they are supplied in the summary table at the end. It is again unlikely that, in a settled Communist economy, differences in weighting will be important over five years. A much more serious problem is the absence of statistics in China, and their suspect nature in Rumania and Albania (qq.v.). If Mr Kaser's confidence in these figures is very moderate, mine is still more so. Rumania and Albania have never been checked as thoroughly as the other countries treated here.

Another problem has greatly exercised us: the valuation of sophisticated defence durables. Dr Klatt estimates China's nuclear effort at about 1 % of the national income since research

---

[2] It is therefore not surprising that the same pattern of errors shows itself in French planning. But it is surprising that the errors, over a five-year period, are the same in France and USSR (except for Soviet agriculture) – Wasserman and Wiles in *Economica*, 1970.

[1] Cases are even reported where a plan is announced as fulfilled by such-and-such percentages in such-and-such categories, so that one is tempted to infer the actual achievement from the original plan; but meanwhile there have been secret changes, and reference is being made to another set of targets.

[2] 'Global' is Mr Kaser's surely less misleading translation of Russian *valovoi* – not to mention Polish *globalni!*

began, *at factor cost*. A market price valuation however would show a much larger sum, considering the value to China on the world stage of possessing even rudimentary nuclear weapons. One of the principal failures of economic measurement is the absence of a reasonable 'market price' for advanced weapons. Any country that develops them has a higher rate of growth than orthodox methods imply. This goes, of course, for France, USA and USSR as well. In addition the space-race has been valued at factor cost. Nay more, in a very general way all sorts of goods and services are valued at factor cost; so presumably undervalued; and this sets up an important bias against the most developed countries.

(7) The inspirer of this effort, Bertrand de Jouvenel, expressed the hope that contributors would give utterance on general social changes as well. Being an economist, and exacting contributions from other economists, I am bound to disappoint him. But at least we can speculate on the effects of general social changes on economic performance. Such change will be greatest where new models are most radically different: Czechoslovakia on the one hand and China on the other. (*The passage that follows, embodying as it does some predictions, has not been changed since 1967.*)

I lift one view of the effect of the new Czechoslovak model from Professor Pesek:[1]

whether the new model will succeed in bringing significantly more rational allocations is, I believe, one of the most fascinating economic issues of this decade. Much depends on the political leadership in Eastern Europe. Will it be able to override the resistance that is now forming among the high echelons of the civil service who see both their ideological orthodoxy and their jobs in danger? Will the leadership be able to withstand the heat generated by the enraged public which, at first, will face only the sacrifices but not the rewards? Much depends also on the economy itself: how fast will a price system be able to bear fruit? If the fruits come fast, the conservative element in the upper civil service will be discredited and popular resistance weaken and possibly be converted into support. Thus, absurdly enough, the only hope of the new economic model is that those Western economists who believe the price system to be a slow and ponderous machinery be proven wrong and those – like Milton Friedman – who believe that the

[1] In another piece, presented to a conference at Berkeley, 28–9 December 1966.

price system is one of the most sensitive instruments ever devised by man be proven right. The West German upsurge following the monetary reform and restoration of the market economy in the middle of 1948 gave to the believers in inherent flexibility of the market-directed economy the first round; we shall all wait most anxiously, I am sure, to see who will win the no less important second round about to start in Eastern Europe.

This is also the view of the resident revisionist radicals. They – and Professor Pesek – add that managers with better commercial education must be installed, and that competition will improve performance at all levels. At present

highly educated people receive less than the average workers; the workers themselves face what is called 'wage ceilings' so that each worker makes sure that he does not exceed 'permissible' output and the management welcomes this 'self-discipline' of its labor force. The press speaks about the conspiracy of mediocrity. Equality of incomes – with departures in the wrong directions – and almost absolute job security is the order of the day. The new economic model is explicitly designed to change all this ... Obviously, the reintroduction of the labor market, denivelization, the reintroduction of income inequalities, and the firing of some workers promise to be an infinitely painful process in a nation in which it became customary to pay irrespective of merit, importance, and quality of work but by the number of children and which became accustomed to almost absolute job security from enterprises viewed as social security institutions.

In a similar vein Dr Seton (in private correspondence) will not include the diminution of planner's tension in USSR as an offset to the increased allocative efficiency of the new model there.

The alternative view must be the editor's own. The claim of greater managerial efficiency must be conceded. Even if this greater efficiency is in part applied to monopolistic restriction (which is what lowered planner's tension permits), surely it will promote both allocative rationality and technical progress. But I do not concede that workers will work more for an economically trained manager than for a terroristic state. Quite the contrary: bonuses out of 20% of profit work out at ludicrous sums per head, and the principal differences will be enhanced trade union activity and lowered labour discipline.

Cost inflation, and an actually lowered will to work, are the order of the day. Balance of payments crises are thus more likely. But while the command economy had excellent means of isolating the effects of such crises, the new regulated market economy must operate through more general, and therefore more deflationary, counter-measures.

Will investment funds be wasted, and especially by spreading them around in small packets, more or less than in the past? It is difficult to be sure. The more rational and critical atmosphere makes it less likely; the relaxation of social discipline and central authority, more. The Yugoslav example is not encouraging either in this matter or in that of cost inflation.

In sum, the West German *Wirtschaftswunder*, to which Professor Pesek refers, came about through the substitution of a market economy and a stable currency for a non-economy and a cigarette currency. The case is therefore not parallel. It remains to be seen whether Friedman or Stalin was the better economist (outside agriculture).

Thus I am pessimistic about the new Czechoslovak model, whether or not it is successfully enforced, while Pesek is only pessimistic about its being enforced. On the new Chinese model, however, we are doubtless both at one with Dr Klatt. Rule by some state, even direct rule by a Communist Party as in China under Liu Shao-chih, is better than anarchy. Demonstrations cut into working time; managers *must* be 'Expert', whether or not they are 'Red'. Beyond doubt the new Maoist anarchy has accentuated the already very strong features of market socialism in China; for in the absence of bureaucrats the Chinese central command economy has always been mostly talk. But command features, irrational allocations and sheer prejudice against education and efficiency will increase along with the restoration of the market in minor matters. Maoism, which reduces Communism to a state of mind, is almost a wilful rejection of economic progress.

2

THE PLANNING OF INDUSTRY

Comparative Analysis

ED. PETER WILES, 1969

In every country, even in Hungary and certainly in Czechoslovakia, the changes in methods of administration have been so gradual, or have gone in practice so short a way, that they could hardly affect our short-term predictions. It is not the actual change of model in Czechoslovakia, but political uncertainty and the absence of a definite plan, that have affected performance. The only exception is China (see below, p. 16). Had *agricultural* institutions been in a state of flux, the prediction of performance would no doubt have been affected more; for collectivization certainly lowers current output, and decollectivization probably raises it. But there has been curiously little recent change in agriculture. Notably, Czechoslovakia has not toyed with decollectivization.

Nevertheless it would have been to miss a great opportunity, with interest in institutions running so high, not to pester so distinguished a body of experts for comparative information. This paper, then, an expansion of 1967's, tries to systematize our knowledge of a very small part of the total field of organizational reform: the current operation of state industry. Since many write as if this were the whole field, it is worth while to specify what is excluded:

(i) changes in Marxist ideology;
(ii) changes in economic theory;
(iii) construction, and therefore also the actual expenditure by industry of its investment funds;
(iv) transport, agriculture (including state agriculture), shops and all services;
(v) private and co-operative crafts and industry;
(vi) personal taxation;
(vii) research and development; and probably
(viii) defence.

11

Within the chosen field the questions are divided as follows. Question 1 concerns the exact structure of the *planning hierarchy* – until recently the principal bone of contention in USSR, though not elsewhere. Note most particularly the role of the association or large firm. Where these have command powers over the actual enterprise but are themselves few in number nothing much has changed (e.g. Bulgaria). In a true market economy associations are weak and numerous, or non-existent.

Questions 2 and 3 ask to what extent *physical command* is still practised. Note that unless the Gossnab[1] or its equivalent is abolished there remains by definition physical command over inputs, and unless the *sortament*[2] indicators are abolished the same is true for outputs. The centrally supervised long-term contract between enterprises is less severe, but serves as a substantial brake on the market.

Questions 6 to 8 deal with the *disposition of the surplus*, both centralized and decentralized. Note that subsidies out of the budget are by no means the only ones: in the more centralized countries the association transfers a great deal of money from profitable to losing enterprises under its command (8d).

The remaining questions speak for themselves, except perhaps numbers 9(e) and 11. In the more decentralized systems, as in Yugoslavia, wages are paid out of 'enterprise income', which is more or less what we would call 'value added', a much more inclusive magnitude than gross profit. That is to say, the virtual government guarantee of wages falls away, and the principles of Khozraschet are greatly strengthened. The distinction between incentive payments out of the wages fund and incentive payments out of profit is obliterated, since there is no separate wages fund any more. The 'value added maximand' goes with workers' self-administration. It developed out of the latter, historically, in Yugoslavia. Both principles were accepted together for the new Czechoslovak model (question 9(e)). Their absence is the one blemish on the Hungarian record of liberalism. The presence of the first of them is the sole Bulgarian claim to liberalism.

As to planner's tension (question 11), this occurs when the enterprise's plan can be screwed tight, as an incentive to output

---

[1] The bureaucracy that distributes raw materials.
[2] The list of particular qualities and types that must be produced.

if not to efficiency. Tension is only possible if minimum output and maximum input orders are given. Physical command leads almost inevitably to tension, for it also appeals to the Bolshevik mentality. Market systems cannot generate it, though excess demand coupled with sticky prices comes close to planner's tension. Monetary commands too could easily cause genuine tension; the question is not, in what form are commands issued, but, are they issued?

We have concentrated, in answering these questions, not on what has been suggested in learned journals, nor even on what has been promised in Party resolutions, but on current practice, or at least – it is not the same thing – on current law (in Bulgaria the quoted Party theses are indeed current practice). It is by no means so easy to describe actuality as to précis an article or resolution; and we cannot pretend to exact knowledge or complete coverage. The consolation is that probably not more than a few officials in each country are much better informed – institutional information about how people do things lags far behind statistical information about how much people do.

Turning to the results, three general tendencies may be observed: conservative, radical and Chinese. The most conservative country is Rumania, which has hardly moved from the Stalinist system.

The next most conservative are the USSR, Poland and the DDR. Take first the question, how genuine is the market and how free is the enterprise? Each country has kept a Gossnab, a planned output *sortament* and central price control; each has put a brake upon market-like phenomena by stressing the 'association' – an intermediate body that was introduced long ago in Poland to be the creature of the enterprises composing it, but quickly became a mere link in the command hierarchy. Simultaneously, however, these countries have enhanced the status of profits as an indicator – though it remains far from being the only one – by permitting, under close restriction, greater retention at the enterprise. However there are also differences. With its uniquely gradualist approach the USSR has nevertheless set no bounds to her movement, and may yet go very far. The DDR seems wedded to the more rational centralization she has now achieved, and is indeed the most centralized country after Rumania.

Poland, the erstwhile pioneer, indecisive in this as in all things, wobbles between them. In this connexion Mr Mieczkowski writes:

The debate over the role of the market in the planned economy has recently become more acrimonious and seemingly more polarized. Its essence, though not its formal content, is political, as recognized openly by an economic weekly.[1] The 1956–57 discussion on the economic model helped to crystallize three views based on: (1) Primacy of the market, with a decentralization of all economic decision-making. This view, represented mainly by S. Kurowski, was put out of existence, chiefly by muzzling of its proponents. (2) Broadening of the scope of the law of value (through a semi-autonomous operation of the market), while guaranteeing the role of central planning in basic economic decisions, with a decentralization of other decisions. This view is represented chiefly by Wlodzimierz Brus, Tadeusz Kowalik and Ignacy Sachs. All three, but especially Brus, have come recently under vituperative attacks,[2] and have been either expelled form the Party or divested of at least some of their jobs.[3] It appears, therefore, that this view, at least temporarily, is also on the way out. (3) The final view is against broadening of the scope of the law of value, and against decentralization, while allowing for improvement within the framework of the existing, centralized system.[4] This hard-line view, supported additionally by a number of opportunists who have decided it safer to ride on the coat-tails of the Partisan group in its quest for political power, seems to have been left alone in the field, at least for the time being, and the ascendancy of the command system seems assured in the short run.

My own feeling is that in the long run, with the example of Yugoslavia, Czechoslovakia and Hungary, and under popular pressures at home, the hard line will have to be softened and some

[1] *Życie Gospodarcze* (Warsaw) 15/68, p. 5, states that '... the views of Prof. W. Brus have recently come under sharp political criticism'. [Mieczkowski's note.]

[2] Among others, *Trybuna Ludu* (Warsaw) 29 March 1968; *ibid.*, 23 April 1968; *Miesiecznik Literacki* 6/67; *Życie Gospodarcze* nos. 17, 18, 20, 21 and 23 (1968). [Mieczkowski's note.]

[3] *East Europe* 6/68, pp. 49 and 51. Brus, additionally, was listed as one of the editors of *Życie Gospodarcze* in the 17 March 1968 issue (no. 11), but not in issues starting with the one of 24 March (no. 12). In the classical Communist tradition, Brus obviously has not been allowed to make any rejoinder to the attacks on his views and himself. [Mieczkowski's note.]

[4] J. Glowczyk, 'The evolution of views concerning the system of administration and planning in Poland', Part 1, *Życie Gospodarcze* 15/68. [Mieczkowski's note.]

modicum of a market system will become acceptable and will be duly reconciled with Marxian orthodoxy.

After their invasion of Czechoslovakia the Polish authorities hardened their line against decentralization, as Mr Gamarnikow (writing after that event) shows. It is almost certain, reading between the lines, that anti-semitism plays a large part in Polish economic policy. Not only is their own Professor Brus a Jew, but so also is the occupied country's more important Ota Šik. The classic anti-semitic identification of the Jew with the small, grasping trader yields to the new, Communist anti-semitism: decentralization equals Zionism. This augurs ill for the market in Poland. The prospect is hardly less bad in Czechoslovakia, for the Russians also have attacked Šik strongly, though without incurring suspicion of anti-semitism. Moreover the new insistence on more trade within Comecon will mean more centralization, since such trade has always been a stumbling-block to the introduction of domestic markets.

But at the same time USSR is carrying forward its reforms unchecked,[1] and permitting or failing to prevent Hungary from doing the same with her much more radical notions.[2] For as our tables show it was Hungary, not Czechoslovakia, that had gone farthest before the invasion. The latter intended to go further, but had not in fact yet gone so far. Note in particular the weak and small 'associations' of Hungary, as opposed to the large and strong ones of Czechoslovakia. The proposals in the latter country for purely informational or 'French' type planning had not even begun to become reality. Perhaps however a future survey of this kind would have to add a question on the very nature, means and purpose of planning in each country.

Bulgaria lies between these extremes. Its very strong 'associations' are an ambiguous institution, that might behave either like immense oligopolists or like a collusive substitute for central planning. The smallness of the country enhances both these possibilities.

It has not been possible to get a China expert to answer the questionnaire! To call the Chinese economy Protean would be already to say too much: Proteus at least had a definite

---

[1] N. Baibakov (Chairman of Gosplan), *Pravda*, 1 October 1968.
[2] V. Zorza, *The Guardian*, 30 October 1968.

shape from moment to moment. Nevertheless there was an almost stable pattern up to 1967, when the Cultural Revolution finally penetrated the enterprise. This old pattern was also one of decentralization, but with a very different nuance, which one can without paradox call Khrushchevian. Power was devolved not to enterprise managers but to the local party cadres. These acted independently, neither according to the *letter* of detailed *state* instructions nor for *private profit*, but in the *spirit* of general *Party* instructions, for *social benefit*. The rudimentary state machine retained every right of direct intervention and physical command, but exercised them only *ad hoc*. Plans were drawn up by subordinates and ratified by intermediate superiors; their targets were in the form of ranges, and the intermediate superiors checked only perfunctorily with Pekin. If this seems very vague to French, Russian or Czechoslovak readers, it *is* vague. The anti-anarchic mind may however be partially reassured by the enhanced role of the central bank. In what is effectually a market of non-profit-maximizers the bank exercises a very orthodox restraining role: it curbs excess demand for total resources and also vetoes the most absurd particular schemes. Of the post-1967 system in China one would be ill advised to speak. The Party that provided the cadres, has been purged and crippled. It is not clear who runs the enterprise.

Albania seems not to be very Chinese in these matters. She has imitated only the mass, forcible mobilization of labour for special campaigns: both young labour for the new farms and bureaucratic labour to do manual tasks for its spiritual uplift. For the rest Albania, like Mongolia and North Korea, leans towards Soviet practice. On Cuba and North Vietnam I plead ignorance.

However in one extremely important respect China, Cuba and Albania are well known to resemble each other: they have played down, in the first two cases almost abolished, the *bonus* to labour and management, and in general their pay scales are far more *egalitarian*. That is to say, they take seriously the Marxian vision of a new man, who works for honour and social passion, not personal reward. It is precisely this that sets them aside from all other countries, and endears them to the new student left in capitalist countries. Even though all this can be said in one short paragraph it is still very crucial. The main cleft in the economic systems of Communism lies here. Nay more, the essence of the convergence prophecy is that the habitual payment of personal reward will draw together the capitalist and Communist countries that practise it.

But decentralization is not all. The question of rational resource allocation is rather separate. If Stalin could combine irrationality with centralization, Mao has combined it with decentralization, and every European Communist country from the DDR to Czechoslovakia seeks to rationalize. If the Czechs and Hungarians are most eager, centralizing Soviet mathematicians are hardly less eager. It remains however sure that the conservative forces which prevent decentralization act also to preserve Marxist irrationalities. Thus in Rumania there is no capital tax, and in USSR, DDR and Poland the tax is designed only to rationalize the decisions of planners; for, being deducted from planned profits, it has no effect on wholesale prices (question 5(a)). Again, only Hungary and Czechoslovakia have the definite intention to even out the turnover tax.

Chinese resource allocation must be held as surprisingly rational! For so many prices are market-determined, and so much capital is borrowed from the bank. The practical effects of the market cancel, presumably, the anti-rational theory.

Thirdly the status of profit as an indicator has gone up everywhere. In China it is not supposed to have, but after all China *is* more or less a market economy. Profit has been demoted only in this sense, that the bonus to management has been abolished. Even in the more centralized economies profit ranks now directly after the output *sortament*. Its rise in importance as an indicator is in all cases *associated with* a great liberalization of profit retention rules: everywhere the enterprise may use more profit for various purposes of its own.

Greater retention, however, is more or less compatible with a scarcely diminished centralism in matters of output *sortament* and input allocation. If retained profit is to be spent on workers' welfare or bonuses it presses on the retail market in a manner little different from wage payments. If it is to be spent on development it can be built into next year's investment plan; but in USSR at least this has not occurred, and there has been much difficulty in purchasing things with this part of the fund. In other words, in the more conservative countries greater profit retention should be simply a re-routing of financial flows; to the extent that it is more than that, there is an 'inner contradiction'.

N.B. We have not asked what suggestions have been made in the technical press; but what current practice actually is.

1 (a) What are the intermediate planning organs? E.g.: sovnarkhozy; republics; ministries or departments thereof; local soviets or equivalent; state committees (say if merely advisory); chambers of commerce; associations, large firms; other.
    (b) How are powers divided between these organs and the centre?

2 *Indicators, and the decision of output*
    (a) What input, output, technological and financial indicators are obligatory on the enterprise? Rank these indicators in order of importance.
    (b) Do arrangements differ between sectors? E.g. heavy and light industry.
    (c) In the absence of obligatory output indicators, must there be long-term inter-enterprise contracts? What power has the centre to interfere with these?

3 What is the system of *distribution* of semi-fabricated goods in inter-enterprise transactions? To what extent is it determined by
    (a) the producing enterprise's plan, or a centralized raznaryadka;[1]
    (b) decentralized kontraktatsia[2] with some wholesale organization;   (c) a free market?
    (d) Is there a Gossnab? What does it do?

4 When were *wholesale prices* last reformed? On what principles? E.g.:
    (a) raw material prices imitate world market;
    (b) direct cost plus profit as a rate on capital: average for the given industry (*Produktionspreise*);
    (c) direct cost plus profit as a rate on it: average for the given industry (*Werte*);
    (d) combination of (b) and (c) (two-channel prices);
    (e) (b), (c) or (d) in the marginal enterprise;
    (f) free competitive market;

---

[1] A separately planned distribution of claims, in this case by the Gossnab.
[2] The compulsory drawing up of a legally binding contract, under the supervision of some central authority.

(g) historical chance and political influence;

(h) semi-free inter-enterprise contract.

(i) What percentage (and how is this percentage calculated?) of wholesale prices is: freely set, limited by a maximum, simply fixed by the plan?

5 (a) Does the *capital charge* on budget-provided capital affect the product price or the enterprise's incentive funds, or is it simply a deduction from the given profits taxes?

(b) How does it differ by branches? How big is it, and on what precisely is it levied?

6 *The financing of capital*

(a) What authority mainly spends amortization quotas? (Other than the part spent on 'capital repairs', which have always been financed by the enterprise.)

(b) Can any fixed capital be borrowed from a bank, governmental agency, or other enterprise (as opposed to budgetary allocation)?

(c) What is the role of intermediate planning organs?

7 *The turnover tax*

(a) On what goods (and services if any) is the turnover tax levied?

(b) What is its proportion to the profits tax in the budget?

(c) Is it paid by the producer or (where appropriate) the retailer?

(d) Is it levied on: total output; 'commodity' output; completed sales; other?

(e) How uniform a percentage is it of the cost of the article on which it is levied? Has it been recently made more uniform?

8 *The disposal of profit*

(a) What rates of profit tax are there, and on what products?

(b) Precisely what is the tax base?

(c) Are capital charges a part of, or additional to it?

(d) What is the status of intra-branch subsidies?

(e) What is the status of central subsidies?

(f) How much of profit is retained by the enterprise?

(g) Into what funds, if any, must retained profit be divided?

9 *Wages and employment*

(a) Who regulates basic wage-rates?

(b) Who regulates bonuses and the like?

(c) Who hires and fires?

(d) Anti-inflationary controls on the wage-bill.

(e) What is the proportion of the wage-type payments out of profit to the wage-fund, or are they both merged in 'enterprise income'?

(f) How are the unemployed cared for?

(g) Is there any kind of workers' council, as in Yugoslavia?

10 *How are retail prices fixed?* E.g.:

(a) central command plus variable turnover tax;

(b) central command plus rationing;

(c) uniform taxes plus centrally commanded output adjustments;

(d) free competition;

(e) free kontraktatsia between designated partners;

(f) what percentage (and how is this percentage calculated?) of retail prices is: freely set, limited by a maximum, simply fixed by the plan?

11 *Planner's tension*

(a) Is tension specifically condemned?

(b) What new provisions are there *re* the desired level of raw material stocks?

(c) Ditto cash in hand or at the bank?

(d) Ditto reserve plant?

(e) Do the plan figures themselves contain upper and lower limits?

12 What special provisions are there for the *export* sector?

13 (a) Who makes *investment decisions*, up to what limits of cost?

(b) What are the principal investment criteria?

14 *Bankruptcy*

(a) Is there an existing law, and has it ever been used?

(b) Is there a new law?

(c) When would it be used?

(d) What is the priority order of creditors?

RESPONSES

Albania[1]

1 (a) Ministries for important products. Local authorities (*rreth* councils) for 'local industry' and co-operatives.

(b) No participation by local authorities for industrial goods not directly subordinate to them, but dual control for farming (Ministry of Agriculture), education and similar public services

[1] Mr Kaser.

(Ministry of Education etc.). Balance of power between Ministries and Plan Office in favour of latter.

2 Global production; physical output for approximately 100 products for which material balances are elaborated; cost of production; payments to the budget. There is no difference between sectors except that 'local' industry is not given any centrally set physical output targets.

3 Centralized raznaryadka for 'funded' goods, producing enterprise's plan for other 'ministerial' goods, decentralized kontraktatsia for local industry. No Gossnab exists.

4 1966; principles not stated.

5 No capital charge.

6 (a) Amortization at disposal of ministry.
   (b) Very little loan capital available; grants still predominate.
   (c) Executants only: Ministry of Finance decides in consultation with Plan Office.

7 (a) Consumers' goods.
   (b) 2·4 times (1963).
   (c) Not known.
   (d) Not known.
   (e) Variable percentage with supplementary 'excise' element for 'luxuries'.

8–9 Not known, except 8(f): no official fund-unemployables are returned to their native commune. 8(g): none.

10 (a)

11 Not known.

12 Priority in supply of inputs, packaging materials etc.; otherwise none.

13 Plan Office and Ministry of Finance, except for rreth industry (from overall limits given by Ministry of Finance) and cooperative farms (with loan capital regulated by State Bank).

14 Not known.

Bulgaria

The Party's 'Theses' of April 1966[1]

1 (a) The Ministries were turned into State Committees in imitation of Khrushchev's 1958 reforms, and so remain. Under them

[1] Cf. Wolfgang Eggers in ed. Thalheim and Höhmann, *Wirtschaftsreformen in Ost-Europa* (Cologne, 1968).

come very big 'concerns' on the production principle, each one covering every enterprise in the country.

(b) The center uses mainly persuasion and monetary means on the concern, the latter mainly commands the enterprise.

2 (a) Basic output sortament, basic input ratios, profit. But the association can impose many more detailed indicators.
(b) ?
(c) Yes: no exchange may take place without a contract. The center retains full powers of veto.

3 ?

4 Price reform is all in the future, and will be gradual. Principles are (a), (c) and (f).

5 (a) No effect on prices.
(b) Can vary by branches. Is mostly 6%, on all fixed and circulating capital derived from the state (bank credit of course attracts interest as before). There is also a differential rent in mining and agriculture.

6 (a) ?
(b) Most is supposed to be so borrowed, or ploughed back (see 8(g)); only heavy industry will draw extensively from the budget.
(c) Very great: cf. 2(a).

7 (a) Mostly consumption.
(b)–(e) ?

8 (a) Progressive, for all products.
(b) ?
(c) Additional.
(d) These are common, and are operated by the powerful concerns.
(e) ?
(f) ?
(g) 'Development and technical improvement', 'new products', 'wage reserve' (see 9).

9 (a) The center, but the enterprise is legally bound to pay these minima, and must even borrow from the bank at interest in order to do so. Hence the 'wage reserve fund' of 8(g).
(b) The enterprise or the association.
(c) The enterprise.
(d) ?
(e) All wages, minimal and bonus alike, are paid out of enterprise income; the center guarantees nothing (see 9(a)).

(f) ?

(g) 'Production committees' have only the right to make suggestions.

10 Mainly (a), but (d) is to increase.

11 ?

12 The two agricultural procurement, canning and distribution concerns, Bulgarplod and Rodopa, operate also as import/export enterprises. The industrial foreign trade enterprise Texim has unusual freedom to innovate and spend currency outside the plan (e.g. it bottles Coca Cola).[1] In other fields little change from the classical system.

13-14 ?

Czechoslovakia

The 'General Guidelines for Enterprise Operation' of 1967[2]

1 (a) Branch directorates of ministries, trusts and – for small products – national councils.
(b) See 8(d). The role of trusts is very ill defined. Their apparent object is to reduce enterprise independence.

2 'Disposable income' as in Pesek's 1967 article; hardly any other.
(b) No.
(c) Contracts are common.

3 Systems (b) and (c). (d) to be abolished. But it still exists and functions (early 1968). The anti-monopoly law of late 1966 implies that any enterprise may buy from any other.

4 1 January 1967. (a), (d), (e), (f) are the principles used. (d) predominates. 80% of wholesale prices are controlled, in that each enterprise may raise its average price only so much, while individual prices are free.
(i) 92% blocked, 8% free. Subsequently all were blocked for January–July 1967. But there are very many loopholes.

5 (a) Yes.
(b) Not much; it is a uniform 6% on net productive fixed assets.

6 (a) The enterprise, with some, mainly transitional, exceptions.
(b) Most of it must be so borrowed. However in 1967 there still remain kcs 10 md. of investment subsidies.

---

[1] Dariusz Fikus in *Polityka* (Warsaw, 14 October 1967).
[2] Translated in *New Trends in the Czechoslovak Economy* (Prague), no. 6. Also Mr Pesek's contribution to *Analyse et Prévision*, Nov. 1967; sundry conversations with Czechoslovak economists.

(c) See 8(d), 1(b). They are in any case the major decision-makers.

7 (a) Consumer goods and a few others in special circumstances. Note possibility of confusion with 8(a). Local governments also collect a 5% sales tax.
(b) About equal.   (c) The producer.
(d) Total output.   (e) Is to be made more and more uniform.

8 (a) A uniform 18%.
(b) Additional.   (c) Gross income.
(d) Transitional only, but large. Special funds provided for.
(e) New wholesale prices *should* abolish them.
(f) ?   (g) ?

9 (a) The centre.   (b) The enterprise, out of profits.
(c) The enterprise.
(d) A high tax on additions to the wage-fund. Also a limit on average wages (which is evaded by hiring as much low-paid labour as possible, to balance wage increases elsewhere).
(f) Vague official mention of new measures only: no dole as yet, or officially proposed.
(g) Some beginnings of it in June 1968, virtually abandoned in October 1968. Actually like Bulgaria.

10 (a) Mostly (a) and (d).
(e) One third to be free, one third to have a maximum, one third to be centrally fixed.

11 (a) No, but it is incompatible with so decentralized a system.
(b) Notice tax on inventories in Pesek's table. The banks are free to increase the tax rates to achieve desired level of inventories.

12 Export enterprises are to get a share of the foreign exchange they earn. This is to stimulate export drives and enable enterprises to buy foreign investment goods.

13 (a) Enterprises, except in mining, electric and water power, transport, agriculture.
(b) For borrowed funds, speed of promised repayment. I.e. very nearly profit, but there are various political and regional preferences.

14 There is no law. Enterprises now being liquidated shift all their assets and liabilities to the ministry responsible. But a law is expected.

Miscellaneous. The law referred to under 3(d) establishes the principle of suing the state; but only where a new state order forces enterprise A to break a contract with enterprise B. Then if A must pay damages to B it may sue the organ issuing the new order.

DDR

The 'New Economic System', gradually introduced since 1963[1]

1 (a) Ministries or their departments, trusts (*Vereinigungen Volkseigener Betriebe*), and district economic councils for minor products.
(b) The about 90 VVBs are very important indeed; comparatively free vis-à-vis ministries, and dominant over enterprises.

2 (a) Physical output sortament, quality, physical input and input/output, cost, profit.
(b) More centralization in heavy industry.
(c) ?

3 (a) and (b).   (c) No.   (d)?

4 Piecemeal since 1964. The principle is mainly (c), but prices remain lower for producers' goods.
(i) Practically all are fixed by the plan.

5 (a) No.   (b) Not uniform; varies, mainly according to capital intensity, from o to 90%. Is levied on gross value of fixed and circulating capital, including land.

6 (a) The VVB and the enterprise.
(b) Yes: by banks only.
(c) The VVB may redistribute between enterprises for investment purposes.

7 (a) 'Production and service tax': mainly on consumer goods.
(b) ?   (c) The producer.
(d) 'Commodity' output.   (e) Still very various.

8 (a) Various.   (b) Planned profit.
(c) At present additional; they are planned to replace profit taxes.
(d) There are, and are meant to be, many: but only profit transfers.
(e) The new wholesale prices should abolish them.
(f) ?   (g) ?

9 (a) State authorities.
(b) The enterprise, according to available funds.
(c) The firm.
(d) Strict price controls by government authorities.
(e) Less than 5%. There are also bonuses in the wage-fund, and 'enterprise income' is not an operative concept.

[1] Mainly from Hans Boehme's paper for CESES (Sept. 1966); Miller and Trend in *Problems of Communism* (March–April 1966); and Dr Seidler.

(f) Low unemployment benefit (up to 2 M per day).
(g) No.

10 Central command on the basis of costs and variable turnover tax.
(f) 100% fixed by the plan.

11 (a) Planning targets on the basis of full use of capacity.
(b) Capital levy charged on excess stocks by banks.
(c) No cash holdings; cash at bank restricted.
(d) Not provided.
(e) Not as far as firms are concerned.

12 Stimuli by participation of export firms in surplus export
receipts of foreign currency.

13 (a) Central authorities, VVBs and firms according to the general
plan. Financing of new plants by the government.
(b) Rationalization, profitability, completion of the economic
structure.

14 (a) Not for socialist enterprises. Reconstruction measures instead
of bankruptcy.
(b) No.   (c) —.   (d) —.

Hungary[1]

1 (a) Ministries and departments thereof: Those few industrial
directorates (sectoral departments of ministries) retained in 1963
industrial reorganization have been dissolved. Each enterprise
and trust now under supervision of a deputy minister. Ministry
appoints enterprise director and his associates and fixes their
remuneration. Ministry also oversees development of its sector,
including preparation and proposal of State investment projects
(see 13(a)).
    Functional ministries and banks (see 1(b)).
    National Technical Development Committee is only important
State committee; it is advisory.
    Chamber of Commerce has advisory role in foreign trade.
    Large enterprises created in 1963 reorganization remain
untouched. A few horizontal trusts have been broken up, and
about a dozen trusts (mainly vertical) remain (with substantial
powers). About a dozen 'associations' have been created, some
by ministerial decree, some on initiative of participating enterprises; these are not separate legal entities (as are trusts), but
rather undertake to co-ordinate certain functions (marketing,

---

[1] Mr Portes.

investment, etc.) on behalf of participating enterprises; they have no power to direct enterprises.

Local council executive committees run local industry (council, co-operative, and private industry). The appropriate ministry also had a role up to 1968 (dual subordination); but this has ceased.

(b) Functional ministries and banks have gained at expense of line industrial ministries and Planning Office; many former duties of line ministries are transferred to enterprises; division of authority between line ministries and Planning Office roughly the same; Materials and Price Office takes over material allocation from Planning Office and becomes very powerful.

2 (a) Some physical import and export quotas. For the rest all indicators are financial and indirect: depreciation charges; capital charge; profit taxes, land tax, communal tax, 'production tax', payroll tax, social security contribution. Some major investment projects are also centrally ordered.

(b) Very little: different depreciation rates for different industries; a few 'special cases' for taxation and capital charge (usually at industrial branch, not enterprise level). There is also a special percentage tax on profit or sales for some enterprises (with rate fixed individually for enterprise); total amount will come to about 17% of total (pre-tax, but after capital charge) profits in industry; this 'production tax' is meant to collect rents.

(c) Signing contracts obligatory only in certain cases: in particular, defense and State investment projects. Compulsory signing of contracts can be enforced by Economic Arbitration Committee in order to maintain long-standing supply relations through transition period, but only if breaking them would cause undue hardship to one of the parties (with no recourse to another partner).

3 Mainly (c) with some (b): some direct inter-enterprise deliveries, some through the two dozen producer goods trade enterprises, which act as genuine wholesale trade firms. New law forbids agreements 'in restraint of trade'.

(d) In addition to its pricing functions, the Materials and Price Office allocates a few products in detail (some domestically produced, some imports) and specifies suppliers and/or users for some others.

4 Price reform 1 January 1968, mainly on system (d). 'Multi-channel prices' (branch average) include uniform capital charge and payroll tax, and profit calculated as percentage of capital

employed (rates varying between industrial branches – average 6·5% in all industry); also (a), (f), and (h); and early-warning system, with Materials and Price Office empowered to delay increase (for certain prices) for up to three months.
(i) Percentages calculated on expected sales volume:

	Fixed	Max.	Limits or rules	Free
Domestically produced raw mat. and semi-finished goods	30	40	2	28
Finished goods	3	16	3	78

5 (a) Affects product price (see 4). Accounted as cost.
(b) Uniform 5% on undepreciated value of fixed and working capital, with a few exceptions for particular industrial branches (e.g. mining, electricity generating). Also land tax (rent), accounted as cost, with rates varying with type of land used (and initial charge for land for new investment projects, assessed at 20 times annual tax).

6 (a) In general, 60% left to enterprises, to go into their development funds (a few exceptions – e.g. 100% for transport, project-planning and some other enterprises); but this base percentage is augmented, or conversely a certain proportion is 'blocked', until 1971, according to the amount invested in the enterprise during 1964–7. Remainder to Budget.
(b) From Investment Bank, to be repaid out of development fund (see 8). Current figures for investment financed out of various sources are meaningless, since much of the 'decentralized' funds are being used to pay for State projects in process at the time of the changeover to the reforms.
(c) Sectoral ministries prepare and propose State investment projects. Investment Bank has wide latitude for choice among enterprise project proposals, subject to 'credit policy guidelines' formulated by high-level interdepartmental committee and approved by Council of Ministers, and taking advice on suitability of project from industrial and functional ministries.

7 (a) Consumer goods and services.
(b) Percentage division of estimated 1968 Budget receipts:

Capital charge and amortization	21
Payroll tax (8% of wage bill in all enterprises) and social security contribution (17% of wage bill)	17
Profit and income tax	35

'Production tax' (see 2(b)) and rents   3
Turnover tax   7
Tariffs   4
Other   13

(c) Paid by enterprise which sells commodity to retail trade (for services, enterprise which provides service).
(d) Sales to retail trade.
(e) Formerly about 2,500 separate 'keys'; now about 1,000. Thus still pretty highly differentiated.

8 (a)(b) and (g) Profit is divided, on the basis of the enterprise's capital employed and its wage bill (with variations for some industries in the standard 1:2 weighting), into 'development portion' and 'sharing portion'.[1] Former taxed at flat 60% rate (with a few exceptions); remainder is 'developmental fund'. Latter taxed progressively, at rates varying with ratio of sharing portion to wage bill (from no tax on that part of sharing portion below 3% of wage bill to 70% tax on that part of sharing portion greater than 13% of wage bill); remainder is 'sharing fund'. Sharing portion tax rates quoted are for 1968; rates for 1969 and 1970, already published, go down from year to year. 10% of each fund must be set aside in 'reserve fund'. 'Production tax' (see 2(b)) paid out of profits; communal tax (between 1 and 2% of wages) paid out of development fund.
(c) Capital charge accounted as cost; thus additional (prior) to profit tax (see 5(a)).
(d) None, except within trusts. These, however, are not very strong.
(e) Central subsidies to a small number of enterprises, fixed in advance for 1968–70. Also export rebates (see 12).
(f) Over 1968–70, it is anticipated that 60% of profit will be taken in taxes, 25% will go to development funds, and 15% to sharing funds (another estimate suggests 56% in taxes, 44% left with enterprises).

9 (a) Center (Ministry of Labour).

[1] Thus normally

$$\pi_d = \pi \cdot \frac{K}{K+2W}, \qquad \pi_s = \pi \cdot \frac{2W}{K+2W},$$

using obvious notation. π here is net enterprise income, with costs including materials, wages (only that part corresponding to average wage equal to 'base' level; see 9(d)), depreciation, capital charge, land tax, payroll tax and social security contribution. W here is also employment times 'base' average wage. K includes both fixed and working capital.

(b) Enterprise director (except his own and those of his deputies; see 1(a)), out of sharing fund.

(c) Enterprise director.

(d) Limit of 4% increase in 'average wage' (over 'base' level of 1967, somewhat modified to enterprise disadvantage) in 1968 only; also, in 1968–70, any increase in total wage bill attributable to increase in average wage over base level must be financed out of sharing fund.

(e) Estimated 10–12% for 1968; should rise from year to year (see 8). The managerial bonus is a much bigger percentage.

(f) Labour exchanges. There seems to be no unemployment benefit.

(g) No; trade unions rights have increased and could possibly become significant in practice.

10 Various ways: a, b (queueing), d, e, and fixed turnover tax (rate or amount) with freely varying wholesale price.

(f) Percentages calculated on expected retail turnover for 1968:

	Fixed	*Max.*	*'Loose' limits or rules*	*Free*
Foodstuffs	31	29	27	13
Clothing	0	21	54	25
Building materials	20	70	0	10
Domestic fuels	100	0	0	0
Mixed industrial consumer goods	7	50	22	21
Other	0	0	10	90
Total	20	30	27	23

11 (a) Yes.

(b) No officially prescribed inventory norms.

(c), (d), (e) No.

12 Some export quotas, especially in trade with CMEA partners; but even here no export contract is valid unless countersigned by producing enterprise. There is a far-reaching export rebate system, with rates differing between enterprises. Number of industrial enterprises entitled to engage directly in exporting has been increased. Foreign trade enterprises now do almost all their business on commission or profit-sharing basis, rather than buying on own account.

13 (a) State, for new factories or significant extensions, called 'individual large state investment projects'; projects costing

less than 300 million Ft. in mining, electricity and chemicals, less than 200 million Ft. in metallurgy, engineering, construction and building materials, and less than 100 million Ft. in light industry do *not* enter this category. (At rate used to convert the dollar to domestic prices, 60 Ft. = $1.) Also some investment *programs* (mainly infrastructure) are handled centrally. Remainder enterprise decisions.

(b) Enterprise initiative. But for long-term (3–6 years) credits, expected rate of profit on capital (minimum 7%) and proposed repayment period of loan; for medium-term credit, simply enterprise's 'capacity to repay'. Also special sectoral preferences and concessions and special attention to balance of payments effects. State investment guided by ministry and Planning Office conceptions of sectoral development.

14 (a) Not like the new one.
(b) Yes.
(c) Ministry appoints investigator if enterprise shows deficit which can't be covered out of reserves (which if necessary must be augmented for this purpose by a certain percentage of managers' pay). But no liquidations are likely for a few years; if necessary, Budget will pay subsidies.

Poland

The 'Reform' of 1965[1]

Note that this reform's main object was to improve planning, not to decentralize. It increased planned reserves of all sorts, reduced planner's tension.

1 (a) Ministries or their departments, trusts and – for small products – national councils.
(*b*) The associations (*zjednoczenia*) have recently been much strengthened, restoring them to the independence they were originally meant to have. For instance the association appears to decide on its own the volumes and even the prices of transfers between enterprises subordinate to it. But they remain far less important than in Bulgaria.

2 (a) Profit as rate on cost; value added; gross output; main physical output targets.
(b) Yes: consumer goods much more decentralized. See 6(b).
(c) ?

[1] Mainly from Leon Smolinski in *Problems of Communism* (July–Aug. 1966). The new regulations for zjednoczenia are in *Życie Gospodarcze*, 8 Jan. 1967.

3 (a) predominates, except for consumer goods (b).   (d) No.

4 Last thorough reform 1959. Nothing radical envisaged except
   for exporting enterprises. Main principles remain (a), (c), (g)
   and (h).
   (i) Prices all centrally set.

5 (a) Initially deducted from profits.
   (b) Varies, but excludes ground sites.

6 (a) Associations and enterprises.
   (b) 60% of public investment is to come from banks (interest
   only on delayed repayment or excess cost).
   (c) The association may freely transfer funds between enterprises.

7 (a) Most.   (b) ?   (c) ?   (d) ?   (e) Not at all; no.

8 (a), (b), (c) ?   (d) Large and unchanged.
   (e) Large and unchanged.   (f), (g) ?

9 (a) Centrally determined.
   (b) In principle determined at the enterprise level by the director
   and the representatives of workers' self-government conference
   (party organization, trade unions and workers' council). But
   are subject to approval by the relevant Industrial Association.
   (c) Enterprise director.
   (d) No special new mechanisms.
   (e) About 4 to 6%. The distinction between the funds is fully
   maintained.
   (f) There are no statutory unemployment benefits, however
   each local authority has an 'intervention fund' (*Fundusz Inter-
   wencyjny*) out of which it can finance a limited amount of 'public
   works' or in exceptional cases pay certain benefits toun employed.
   Only unemployed heads of families (with no other bread-
   winner in the household) are eligible.
   (g) Nominal workers' councils remain from 1956, but are much
   overshadowed by the Party and the trade union.

10 (a) predominates, subject to a small influence on retail prices of
   6(b). The turnover tax remains variable.

11 (a) Yes.
   (b) The current fashion is for adequate reserves (from the
   national plan downwards). However there are no specific and
   concrete provisions in respect of norms for such reserves.
   (e) Some national plan targets are in ranges.

12 There is, for instance, a special speedy procedure for obtaining

credit for export production which is expected to bring in quick returns. There is a special central fund out of which this type of export output is financed. The basic advantage is that one can cut across red tape in promoting extra-plan output. Selected enterprises have great freedom, especially in settling the assortment. Polfa, the chemical concern, even imports freely, provided it can promise greater re-exports. Polfa is almost an independent island in the economy.

13 (a) 'Essential' investments (whatever that may mean) are decided upon by the central planners and paid from the state budget. All other investments may be decided upon at the enterprise level (with approval from the association) and ought to be financed by an interest bearing credit. In practice all new investments which pertain to complete plants (with the exception of small enterprises of local interest) are decided upon centrally. (b) The 'plan', whatever that means.

14 The law on bankruptcy stands, although it is not applied in the accepted sense, except in the case of co-operative and private undertakings. If a state enterprise cannot pay its way, it may be liquidated, or transferred to another branch of industry. This procedure is followed if the banks refuse further credits because of the financial state of the undertaking.

In all cases the order of creditors is as follows: (1) wages, (2) financial commitments to the state, (3) money due to co-operative and private contractors or creditors.

Rumania[1]

The legal instruments of the reform, the principles of which were approved by the RCP Central Committee in October, by the RCP Congress in December and by the Grand National Assembly also in December 1967, will not all be formulated before 31 December 1969 (Law of 26 December 1967). Those provisions already enacted are appropriately indicated below.

1 (a) Ministries, State Committees and, for 'local industry', local authorities (which were reformed on the pre-1950 *judete* pattern in February 1968). Dual subordination is not employed in Rumanian administration. But central offices, or industrial associations (*centralele*) began to be established in April 1969 and will be extended to cover all enterprises hitherto administered by industrial ministries.

(b) Balance of power probably in favour of industrial ministries.

[1] Mr Kaser.

2 Marketable production sold and paid for; global production; cost of production; profits; labour productivity. In 1966 physical output targets were set for 232 goods by the Council of Ministers and for 1,200 goods by ministries. There is no variation by sector, and little change since that date.

3 Centralized raznaryadka, but with decentralized kontraktatsia becoming more common between enterprises. Currently these latter transactions are supervised by 'co-ordinating forums' of representatives of the ministries concerned; Gossnab activities are operated by the Plan Office. It is proposed that transactions be increasingly devolved to the 'central offices'.

4 1963; a price reform is in preparation. Many new products (e.g. synthetic fibres) appear to be priced at the world-market ratio to their traditional substitutes (viz. approximately version (a)), but most products are (c). Price determination is currently highly centralized under the State Committee for Prices (recently strengthened), most prices being fixed but a few (no percentage available) set as maxima. Under the reform there would be significant devolution to 'central offices'.

5 No capital charge is envisaged in the reform.

6 (a) Amortization is divided between enterprise, central office and ministry.
(b) Small 'modernization' loans available from the banking system.
(c) Unclear.

7 (a) Turnover tax is levied on consumers' goods – but a similar tax was introduced on some producers' goods in 1963.
(b) 1·6 times (1965).
(c) Producer.
(d) Commodity output.
(e) Variable.

8 (a), (b) Not known.
(c) No capital charge.
(d) These will be operated by the 'central offices'.
(e) Central subsidies are to be terminated.
(f) 5% of planned profit (and higher percentages of above-plan profit) must be paid to the Director's Fund. From 1968 the obligatory payment from profit to the Premium Fund was reduced; other payments must be made in execution of the Annual Collective agreement. All these amounted in 1966 to 7·1% and in 1967 to 6·4% of planned profits.
(g) See (f).

9 (a) State Committee for Problems of Organization and Wages abolished in March 1969. Now Ministry of Labour.

(b) The Board of Management of each enterprise, subject to regulations on the percentage of salary which can be paid as bonus and maximum and minimum limits for bonuses to (i) the director and his deputies (ii) other managerial staff (iii) technicians and clerical personnel and (iv) operatives. In June 1968 the percentages allowable for (i) and (ii) were significantly reduced, so that earnings differentials from bonuses have been narrowed.

(c) The manager of the enterprise.

(d) None.

(e) Not known; but the 'enterprise income' or 'value added' policy does not apply.

(f) No employment benefit.

(g) In May 1968 'Boards of Management' were authorized, to be elected by the 'General Assembly of Employees' (formerly the Production Conference).

10 (a)

11 No new developments.

12 Creation of a Foreign Trade Bank in July 1968. Under the reform 'central offices' will have the main oversight of foreign trade operations, subject to participation by the Ministry of Foreign Trade in 'major' deals.

13 (a) All but the smallest investments are determined by the Plan Office, Ministry of Finance and appropriate industrial ministry. Approximately 60% of all state investment is effected by budget grant, as is about 90% of increments in working capital.

(b) Little new discussion.

14 Not definitely known: there appears however to be no law.

USSR

The 'New System' of 1966[1]

N.B. This system is nowhere authoritatively described, and it varies from branch to branch. It is being introduced piecemeal.

1 (a) Branch directorates of ministries (*glavki*), associations (*firmy*,

---

[1] There is no systematic official source. This is mainly from Keith Bush in *Problems of Communism* (1967); *idem*, 'The Soviet Economic Reforms after Two Years', Radio Liberty (18 December 1967); *idem*, 'An Appraisal of the Soviet Economic Reforms', Radio Liberty (14 March 1968).

ob'edineniya), State Committees, Republican Gosplans; for very light industry, local soviets.

(b) The glavk is to be on 'full Khozraschet' ('full' implies that it finds its own capital), so will presumably play a role somewhat independent of Gosplan. The role of the association (*firma*) is very ill-defined in the new system. It seems to exist in order to reduce enterprise independence.

2 (a) Sales (but global output often persists unofficially; for the Ministries in charge of reformed enterprises must still fulfil 'global' targets); the most important physical targets in the sortament; profit or profitability; the wage-fund maximum; payments to the budget; important physical inputs or input/output ratios, and the basic technology.

(b) Hardly.   (c) ?

3 Mostly (a), but (b) for small, decentralized articles. Proposals to abolish the raznaryadka circulate.

(d) Gossnab remains in charge of basic materials, but operates on the territorial principle.

4 July 1967 (last previous thorough reform July 1955). Main principle is (c), but there are many exceptions.

(i) All to be fixed, though some rather decentrally.

5 (a) No: it is formally deducted from the profit tax.

(b) It varies according to planned profitability (see 8(a)). Mostly 6%, it is zero for planned-loss enterprises. It is not levied on land.

6 (a) The glavk or possibly the association, save as noted in 8(g).

(b) Budget allocations are to diminish sharply, but bank credit is to be less important than own resources.

(c) Big: see 6(a). Even profits can be transferred between the enterprises of one authority, quite outside the budget.

7 (a) Consumer goods, and a few others in special circumstances.

(b) ?   (c) The retailer.

(d) Completed sales.   (e) Not at all; no.

8 (a) Various. The tax on capital is regarded as a profits tax; there are differential rent charges ('fixed payments from profits'), and the 'free remainder' after forming the various funds goes automatically to the budget. Most charges are lower on producers' goods.

(b) Net enterprise income.

(c) Effectively a part of it.

(d) There are many.

(e) The new wholesale prices *should* abolish them, but will not in fact: see 7.

(f) *c.* 35%. (g) Material incentives fund, *c.* 12%; social-cultural fund, *c.* 4%; production development fund, *c.* 5% (to which is added 30–50% of amortization plus the negligible revenue from sales of surplus equipment); capital charge *c.* 41%; *c.* 16% to budget to 'finance centralized investment, including credit repayment and expansion of working capital'; *c.* 22% to budget as 'free remainder'.[1] I.e. 21% only retained.

9 (a) The center. (b) The enterprise, out of profits.
(c) The enterprise.
(d) Upper limit to wage-fund.
(e) About 7%.[2] Most bonuses come out of the wage-fund.
(f) Dole proposed unofficially. Some labour exchanges.
(g) The 'production conference', of workers, management and Party, meets from time to time and received a legal boost in 1958; it has little power even so.

10 Mostly (a).

11 ?

12 ?

13 (a) Investment for modernization and rationalization: the enterprise.
(b) These remain very various and political.

14 (a) The first stage, according to the existing law of August 1954, has often been used: the bank establishes a special supervisory regime. But thereafter subsidies invariably continue.
(b) No.
(c) Not applicable.
(d) Wages, suppliers' bills, taxes.

---

[1] *Ekonomicheskaya Gazeta*, 39 (1967), p. 15.
[2] R. 195·7 million among over 2 million workers and employees in 704 enter-prises in 1966 (Bush, op. cit. (Dec. 1967), p. 5). Mr Bush tells me that bonuses out of the wage-fund were definitely separate.

3

OWNERSHIP AND PLANNING IN SOVIET AND EAST EUROPEAN AGRICULTURE

EVERETT M. JACOBS, 1969

The purpose of this questionnaire-type study is to provide easy-to-use material for the assessment of the agricultural sectors of the Soviet and East European economies. Measurements have been standardized as much as possible in order to facilitate comparisons between and among the countries involved. Of course not all the factors influencing performance could be considered in a work of this type. For instance, the examination of such factors as soil conditions, weather conditions, the development of animal and plant breeding, and the number and distribution of agricultural specialists was beyond the scope of this study. Nor was it possible to go into the causes or reasons for the particular characteristics found in the agricultural sector of one country or another.

The first part of the questionnaire deals with the ownership (in the loose sense) of land and the means of production. In addition, it includes data on agricultural production, the size of the labour force engaged in agriculture, recent trends in the structure of the farms, and the organization of farm work. Despite the problems connected with the accuracy or completeness of the official statistics, they have been used where available for the sake of consistency.

The absence of complete information is most apparent for the questions pertaining to the proportion of total agricultural output by sectors and the size of the agricultural labour force by sectors. In both cases, the lack of information seems to be the result of an attempt by the régimes to conceal their dependence on the production and work force of the non-socialist sector to provide the population with food. Another difficulty concerns determining the effective size of the tractor parks, since the official figures make no allowance for the large numbers of

machines out of service for long periods because of inadequate
maintenance and repair facilities.

In spite of the difficulties encountered in standardizing the
statistics, much information can still be gained from a comparative analysis of the data. Perhaps most important, the true
extent of the diversity in agricultural organization and ownership in the Soviet Union and Eastern Europe becomes readily
apparent. It is clear that there are wide differences in the
importance the regimes attach in practice to collective farms as
the main form of socialist agriculture. Poland and Yugoslavia of
course are uncollectivized, while the collective farm sector
covers between 60–80% of the arable land in the other East
European countries, and only about 50% of the arable land
in the Soviet Union. Moreover, it should be noted that although
the Soviet Union eliminated all other types of collective farms
in favour of the kolkhoz during the period of mass collectivization, almost all the East European countries still maintain two
or more types of agricultural co-operative with differing degrees
of collective ownership. The exception is Bulgaria, which from
the first adopted a kolkhoz-type farm as the sole form of
collective. As seen for instance in Hungary and Rumania, the
general policy in Eastern Europe has been to eliminate the
lower types of co-operatives by upgrading them until they reach
the kolkhoz level.

There are considerable differences in the extent of the state
farm sector. It is most developed in the Soviet Union, where it
covers almost 50% of the arable area. In most of the East
European countries the figure is only 12 to 14% (the figure is
somewhat higher in Czechoslovakia and Rumania, and somewhat lower in East Germany and Yugoslavia). State farms are
rather more important in Poland and Yugoslavia than their
relative area suggests, since they represent almost the only kind
of socialist farms in those countries.

Both Poland and Yugoslavia are currently trying to increase
the size of their socialist sectors without resorting to collectivization.[1] In Poland, the number of agricultural circles has been
expanding at a rate of more than 15% a year since 1963, and

[1] For a fuller description of these attempts, see the author's 'Landwirtschaft im
kommunistischen Osteuropa: Entwicklung, Leistung, Reformversuche', *Osteuropa*,
no. 10 (1969), pp. 723–5.

the government seems determined to transform the circles eventually into some sort of producers' co-operatives. At the same time, the Party is going ahead with its plans to increase the area covered by state farms in Poland from 15% of the agricultural land at present to about 30% by 1975. State farms have been acquiring land as a result of a January 1968 law which provides for socialist and private farms to exchange one plot of land for another in order to consolidate their holdings. The law also allows aged peasants to transfer their plots to the state in return for a pension. In practice the law has been applied mainly to consolidate land held by the State Land Fund and state farms.

A land consolidation law also operates in Yugoslavia, though the state has been relying on land purchases from the peasants to expand the socialist sector. This policy has run into difficulties in recent years since the peasants have been reluctant to sell their land now that farming has become more profitable for them. Yugoslavia is also trying to expand the socialist sector by encouraging a greater number of private farmers to collaborate with socialized farms and enterprises.

The proportion of arable land devoted to personal plots is not necessarily a good measure of the severity or leniency of the régime's policy towards the collective farmers and other groups of the population. In most cases, the total area covered by personal plots reflects the relative size of the collective farm population. The average size of each personal plot is a more accurate indicator of the regime's policy. Using this as a guide, it is evident that the Albanians have adopted a hard line towards the peasants, and the Hungarians a comparatively soft line, with the other countries somewhere in between.

Another feature brought out by the data is the diversity in the size of farms within the socialist sector. Generally speaking, most of the East European régimes have followed the Soviet example of creating state farms several times as large as the average collective farm. The exceptions are Bulgaria, where state farms are somewhat smaller than co-operative farms, and East Germany, where state farms are about the same size as Type III co-operatives. On the other hand, there are great variations in the average arable area covered by a state farm, ranging from 8,300 ha. in the Soviet Union and 4,800 ha. in

Rumania, to less than 670 ha. in East Germany and 330 ha. in Poland. Considerable differences are also apparent in the size of collective farms. Only Bulgaria, Rumania, and Hungary have followed the Soviet example of setting up very large collective farms (Bulgarian co-operatives are actually bigger on average than Soviet kolkhozes), whereas collective farms in East Germany, Czechoslovakia, Albania, Poland and Yugoslavia are relatively small (not more than 660 ha. of arable land on average).

Compared with Western standards, all of the Communist countries except Czechoslovakia and East Germany are badly undermechanized and are also undersupplied with fertilizers (Tables 3.1 and 3.2, pp. 43 and 44). After Czechoslovakia and East Germany, the most technically advanced countries are Bulgaria and Hungary. In general, the yields in both the crop sector and the livestock sector of the Communist countries are still quite low by Western standards (Tables 3.3 and 3.4, p. 45). However, it should be noted that Czechoslovakia and East Germany have been regularly able to surpass the average wheat yield for non-Communist countries in Europe, while Bulgaria has bettered this average since 1965 thanks to a significant increase in tractor power and fertilizer consumption. As might be expected, there is an almost exact correlation among Communist countries between rank in terms of fertilizer consumption and rank in terms of wheat yield. A strong link is also evident between general technical standards and milk yield.

An interesting feature of Communist mechanization policy is that the large-scale fieldwork brigade, consisting of scores of peasants, appears to be an intermediate form of labour organization. When mechanical power was scarce, work units tended to be small, and much work was done by manual labour. An increase in tractor power and in the size of farms led to the abandonment of small work units for extensive farming. Large work brigades were formed in order to absorb surplus manpower and provide closer organizational control over the work units. With a further increase over the years in tractor power, coupled with an increase in the number of skilled machine operators and a decline in overall farm population, the trend has been to adopt smaller work units, called brigades,

Table 3.1 *Tractor power in the Soviet Union and Eastern Europe, 1960–67 (tractors in 000's of 15-h.p. units; intensity of tractor use in hectares of arable land per 15-h.p. unit[a])*

	1960 units	1960 ha./unit	1963 units	1963 ha./unit	1965 units	1965 ha./unit	1966 units	1966 ha./unit	1967 units	1967 ha./unit
USSR	1,985	112	2,612	86	3,032	74	3,233	69	3,485	64
Albania	4.5	103	7.0	72	7.6	67	8.2	65	9.0	60
Bulgaria	40.3	113	54.6	84	66.4	68	71.8	63	76.0	60
Czechoslovakia	94.3	56	161.6	33	179.5	29	185.9	27	195.2	26
East Germany	88.0	55	139.0	36	156.9	30	167.3[b]	28	174.8[b]	27
Hungary	47.9	110	71.8	78	91.5	59	96.9	52	98.2	52
Poland	77.2	207	113.5	139	146.1	106	160.5	95	183.4	83
Rumania	65.3	160	100.9	105	133.0	74	151.1	65	155.7	63
Yugoslavia[a]	35.8	214	43.3	177	45.3	168	51.0	148	47.0	161

[a] For Yugoslavia, tractors in 000's of physical units, and intensity of tractor use in hectares of arable land per tractor.
[b] Estimate based on physical units.
Sources: statistical yearbooks.
Tables 3.1 to 3.4 have already appeared in *Osteuropa*, no. 10 (1969). We reproduce them here by courtesy of that journal.

teams, or links of complex mechanization, for extensive farming. This development is clearest in the Soviet Union, but Bulgaria has also adopted this policy, and other countries are likely to follow in the near future. Hungary's Nádudvar system, which makes use of small work units, has not yet been applied to mechanized extensive farming there.

Table 3.2 *Consumption of chemical fertilizers in the Soviet Union and Eastern Europe, 1960–68* (pure nutritious matter: kg./ha. arable land)

	1960	1964/65	1965/66	1966/67	1967/68[a]
USSR	11.9	19.5	24.8	25.8	28.7
Albania	15.0[b]	12.8[b]	16.0[b]	16.2[b]	26.1[b]
Bulgaria	36.3	62.2	79.1	97.5[b]	133.0
Czechoslovakia	97.1	152.3	166.3	172.7	186.1
East Germany	195.9	256.1	262.7	279.0	280.0
Hungary	31.5	60.7	62.5	68.6	91.0
Poland	48.6	70.6	83.1	100.9	112.2
Rumania	7.4	22.0[b]	25.4	32.0	44.6
Yugoslavia		56.3[b]	54.8	60.7	62.5
Europe (excluding USSR)		112.9	118.8	125	137

[a] Preliminary.   [b] Unofficial estimate.

Sources: statistical yearbooks; *Economic Survey of Europe in 1962* (United Nations, New York, 1963), part 1, chapter I, p. 13; *Fertilizers: An Annual Review of World Production, Consumption, and Trade, 1966* (FAO, Rome, 1967), p. 22; *Fertilizers . . ., 1967* (Rome, 1968), p. 20; *Monthly Bulletin of Agricultural Economics and Statistics* (FAO, Rome), xviii, no. 2 (February 1969), 16.

The section of the questionnaire on planning is descriptive rather than statistical. Albania has been excluded for lack of information. Perhaps the most convenient way of evaluating the findings is in terms of the degree of decentralization in the various aspects of planning in the socialist sector of agriculture. If it is possible to rank the countries in such terms, Hungary would lead the list, followed by a group composed of Bulgaria, Czechoslovakia, the Soviet Union, and Yugoslavia. Centralization is strongest in East Germany, Poland, and Rumania.

The greatest amount of on-farm planning in the socialist sector of agriculture is found in Hungary. There is only a very

Table 3.3   *Wheat yields in Eastern Europe and the Soviet Union, 1952–67* (100 kg./ha.)

Country	1952–56	1963	1964	1965	1966	1967
Eastern Europe	13·3	17·6	17·4	22·0	22·1	24·6
Albania	10·3	7·1	9·6	9·6[a]	8·8[a]	8·8[a]
Bulgaria	13·8	15·9	17·7	25·5	28·0	30·6
Czechoslovakia	19·8	24·6	22·2	24·2	25·3	27·1
East Germany	28·4	30·0	31·1	36·7	31·4	37·8
Hungary	13·9	15·7	18·6	21·7	21·7	25·9
Poland	13·6	19·9	18·7	20·6	21·5	22·4
Rumania	10·5	13·2	12·9	19·9	16·7	20·0
Yugoslavia	10·5	19·3	17·6	20·6	25·1	25·6
Soviet Union	9·1	7·7	11·0	8·5	14·4	11·6
Europe, excluding Soviet Union	16·2	19·7	21·1	23·4	22·4	26·0
Europe, excluding Soviet Union and Eastern Europe	17·8	20·9	23·1	24·2	22·5	26·8

[a] FAO estimate.
Source: *Production Yearbook, 1968*, vol. 22 (FAO, Rome, 1969), pp. 37–8.

Table 3.4   *Milk yields in Eastern Europe, the Soviet Union and selected West European countries, 1952–67* (average annual yield in kg. per milking cow)

Country	1952–56	1963	1964	1965	1966	1967	% increase, 1963–67
Albania	392[a]	675[a]	675[a]	680[a]	680[a]	685[a]	1
Bulgaria	621	1,375	1,627	1,741	1,914	2,109	53
Czechoslovakia	1,614	1,812	1,975	2,015	2,146	2,239	24
East Germany	2,267	2,650	2,719	2,982	3,090	3,166	19
Hungary	1,654	2,307	2,359	2,214	2,410	2,554	11
Poland	1,798	2,083	2,094	2,252	2,365	2,356	13
Rumania	1,027	1,371	1,435	1,543	1,686	1,785	30
Yugoslavia	1,040	1,125	1,212	1,221	1,243	1,233	10
Soviet Union	1,479	1,600	1,618	1,853	1,880	1,948	22
France	2,027	2,609	2,622	2,756	2,912	3,170[a]	22
United Kingdom	2,903	3,662	3,676	3,797	3,755	3,830	5
West Germany	2,892	3,498	3,572	3,642	3,649	3,707	6

[a] FAO estimate.
Source: *Production Yearbook, 1968*, vol. 22 (FAO, Rome, 1969), p. 395.

limited degree of planning decentralization in the other countries, and at the bottom of the scale it seems that few if any planning decisions are taken at farm level in East Germany. Various forms of compulsory planning or production indicators still abound in the Communist countries. However, only Poland has retained a system of compulsory deliveries to the state at very low prices. The continued failure to solve the grain problem in the Soviet Union and Eastern Europe is evident from the fact that compulsory indicators for the sowing, production, or delivery of cereal crops are still in force in all the countries, though the private sector of Yugoslavia is exempt from them. Compulsory indicators imposed from above for grain crops seriously limit the scope of on-farm planning, since a significant area of the farm must be set aside for cereals and cannot be devoted to perhaps more suitable or more profitable crops.

All the Communist countries have introduced at least some degree of flexibility in their pricing policies and are making use of economic means to encourage production of certain crops. Pricing policy is so far the most flexible in Hungary and Yugoslavia, but more changes in this area can be expected from the other countries as their economic reforms progress. Only Bulgaria has introduced full khozraschet for all farms, though it has been introduced for all kolkhozes and 30% of the sovkhozes in the Soviet Union, and for all the state farms in Rumania. The successful application of the principles of full economic responsibility for the operation of the farms will depend on how much more the régimes are willing to do to put the farms on a firm financial basis.

A. QUESTIONNAIRE ON THE OWNERSHIP OF AGRICULTURE

1 What percentage of (a) arable land, (b) agricultural output, and (c) agricultural labour force is accounted for by the following sectors:
   (i) state farms and other state institutions;
   (ii) collective fields of collective farms;
   (iii) personal plots of collective farmers;
   (iv) other personal plots, including workers in (i);
   (v) individual (private) farms;
   (vi) other farms?

2 What percentage of collective farms belongs to the looser or stricter types? Where applicable, what percentage of individual farms co-operate with socialized enterprises?

3 (a) How many workers are there on an annual basis in the average state farm? (b) How many hectares of arable land? (c) How large is the average tractor park?

4 (a) How many families are there in the average collective farm? (b) How many hectares of arable land? (c) How large is the average tractor park?

5 (a) How large is the average private peasant farm? (b) What is the legal maximum?

6 How large is the average personal plot of (a) the collective farmer, (b) the state farm worker, and (c) other people?

7 Are small tractors or cultivators suitable for small farms (a) made in the country, or (b) imported in reasonable quantity?

8 What provisions are there for the supply of (a) artificial fertilizers, (b) insecticides, (c) fodder, or (d) farm animals for private activity?

9 (a) How large is the tractor park of an average Machine–Tractor Station? (b) How many workers are there in an average MTS? (c) What is the present position of the MTS? Where applicable, when was the MTS abolished?

10 What share of tractor power in (a) 15-h.p. units and (b) physical units is accounted for by:

(i) state farms;
(ii) collective farms;
(iii) other farms, including all personal plots and private farms;
(iv) MTS;
(v) other agencies?

11 What recent movement of farm amalgamation and/or sovkhozization has there been?

12 Has there recently been any movement to decentralize within the collective or state farm, e.g. by forming 'links' or other small labour units?

13 What percentage of total capital investment in the economy is devoted to agriculture?

RESPONSES

Albania (1967)[1]

1 (a): (i) 17·8% (state farms alone, 13·5%); (ii) 77·6%; (iii) 4·0%; (v) 0·6%.

3 (b) 1,990 ha.; (c) 71 15-h.p. units (49 physical units).

4 (a) 150 families; (b) 330 ha.; (c) tractor work done by MTS.

6 (a) 0·11 ha. arable land per family (indicating that the order of early 1967 limiting personal plots to 0·1 ha. had not been fully implemented by the end of the year).

7 (a) no; (b) no.

9 (a) 221 15-h.p. units (120 physical units); (c) Collectivization was completed in 1967, and 6 more MTS were set up; as a result, the average number of tractors per MTS between 1966 and 1967 decreased by 23·3% (15-h.p. units) and by 12·4% (physical units). There are no plans to sell the MTS machinery to the farms.

10 (a): (i) 25·8%; (iv) 73·1%; (b): (i) 30·5%; (iv) 67·9%.

11 Between 1966 and 1967, the number of state farms dropped from an all-time high of 37 to 33; the total area covered by state farms was almost unchanged, indicating that some state farms had been amalgamated. Amalgamations of co-operative farms between 1960 and 1966 reduced the number of co-operatives from 1484 to 819; the total area covered by co-operatives rose by 10·6%. The period of amalgamations ended in 1967 when 389 new co-operatives were added during the drive to complete collectivization; the total area covered by co-operatives rose by 14·6% in that year.

12 No.

13 Socialist sector of agriculture only: 16·2% in 1967 (11·7% in 1966).

Bulgaria (1967)[2]

1 (a): (i) 16·9% (state farms alone, 12·5%); (ii) 70·9%; (iii) 8·6%; (iv) 3·0%; (v) 0·5%.

---

[1] Source: *Vjetari Statistikor I Republikës Popullore Të Shqipërisë, 1967–1968* (Tirana, 1968).

[2] Sources: *Statisticheski Godishnik na Narodna Republika Bulgaria, 1968* (Sofia, 1968); *World Marxist Review*, no. 8 (1966), p. 5, and no. 6 (1969), p. 28.

(b) [comparable prices for 1962]: (i) 15·5% (state farms alone, 9·3%); (ii) 63·2%; (iii) 15·6%; (iv) 5·4%; (v) 0·3%.
(c) [incomplete figures]: (i) 168,862 state farm workers and employees, and 14,955 MTS workers and employees; (ii) 1,070,513 economically active members of co-operative farms; (v) [at end of 1965] 21,465 economically active non-co-operating farmers.

2 All co-operative farms are of a single type, the Co-operative Labour Agricultural Farm [TKZS], which is similar to the Soviet kolkhoz.

3 (a) 1,118; (b) 3,446 ha.; (c) 60 15-h.p. units.

4 (a) 1,103 households; 1,236 persons permanently engaged in agriculture; (b) 3,808 ha.; (c) 52 15-h.p. units [not including MTS tractor park – see 9(c)].

6 (a) 0·46 ha. agricultural land (0·38 ha. arable land) per household (legal limits: up to 0·20 ha. arable land in intensive farming regions; up to 0·50 ha. arable land in grain growing regions; up to 0·50 ha. arable land with up to 0·50 ha. of land not suitable for machine cultivation in mountainous regions).

8 (a) If a peasant sells a pig to the procurement agency, he receives a fodder bonus.

9 (a) 191 15-h.p. units; (b) 211; (c) The MTS were dissolved in all but the hilly and mountainous regions in 1962–63. There were 211 MTS in 1960, 78 in 1966, and 71 in 1967. MTS equipment is either sold to the co-operatives or transferred to other MTS.

10 (a); (i) 11·9%; (ii) 60·0%; (iv) 17·9%.

11 Large-scale campaign to amalgamate co-operatives in 1958; many amalgamated farms proved to be too large to manage and were split up within a year. Since then, a policy of converting economically weak co-operatives in mountainous and semi-mountainous regions into state farms. After 1966, sovkhozization in abeyance. There were 3,202 co-operatives in 1957, 932 in 1960, 920 in 1965, and 866 in 1967; for state farms, the figures are 49, 67, 104, and 151.

12 'Accord system' in use since mid-1960s: small work units farm set areas of cropland, and payment is by results (trudodens plus 50% of above-plan crop output). Most of the work is un-mechanized, but mechanized teams are also being introduced [*Ekonomika stran sotsializma: 1964 god* (Moscow, 1965), p. 66]. Brigades of complex mechanization, having on average about

12 machine operators, were introduced in 1968–69 for the production of cereal crops [*Ekonomika Selskogo Khozyaistva*, no. 12 (1969), p. 112].

13 17·3% in 1967 (19·2% in 1966).

Czechoslovakia (1967)[1]

1 Notes: (ii) Type III and IV co-operatives only; (iii) Personal plots of members of Type III and IV co-operatives; (v) Individual (private) farms and Type II co-operative farms.
(a): (i) 28·6% (state farms alone, 20·7%); (ii) 60·5%; (iii) 4·1%; (v) 6·7%.
(b): (i) 24·3%; (ii) 53·9%; (iii) 9·5%; (v) 12·2%.
(c) [Persons permanently engaged in agriculture; incomplete figures]: (i) 291,000 persons in the state sector (without MTS), of which 196,000 on state farms; 25,800 MTS workers; (ii) 717,000 persons; (v) 160,000 persons.

2 There are three different types of Unified Agricultural Co-operatives (JZD): Type II – land pooled, but products distributed according to the value of land; cattle and machinery put at disposal of co-operative; Type III – consolidation of land holdings, and animal husbandry is also pooled; income distributed according to work done, with a maximum of 15% distributed according to value of property contributed to co-operative; Type IV – similar to Type III, but income divided solely according to work done. Type IV farms 'predominate'. Only members of Type III and IV farms have personal plots in the kolkhoz sense.

3 (a) 570 persons permanently engaged in agriculture; (b) 3040 ha.; (c) 123 15-h.p. units.

4 (a) 112 permanently active farmers; (b) 509 ha.; (c) 20 15-h.p. units [not including MTS tractor park – see 9(c)].

5 (a) 75·4% of all private peasant farms (not including Type II co-operatives) covered less than 0·50 ha. of agricultural land each, and accounted for 25·0% of the total agricultural land in the private sector; the average size of these farms was 0·26 ha. agricultural land. In contrast, 24·6% of all private peasant farms covered 0·50 ha. or more of agricultural land each, and occupied 75·0% of total agricultural land in the private sector; the average size of these farms was 2·40 ha. agricultural land.

[1] *Sources: Statistická Ročenka ČSSR, 1968* (Prague, 1968); *Czechoslovakia: Statistical Abstract* (Prague, 1968).

SOVIET AND EAST EUROPEAN AGRICULTURE   51

There were 1957 Type II agricultural co-operatives (all in Slovakia), each averaging 32·4 ha. agricultural land.

6 (a) 0·32 ha. arable land. [Note: there were 850,984 members of Type III and IV co-operatives in 1967, but only 649,268 personal plots.]

7 (a) Small tractors produced, some of which exported to Hungary (exact data not available).

9 (a) 98 15-h.p. units; (b) 266 workers; (c) Most MTS were abolished in 1959–60, their equipment being sold to co-operative farms. Some (97) MTS were still functioning in 1967 to carry out large-scale field work and help economically weak co-operatives.

10 (a): (i) 21·7%; (ii) 63·9%; (iv) 4·9%.

11 Most co-operative farm amalgamations were completed between 1959–64; the campaign slowed down in 1965 and 1966, and there was little change in the number of co-operatives in 1967 (a drop of 68 to 6,395). The number of state farms has increased in recent years (329 in 1965 to 344 in 1967) while the area covered by them has remained fairly constant, indicating that several large state farms have been divided into smaller units.

12 Nothing reported.

13 [1964 prices] 13·8% in 1966.

East Germany (1967)[1]

1 (a) [agricultural land – mid-year]: (i) 6·8%; (ii) 76·0% (of which, Type I and II Agricultural Production Co-operatives (LPG), 17·6%, and Type III LPG, 58·4%; (iii) 9·8% (of which, Type I and II LPG, 6·6%, and Type III LPG, 3·2)%; (v) 5·9%; (vi) Horticultural Production Co-operatives (GPG), 0·3%.
(c) [incomplete figures]: (i) 74,103 state farm workers and employees (including apprentices); (ii) 875,278 LPG members permanently engaged in agriculture (of which, 258,432 belong to Type I and II LPG, and 616,846 belong to Type III LPG).

2 Type I LPG: arable land is cultivated collectively; Type II LPG: arable land, orchards, pastures and other usable areas are cultivated collectively, and farm machinery and draught animals are used collectively; Type III LPG: all land, farm

[1] Sources: Statistisches Jahrbuch, 1968 (Berlin, 1968); K. I. Milkulsky and M. V. Senin, eds., Sotsializm na nemetskoi zemle: dva desyatiletia stroitelstva novoi Germanii (Moscow, 1969), p. 125.

machinery, and draught animals, and almost all livestock are used collectively (kolkhoz-type co-operative). GPG operates on basis of Type III LPG rules. In Type I LPG, 40% of farm's money income is distributed according to the land shares contributed to the farm when the peasant entered; Type II, 30%, and Type III 20%. The remaining part of the farm's money income is distributed according to work done in the collectively farmed sector.

Proportion of LPG's belonging to Type I and II, 54·5%; Type III, 45·5%. Proportion of agricultural area of LPG's occupied by Type I and II, 27·5%; Type III, 72·5%.

3 (a) 114; (b) [agricultural land – mid-year] 668 ha.; (c) 17 physical units.

4 [September 1967]: (a) Type I and II LPG, 41 members; Type III LPG, 73 families (114 members); GPG, 53 members; (b) [agricultural land]: Type I and II LPG, 209 ha.; Type III LPG, 662 ha.; GPG, 53 ha.; (c) average for all types of LPG, 9 physical units.

5 [mid-year]: (a) 3·2 ha. agricultural land.

6 *Note:* Only members of Type III LPGs have personal plots in the kolkhoz sense of the term (legal limit is 0·5 ha. agricultural land per member); members of Type I and II LPGs have areas of land set aside for their own use.
(a) [agricultural land]: Type I and II, 1·44 ha. per member; Type III LPG, 0·30 ha. per member; personal plots in GPGs covered only about 200 ha. of agricultural land (out of about 18,000 ha.) in 1967.

9 Decision to abolish MTS in 1963. Machinery was transferred free of charge to Type III LPGs; Type I and II LPGs could purchase machinery, or could be served by reorganized MTS/RTS for a fee.

10 (b): (i) 7·7%; (ii) 85·3%.

11 State farm amalgamations between 1958–63; some larger farms split up again in 1964; evidence in 1967 of new amalgamations and possible conversion of LPGs to state farms as the number of state farms decreased and the area increased. Since the final collectivization drive in 1960, the number and area of Type I and II LPGs has fallen continuously because of amalgamations and the policy of upgrading these farms to Type III status. Amalgamation of Type III LPGs began in 1964 and continues to present (1967). Overall decline in area covered by LPGs in 1967 indicates conversion of some LPGs to state farms.

12 Nothing reported.

13 Agricultural and forestry: 14·0% in 1967 (14·4% in 1966).

Hungary (mid-1967) [1]

1 (a): (i) 14·2% (state farms alone, 13·1%); (ii) 70·8%; (iii) 9·6%; (iv) 2·5%; (v) 2·9%.
(b): (iii) 21–22% in 1968 (*Népszabadság*, 22 January 1969).
(c) [incomplete figures – second quarter, 1967]: (i) 175,414 state farm workers and employees, and 37,485 workers and employees of state agricultural machine stations; (ii) 791,405 co-operative farm members permanently engaged in agriculture.

2 'Simple co-operatives' (also called 'lower level co-operatives'), specialize in wine, fruit and vegetable production. In 1968, they covered 3·4% of arable land. Changes introduced in 1969 brought the 'simple' co-operatives closer in form to the kolkhoz-like agricultural producers' co-operatives.

3 (a) 835; (b) 3160 ha.

4 (a) 340 co-operative farm members per farm; (b) 1280 ha.

5 (a) 1·6 ha. arable land.

6 (a) 0·47 ha. arable land per farm member (legal maximum: 0·57 ha.); (b) legal maximum is 0·285 ha. arable land; (c) legal limits are from 0·07 to 0·14 ha. arable land.

7 (a) Domestic production of small machinery, including tractors, in 1967 met only 40–45% of demand (*Dunántúli Napló*, 1 December 1967). Imports of small tractors from Czechoslovakia (no data available). The National Savings Bank grants co-operative farm members short-term credits (2–5 years) of from 5,000–15,000 forint for the purchase of small machinery for their personal plots (Sandor Kiss, 'Hungarian Agriculture Under the NEM', *East Europe*, no. 8 (1968), p. 16, and *East Europe*, no. 4 (1967), p. 34).
(b) Hodmezovasarhely Agricultural Machine Repairing Enterprise and the West German HANKO Works signed an agreement in May 1969 to manufacture jointly 500 small tractors each year (*Magyar Hirlap*, 13 May 1969).

8 (a) A scheme began in 1970 to sell fertilizer in small parcels (5 to 10 kg.) for use on all types of personal plots; (b) Various plant protection agents have been available in small parcels for use on all types of personal plots since the late 1960s; (c) Arrangements

[1] *Sources: Statistical Pocket Book of Hungary, 1968* (Budapest, 1968); *Statistical Yearbook, 1967* (Budapest, 1968).

have been made to provide mixed concentrates in small parcels for use on all types of personal plots (*Dunántúli Napló*, 27 January 1970); (d) The state subsidy given to persons buying heifers in calf was raised to 8,000 forint (from 5,000) on 1 January 1970 (*Magyar Hírlap*, 5 December 1969). Also, co-operative farm members can buy sows with interest-free state loans and pay later in kind with young pigs and fattened pigs (Radio Budapest, 12 September 1969).

9 Decision to abolish MTS in December 1964: most machinery sold to agricultural co-operatives, but very large tractors assigned to state agricultural machine stations which also serve as repair stations.

11 State farm amalgamations between 1960–63 reduced their number from 333 to 210; since then, little change in this sector. In co-operative farm sector, continuous process of farm amalgamation from the end of collectivization to the present (1960–67), during which the number of farms fell from 4,265 to 3,033. Little or no sovkhozization.

12 Under the 'Nádudvar system' in use on more than 80% of the co-operative farms, a farm member, farm family, or other small work unit is assigned a specific piece of land for the cultivation and harvesting of highly specialized row crops (e.g. maize, sugar beets, potatoes), or for intensive farming (e.g. vineyards, livestock production). The farmers receive a guaranteed percentage of the total output regardless of results, plus a payment for their work based on trudodni.[1] The Nádudvar system is not used for mechanized extensive farming, such as grain production.[2]

13 Socialist sector of agriculture only: 14·9% in 1967 (15·8% in 1966).

Poland (mid-1968)[3]

1 (a): (v) 84·8%; (i) 13·7%; (ii) 1·1%; (iii) est. 0·06%; (vi) collective husbandry of agricultural circles, 0·4%.
(b) [1967]: (v) 86·7%; (i) 12·0%; (ii) [including (iii)] 1·1%.
(c) [Incomplete figures]: (v) 5,822,000 persons engaged 'exclusively' in private farming, and 276,000 engaged 'mainly' in

[1] 'Labour-days': accounting units credited to each worker on the basis of job classification (depending on skill), fulfilment of work quota, and quality of work, at centrally determined rates. The value of the unit is settled annually *ex post*, according to the financial results of the whole farm.
[2] See my op. cit., 1969, p. 727.
[3] *Sources: Rocznik Statystyczny, 1968* (Warsaw, 1968); *Concise Statistical Yearbook of Poland, 1969* (Warsaw, 1969).

private farming (in 1960); (i) 363,000 full-time employees on state farms subordinate to the Ministry of Agriculture (end of 1968); 139,000 full- and part-time employees in agricultural circles (end of 1968); (ii) 33,200 members of co-operative farms distributing income (end of 1967).

2 Agricultural circles were established after 1956 to acquire farm machinery and equipment for the collective use of individual peasants. They also provide collective supplies of fertilizers, plant protection agents, and building materials, and engage in a variety of collective production tasks (including cultivation of land, milk processing, and livestock breeding). At the end of 1968, there were 34,800 agricultural circles, with 2,330,000 members (about 38% of the private farmers). In all, only 25,100 of the circles (72%) conducted economic activities. In June 1968, 3,700 of the circles conducted collective farming on about 60,000 ha. of arable land belonging to the State Land Fund. Two types of farms exist in the co-operative sector: Type I co-operatives, in which only land is pooled; and Type II co-operatives (similar to kolkhozes) in which land and livestock are pooled. At the end of 1967, there were 171 Type I co-operatives and 959 Type II co-operatives distributing income.

3 [State farms subordinate to the Ministry of Agriculture, mid-1967]: (a) 57 full-time employees; (b) 330 ha.; (c) 12 15-h.p. units (9 physical units). [Note: there were also 2,376 other state farms, covering only 55,800 ha. of arable land.]

4 (a) [Co-operative farms distributing income, end of 1967]: Type I co-operative, 15 members; Type II, 32 members; (b) [total land area]: Type I, 130 ha.; Type II, 230 ha.; (c) [all income-distributing co-operatives]: 6 15-h.p. units (4 physical units).

5 (a) Approx. 4·7 ha. of agricultural land (including approx. 3·6 ha. arable); (b) 40 ha. agricultural land.

6 (a) [Total land area per member, end of 1967]: Type I co-operative, 0·35 ha.; Type II, 0·30 ha.

7 In December 1967, a decision was announced to sell repaired old tractors and agricultural machines withdrawn from service to individuals. Shortage of tractors necessitated postponement of any decision to sell new tractors to private farmers [see *East Europe*, no. 2 (1968), p. 51], though peasants can buy new tractors with hard currency sent from abroad.

8 (a) A law establishing minimum quantities of fertilizers to be used on farms in various categories was passed in June 1967. Peasants who sell grain to the state under contract receive a

56   EVERETT M. JACOBS

discount on fertilizer purchases [see *East Europe*, no. 7 (1967), p. 49].

9 The MTS were converted into state machinery and repair stations after 1956, and most of their machinery was sold to the co-operative farms and agricultural circles. The stations now serve as repair shops for tractors and other equipment owned by individual peasants and the agricultural circles. They also engage extensively in rural transportation and provide a heavy machinery service to private and co-operative farms for a fee. At the end of 1968, there were 357 state machine stations and 634 branches [*Ekonomika Selskogo Khozyaìstva*, no. 10 (1969), p. 110]. Peasants who require mechanization services can use the agricultural circles.

10 [Not including garden tractors]: (a): (i) 39·6%; (ii) 3·4%; (iii) 13·7%; (v) agricultural circles, 39·4%; state machinery stations, 3·8%; (b): (i) 36·1%; (ii) 3·2%; (iii) 14·0%; (v) agricultural circles, 42·9%; state machinery stations, 3·7%.

11 No sovkhozization. Amalgamation of state farms subordinate to the Ministry began in 1965 (6,515 state farms at the end of June 1965; 5,792 at the end of June 1968). The area covered by state farms has increased mainly through acquisitions from the State Land Fund, but also as a result of acquisitions from individual peasants following the land consolidation law of January 1968. After the decollectivization of 1955–56, the number of co-operatives and the number of members continued to decline through 1962. From 1963 to present, there has been a gradual expansion of area and number of members, with a limited degree of amalgamation (1,342 co-operatives distributing income at the end of 1963; 1,130 at the end of 1967).

12 No special arrangements because of the small size of socialized farms.

13 [Current prices] 15·9% in 1968 (15·2% in 1967).

Rumania (1967)[1]

1 (a): (i) 20·2% (state farms alone, 16·8%); (ii) 66·9%; (iii) 8·2%; (v) 4·6%; (vi) agricultural associations (lower form of agricultural co-operative), 0·1%.

---

[1] *Sources: Anuarul Statistic al RPR, 1968* (Bucharest, 1968); George Cioranescu, 'How Efficient Is Rumanian Agriculture?', *East Europe*, no. 9 (1967), p. 13; *Ekonomika stran sotsializma: 1966 god* (Moscow, 1967), p. 191; Row 1(b): John Michael Montias, *Economic Development in Communist Rumania* (London, 1967), p. 104; Radio Bucharest, 31 May 1970.

(b) [1964]: *Crop output:* (i) 20·2% (state farms alone, 18·0%); (ii) 60·9%; (iii) 13·6%; (v) 4·3%; (vi) agricultural associations, 1·2%. *Animal output:* (i) 18·6% (state farms alone, 16·9%); (ii) 19·5%; (iii) 46·2%; (v) 15·6%; (vi) agricultural associations, 0·1%.
(c) [Incomplete figures]: (i) 287,200 registered employees engaged in agricultural work on state farms; 96,012 registered employees engaged in agricultural activity in MTS; (ii) 3,441,200 families belonging to agricultural co-operatives.

2 The remaining agricultural associations are gradually being up-graded to full agricultural producer co-operatives. In 1967, they occupied only 0·3% of total agricultural land.

3 (a) 837 registered employees engaged in agricultural work; (b) 4,800 ha.; (c) 136 15-h.p. units (80 physical units).

4 (a) 736 families; (b) 1,570 ha.; (c) tractor work done by MTS.

6 (a) 0·23 ha. arable land per family (legal maximum, 0·30 ha.).

8 (c) Since June 1970, co-operative farmers and individual peasants in the hilly regions and river meadows have been permitted to buy annually from the state 100 to 150 kg. of maize for each cow from which they deliver 700 to 1,000 or over 1,000 litres of milk respectively, on the basis of a contract; (d) Since June 1970, cash incentives and some tax benefits have been offered to co-operative farmers and to individual peasants who sell young cattle to the state or to co-operative organizations.

9 (a) 369 15-h.p. units (221 physical units); (b) 332 registered employees engaged in agricultural activity; (c) the number of MTS and the average size of each tractor park continues to increase year by year: 264 MTS in 1965, 273 in 1966, 289 in 1967. There are no plans to sell the MTS machinery to the farms.

10 (a): (i) 30·0%; (iv) 68·4%; (b): (i) 29·5%; (iv) 68·9%.

11 Intense campaign to amalgamate state farms in 1967: their number dropped from an all-time high of 731 in 1966 to 343 in 1967. Some amalgamation of co-operative farms in connection with collectivization drive between 1961–63. Number and area of co-operatives has remained steady since 1964. No sovkhozization.

12 Small work units for certain labour-intensive crops (e.g. fruits and vegetables); defined part of harvest (in addition to trudodens) paid to unit members.

13 [1963 prices] 16·3% in 1966.

USSR (1967) [1]

1 (a): (i) 47·8%; (ii) 49·2%; (iii) 1·8%; (iv) 1·1%.
(b) approx. (i) 43%; (ii) 31%; (iii) 17%; (iv) 9%.
(c) [Incomplete figures]: (i) 7,889,000 workers and employees; (ii) 18·2 million kolkhoz members taking part in the work of the kolkhoz; (v) 40,000 private farmers [in 1966].

2 All collective farms are of the kolkhoz type.

3 (a) 617; (b) 8,300 ha.; (c) 115 15-h.p. units (55 physical units).

4 (a) 418; (b) 3,000 ha.; (c) 45 15-h.p. units (24 physical units).

6 (a) 0·30 ha. arable land per household (0·50 ha. legal maximum);
(b) 0·30 ha. per family legal maximum;
(c) 0·15 ha. legal maximum.

7 (a) No; (b) No.

8 (c) Since December 1964, the State Committee for Procurement has been responsible for providing additional feed grain to kolkhoz members and to workers and employees owning livestock; (d) Since December 1964, Gosbank has been permitted to extend credit for the purchase of cows and heifers to kolkhoz members and to workers and employees. A five-year credit of up to 300 roubles per family for buying cows and up to 150 roubles for buying heifers may be granted.

9 The MTS were reorganized into repair stations in 1958 and the machinery was sold to the collective farms.

10 (a): (i) 42·0%; (ii) 47·1%; (b): (i) 40·3%; (ii) 49·2%.

11 Little sovkhozization since the fall of Khrushchev in late 1964. Previously two great waves: 1954–56 and 1959–60. Amalgamations of kolkhozes began in 1950: large-scale campaign in 1950 and also 1958–60, but process came to virtual halt after Khrushchev's ouster. Number of sovkhozes increased from almost 5,000 at the end of 1950 to close to 13,000 at the end of 1967; number of kolkhozes dropped from 254,000 at the end of 1949 to around 36,200 at the end of 1967.

12 Original zveno (link) system, with 5–6 kolkhoz members farming a small plot of land, was dropped in 1950 on the grounds that it hindered the introduction of mechanization. New system of mechanized zvenos, consisting of 5–6 highly-

[1] Sources: Narodnoe Khozyaistvo SSSR v 1967 g. (Moscow, 1968); Strana Sovetov za 50 Let (Moscow, 1967). Row 1(b): Karl-Eugen Wädekin, 'Private Production in Soviet Agriculture', Problems of Communism, no. 1 (1968), p. 23; idem, Die Sowjetischen Staatsgüter (Wiesbaden, 1969), p. 52; P. J. Wiles in Analyse et Prévision (Sept. 1966), pp. 601–2; Wädekin, op. cit. (1969); Izvestia, 2 April 1965.

skilled machine operators who cultivate and harvest crops on a specific piece of land, introduced in mid-1960s. Mechanized zvenos are used for row crops, intensive farming, and also extensive grain farming. Members of zveno receive their usual tradodni plus bonuses for the over-fulfilment of production plans. Approval for wide application of system, subject to local conditions, in May 1969 (*Komsomolskaya Pravda*, 11 May 1969).

13 17·6% in 1967 (17·9% in 1966).

Yugoslavia (1967) [1]

1 Note: 'Social holdings' are composed of the following: state sector – agricultural farms, estates, and combined establishments; co-operative sector – peasants' producer co-operatives (i.e. kolkhoz-type collective farms) and agricultural co-operatives (simple-type co-operatives); other social holdings – holdings of such official institutions and enterprises as agricultural institutes, schools, stations, etc. Farms of peasants who are members of agricultural co-operatives and also of peasants who co-operate with social holdings are considered to be private farms. Most agricultural co-operatives conduct their own economic activities, and all the land, animals, and machinery owned by the agricultural co-operatives is part of the social sector. 'Arable land' refers to arable land and gardens.

(a): (v) 84·3%; (i) 10·1%; (ii) agricultural co-operatives, 4·3%; peasants' producer co-operatives and other social holdings, 1·2%.

(b) [Social product, i.e. national income plus depreciation]: (v) 71·4%; (i) [including peasants' producer co-operatives] 16·4%; (ii) agricultural co-operatives, 8·6%; other social holdings, 1·2%.

(c) [Incomplete figures]: (v) 5,585,000 agriculturalists and females who work mainly or periodically on private holdings (1960 figure); (i) 143,874 persons employed; (ii) agricultural co-operatives, 95,026 persons employed; peasants' producer co-operatives and other social holdings, 17,070 persons employed.

2 In 1967 there were about 1,600 agricultural co-operatives and 17 peasants' producer co-operatives (as well as 287 farms in the state sector and 334 other social holdings). Agricultural co-operatives accounted for 63·7% of the total number of social

[1] *Sources: Statistički Godišnjak FNRJ, 1962* (Belgrade, 1962); *Statistički Godišnjak Jugoslavije, 1968* (Belgrade, 1968); *Statistical Pocket-Book of Yugoslavia, 1968* (Belgrade, 1968); *Statistical Pocket-Book of Yugoslavia, 1969* (Belgrade, 1969).

holdings. Peasants who are members of agricultural co-operatives keep their own property and derive their income from what they have produced on their land; tools are loaned to, or borrowed from, the co-operative, rent being paid to the owners. Agricultural co-operatives purchase and market surplus agricultural products, process agricultural products, and provide seeds and equipment for members. Machinery from social holdings is also used to cultivate privately owned land: in 1967, 17·3% of total cultivated land in the private sector was cultivated by socially owned machinery. About 20% of the individual peasants engaged in some form of co-operation with social holdings in 1967.

3 (a) 501 persons employed; (b) 2,675 ha.; (c) 65 physical tractors.

4 (a) Agricultural co-operatives, 60 persons employed; peasants' producer co-operatives and other social holdings, 49 persons employed; (b) agricultural co-operatives, 205 ha.; peasants' producer co-operatives and other social holdings, 255 ha.; (c) agricultural co-operatives, 9 physical units; peasants' producer co-operatives and other social holdings, 4 physical units.

5 (a) 4·7 ha. agricultural land (of which 2·4 ha. arable); (b) 10 ha. arable land.

6 (a) [Peasants' producer co-operative] 1 ha. arable land legal maximum.
(c) maximum of 3 ha. of arable land, or 5 ha. of woodland.

9 (c) MTS were disbanded between 1951–52 and their machinery was turned over to the then-operating peasants' producer co-operatives.

10 (b): (i) 40·0%; (ii) agricultural co-operatives, 30·8%; peasants' producer co-operatives and other social holdings, 3·3%; (iii) 25·9%.

11 The decision in 1953 to abandon the policy of forced collectivization led to the almost total elimination of peasants' producer co-operatives by the early 1960s. The disbandment of some agricultural co-operatives and the amalgamation of others reduced the total number from 7,114 in 1953 to 3,228 in 1961. Total arable area covered by agricultural co-operatives remained fairly steady between 1962–67, but the number of co-operatives fell to around 1,600 because of amalgamations. Large-scale amalgamation campaigns in the state sector between 1958–60 and 1962–64 reduced the number of holdings from 776 in 1957 to 287 in 1967.

12 Nothing reported for state sector. No special arrangements necessary for other types of social holdings because of small size of units.

13 Agriculture and fisheries: 8·5% in 1967 (8·6% in 1966).

B. QUESTIONNAIRE ON THE PLANNING OF AGRICULTURE

1 *Intermediate planning organs*
   (a) What are the intermediate planning organs?
   (b) How are the powers divided between these organs and the centre?
   (c) Is Party influence direct or indirect?

2 *Indicators and the decision of output*
   (a) What input, output, technological, and financial indicators are obligatory on the farm?
   (b) Do arrangements differ between state, collective, and private agriculture?
   (c) In the absence of obligatory output indicators, must there be long-term inter-enterprise contracts? What power has the centre to interfere with these?
   (d) Who decides the sowing plan?

3 What is the *system of procurement* in the three sectors, and to what extent is it determined by:
   (a) a zagotovka (compulsory delivery at low price)?
   (b) a zakupka (semi-compulsory delivery at more-or-less market price)?
   (c) kontraktatsia (contract delivery at prices agreed between farms and procurement agencies)?
   (d) a free market, even if only a marginal one?

4 When were *wholesale prices* of produce last reformed, and on what principles? Do they differ by region or type of ownership?

5 Upon what principle are *industrial inputs* allocated? Is there discrimination by price or quality among the ownership sectors? What turnover tax is levied?

6 *Capital charge*
   (a) Is there a capital charge on budget-provided capital? How does it differ by sectors of ownership, how big is it, and on what precisely is it levied?
   (b) Does the capital charge affect the product price or the enterprise's incentive funds, or is it simply a deduction from the given profits taxes?

(c) Is there any rent of land or its equivalent (e.g. differentiated procurement prices, the inclusion of land value in the capital charge, etc.)?

7 *The financing of capital*

(a) What authority mainly spends amortization quotas (other than the part spent on 'capital repairs', which has always been financed by the enterprise)?

(b) Can any fixed capital be borrowed from a bank, governmental agency, or other enterprise (as opposed to budgetary allocation)?

(c) What is the role of intermediate planning organs?

(d) Is there 'full khozraschet', and if so, what does it mean?

8 *Disposal of profit in the state sector*

(a) What rates of profit tax are there, and precisely what is the tax base?

(b) Are capital charges part of, or additional to, it?

(c) What is the status of intra-branch subsidies; of central subsidies?

(d) How much profit is retained by the enterprise, and into what funds, if any, must retained profit be divided?

9 *Disposal of collective farm income*

(a) Into what funds, including tax, is collective farm income divided?

(b) How much goes into each?

10 *Investment decisions*

(a) Who makes investment decisions, and up to what limits of cost?

(b) What are the principal investment criteria?

11 *Bankruptcy*: Is it possible for a state farm or collective farm to go bankrupt? What procedure is used in dealing with bankrupt farms? Have any farms been declared bankrupt?

RESPONSES

Bulgaria[1]

1 (a) Local People's Councils, in conjunction with the district co-operative union (for co-operative farms) and district

[1] Sources: Ekonomika Selskogo Khozyaistva, no. 4 (1967), pp. 120–1, no. 3 (1969), pp. 117–19, and no. 12 (1969), pp. 110–11; E. V. Rudakov, S. A. Mellin, and V. I. Storozhev, Ekonomicheskaya reforma v selskom khozyaistve sotsialisticheskikh stran (Moscow, 1968), pp. 55, 57, 60, 69, 72–3, 93, 96–9, 105, 139; World Marxist Review, no. 8 (1966), pp. 6–7, no. 1 (1968), pp. 13–15, and no. 6 (1969), p. 28.

amalgamated enterprises of state farms (for state farms), for the sale of nine 'fixed items' (cereals, rice, beans, sunflower seeds, meat, tomatoes, tobacco, milk, and eggs); local branches of procurement agencies for other products.

(b) Plans for the sale of the nine fixed items in (a) are drawn up by the State Planning Committee. Local People's Councils and district co-operative or state farm agencies draw up local plans based on the central figures. Plans for the sale of all other products are worked out by the co-operative or state farms in agreement with the appropriate procurement agencies. Government, procurement, and planning authorities at the province level must approve these plans. Finally, the State Planning Committee can amend these plans, which are then incorporated into the national plan.

(c) Direct Party influence through representation on the farms and in local People's Councils and farm agencies; also, in hilly and mountainous regions, through Party workers attached to MTS.

2 (a) The only obligatory indicators are for the sale of the nine fixed items in 1(a).

(b) Co-operative and state farms are treated the same under 2(a). Private farms are exempt from obligatory indicators.

(c) For products without obligatory sale indicators, the farms must conclude contracts with the various procurement organizations. The Council of Ministers sets targets for the procurement agencies for eight items (including cotton, hemp, flax, potatoes, grapes, and apples), and the agencies offer such incentives as higher prices, bonuses, and supply of deficit equipment to encourage the sale of these items. Central planners can also use economic means (e.g. prices, bonuses, etc.) to encourage greater contract commitment. If this fails, they can resort to exerting pressure on local procurement and government agencies to conclude larger contracts.

(d) Farms decide their own sowing plans, which must be geared to meet their obligatory sales quota [see 1(b)].

3 (b) There is no practical difference between procurement by obligatory delivery or by contract delivery [see 2(a–c)]. Peasants can sell produce from their personal plots to procurement agencies. Unified purchase prices are applied for all categories of farms.

(d) A free market operates for the sale of produce from personal plots; volume n.a.

4 Wholesale prices were reformed in 1964 in order to put production of many commodities (e.g. wheat, milk, maize, etc.) on a

profitable basis for the first time. Additional charges were made in 1969. Unified purchase prices have been established for all categories of farms, through farms located in mountainous and semi-mountainous areas receive zonal price increases of up to 50% over purchase prices for various items (including milk, meat, wool, fruits, and grapes) in order to put their production on a sufficiently profitable basis. The price scale is based on indicators of quality [see *Ekonomika Selskogo Khozyaistva*, no. 1 (1969), pp. 112–13]. There are bonuses for above-contract sales to procurement agencies if such sales are envisaged in the contract; if not, there is a smaller bonus. Procurement agencies can raise prices in order to encourage deliveries. Among all the fruits and vegetables, only potatoes, grapes, and apples have centrally fixed prices.

5 In addition to being able to purchase industrial inputs through the normal channels (which include the State Farms Economic Concern for state farms, and the Co-operative Farm Union for co-operative farms), the farms can receive certain inputs (in particular, concentrated fodder) at favourable prices for concluding special contracts with procurement agencies or for making above-contract sales. Favourable terms for the purchase of fertilizer and 'other means of production' are also offered on a similar basis [see 2(c) and 3(b)].

6 (a) State farms pay a capital charge of 1% to the state on the value of their machines, equipment, and buildings (this charge does not affect gardens or vineyards). The charge is established for each district amalgamated enterprise of state farms, which then apportions it by individual farms. Co-operative farms, n.a.
(b) The capital charge for state farms is deducted from total actual profits, so does not affect price. Incentive funds are formed after deduction of the capital charge.
(c) Farms located in mountainous and semi-mountainous areas receive zonal price increases [see 4].

7 (a) The entire amortization quota remains at the disposal of the enterprise.
(b) Budget-provided capital, free of interest, is supplied only to state farms and only for the creation and care of new long-term plantations, or for the formation of a basic herd in state farms set up on the basis of co-operative farms in mountainous and hilly regions. All other capital for state and co-operative farms is in the form of interest-bearing credits from banks. Co-operative farms can receive credits for capital investment at an annual interest of 2%. The emphasis is mainly on providing short-term

credits, though the upper limit is 20 years. State farms can receive short-term bank credits at an annual interest of 2%.

(c) As the need for credits must be foreseen in the enterprise's plan, the intermediate planning organs presumably exert considerable influence in the approval and allocation of credits.

(d) Full khozrashchet operates for both state and co-operative farms. Each farm is supposed to be economically independent and self-financing (with the use of credits if necessary, but no state grants), and operations are to be based on the law of value.

8 (a) Turnover tax is levied on the total revenue received by the farm, including any receipts from the fund for crop failure and natural calamity. There is no profit tax as such.

(d) Profits are allocated to a fund for expanding production and improving techniques (to augment basic and turnover funds, to raise the technological level production, and to train personnel); a social and cultural fund; and to a reserve wages fund (for payments for state social security, for individual bonuses for workers and employees, and for bringing wages up to the guaranteed minimum level). The rest of the profits goes into a general wages fund, from which the workers and employees are paid (minimum wages are guaranteed).

9 (a) Co-operative farm income is divided into a fund for expanding production and improving techniques; a social and cultural fund; and a reserve wages fund. The remaining income goes into a general wages fund (minimum wages are guaranteed); information on taxes n.a.

10 n.a.

11 No.

Czechoslovakia[1]

1 (a) District Agricultural Associations (DAAs).

(b) Central planners set obligatory plan indicators to DAAs for marketable produce for the following: cereals (including wheat, rye, and barley), potatoes, rape-seed, industrial sugar beets, meat, eggs, and milk. DAAs are assigned shares of the obligatory central plan indicators according to the specialization

[1] *Sources:* East Europe, no. 5 (1967), pp. 37–9; *Economic Survey of Europe in 1966* (UN, New York, 1967), part 1, chapter II, p. 24; *Economic Survey of Europe in 1968* (UN, New York, 1969), p. 141; *Ekonomika Selskogo Khozyaistva*, no. 4 (1967), p. 121 and no. 3 (1969), p. 120; *Ekonomika stran sotsializma: 1966 god* (Moscow, 1967), p. 232; Gregor Lazarcik. 'The Performance of Czechoslovak Agriculture Since World War II', in Jerzy F. Karcz, ed., *Soviet and East European Agriculture* (Berkeley, 1967), p. 403; E. V. Rudakov, S. A. Mellin, and V. I. Storozhev, op. cit., pp. 55–7, 71, 106, 115, 140–1; *World Marxist Review*, no. 9 (1967), pp. 36–8.

of the farms in their district. The only obligatory plan indicator passed on by DAAs to co-operative and state farms is for marketed produce in cereals. For the rest, the farms use the DAA's plan as the basis of their own plans. Combined plans of DAAs make up the draft national plan, which central planners can modify by the use of economic levers or by using binding directives to set new targets in marketable produce (chiefly cereals).

(c) Party organizations in rural areas act as overlords to state agencies in economic, political, and social matters [see *Život Strany*, no. 3 (1970)].

2 (a) State and co-operative farms have obligatory indicators only for marketable produce in cereals.

(b) Both state and co-operative farms are subject to the conditions in 2(a). Private farmers are no longer required to meet delivery quotas. They decide what to produce and what to sell, and can conclude contracts with the procurement agencies [see *Zemědělské Noviny*, 7 December 1968].

(c) State and co-operative farms must conclude contracts with procurement agencies on the basis of the farms' marketable produce plan. The obligatory indicators for marketable produce in cereals are incorporated into contracts. Private farmers can also conclude contracts. All contracts are binding.

(d) Farms decide their own sowing plans, which must be geared to meet their obligatory plan indicator for marketable produce in cereals [see 1(b)].

3 (c) Procurement is based on a combination of zakupka and kontraktatsia [see 2(b–c)]. There are fixed prices for such major staple commodities as wheat, rye, barley, sugar beets, hops, potatoes, beef cattle, hogs, milk, and eggs. These prices are based on the average production costs in the regions accounting for the bulk of the given product. In addition, differential bonus payments are made to farms located in poor natural or climatic conditions. Free prices, based on supply-and-demand, are in force for fruits and vegetables, lambs for slaughter, millet, buckwheat, forest fruits, mushrooms, freshwater fish (except carp), rabbits, and several other products. Farms have the right to set prices on the basis of agreements with procurement organizations for above-plan produce delivered. Also, procurement organizations have the right to offer price incentives to farms. Bonuses are paid for increases in marketable produce (compared with the average for the three previous years) for milk, cereals, sugar beets, and several other products. (d) A free market operates for the sale of produce from personal plots; volume n.a.

4 Wholesale prices were last reformed in 1966 in a plan to bring the net income of an average state farm worker and co-operative farmers up to the level existing in the non-agricultural sector. There are no distinctions of price between classes of ownership, though regional price differences do exist [see 3(c)].

5 n.a.

6 (a) No.

(c) A land tax is payable on the total agricultural area of a farm. Also, differential bonus payments are made to farms located in conditions worse than those on which the uniform purchase prices are based.

7 (a) n.a.

(b) Budget-provided capital is granted free of charge (in the form of a subsidy) to state and co-operative farms for the following: stabilization and enlargement of the labour force; partial compensation for productive and non-productive capital investments; cattle breeding; and improvement in living conditions. Credits are granted to state and co-operative farms on the same basis: credits for working capital, 3% annual interest; short-term credits for capital investment, 3% annual interest; long-term credits for capital investment, 5% annual interest; special short-term credits and special long-term credits, 5% annual interest.

(c) n.a.

(d) No.

8 (d) Profits are divided into the renewal and development fund for capital investments and the expansion of the means of production; the working capital fund; the reserve fund; the cultural and social fund; the fund for improvement of living conditions; and the fund for labour remuneration.

9,10 n.a.

11 No.

East Germany[1]

1 (a) District Agricultural Councils, together with District Production Administrations, for co-operative farms: Regional Agricultural Councils (encompassing several districts), together with Regional Production Administrations, for state farms.

[1] Sources: Ekonomika Selskogo Khozyaistva, no. 4 (1967), p. 120, and no. 3 (1969), pp. 118–19; E. V. Rudakov, S. A. Mellin, and V. I. Storozhev, op. cit., pp. 34–6, 50, 56–9, 71, 73, 105–8, 116–17, 136–9 Gerhard Grüneberg, Ot krestyanskoi vzaimopomoshchi k sotsialisticheskomu selskomu khozyaistvu v GDR (Moscow, 1967), pp. 192–3.

(b) District Production Administrations 'put the decisions of the District Agricultural Councils into practice' and are responsible for the effective guidance of the agricultural co-operatives within the district. Regional Production Administrations are responsible for all the farms (co-operative and state farms) within the region. They also co-ordinate the activities of enterprises producing the means of production for agriculture, as well as the work of purchasing organizations and processing enterprises. The centre exercises firm control through the production administrations, which are much more powerful than the corresponding agricultural councils.

(c) Direct Party influence through farm Party organizations and representation on key administrative bodies.

2 (a) The only obligatory indicators for co-operative farms are for the production and sale of grain and potatoes. State farms, n.a.

(c) The obligatory indicators of sales [see 2(a)] are incorporated into contracts with procurement bodies. For products without obligatory indicators, the farms must conclude contracts with procurement agencies.

(d) Farms decide their own sowing plans, which must be in keeping with the obligatory indicators for the production and sale of grain and potatoes.

3 (a) Zagotovka procurements for crops and most livestock products were abolished in 1964. The remaining livestock zagotovka procurements were abolished on 1 January 1969. In 1966, compulsory deliveries of livestock products accounted for more than 30% of the cattle, 28% of the milk, and 11% of the eggs procured.

(b) All procurements have been on the basis of zakupka purchase contracts since 1 January 1969 [see 2(c) and 3(a)]. (d) A peasant free market operates; volume n.a.

4 Some wholesale prices were reformed in 1964 and the rest in 1969 [see 3(a)] in an effort to ensure the profitability of production and secure a reasonable income for co-operative farmers. Produce prices are differentiated according to the quality of the land (the better the land, the lower the prices) and according to the quality of the produce. Since 1964, co-operatives have received premia for increasing the production and sale of milk, pork, beef and eggs in comparison with the previous year. The premium differs according to the area of the country and is progressive according to the degree of increase over the previous year. Procurement organizations and enterprises cannot establish prices for agricultural produce. However, local organs have the right to vary

the prices within the established limits for co-operative farms. In addition, the District Production Administration, in conjunction with the procurement organizations, can arrange for a special extra premium to be added to the purchase price paid to individual farms. State farms receive the same prices for produce as co-operative farms. Also, the system of premium payments for state farms has been substantially the same as that for co-operative farms since mid-1966.

5 n.a.

6 (a) n.a.

(c) Land is rated below or above 100 points for quality, and produce prices vary accordingly. Also, premia on procurement prices are differentiated according to region [see 4].

7 (b) Co-operative farms can arrange for long-term credits through the agricultural bank. Interest ranges from 1·5% to 3·5% a year. Short-term credit can be obtained by co-operatives for rationalization and the introduction of necessary technology. Annual interest on short-term credits of up to three years is 1·5%; on credits of more than six years, 5%. Credits for replenishing working capital are available to co-operatives at 2% annual interest.

(d) No.

8,9,10 n.a.

11 No.

Hungary[1]

1 (a) District Councils (only for compulsory sowing of bread grains); all other planning is decentralized and is based in part on contract relations between the farms and procurement and processing enterprises.

(b) District Councils receive their targets for compulsory sowing of bread grains from the centre. The purchasing policy of the procurement and processing agencies is determined at the centre, and this affects the nature of the contracts these agencies conclude.

(c) n.a.

[1] *Sources: East Europe*, no. 4 (1967), p. 34; *Economic Survey of Europe in 1967* (UN, New York, 1968), part I, chapter II, p. 28; Sandor Kiss, 'Hungarian Agriculture Under the NEM', *East Europe*, no. 8 (1968), pp. 12–16, 18; *Magyar Hirlap*, 3 December 1968, 16 January 1969 and 17 May 1969; *Népszabadság*, 10 December 1968; E. V. Rudakov, S. A. Mellin, and V. I. Storozhev, op. cit., pp. 56–7, 69–70, 73; *World Marxist Review*, no. 4 (1967), pp. 16–17.

2 (a) None [see 2(d)].

(c) Inter-enterprise contracts between the co-operatives and state procurement and processing agencies are necessary only for products over which the state maintains a monopoly (e.g. bread grain, beef cattle, slaughter pigs, tobacco, raw hides, wool, and paprika). Such produce from individual farms and from personal plots of co-operative farm members must also be sold to the state agencies.

(d) All state, co-operative, and individual peasant farms are assigned compulsory targets for the sowing of bread grains [see 1(a)]. Suggestions have been made to change this to a quota for grain deliveries (*Nograd*, 5 October 1968; and Radio Budapest, 13 August 1969).

3 (b) Only products over which the state has a monopoly must be sold through contract arrangements to state procurement and processing agencies [see 2(c)]. (d) Aside from contract deliveries and the sale of produce affected by state monopoly, co-operatives have the right to sell their output, and also the produce grown by their members on their personal plots, to the following: state procurement and processing organizations, state or co-operative wholesale or retail outlets, export agencies, hotels, restaurants, other organizations, and also directly to consumers in their own shops. Co-operatives can operate their own processing facilities and can market produce jointly with other co-operatives. However, they are not allowed to buy and resell produce, except in specified cases, nor can they assume the functions of wholesale trading organizations. Volume of free market sales n.a.

4 Wholesale prices were last reformed in 1965 when a single price system was introduced for all farms. Agricultural procurement prices were raised in 1966 and 1968 and again (for livestock products) at the beginning of 1970. The new prices are designed to encourage the production of export commodities and raw materials, as well as to stimulate overall production. Prices for staple products (40% of agricultural products) are fixed centrally; other products with considerable free-market turnover (e.g. vegetables, fruit, poultry, eggs, and wine – in all, 40% of agricultural products) are priced within centrally established guidelines; the remaining products are purchased by the state at market prices. Procurement organizations pay supply-and-demand free prices for produce sold to them above the quantity specified in the contract. Co-operatives operating under un-favourable natural and/or economic conditions receive addi-

tional price subsidies for produce sold at centrally-fixed price to the state.

5 n.a.

6 (c) Since the end of 1967, all farmland has been subject to a land tax, which must be paid in cash. The tax varies according to the quality of the land taxed; the lower the quality, the less the tax.

7 (a) The entire amortization quota remains at the disposal of the enterprise.

(b) Co-operatives can receive long-term bank credits (up to 35 years) for capital investments at 1% annual interest. Since the beginning of 1969, state and co-operative farms have been able to get medium-term loans repayable in 48 months at a preferential annual interest rate of 5% (industrial enterprises must pay 6% for 36-month loans). Also, long-term loans for 10 to 15 years are available at 5% per annum. Apart from those facilities, co-operatives receive subsidies covering 50% of costs for construction of modern cattle-sheds, hog farms, and breeding places (cut from 70% in 1970); 70% of costs of new orchard plantations; and 100% of costs of melioration work. The subsidy of 50% of costs for machinery repair was eliminated in 1969 for obsolete machinery and reduced to only 23% for the rest in order to encourage the purchase of new machinery. This subsidy was abolished entirely in 1970 to compensate for the cost of the increased livestock prices. Credits for working capital are provided to co-operatives only if they have increased their working capital over the previous year or if they have insufficient working capital (the latter provision is designed to help weak co-operatives to take advantage of the subsidies). Credits for working capital are provided only for productive purposes, for an average of four years, at 3% annual interest. Co-operative farm members can obtain bank credits of from 5,000 to 15,000 forint for 2 to 5 years for the purchase of small machinery for their personal plots.

(d) No.

8 n.a.

9 (a) Co-operative farm income after tax is allocated to development funds (including an amortization fund and an income-sharing fund for wages), social and cultural funds, and a reserve fund.

10 (b) The profit criterion has been applied to investments in the

agricultural sector of the economy. The general investment criteria are to increase the productivity of labour and to provide for the economic independence of the farms.

11 Co-operative farms with chronic annual deficits can be declared bankrupt if attempts at economic rehabilitation fail. An independent committee is set up by the county council to assess the farm, ascertain reasons for the deficit, and offer suggestions to rectify the situation. If the farm fails to improve its position, it can be granted an economic rehabilitation credit or it can be merged with another farm. As a last resort, the farm's licence can be revoked. Under this procedure, in May 1969 a weak co-operative was disbanded and its workers and production assets were allocated to other farms [see *Magyar Közlöny*, 25 October 1968, and *Szabad Föld*, 16 March 1969 and 11 May 1969].

Poland[1]

1 (a) Powiat (district) State Farm Inspectorates, for state farms; powiat Co-operative Unions, together with powiat procurement agencies, for co-operatives; powiat planning agencies for compulsory deliveries from farms of individual peasants.

(b) Plans drawn up by the state farms in conjunction with the powiat State Farm Inspectorate must be approved by the voivodship (county) State Farm Administration, which then formulates an overall plan for the voivodship. This plan must be approved by the Ministry of Agriculture, after which it is incorporated into the national plan for state farms. The planned output indices for state farms have the force of law. Co-operatives plan their output on the basis of contracts concluded between themselves and the procurement agencies. The powiat Co-operative Union gives only general guidance. Contracts between co-operatives and procurement agencies must be approved by higher procurement organizations. Compulsory deliveries for individual farms are based on quotas sent down from central agencies.

(c) The Party exerts a direct influence in state farm planning since the local Party organization is represented at the conference

[1] *Sources:* Marek Celt, 'Another Round: Peasant and Party in Poland', *East Europe*, no. 2 (1968), pp. 2–3, 5–7; *Concise Statistical Yearbook of Poland, 1969* (Warsaw, 1969), pp. 156, 170–4; *East Europe*, no. 8 (1967), p. 49, and no. 7 (1968), p. 53; *Ekonomika Selskogo Khozyaistva*, no. 4 (1967), p. 121; Michael Gamarnikow, 'Reforms in Agriculture', *East Europe*, no. 11 (1966), pp. 19, 21; E. V. Rudakov, S. A. Mellin, and V. I. Storozhev, *op. cit.*, pp. 43–4, 53–4, 72, 84–5, 87–9, 102; *Życie Gospodarcze*, 12 January 1969.

to draw up the state farm inspectorate plan. A similar situation presumably exists when the co-operatives conclude their contracts with the procurement organizations. The Party has little or no direct influence over the individual farms, though Party members are active in the work of the agricultural circles.

2 (a) Individual farms are still subject to deliveries of grain, meat, and potatoes. Also, a law passed in 1967 defines the minimum quantity of fertilizers to be used by all types of farms. If the minimum amount of fertilizer is not used, fines can be applied up to the total cost of the fertilizer that should have been employed.

(b) Only individual farms have compulsory delivery quotas; all farms have fertilizer input targets.

(c) Co-operative and state farms must conclude contracts with procurement agencies for the sale of produce to the state. These contracts must be approved by higher bodies [see 1(b)]. Individual peasants can sell produce to the state on a voluntary basis through contracts. Contract deliveries can be made only after compulsory delivery quotas have been met. Farmers who sell grain under contract to the state receive a discount on their fertilizer purchases. Central planners use economic means (prices, bonuses, etc.) to encourage contract commitments and stimulate production of desired products.

(d) State farm sowing plans are determined by the farm in conjunction with the powiat State Farm Inspectorate. Co-operative farms decide their own sowing plans. Individual peasants decide their own sowing plans, making provision for compulsory deliveries.

3 (a) Individual farms are subject to zagotovka procurements of grain, meat, and potatoes. Compulsory deliveries are calculated according to a six-category scale of 'social land classification' based on nominal income per ha. The rates are sharply progressive. Obligatory deliveries in 1968 made up 27% of total cereal grain purchases, 21% of total meat purchases (without poultry), and 38% of potato purchases. These deliveries accounted for less than 7% of total cereal grain production, for 15% of total meat production (without poultry), and 4% of total potato production. The state's proceeds from the obligatory deliveries (the difference between the low price for compulsory deliveries and the higher regular contract price) are put into the Agricultural Development Fund which is used to finance machinery purchases and other investments by the agricultural circles. [For a description of the functions of agricultural circles, see

the ownership section of the questionnaire for Poland, question 2.]

(b) Procurements from state farms and co-operative farms are by zakupka, with obligations incorporated into contracts. Individual peasants can also conclude contracts for the delivery of produce. All producers receive the same prices for contract deliveries.

(d) Individual peasants can sell their produce on the free market after they have met their obligatory delivery quotas. The state maintains a virtual monopoly over bulk buying, and prices offered by socialized purchasing agencies for non-contract purchases are invariably lower than for contract purchases, though higher than for obligatory deliveries. Sales by peasants direct to consumers in the licensed markets fetch the highest prices of all. For instance, in 1968 the average price for one quintal of wheat was 232 zlotys for obligatory deliveries, 369 for non-contract purchases, 395 for contract purchases, and 450 for peasant market sales. Individual peasants provided 80·7% of the market output in 1967. Free market volume n.a.

4 Wholesale prices were reformed in 1957, and there have been further price increases since then. The object has been to provide financial incentives for increased production.

5 n.a.

6 (c) Individual peasants pay a land tax based on the same scale of 'social land classification' as their compulsory deliveries [see 3(a)]. The rates are sharply progressive. The private sale of land is governed by a law of 1963 which prohibits the division of farms into plots smaller than eight ha., and by a law of 1964 which forbids private purchases of land unless the buyer already owns from 2 to 5 ha., depending on the region. It was reported in March 1969 that general taxes on land transfer had been abolished, but that a new tax was being prepared [see *East Europe*, no. 5 (1969), p. 50].

7 (b) Co-operative farms can receive long-term credits from the state (from 5 to 36 years) for capital investments at an annual interest of 1%. Subsidies are also available to co-operatives for the purchase of pedigree livestock (up to 70% of costs), electrification (75% of costs), and land melioration on collectively farmed land (up to 40% of costs). State farms receive various special-purpose subsidies from the state. Subsidies are paid for production of high-grade seeds, seed potatoes, and pedigree cattle; for the development of land received from the

State Land Fund; for the wages of probationer students and young specialists; and for the upkeep of crèches. Grants are also made for the acquisition of fuel and lubricants and, for economically weak farms, for spare parts and construction materials. Finally, additional subsidies are given to individual voivodships having economically weak farms.

(c) n.a.

(d) No, except, in a sense, for private peasants.

8,9,10 n.a.

11 No, but the state can take over privately owned farms declared by their owners and appraised by the local authorities to be economically ruined or those mortgaged above their value. Under a law of 1968, land not rationally exploited by the user is liable to be put up for sale at public auction.

Rumania[1]

1 (a) For state farms, local 'state agricultural enterprises'; for co-operative farms since October 1969, county agricultural directorates.

(b) In the state farm sector, the basic production unit is the specialized crop or livestock farm. State agricultural enterprises hand down certain plan indicators from above and direct and manage small groups of close-together state farms with the same specialization (i.e. local state agricultural enterprises for the crop sector are responsible only for farms specializing in crop production; local state agricultural enterprises for the livestock sector are responsible only for farms specializing in livestock production). County trusts of state agricultural enterprises are responsible for all the state agricultural enterprises, regardless of specialization, within the county. Since October 1969, the department for state agricultural enterprises within the Ministry of Agriculture and Forestry directs and co-ordinates the work of the county trusts. For co-operative farms, county agricultural directorates, which are subordinate to both the executive committee of the local People's Council and the Ministry of Agriculture and Forestry, approve local plans and pass them to the Ministry for final approval and co-ordination.

(c) Direct Party influence through the principle that a single

---

[1] *Sources: East Europe*, no. 5 (1967), p. 48; *Ekonomika Selskogo Khozyaistva*, no. 4 (1967), p. 121, and no. 3 (1969), p. 118; Radio Bucharest, 1 February 1969 and 31 May 1970; E. V. Rudakov, S. A. Mellin, V. I. Storozhev, op. cit., pp. 35–6, 50, 57, 85–7, 91.

Party leader should be in charge of both Party and state affairs in a given field. In December 1969, the National Union of Agricultural Production Co-operatives was placed directly under the Central Committee. Also, the county agricultural directorates were placed under the direct supervision of the CC and the Party committees of the respective counties.

2 (a) Co-operative farms have obligatory output indicators for wheat, maize, sunflower seeds, sugar-beets, and potatoes. Beginning in 1971, central planning for co-operatives farm production of cereal crops and animal products will be done only for the quantities contracted by the state (*Scînteia*, 25 December 1969). All plan indicators from above for state farms are compulsory. However, the number of such indicators has been declining since 1967.

(b) Private farms and personal plots of farmers are not subject to obligatory indicators.

(c) Co-operative farms must conclude contracts with procurement agencies for the sale of their produce. Private farmers can enter into such arrangements if they want. State farms must conclude contracts with agro-industrial processing units and procurement organizations. Also, state farms can sell their surplus produce in their own stores.

(d) Co-operative farms decide their own sowing plans, which must be geared to meet their obligatory output indicators [see 2(a)]. State farms, n.a.

3 (b) State farms receive zakupka prices for their contract sales.

(c) Kontraktatsia prices are paid to co-operative and private farms for their contract deliveries. They receive bonus prices for their above-contract sales. County People's Councils have the right to establish contract prices for some types of vegetables and fruit, but prices for other types of vegetables are based on agreements between the co-operatives and local trade organizations.

(d) Produce from private farms and personal plots can be sold on the free market; volume n.a.

4 Prices for certain animal and vegetable products were raised in May 1965 and subsequently. New price increases for the purchase of livestock by the state were introduced in June 1970: a 28.3% increase for top-quality mature cattle, for all categories of producers; a 12.5% increase for top-quality pigs, for co-operative farms, their members, and individual farmers; prices for cow's milk, depending on season, were raised to between

0·10 lei and 0·45 lei per litre for co-operative farms, their members, and individual farmers, and to between 0·10 lei and 0·25 lei for state farms.

5 n.a.

6 (c) Private farms and Agricultural Associations pay a land tax based on the state's calculation of the average per ha. income of the farms. There are five categories of land fertility upon which the incomes are estimated. The per ha. tax differentiated by areas of fertility was abolished for co-operative farms in 1969 and was replaced by a tax based on farm income. State farms, n.a.

7 (a) n.a.

(b) Co-operatives can receive long-term loans from the Agricultural Bank at 3% annual interest for investment projects being carried out at their own expense or on contract, as well as for planting and tending vineyards until they start bearing fruit. Short-term loans at 3% annual interest are also available to cover production costs, transport, and development of annexes, and other temporary needs. The Agricultural Bank maintains control over these transactions. State farms can obtain loans from the State Bank to help finance their operations.

(d) 'Full khozraschet' has not yet been introduced for co-operative farms, though it has been in force for state farms since 1968. Each state farm operates as an independent unit (state agricultural enterprises notwithstanding), has full powers in the administration of its assets, has its own financial responsibility, and is responsible for the tasks concerning marketable output and the fulfillment of the income and expenditure plan.

8,9 n.a.

10 (a) The Ministry of Agriculture and Forestry has had overall responsibility for investment decisions since October 1969.

(b) n.a.

11 No.

USSR[1]

1 (a) Raion (district) or inter-raion agricultural production administrations, together with raion planning commissions, for both sovkhozes and kolkhozes.

[1] *Sources:* G. A. Gaponenko, M. K. Gritsov, and I. K. Popova, *Osnovnye printsipy planirovania selskogo khozyaistva* (Moscow, 1965), p. 15; I. E. Apalkov and A. S. Smirnov, *Ekonomika, organizatsia i planirovanie selskokhozyaistvennogo proizvodstva*

(b) USSR Gosplan's plan for the volume of state procurements is approved by the USSR Council of Ministers. The plan is allocated according to union republics, and within them, according to autonomous republics, oblasts (provinces) or krais (territories), and raions. Using the procurement plan as a basis, the raion agricultural production administration and the raion planning commission 'guide' the farms in drawing up their production and procurement plans. The raion agricultural production administration and the raion planning commission are branches of the raion soviet executive committee. The raion's production and procurement plans are approved by the raion soviet executive committee, which sends them for approval to the oblast (krai) agricultural, planning, and soviet bodies. The oblast (krai) agricultural administration and planning commission make the necessary changes and additions, and the oblast (krai) plan, as approved by the soviet executive committee, is then passed to the republic Ministry of Agriculture and Gosplan for approval. Republic plans are combined to form a national plan. All territorial procurement plans must meet the minimum requirements for procurements set by USSR Gosplan; if they do not, they are returned to the farms for the necessary changes. The USSR Ministry of Agriculture compiles its plan for the development of agricultural production for kolkhozes and for the sovkhozes subordinate to it on the basis of republic plans for production and procurement. Plans for sovkhozes subordinate to other ministries are drawn up by those ministries. In 1965, the government set a 'fixed and unalterable' grain procurement quota of 55·7 million tons a year for 1965–70. A quota of 60 million tons a year will be in force for 1971–75.

(c) Direct Party influence at all levels of planning. For example, representatives of raion Party, soviet, and Komsomol organizations are active on raion agricultural production administration

(Moscow, 1969), pp. 386–97; Keith Bush, 'Agricultural Reforms Since Khrushchev' in *New Directions in the Soviet Economy* (Washington, D.C., 1966), part II–B, pp. 456–62; Roger A. Clarke, 'Soviet Agricultural Reforms Since Khrushchev', *Soviet Studies*, vol. 20, pp. 163–4, 176; *Ekonomicheskaya Gazeta*, no. 16 (1967), pp. 2–3; *Ekonomika Selskogo Khozyaistva*, no. 12 (1968), p. 5; *Ekonomika selskokhozyaistvennykh predpriatii* (Moscow, 1965), pp. 81, 297–8, 317, 320; Jerzy F. Karcz, 'The New Soviet Agricultural Programme', *Soviet Studies*, vol. 17, pp. 135–40; Yu. M. Kozlov, ed., *Administrativnoe pravo* (Moscow, 1968), pp. 383, 387; A. E. Lunev, ed., *Administrativnoe pravo* (Moscow, 1967), pp. 307–11, 318, 320; *Pravda*, 23 May 1969; N. V. Tsapkin and V. I. Pereslegin, eds., *Planirovanie narodnogo khozyaistva SSSR* (Moscow, 1967), pp. 126–32; *Narodnoe khozyaistva SSSR v 1967 g.* (Moscow, 1968), pp. 714, 762.

councils, which decide local agricultural policy. Farms have their own Party organizations, which directly influence on-farm planning.

2 (a) Sovkhozes on full khozraschet [see 7(d)] have the following plan indicators handed down from above: volume of sales to the state of major products (in physical terms), the total wage fund, the total sum of profits, allocations from the state budget, the capital charge on fixed assets, the total volume of centralized capital investments, and the volume of deliveries of tractors, machinery, fertilizer, and so on. Total planned profit is determined by the farm and confirmed by superior organs. Obligatory plan indicators for sovkhozes not on full khozraschet include volume of sales to the state, limits on the number of workers and the wage fund, targets for reducing the cost of basic types of agricultural produce, targets for accumulations and the volume of capital investments, and the limits of financing from the state budget and from the farm. Kolkhozes have obligatory indicators only for the volume of sales to the state.

(b) There are no obligatory indicators for personal plots.

(c) Sovkhozes and kolkhozes must conclude contracts with state procurement agencies for the sale of their planned marketable output. These contracts have the force of law. The raion agricultural production administrations are responsible for organizing the conclusion of contracts between the farms and the procurement bodies. They are also charged with securing the observance of the contracts. The oblast (krai) agricultural administrations check the work of the raion agricultural production administrations.

(d) Sowing plans are worked out by the farms, with the help of the raion production administrations, in accordance with their obligatory plan indicators for the volume of sales to the state.

3 (b) Zakupka is used for the procurement of planned marketable produce from kolkhozes. Although procurements are made through contracts, the contracting agencies have no power to change centrally-fixed prices. Sovkhozes also sell their marketable produce through contracts, but most of them receive fixed prices which are lower than the zakupka price [see 4(a) and 7(d)]. Co-operatives and other purchasing organizations pay kolkhoz zakupka prices for voluntary sales of produce to them from personal plots.

(d) Produce from personal plots can be sold at free market prices in the kolkhoz markets. Volume of the kolkhoz market in 1967 (without sales of consumer co-operatives) was 3,866 million roubles (4·9% of sales of foodstuffs in state, co-operative, and kolkhoz trade).

4 Wholesale prices were last reformed in 1965 to increase the profitability of farm production and to provide financial incentives for farms and farmers to produce more. Purchase prices for several products, including grain and meat, were increased substantially. Prices for such products as wheat, rye, sugar-beets, sunflower seeds, milk and meat are set by union republic Councils of Ministers and are differentiated by zones. Prices for flax, potatoes, buckwheat, millet, rice, and several other products apply for all areas of the country. Kolkhozes and sovkhozes receive the same prices for buckwheat, millet, rice, milk, and sunflower seeds, but for most other products, prices paid to kolkhozes are higher than those for sovkhozes. Sovkhozes on full khozraschet receive the same prices for their produce as kolkhozes in the same zone. All kolkhozes and sovkhozes receive bonus payments of 50% on the normal procurement price for above-plan deliveries of wheat, rye, millet, feed barley, oats, maize, and peas. Bonus schemes also operate for sunflower seeds, rice, and other crops [see *Ekonomika Selskogo Khozyaistva*, no. 11 (1968), p. 59]. While plans for grain deliveries are supposed to be fixed and unalterable, there is much official pressure for farms to make above-plan deliveries [see *Ekonomika Selskogo Khozyaistva*, no. 3 (1968), p. 24, and no. 12 (1968), p. 51].

5 The old practice whereby kolkhozes paid higher prices than sovkhozes for certain inputs has been abolished; i.e. kolkhozes no longer pay turnover tax.

6 (a) Sovkhozes on full khozraschet pay the state an annual charge of 1% of the value of their capital (excluding livestock and perennial plantations). However, this charge does not apply to sovkhozes whose profit rate on direct cost is less than 25%.
(b) Payment of the charge is deducted from total actual profits, so does not affect price. Incentive funds are formed after payment of the capital charge.
(c) Differentiated procurement prices [see 4].

7 (a) 'Higher sovkhoz authorities' decide on the disbursement of sovkhoz amortization quotas for capital investments. The use of kolkhoz amortization quotas for capital investments (and likewise the use of the indivisible fund for capital investments) must be foreseen in the farm's financial plan, which must be approved by the raion agricultural production administration and higher agricultural administrations.

(b) Sovkhozes on full khozraschet can receive short-term credits from Gosbank under the same terms and interest rates as kolkhozes. Long-term credits are also available (at kolkhoz interest rates), but the farms are supposed to finance most capital investments out of profits. Sovkhozes not on full khozraschet sometimes receive short-term credits at a set interest for specific purposes. Also, the state provides them with non-repayable grants for their capital investments. Kolkhozes can receive short-term credits (up to one year) at 1% annual interest, and long-term credits (up to 15 years) at 0.75% annual interest. For loans on which payment is overdue, kolkhozes must pay 3% annual interest for the entire period exceeding the time limit.

(c) Republic Ministries of Agriculture and local planning commissions are responsible for planning the extent of credits. The financial plans of the farms must be approved by the raion agricultural production administration.

(d) Full khozraschet had been introduced in 3,731 sovkhozes (about 30% of the total number) by mid-1969 [*Voprosy Ekonomiki*, no. 7 (1969), p. 45]. The number of sovkhozes on full khozraschet is scheduled to reach 5,300 (about 40% of the total number) by the end of 1970 [*Pravda*, 17 December 1969]. These farms are expected to cover all their production costs, productive capital investments (except housing and cultural and social amenities), increases in working capital, the formation of incentive funds, and repayments of bank credits out of their own revenue. All kolkhozes are on full khozraschet, which means that they are supposed to cover operating expenses and provide for new investment out of their own income.

8 (b) Only sovkhozes on full khozraschet pay capital charges [see 6(a)].

(c) In sovkhozes not transferred to full khozraschet, state subsidies cover any financial losses and provide a 'significant part' of the funds for capital investments. Sovkhozes on full khozraschet receive central subsidies only for the construction of housing, schools, hospitals, crèches, clubs, baths, and other social amenities, and also for irrigation, land improvement, electric power transmission lines, the construction of new enterprises for the factory production of pork, and similar investments.

(d) Since the beginning of 1969, sovkhozes not on full khozraschet have retained at least 42% of their profits after repayment of bank loans: 8.5% of profits goes to the fund for material incentives and social–cultural measures, which fund must not

exceed 10% of the planned annual wage fund with its recalculation for fulfillment of the production plan; 12% to the production development fund; 20% to the insurance fund; and 1·5%
for bonus payments to leading workers and specialists (except
office workers) for obtaining profits. The remaining part of
profits is allocated for premia for socialist competition, for
financing the farm's working capital, for the formation of a
basic herd, for payment of planned losses for the housing–
communal part of the economy, and so on. Also, 'appropriate
deductions' for the state budget are made from this part of the
profits. For sovkhozes on full khozraschet, after payment of the
capital charge [see 6(a)], the remaining profit is retained by the
farm. From total actual profits, the farm must pay the following:
15% of planned profits (and from 7·5 to 15% of overplan profits)
to the material incentives fund, the size of which cannot exceed
12% of the planned annual wage fund; 10% to the fund for
social–cultural measures and housing construction; 20% to the
insurance fund; 10% to the production development fund; and
1·5% for the bonus payment fund. The rest of the profits is to be
used for expanding the farm's working capital, financing
capital investments, repayment of credits, repayment of expenditures on forming the basic herd, and so on.

9 (a) Kolkhoz income is divided into the following funds: fund
for monthly guaranteed wages, tax fund, centralized social
security fund, insurance fund, indivisible fund, reserve fund,
bonus payments fund, fund for social–cultural measures, and
kolkhoz pension fund.

(b) A standard tax of 12% is levied on that portion of a kolkhoz's
net income which exceeds a profitability rate of 15%. In addition, tax at the rate of 8% is levied on that portion of the wage
fund which exceeds the tax-free maximum of 60 roubles per
month for each kolkhoz member. The wage tax is deducted
directly from the wage fund. Deductions for the centralized
social security fund amount to 4% of gross farm income. The
size of most other allocations varies with the particular farm.
The pay of kolkhoz members has first claim on the farm's income;
allocations to the indivisible fund are now made after paying the
peasants and meeting taxes and social security fund contributions.

10 (a) The farms themselves make investment decisions, guided by
the advice of raion agricultural and planning authorities. The
raion agricultural production association has to approve the
farm's financial plan.

11 No.

Yugoslavia[1]

1 (a) Chamber of Economy of the district assembly, for the social holdings. In the private sector, planning is indirect and is carried out through contract agreements between individual peasants on one hand and co-operative farms and other procurement agencies on the other.

(b) For planning in the social sector, each republic has a production plan, on the basis of which each district is assigned a particular specialization. The farms within the district base their plans on the district's plan. The plans of the farms are then approved by the Chamber of Economy of the district assembly. But since no plan is binding, the market determines most actions. In the private sector, the centre's role in planning is confined to encouraging or discouraging the production of certain items by regulating the guaranteed prices paid to peasants for the sale of their produce to socialist procurement agencies.

(c) The Party has little or no direct influence over the individual peasants, and its plans have slight influence on socialist enterprises.

2 (a) District assemblies cannot give social holdings compulsory directives on how much land must be devoted to a particular crop or how much produce must be sold. Nevertheless, the government exercises surveillance over the dimensions of sown areas and production on them, and also establishes guiding figures for social holdings for the sale of grain, meat, and milk. For the private sector, district assemblies can set various requirements for land cultivation or other agro-technical measures which the owners of land must meet. It can in addition prescribe certain land reclamation measures. Special regulations govern the obligations of farmers possessing holdings in land reclamation areas or in areas where anti-erosion and torrent control schemes are being systematically implemented.

(b) Private farms receive no guiding figures from the government.

(c) No.

(d) All farms decide their own sowing plans.

3 (c) Procurement agencies (mainly agricultural co-operatives)

---

[1] *Sources:* L. F. Karinya, Yu. K. Knyazev, and L. V. Gyalunenko, *Ekonomika Yugoslavii* (Moscow, 1965), pp. 71, 74, 88, 91–4, 103; *Yugoslav Survey*, no. 25 (1966), p. 3604, no. 4 (1967), pp. 85–7, no. 1 (1968), pp. 19–20, no. 4 (1968), pp. 101–18, and no. 3 (1969), p. 65; *Privredni Pregled*, 12 January 1968; *Ekonomika stran sotsializma: 1967 god* (Moscow, 1968), p. 252.

buy produce from the private farms by a form of kontraktatsia. Such arrangements are voluntary on the part of the peasants. Guaranteed prices are paid to the peasants for the sale of a specified quantity of certain produce (grain, technical crops, some types of vegetables, and so on), but only on condition that the peasants meet certain agro-technical requirements (e.g. depth of ploughing, time of sowing, quality of seed, defined quantity and type of artificial fertilizer, etc.). In meeting these requirements, the peasants are often forced to rely on the sales facilities (e.g. for seed and fertilizer) and services (e.g. agricultural experts and mechanization) of the agricultural co-operatives, for which they pay, most often in kind. Social holdings sell their produce to processing and procurement agencies through purchasing agreements. Prices, which are set by direct arrangement between the farms and the agencies, must not exceed the centrally-fixed upper limit for the particular product and must be approved by the chambers of economy and the central co-operative union.

(d) Peasants are free to sell their produce on the free market. About 10% of the marketable produce of the individual peasants is sold in this way, the rest being sold through socialized purchasing agencies.

4 Wholesale prices were last reformed in 1965 to ensure, in principle, the free formation of delivery prices at which the state and socialist organizations purchase agricultural products direct from the producers. The goal is for the delivery prices to reach the level of world prices. Supply-and-demand free prices apply to most agricultural products, but there is also a system of minimum guaranteed prices which affects certain key products: grain crops (wheat, rye, maize, barley, oats, and rice), sugar beets, oil crops, tobacco, cotton, meat, and milk. Only farms in the social sector and peasants selling the specified produce through the co-operative farms and other procurement agencies qualify for guaranteed minimum prices. Under this system, the state purchases all otherwise unsold produce at the minimum price and also makes up any deficiencies between the price at which the processing agencies are willing to buy the produce and the minimum price. Purchasing agreements between farms in the social sector and the processing agencies are subject to maximum price limitations [see 3(c)]. Premia are paid for sales of milk, cotton, and pigs 'in the expectation of their eventual abolition'.

5 Machinery and artificial fertilizers are sold at preferential

prices to farms in the social sector. Individual farmers do not receive the preferential prices, and there are restrictions on the type of farm machinery they can buy. Private farmers must pay a tax on large mechanically-operated machines. Republican legislation specifies which machines are considered large, and thereby subject to tax, and communes fix the tax. In 1967, the average tax on a privately owned tractor was 7,300 dinars (about $600 at the official rate of exchange). Agricultural organizations are not subject to the tax, but instead must pay depreciation charges on such equipment as part of their fixed assets. The average depreciation period for agricultural plant and equipment is about 10 years.

6 (a) n.a.

(c) Private farmers pay a tax based on 'cadastral revenue', i.e. of average revenue that could accrue from the land of a definite category. Cadastral revenue for a given category of land is estimated from the average income of crop and livestock production over the past few years (at present, 1959/62), in accordance with purchase prices prevailing in the year it was calculated (at present, according to 1964 prices). There are certain exemptions from this tax [see *Yugoslav Survey*, no. 4 (1968), p. 116]. Privately owned land can be leased or sold providing that it is first offered for lease or sale to the socialist sector, and that a private farm household cannot lease and/or own more than 10 ha. of arable land. Republican tax laws provide for a reduction in land revenue taxes for taxpayers leasing land to socialist holdings for more than three years. The level of such reductions depends on the duration of the lease contract. Sales of privately owned land to the socialist sector have declined since 1965 (only 2,500 ha. were sold in 1967) because the economic reforms have enabled private farmers to earn more from their land, thus making private farming more attractive than formerly. The price of land has risen sharply: before the July 1965 reforms, it varied from 800 to 2,000 new dinars per ha.; in 1967, the price was reported to be 'several times' that.

7 (a) Amortization quotas affect only the social sector. The farms themselves spend such quotas. The funds can be used to purchase new fixed assets, for working capital, for the repayment of credits, etc.

(b) Social holdings can receive credits from banks for investment capital and working capital. Social holdings which are being run on a profitable basis have first priority. Agricultural credits carry lower interest charges than industrial credits: for investment credits, the annual rates are 2% instead of 4%; for credits for working capital, 2·5% instead of 5·3%. Individual peasants cannot receive investment credits. However, peasants who enter into contract agreements with agricultural co-operatives for the sale of a specified quantity of produce can receive credits for working capital.

(c) Intermediate planning organizations must approve the finance plans of social holdings before they can apply for credits. Nevertheless, the banks have final say on which farms can receive credits and how much.

(d) No.

11 No, but the socialist sector can aquire land from the peasants by means of its right to purchase land not properly cultivated by families having outside economic interests.

4

GENERAL NOTE ON PROJECTIONS
FOR ALBANIA AND RUMANIA

MICHAEL KASER, 1967

The macroeconomic assessment of future activity in Albania and Rumania involves a difficulty with statistics no longer met by those studying the other eastern European states: the official estimates by the National Statistical Office of each country are published only in percentage form. It has been possible for earlier years to reconstruct approximate estimates of the official series, but price changes since intervening have nullified their value in connection with reported data for 1965 and 1966 and the plans for 1967 and 1970. The price basis for the Albanian national income was of the year 1956 until 1960, of 1960 until 1965 and is currently of the year 1966; investment statistics were respectively in 1958, 1961, and now 1966 prices. The price basis of Rumanian national accounts has been changed from 1955 to 1963 prices, and investment statistics have been changed from a 1959 price basis to 1963. The Albanian national income series was very rudimentary in composition until 1960, and the Rumanian series underwent methodological change in 1964.[1] The figures put forward in the present note are hence offered only as rough orders of magnitude.

The two countries also have in common a high degree of caution in approaching reform of economic management, progress in which is substantial in all other countries of eastern Europe. The Albanian authorities have explicitly denounced the measures now being adopted elsewhere as 'revisionist', and have stated that derogations to the present centralized system are not envisaged. The manner of industrial administration is not perhaps of major importance in a country where some four-fifths of industrial production is generated in about one hundred enterprises: contact between the central planning

[1] See M. Kaser, 'An estimate of the national accounts of Rumania following both Eastern and Western definitions', *Soviet Studies* (July 1966), pp. 86–90.

office, the ministries and the enterprise directors is virtually on a personal basis. There is no devolution of rights to enterprises, and no need to copy the Chinese devolution to provinces. Small-scale plants and handicrafts are controlled by the local authorities (factories being transferred to 'centralized administration' when expansion of scale or equipment so justifies). Until mid-1966 a similar attitude seems to have inspired the Rumanian government, although motivated by the view that successful industrial expansion did not justify any change of a fundamental nature in economic management. There have been numerous indications since the speech of the General Secretary of the Rumanian Communist Party, Mr Nicolae Ceausescu, at a meeting of engineering workers on 1 June 1966, that changes are being seriously considered: a reform of planning practice in retail and wholesale trade has since been introduced and a transfer of much of industrial investment from budget finance to bank loans can be predicted with some confidence for 1968; banks have now been authorized with effect from last year to grant modernization loans to state industrial enterprises.

The forecasts for the period of the current Five-year Plans of each country follow such indications as have been given in the respective Plan documents, established in both countries on the assumption that there would be no major reform of economic management during their validity. Unplanned change in management methods could affect the projection in either direction, though in the short term the predominant influence on industrial activity would be downward and in the longer term upward.

5

ALBANIA

MICHAEL KASER, 1967

The basic projections for the Albanian economy are set out in
Table 5.1 (p. 93). 1967 represents the basic estimate and the
forward perspective is taken as 1970. A view a full five years
ahead has not been adopted, in order to utilize the official
targets of the Five-year Plan, ratified in November 1966.
These targets are sufficiently detailed to be worthy of study, the
more so since the degree of external aid is the major determinant
of the expansion of domestic capacity.

The Albanian economy, since the creation of the country as
an independent state, has always been dependent on foreign
aid. A review of these problems is available in chapter VI of
the *Economic Survey of Europe in 1960* (Economic Commission for
Europe, Geneva 1961).

That review described the post-war assistance of Albania by
the Soviet Union, and set out the targets of the third Five-year
Plan (1961–65), which subsumed that Soviet development
aid would continue, and that Albania would gain by the
specialization of production within the framework of the
Council for Mutual Economic Assistance. Both subsumptions
were disrupted by the well-known dispute with the Soviet
Union and the Albanian political alliance with China. It seems
necessary therefore to preface the projections with a brief
summary of the conditions under which the third Five-year
Plan operated.

ECONOMIC ACTIVITY 1961–66

Albania first publicly indicated its political support for China
at the Third Congress of the Rumanian Workers' Party in
June 1960. Relations deteriorated with those Communist
Parties following the Soviet lead, and the dispute was transferred
from Party to a State basis in December 1961 when the USSR
broke off diplomatic relations with Tirana and Albania failed

89

to appear at the Executive Committee of the Council for Mutual Economic Assistance. Soviet aid, both technical and financial, ceased and trade between the two countries was eliminated by 1962: Albanian imports from the USSR which had been 3·5 billion[1] foreign exchange leks in 1960 were 1·3 million in 1962 and zero in 1963. Only two members of the CMEA, Rumania and Poland, have increased their trade with Albania since 1961. The reduction of trade by the other members and the total Soviet boycott has been described by the Albanian Government as an economic blockade. Chinese trade and assistance partly replaced that previously furnished by CMEA members and already in 1962 China was exporting to Albania as much as the USSR had done in 1960 (3·3 billion leks). Inevitably, however, the composition and magnitude of Chinese capital aid could not match the support from outside which underwrote the original text of the third Five-year Plan.

The targets of the Plan were all under-fulfilled: expressed as the annual rate of growth from 1960 to 1965, the official results of the Plan compared as follows with the original targets. Net material product (defined in the conventional Marxist production boundary as excluding 'non-productive services') rose 5·8% against a goal of 9·3%; the global output of industry (again computed on the Soviet practice of aggregating gross outputs of enterprises) rose 6·8%, compared with the target of 8·7%; whereas the Plan had envisaged global agricultural output (duplicating fodder inputs with livestock production and non-farm inputs into all branches) expanding more rapidly than industrial output, the reverse was the case, with the annual agricultural expansion averaging 6·4% against a Plan of 11·5%. Retail turnover in state and co-operative shops expanded by 4·1%, compared with a goal of 6·7%. The annual increment in state investment was 8·7%, compared with a plan target of 8·6%, but in real terms there must have been a significant under-fulfilment. The cost of small-scale local engineering and the manufacture of spare parts by processes which can only be described as handicraft must have raised the cost of the equipment component per unit much above that envisaged in the Plan when reliance was placed in a 300 million old rouble

[1] 1 billion = 10^9.

(= $75 million) loan from the USSR and trade and credit from other CMEA members. Engineering imports from China would almost certainly have been more costly per unit than those planned from the USSR, the GDR and Czechoslovakia.

The Albanian authorities did remarkably well in mobilizing local resources, particularly in engineering: the annual expansion in this sector has been and continues to be extremely high, although a considerable part of the annual increment must be attributed to the manufacture of new products at high cost. Although the shift of surplus agricultural labour into the expansion, and melioration, of land was slower than might have been expected, much was done to promote activities not dependent on imports. A notable beneficiary of this concentration on domestic-based projects was education. The number of pupils and students in all forms of education (other than in pre-school institutions) was 315,500 in 1960,[1] numbers were to have risen to 419,000 in 1965. In fact enrolment was 425,000 in that year and a 1970 target has been set of 540,000. It was planned in 1965 that 80% of primary school leavers would enter secondary school (with an eight-year curriculum, inclusive of primary schooling): in fact the rate achieved was 88%.

In general, the Albanian economy was able to survive the sharp change in its external relations by its previous policy of building small-scale plants closely related to the exploitation of natural resources. The annual rates of growth quoted above are substantial and the Albanian leaders at the Fifth Party Congress in November 1966 had reason to be self-congratulatory.

This sturdy self-sufficiency does not, however, fully explain the ability of the Albanian economy in 1966 and in the plan for 1967 to manage with fewer imports than in 1965. Moreover, from March 1966 to the present, managers and officials have been subjected to 'a successful struggle against the danger of bureaucracy in state and economic agencies'.[2] The campaign then launched (by an 'open letter' of the Central Committee of the Albanian Workers' Party) cannot fail to have caused difficulties in business administration: recent criticisms have, for example, been directed towards the chief engineer of the Dinamo Engineering Shops in Tirana and the Director of a

---

[1] The Plan text cited a preliminary figure of 313,000 for 1960.
[2] *Zeri i popullit*, 5 March 1967.

coal mine near the capital; in line with the Chinese 'Cultural Revolution' public reprimands have been concerned with such points as cigarette packages (one showed a mosque and another was called *Lux,* both of which were seen as harking back to a bourgeois period).

The exact situation in foreign trade cannot be determined. The latest statistical yearbook provides data only up to 1963; the 1966 Plan Results quoted only a 5% expansion in exports, while the 1967 Plan states only that both exports and imports will remain on the 1966 level. It is estimated that about 70% of Albanian trade is with China, which publishes no country-breakdown of its commerce. The estimates published by the United Nations Statistical Office in its annual matrix of world trade can hardly be more than a guess. It is here assumed that imports fell in 1966, largely due to Chinese unwillingness to supply. During April–June 1965 an Albanian delegation in Peking had negotiated a loan for the fourth Five-year Plan, but another mission in March 1966 was unable to gain any supplementary assistance. Poland, moreover, which had reversed its trade balance with Albania in 1965 (importing $1·35 million from Albania more than it delivered), continued that policy during early 1966, although in the latter part of the year it increased its exports significantly. Rumania, which had rapidly expanded its exports to Albania until 1964, levelled these off in 1965; it has not yet published data for 1966 by country. The Five-year Plan (see Table 5.2, p. 94) envisages a lower degree of trade dependence in 1970 than in 1965, together with a reduced balance-of-trade deficit. The slight progress of exports in 1966 and planned for 1967 has put this target in jeopardy; trade protocols signed with Yugoslavia and France for 1967 envisage substantial increases (a 26% rise in turnover with Yugoslavia and a 35% rise in Albanian exports to France). It may well be that the continuing expansion of metal mining and the preference accorded agriculture in the Five-year Plan will provide export goods in sufficient quantity later in the quinquennium; nevertheless, the market for primary commodities is not one upon which the Albanians can depend in western Europe. A very rough calculation of trade dependence during 1967 (if, as expected, neither imports nor exports diverge from the 1966 level) suggests that imports will be 13%

of gross national product; this calculation uses the very hazardous estimates of Table 5.1 and the conversion rate shown in the footnote to Table 5.2. Because the estimate of the degree

Table 5.1 *Forward estimates of Albanian national accounts* (billions of leks at 1966 prices)

	1967		1970	
Net material product 'produced'	4·67		5·60	
of which:				
consumption		3·34	4·02	
accumulation (net of depreciation)		1·33	1·58	
Foreign-trade price-differential *plus*				
domestic value of foreign aid	1·20		1·47	
Net material product 'disposable'	5·87		7·07	
Depreciation	0·62		0·86	
Services:				
consumed by government				
– defence		0·20		0·22
– other		0·70		0·85
consumed by persons (including rent)	1·90	1·00	2·17	1·10
Expenditure on gross national product	8·40		10·10	
of which:				
retail sales		3·05		3·44
personally-used services		1·00		1·10
auto-consumption of goods		1·17		1·72
personal consumption	5·22		6·26	
defence services		0·20		0·22
defence goods		0·07		0·08
total defence	0·27		0·30	
government consumption of				
non-military services		0·70		0·85
government consumption of				
non-military goods		0·26		0·32
government consumption (excl. defence)	0·96		1·17	
gross capital formation	1·95		2·37	

of over-valuation of the Albanian lek can only be guessed at within wide limits (the mid-range value of 3·1 times the official rate probably being the most realistic), the extent of trade dependence must be seen as an order of magnitude.

Among the other results for 1966 (also shown in Table 5.2) considerable caution must attach particularly to the statistics

Table 5.2 *Main published indicators of the Albanian Five-Year Plan (1966–70) and Annual Plan for 1967 (table updated in 1969)*

	Billion leks at 1960 prices		1966–70 Plan index, 1965 = 100	1967 Plan, 1967 actual index, 1966 = 100		1968 Plan index, 1967 = 100
	1963	1965		1967 Plan	1967 actual	
Net material product	—	—	145–50*	(110)	107·5	117
Global industrial production (socialist sector)	3·89	4·45	150·4	(110)	112·8	120·7
heavy	1·93	—	165·9	—	113	122
light	0·96	1·07	133·8	—	—	[i]
minerals	—	0·46	140	—	—	—
metal-working	0·22	—	121·6	(123)	—	126
machine-building	—	0·30	105	—	—	—
harvest-related food	1·64	1·79	120·4	(102)	105	112
building materials	—	0·19	110	—	—	135
textiles, leather and rubber	0·97[a]	—	143·5	(107)	—	—
imported-related	—	—	105	—	—	—
Handicraft output	0·64[b]	—	146	—	—	—
Global agricultural production	3·12[c]	3·05[c]	171·6 (108·3*)	(116)	112	112
crop products	1·56	1·56	215	(120)	—	116
livestock products	1·01	1·01	160	(109)	—	108
Export volume	0·24[a]	—	136	(100)	105	118
Import volume	0·35[d]	—	128	(100)	—	—
Real income of workers	—	—	109–11	—	—	107[j]

Real income of peasants	—	—	—	120–5	—	—	117'
Retail sales (state and co-operative shops)	2·54[a]	2·76[d,h]	107	125–7	(104)	107	—
State investment: non-farm	0·87[e]	1·57	—	140	—	—	—
State investment: farm	0·25[e]	0·16	—	168[f]	(106)	—	—
Construction volume (State sector)	0·74[e]	0·83	—	—	(105)	109	107
Thousands							
Workers and employees in socialist sector[g]	250	—	—	123–5	(107)	—	—

[a] Cannot be distinguished.

[b] Of which 0·62 billion in co-operative and 0·02 billion in private sector.

[c] Includes, in addition to crop and livestock produce, 0·44 billion orchard crops and 0·12 billion forest products and medicinal and decorative plants in 1963 and 0·34 and 0·12 in 1965.

[d] Current prices.

[e] 1961 prices.

[f] May include some outlays in rural areas not covered in data for 1963 (which are investment by Ministry of Agriculture and State Procurement Committee).

[g] Excludes members of craft and farm co-operatives.

[h] Of which 1·01 billion lek from co-operatives. Although in 1963 the private sector had a turnover of 0·02 billion lek, it no longer existed in 1965.

[i] Coal 115; chrome 118; copper 150.

[j] 1965 = 100.

Note: Between 16 August and 15 October 1965 a monetary reform required the exchange of 10 old leks for one new lek; 1963 values are shown in new leks. The exchange rate for 100 leks was adjusted from 2 US cents to 20. The official rate is overvalued by an estimated 3·1 ± 0·4 times; the tourist rate has been three times the official. GNP is very roughly suggested to lie between $235 and $300 per capita in 1967.

Sources: 1963 – _Vjetari statistikor i RPSh 1964_; 1966 – _Zeri i popullit_, 29 January 1967; (except for data marked * which are from _Rruga e Partise_, I (1967), pp. 3–4;) 1967 Plan – _Zeri i popullit_, 23 December 1966; 1967 actual – _Information Bulletin du C.C. du Parti Ouvrier Albanais_, I (1968), pp. 73–9; 1970 Plan – _ibid._, 6 November 1966 and 23 December 1966; 1968 Plan – as for 1967 actual, pp. 49–73.

for net material product and agricultural production. Both figures have been extracted from a journal of the Albanian Workers' Party, the official report of the Statistical Office making no mention of either.

PROJECTIONS FOR 1967 AND 1970

The estimates of Table 5.1 for 1967 utilize Albanian statistics almost solely on the consumption side: auto-consumption only is based upon data of production. The period through which Albania is passing has some of the elements of a quasi-Chinese 'great leap forward', during the course of which exaggerated claims are to be expected both from the centre – to promote the campaign – and from local officials – to promote themselves. It is perhaps for this reason that the Albanian Statistical Office did not include a figure for the increment for global agricultural production in its 1966 Annual Plan Results; a statistic appeared only in the Party journal, as the sources to Table 5.2 indicate. The estimate made in the present study assumes that no falsification takes place in the recording and publication of outlays, viz., state investment, government consumption, and retail sales. Inevitably the calculation of auto-consumption on farms relies upon Albanian indications of total output, and no independent work can be carried out on the real state of farm supply. The projections for 1970 fall into an altogether different category. They are not projections in the sense of representing the author's best guess of activity in 1970, but his estimate of what is feasible on the working hypothesis that the Albanian government will do what it seems to be undertaking. This exercise seemed to be necessary because, true to the traditions of a 'great leap forward', the government has not revealed the real bases of its optimism. As is shown in the section on Rumania, the corresponding 'leap' in agricultural output planned by the Rumanian government for 1960–65 ended in failure: in perhaps over-simplified terms, the Rumanian plan assumed that a rise in farm inputs generally to the level of the favoured state-farm sector would bring automatic returns even in conditions of recent collectivization. Examination of the Albanian proposals seems to indicate that, while placing overt stress on farm supplies, the opening up of new land and general patriotic fervour, the government is tacitly seeking to elicit more production by letting farmers keep considerably more of what they produce; in the political conditions of present-day Albania a public appeal to self-interest would be misplaced. There is enough scope for substantial increments in farm productivity in the lowland areas for such incentives to be realistic. The increase in new land, largely in the highlands, will not, obviously, bring equivalent returns, but such potential as these areas possess has been much under-utilized in the post-war years: as in neighbouring Montenegro, the hill farms have been increasingly neglected and deserted. The Albanian government tended to encourage depopulation in the mountainous regions to improve political security. If it can reverse this trend and allow the hill farms (albeit under recent collectivization) to operate normally, some significant contribution could be made to attaining the ambitious farm targets. To set out the potential available for agricultural expansion under present government policies, as is done in the following paragraphs, is not to declare that output will rise as quickly as hoped: the figures for 1970 cannot be other than the highest expected product, for the Albanian Planning Office would not allow itself to be accused of 'under-estimating reserves'. A safer estimate for 1970, in the sense of a juster balance of probabilities, would evidently be lower, but it seemed right at this stage in the projections scheme to put the Albanian Plan into perspective, rather than to build up a more conservative estimate for which the statistical bases were lacking.

The working hypothesis on the achievement of the high targets of the Five-Year Plan is based on two considerations. First, as mentioned above, the net material product seems to be expanding in line with Plan requirements despite a much smaller import-content than originally planned; to that extent, and with relatively low trade dependence for an east European economy (the USSR, of course, excepted), Albania can pursue its policy of self-reliant growth. Secondly, the main emphasis in the Plan is on agricultural expansion, which in Albanian conditions is little affected by imports. The hypothesis of agricultural success in 1970 is tenable if the conclusions implicit in Table 5.1 are correct: in particular that the government will allow collective farmers to consume more. The relatively small increase in retail sales in conjunction with the stated plan for material product 'produced' seems to imply a higher consumption on the farm of the big increment of farm output (or a substantial rise in intra-rural trade in farm produce which is not counted as retail turnover). The planned rise in exports is much less than that for global agricultural output, and exports will in any case include a lot of oil and metals: there hence seems little expectation of disposing much of the additional farm output abroad.

Incentives to farmers – permission to keep more of what they grow if they substantially expand production – are not the only determinant. The plan to expand state credits – in almost the same proportion as global output is to rise – must be supported by capital-goods supplies and the 1967 Plan is not encouraging. The new land being brought into use is marginal and the feasible volume of investment in it will hardly bring yields as large as those on fields now under cultivation. On the other hand the irrigation schemes of the littoral should at last be bearing fruit. Although water supply, land melioration and malaria eradication over the past decade have received substantial investments, returns have been slow to mature. This has occurred partly because the farmers of the region were unused to irrigated agriculture: the only Albanian community traditionally adapted to this sort of farming were the Roman Catholic peasants of the Shkodër (Scutari) region and their coming to teach the Muslim peasants of the middle and southern coastal plains was not without its difficulties. It seems likely that farmers are now better able to cope with the new techniques. A second cause of the delayed returns was the somewhat inefficient manner in which canal digging and soil reinstatement was carried out; the consequences of this inefficiency have almost certainly been by now overcome.

The introduction of new ploughland seems to have been proceeding well. During 1966–70 it is planned to plough up 115,000 ha., and consequentially to expand the sown area by 89,000 ha. In 1965 a big effort started and 11,000 ha. were ploughed up, in 1966 the result was 18,600 ha. (increasing the sown area by 12,000 ha.) and the plan for 1967 is 22,000 ha. Much of this land is, however, in the highland areas: the 1967 budget envisages tax reimbursements to farms in these areas, partly for this purpose and partly to support the recent campaigns of resettlement and collectivization in those districts. It is difficult to say whether the mountain peasantry of the Gheg districts will take easily to the new conditions imposed, as they would see it, by urban leaders of the Tosk group. It is perhaps still relevant to recall that the late King Zog was a leader of the Ghegs and that the Gheg dialect predominated in official usage before the War; Enver Hoxha on the other hand is a Tosk and the Tosk dialect has become the channel of government communication.

The forward estimates (Table 5.1) for both 1967 and 1970 are based on the assumption that the Albanian government will be able to mobilize the Plan resources for investment: the long-term Plan foresees a slight decline in the share of accumulation in net material product (from 28·8% in 1965 to 28·2%). Certainly, the government has been able to expand its revenue from the socialist sector at a remarkably rapid pace, and the growth of investment foreshadowed in the Plan (Table 5.3, p. 100) should be seen in conjunction with the increased public revenue shown in Table 5.4 (p. 101). What is not clear from the published public accounts is the head under which is entered the profit of foreign-trade corporations and proceeds of foreign loans. Formerly, these were shown as a distinct revenue item, and it may be concluded – though tentatively – that the difference between the apparent receipts from turnover tax and deductions from profits and stated 'revenue from the socialist sector' consists largely of funds accruing from external transactions. If defence expenditure, which has been maintained at a remarkably steady level, does not expand beyond 300 million leks in 1970 (against 270 million in recent years) government commitments to the non-State sector can reasonably be met. On the one hand, pensions have been increased this year, but on the other, the State Bank, the loanable funds of which are largely dependent on State fiscal policy, has been cutting down its credits to the only major non-State creditor, the collective farms.

The greatest uncertainty attaches to the projection of the private sector, comprising auto-consumption in agriculture – still important in a country where *Naturalwirtschaft* predominated until recently – private house-building and the provision of private services (including a few handicrafts). For lack of any better basis it has been assumed, as mentioned above, that the government will allow on-farm consumption to expand and will not seek particularly to repress the service sector, and the explicit preference in the Plan for the real income of peasants over that of workers and for house construction in rural areas over that in urban areas seems to indicate some readiness to accept

Table 5.3   *Quinquennial volume (at 1966 prices) of gross domestic investment and foreign trade, 1961–65 and 1966–70 Plan, in Albania*

	1961–65 index	1966–70 index
Construction volume	100	118
Investments	100	134
Export volume	100	136
Import volume	100	128
Turnover of foreign trade[a]	100	131
Investments:	(million leks)	
industry	3,121	4,360
agriculture	978	1,633
transport	727	627
education, health, etc.	242	713
housing	590	530[b]
other	826	887
Total:	6,524	8,750

[a] Imports plus exports.
[b] Percentage increase in dwellings newly built: 1970 will be 5% over 1965 in urban areas, 11% in rural areas.
Source: Zeri i popullit, 6 November 1966.

the rural way of life, with the private inputs that this implies. Certainly, however, this policy could be disrupted by an accentuation of the 'Cultural Revolution' on Chinese lines, while it could be encouraged in further favour of private activity if detente could be achieved with Yugoslavia, and perhaps Greece. The Albanian government has been showing itself more conciliatory towards its neighbours, but serious problems remain (the Albanian minority in Yugoslavia, whose ill-treatment was exposed in connection with the dismissal of

Mr Ranković last year, and the Greek claim to Northern Epirus). To this extent, as well as to the more straightforward problem of foreign aid, political factors underlie any projection.

Table 5.4 *Albanian public accounts 1963–67* (millions of leks; table updated in 1969)

	1963	1965	1966	1967
Expenditure:				
national economy	1,311	1,516	1,933	1,988
social–cultural	712	767	811	837
defence	277	291	278	301
administration	72	74	71	71
other	469	647	328	403
Total expenditure	2,841	3,295	3,421	3,600
Surplus	42	193	194	130
Revenue:				
turnover tax	1,095	1,300	1,531	1,602
profit tax	450	607	643	970
from persons	69	70	68	35
social insurance premia	126	133	144	167
miscellaneous	1,143	1,378	1,239	966
Total revenue	2,883	3,488	3,615	3,730
Profits of state enterprise	—	—	692	837[a]
Investment in state enterprises and institutions (from budget grants, retained profits and depreciation)	—	—	—	1,536[a]
Credits by State Bank to co-operative farms	44	39	58	56
Tax reimbursements to collective farms in highland areas for productive investment	—	—	—	7

[a] Budget.

Source: Vjetari statistikor i RPSh 1967 dhe 1968; Zeri i popullit, 23 December 1966.

6

ALBANIA: AFTERTHOUGHTS

MICHAEL KASER, 1969

The Albanian Statistical Directorate has produced a combined volume for two years: *Vjetari statistikor i RPSh 1967 dhe 1968*, but has roughly halved its contents. There are hence few data which can be used to verify the projections written in March 1967.

Among the estimates then given which could have been checked had previous statistical publication been maintained, are the share of trade with China (said to be 70%), the percentage of accumulation in net material product (thought to be declining to 28% by 1970) and the trend in the marginal propensity to consume of the Albanian farmer (believed to be rising). The latest abstract in fact gives no statistics whatever on the value of foreign trade, limiting itself to volumes in physical units of selected commodities.

The prognosis took achievement of the high targets for agriculture as 'a working hypothesis', but Professor Wiles's note of greater caution in the general review at the time now seems reasonable: thus although global farm output was planned to rise by 16% in 1967 it rose in fact by 12%, although new lands ploughed up were 26,000 ha. against a plan for 22,000. Results seem to have been still more disappointing in 1968.

An assumption which was quickly proved wrong was that defence spending would rise gradually to no more than 300 million leks in 1970: in fact, it leapt from 278 million in 1966 to 310 million in 1967 alone. Even so, the détente with Yugoslavia on which the article concluded has developed – if slowly – and Albano–Yugoslav trade has in consequence expanded.

Finally, it appears in retrospect that the March 1966 Party resolution on the 'struggle against bureaucracy in state and economic agencies' has caused difficulties in business administration, not least because of the later decree requiring managers to be frequently transferred (so that they do not succumb to 'bureaucracy') and to submit to 'working-class control' (enquiries by the staff upon their business acumen and ideological purity). On the other hand, some simplification of planning (including a reduction in the number of 'success indicators') took place in 1966 and soon afterwards 'local' enterprises were freed by the liquidation of the supervision of the Ministry of Local Economy. To date that is the sum total of Albanian economic reform.

7

BULGARIA

ALEXEJ WYNNYCZUK, 1968

Bulgaria is the poorest (after Mongolia) and probably the fastest developing member of the Comecon countries. It is also the only country in Eastern Europe which shows a parallel to the Chinese Great Leap in 1959–60. At the same time Bulgaria is no exception to the observed cyclical pattern in growth rates characteristic for East-European countries since the introduction of comprehensive planning.[1] The swings differ only in amplitude. The relative slowdown in the mid-fifties was more pronounced in 1954 and 1956 due to effects of weather on agricultural output, while the declines in growth rates in the early sixties were milder than for example in Czechoslovakia.

Currently Bulgaria is reaching the halfway mark of its fifth Five-Year Plan and is engaged in 'economic reforms' analogous to those undertaken by a number of countries of Eastern Europe. The best forecast of the future performance of Bulgarian economy could probably be obtained with the help of an econometric model using selected current planned targets as exogenous variables. Since it is impossible to attempt a construction of such a model at this time, the present forecast has to make do with estimating procedures which include a large dose of the author's informed (but still subjective) judgements. Basically, an attempt will be made to project the future in the light of current economic plans and past experience. All economic variables mentioned below conform to the definitions generally accepted by the East-European Statistical Offices. Thus, the term National Income has the standard so-called 'Marxian' meaning, that is net output of

[1] For a quantitative study of fluctuations in East Europe see: Josef Goldman, Tempo Růstu a opakující se výkyvy v ekonomice některých socialistických zemí, in *Planovane Hospodarstvi*, no. 9 (Prague, 1964) (The Growth Rate and Recurring Fluctuations in the Economies of some Socialist Countries); and George Staller, 'Fluctuations in Planned and Free Market Economies', *The American Economic Review* (June 1964).

'productive' sectors valued at market prices, i.e. including indirect taxes. The reason for adhering to the concepts used in Bulgaria is, first of all, that all plans and, of course, the actual performance, are officially measured in terms of these concepts. Any recalculation in terms of Western definitions would mean conceptual precision achieved at the cost of greater imprecision in figures. The drawbacks of using official measures derive from their failure to express properly changes in productive capacity or economic activity of the society. However, it has a great practical advantage in that any forecast can be readily compared with future official announcements published in the Bulgarian press.

NATIONAL INCOME

According to official sources, national income quadrupled between 1948 and 1965, which implies an annual average rate of growth of 8·5%. However, the growth rate has fluctuated considerably around the average. Most of the fluctuations can be attributed to effects of the weather on agricultural production which still constituted a considerable part of total output during the early part of the period. There is no doubt, though, that changes in the weather cannot explain all the deviation in the growth rates of national income, especially not those of the more recent years.[1] The reason is that currently the share of industry in national income, according to official calculations, is some 47% at market prices, while agriculture contributes about 30% to net output.

After the Great Leap of 1959, the average rate of growth of national income declined to 6·7% between 1960 and 1965. Since then the growth rate has picked up again, especially in 1966.

Anticipated by the current Five-Year Plan the average growth rate of national income is about 8·5% between 1966 and 1970, that is equal to the long term trend. So far, for the first two years of the plan, the actual rate has been above the planned average. This experience suggests that no permanent change in the economic behavior of the system has occurred; after the 'cyclical' decline in the growth rate came a strong recovery in

[1] See Table 7·1, line 20.

the form of above-average performance during the first years of a plan.

The introduction of 'reforms' characterized chiefly by recent decentralization of the decision-making process should have a bearing on the current and future aggregative performance. During the current year, all industrial plants are to be freed of the rigid central controls. In the short run, it may be expected that national income as measured by quantity indices would be raised somewhat. This expectation is based on the assumption that within each plant resources will be reallocated towards more expensive (or higher-value-added) commodities and that existing disguised unemployment will be reduced or eliminated. The effects of this reform on growth of output, however, are expected to be relatively short lived, because the existing price system will not allow for efficient allocation of resources within the economy, as well as for faster absorption of new technology. Thus the main characteristic of the economy in the near future will be an improved efficiency in resource allocation within individual plants, while misallocation within the whole system continues.

The national income is then expected to grow at a rate at least equal to the planned average, that is 8.5% in 1968 (assuming some sort of an average weather effect on agriculture) and a decline in the growth rate in the early seventies to less than 7%, or even 6% per year.

INDUSTRIAL PRODUCTION

The major sector of national income is 'Industry'. As mentioned above, this sector – manufacturing, mining and public utilities – contributes almost 50% to total income. (The official figures of course include the turnover tax which is accounted for as being created mainly in manufacturing.) The gross output of industry has grown at a rate of over 14% from 1948. Net output – or value added – has increased at a slower rate. Unfortunately, data on net output are not available. The reason for the disparity between increases in gross and net output is primarily in the different rate of growth of the volume of inputs purchased by firms from other firms (see Table 7.1, p. 108). In other words, the double counting included

in gross output has been increasing faster than the total. This
is true especially of the first part of the period, that is in the
early fifties. As in the case of national income, industrial

Table 7.1   *Industrial output*

	Gross output	Net output	Ratio of actual to trend values of Gross output
1948	28·2	40·3	82·9
1949	38·0	48·1	97·4
1950	45·6	56·4	101·8
1951	54·6	55·1	106·4
1952	63·9	67·8	108·5
1953	73·5	74·8	108·9
1954	80·8	82·0	104·3
1955	86·5	91·1	97·4
1956	100·0	100·0	98·1
1957	116·1	—	99·3
1958	133·8	—	99·9
1959	162·3	—	105·5
1960	184·2	—	104·4
1961	206·5	—	102·1
1962	229·9	—	99·1
1963	254·4	—	95·6
1964	281·1	—	92·1
1965	318·5	—	—
1966	356·7	—	—
1967	404·1	—	—

Gross output: official index of gross output is taken from relevant issues of the
statistical yearbook for the period 1948 to 1964. For later years, the yearly growth
rates as announced in January issues of *Planovo Stopanstvo*, were used.

Net output: this is an index of value added obtained from the difference between
gross output and material inputs, both valued at 1939 prices. From: Kh. Popov:
Sotsialistichesko Razshireno Vuzproizvodstvo (Sofia, 1959), p. 159.

Ratio of actual to trend values: this is a measure of the fluctuation of actual gross
output as indicated in column 1 around the trend. The trend was calculated by
least squares fit to time and the logarithm of the gross output index. The annual
growth rate calculated this way – between 1948 and 1964 – was 14·7%.

production has not grown evenly over the whole period. The decline in the growth rate during early sixties, although considerably smaller than, for example, that of Czechoslovakia, was followed by a recovery already in 1965.

The existing Five-Year Plan calls for an average growth rate of about 12% per year. It is expected that the current year will show a performance at least comparable to the planned average. The longer term prospects will again depend on the continuation of economic reforms, particularly the reforms in the price system. It is expected that after the possibilities of improvements in plant efficiencies have been exploited within the limits of currently introduced reforms, the growth rate of industrial production will slow down to below 10% a year.

The above figures refer to the up to now most widely used measure, namely, the gross output obtained as a sum of final outputs of individual enterprises, and thus including a large share of doublecounting. The most interesting and important aspect of the future development in Bulgaria is an attempt to increase net output faster than gross output of industry which means reducing the rate of growth of inputs purchased by firms from the outside, as shown in the following tabulation:

Planned increase in industrial production
1970/65

Gross output:	170
Material inputs:	166
Net output:	178.5

The planners have probably assumed that the economic reforms will succeed in eliminating unnecessary transactions among firms, i.e. those which have been carried out only for the sake of attaining the main indicator of plan fulfilment – gross output – by means of a faster increase of inputs purchased from the outside. In this respect it is believed that the current reforms will reach the desired objective during the first years after introduction. Accordingly, we expect that this year's net output of industry will increase faster than gross output. However, this source of faster increase of net output may be exhausted very soon.

Leaving improvements due to organizational improvements aside, the increase in industrial output is to be obtained from the increased volume of inputs and increased productivity of the inputs. Available sources imply a planned increase in labor input of about 4% annually during the Five-Year Plan (1965–70), and capital input of about 15% annually. Although the combined inputs productivity is expected to grow, according to the Plan figures, at about the same rate as in the past,[1] the development of input proportions should differ from the past trend.

It is to be expected that industrial employment will grow at a slow pace, since total labor force will grow at about 1% a year, and what may be called excess labor in agriculture will have been exhausted. Part of the need for additional labor will come from the effect of economic reforms upon disguised unemployment in industry, as mentioned above. Thus, we may expect that the 4% of planned growth in employment will probably be a maximum achievable.

The planned increase in capital inputs should be fulfilled by considerable growth of output of machinery industry on the supply side, with the assistance of the new form of financing of capital outlays on the demand side. The first effect of the reform will probably be an increase of investment funds in the hands of industrial enterprises, since retained profits and bank loans will grow faster than budgetary grants decline. This is largely because the shift to more profitable products will raise profits more quickly than output. We could then expect the capital inputs of industry as a whole to grow as fast as planned this year. However, in the early seventies – five-year prediction – the demand for capital goods by industrial enterprises is expected to decline relatively. This is because the retained profits earmarked for investment will fail to grow faster than output due to expected decline in the growth rate of net output as well as due to faster increasing tax payments on fixed capital. The other obvious limitation on capital growth in industry may be the supply of fixed capital. Since imports are not expected to grow faster than total output of the economy, the increasingly major part of fixed capital would have to come from domestic

---

[1] The combined productivity change is calculated here by adding annual growth rates of both inputs and subtracting the sum from output growth rate. The weights used to add the inputs are 0.7 and 0.3% for labor and capital stock, respectively. The 1949–64 growth rates are 7.7% for labor, 13.1% for capital, and 14.7% for output (the last figure pertains to gross output).

production. This, however, seems impossible without considerable increases in imports of raw materials. (There is a possible explanation in that Bulgaria intends to substitute imports of raw materials for imports of finished fixed capital.)

One characteristic of the development of Bulgarian industry during the next five years should be continuing, perhaps even faster change in the structure of output. The three fastest growing sectors have been, and in the near future will continue to be, chemicals, ferrous metallurgy, and machine building. These three sectors are supposed to grow at more than double the rate for total industrial output. As we already indicated, it is hard to see how this can be accomplished without considerable increase in imports of inputs, particularly from the USSR (iron ore, or intermediate products of ferrous metallurgy).

AGRICULTURE

Short-term predictions of agricultural output are the most difficult to make. The small size of the country makes it possible for weather to be uniformly good or bad in all regions, and thus affect the country's total output. In the official estimate of national income, the contribution of agriculture to total net output has decreased to less than one-third. However, this figure has meaning only as a measure of weight in the calculation of the output index for national income. Because of the price system it certainly does not express adequately the opportunity cost of inputs used, or the relative welfare significance of agricultural output. The share of agriculture in national income is influenced either by relative changes in real net output, or simply by arbitrary changes in relative prices. It is safe to say that, in terms of resources, agriculture may still be considered the main sector of the Bulgarian economy. It employs over 40% of the labor force,[1] and some 20% of the fixed capital.

[1] The figure on employment is only an approximation, because of the problem of the accounting of the members of the labor force active in agriculture. It cannot be understood as potential labor force in other sectors. It has been Bulgarian experience, that about 30% of those who leave agriculture do not take employment elsewhere. Most of them become housewives. The figure on capital refers to so called 'productive' capital only, that is capital used by sectors producing goods or productive services only. The major sector excluded thus is housing.

The organizational structure, as it developed during the fifties, can be described as full collectivization. About 77% of agricultural land is in the hands of collectives directly, another 8% tilled by kolkhoz members as their private plots. The remaining part comprises farms directed by the Ministry of Agriculture or by industrial enterprises. The land owned by private farmers is negligible. However, their contribution to total output is disproportionately large in view of their share of agricultural land. The privately operated part of agriculture (including plots of kolkhoz members), contributes about one fourth of the gross production of agriculture and more than one third of the output of livestock and livestock products.

Gross output, according to official statistics, has doubled compared to the prewar period. Although figures are not available, it is believed that final output has increased less during the same period, meaning that intermediate products, e.g. feed grains, did grow faster than gross output. Furthermore, net output, or value added by agriculture, most probably did increase at a considerably lower rate than gross output. The implied average rate of growth of gross output of agriculture since the beginning of comprehensive planning, that is from 1948, has been about 3.5%, with crop and livestock production growing at about the same rate.

The current Five-Year Plan calls for yearly increases of about 5%, with net income growing only slightly less. Since the base year (1965) was characterized by bad weather and thus low agricultural production, it is quite reasonable to expect a faster than long term average growth for the following five years.[1] As far as short term predictions are concerned, the 1968 output or rather the 1968 increase over 1966 may well be small or negative, assuming that it will not be about time for another peak in the climatic conditions. However, longer-term predictions for the performance of agriculture are more optimistic. Given the successes in production of chemicals needed in agriculture, as well as increases in machinery supplies, it is expected that agricultural production will grow at a rate above the average of the whole planning period. Ignoring weather effects, the average for gross production may reach as much as 5% a year.

[1] For example the 1966 output was already 15% above 1965 output.

CONSUMPTION, INVESTMENT, AND PRICES

Since fixed capital is supposed to increase faster than output for the economy as a whole, the share of accumulation in national income will be growing. The fact that lower-than-average increases in inventory changes are planned can hardly reverse this trend. Given the expected national income growth of 8·5% a year and growth of consumption of 7·5%, net investment will be increasing by about 11% a year.[1]

It is assumed that the new economic system should eliminate the former ills of accumulation of 'unneeded' inventories, as well as shortages in the supply of fixed capital, especially finished construction projects. It is our considered estimate that in the current year the planned results can be obtained. However, since prices will continue very strictly, given the continuance of the existing price system, it can be expected that the rate of inventory accumulation will pick up again while deliveries of finished equipment and construction will slow down. Thus, in the early seventies we may expect the ratio of investment to national income to reach the planned 28–30%, but a slower growth of fixed capital stock.

Given the new freedoms of enterprises concerning the output mix, and the profit incentive, it is very probable that wholesale as well as retail prices will increase. Although prices are still determined, and most probably will continue to be determined centrally, there is more room now for individual enterprises to influence actually realized prices as opposed to list prices. Such price increases most probably will not be reflected in the official information. Thus, it would be next to impossible not only to estimate future price changes but even to estimate the actual past rate of inflation.

The general prediction of the performance of Bulgarian economy in the near future may then be summarized in the following way: this year we may expect a continuation of a relatively fast rate of growth (given our assumptions about agriculture and the climatic condition), while within the next four or five years the rate of development will slow down considerably. The degree of the slowdown will also depend on the reaction of the government to the difficulties that will be

[1] This calculation applies a weight of 0·3% to accumulation.

created by the economic reform as it stands now. It is hard to visualize how the present system of price determination can guide the allocation of resources in the absence of central comprehensive planning. As long as prices are not allowed to respond reasonably fast to changes in supply and demand, the decentralization of decisions on what to produce will result in an accumulation of the problems that originally led to the reforms. Deviations of individual prices from what the competitive market prices would be, will lead either to too fast a growth of profits in the hands of some firms or to shortages, and at the same time, accumulation of inventories. Such experiences may again give rise to voices calling for central intervention in resource allocation, and at the other extreme for a reform of the price determination system. It is believed that either change will cause the growth of the economy to slow down during the transitional period.

Sources: Ikonomicheska Misl, nos. 1, 8, 10 (Sofia, Bulgaria, 1966); *Planovo Stopanstvo i Statistika*, nos. 1, 4, 8, 10 (1966) and 1 (1967) (Sofia, Bulgaria); *Statisticheski Godishnik 1964* (Sofia, Bulgaria); *Planovane Hospodarstvi* no. 9 (Prague, Czechoslovakia, 1964); Staller, G., 'Fluctuations in Planned and Free-Market Economies', *The American Economic Review* (June, 1964); Wynnyczuk, A. 'The Growth of Bulgarian Industry 1939' (1948–64). Unpublished manuscript, Research Project on National Income of East Central Europe, Columbia University, New York.

8

CHINA

W. KLATT, 1967

None of the data on which an assessment of the economic performance of a communist country is normally based is available in the case of Mainland China. No budget has been published since 1961, no absolute figures on planned and actual production of industrial and agricultural goods have been released since 1960 and those available for 1958 and 1959 are known to be faulty in the extreme.[1] The last reasonably reliable information thus dates back to 1957, the final year of the first Five-Year Plan.

In 1958 the second Five-Year Plan was inaugurated and some targets for the period up to 1962 are known. However, in the course of 1958, the Great Leap Forward, a huge operation of social engineering, was instigated and the mode of production was changed, first in the countryside and later in the urban areas, from individual 'firms', such as agricultural producer 'co-operatives', i.e. collective farms, and industrial enterprises to communes which were charged with a multitude of functions, some of which were unconnected with matters of economic performance. Due to these measures, not only had the second Five-Year Plan to be abandoned almost immediately after its inauguration, but a year later planning had become impracticable altogether. Although occasional references were made to planning in the publications emanating from official Chinese sources, there is no certainty that even annual plans were in operation in the years of serious economic dislocation immediately following the Great Leap Forward.

Whilst it is no longer of interest to report every bend of Chinese official publicity, the last detailed statement is worth recording. At the turn of the year 1964, the National People's Congress received a report on the economic progress made

[1] Choh-ming Li, *The Statistical System of Communist China* (University of California Press, Berkeley, Cal., 1962).

during the previous twelve months and on the progress expected
in 1965. At the same time Chou En-lai, China's Prime Minister,
gave the news that the year 1966 was to see the beginning of
the third Five-Year Plan. This plan had been due originally
early in 1963, but at that time China's economy was too
dislocated to permit of any planned operations.

A year later the National People's Congress failed to meet,
and a leading article in the Communist Party's official organ,
Jenmin Jih Pao, the People's Daily, had to suffice to fill the gap
in factual information. The article gave the first official account
of what had happened in the years since the Great Leap
Forward. The second Five-Year Plan, launched in 1958, was
said to have been fulfilled in 1960, two years ahead of schedule.
During the next three years, the national economy had been
readjusted in a general way, and in the last two years of the
transition period a new upsurge of the national economy had
been organized, 'creating in every respect sound and adequate
foundations for implementing the third Five-Year Plan'.[1] Some
shortcomings and mistakes were admitted for the years 1959 to
1961, the years following the Great Leap Forward, when the
economy was seriously dislocated and the population suffered
great hardships. However, no indices or absolute data were
made known on China's economic performance prior to 1966,
nor were any forecasts or plan targets published for the period
of the third Five-Year Plan, ranging from 1966 to 1970.

In these circumstances it may seem to be the only legitimate
course of action to abandon all attempts at assessing economic
performance in the past and making any forecasts of likely
achievements in the future. Any such attempt may be regarded
as unscholarly and thus academically indefensible. Such views
could not readily be dismissed, were it not for the fact that
China is the largest nation on earth and a very dynamic
country at that; her economic performance, like her political
behaviour, is bound to leave its mark not only on her neighbours in Asia, but also on the major world powers and on their
relations towards each other. Any misjudgment of China's
performance and intentions might indeed have consequences
which could not easily be reversed with hindsight at some later
stage. Provided that a reasonable assessment of the main

[1] *The People's Daily* (Peking, 1 January 1966).

orders of magnitude can be attained, the attempt should therefore not be rejected out of hand. Can it be done, and if so, how can it be done?

First of all, there are the results of Western scholarly work concerned with China's economy in the immediate post-war period when economic information was more readily available than from 1958 onwards. The first economic survey of communist China was made by Yuan-li Wu who recorded the major features of the economy up to the year 1954.[1] Later Choh-ming Li published an appraisal of the first five years of industrialization in China.[2] The latest review of this kind is Yuan-li Wu's introduction to the economy of communist China which covers the period up to 1962.[3] The same applies to Choh-ming Li's symposium on industrial development in communist China.[4] The most comprehensive study so far on the economy of the Chinese Mainland is that by Ta-chiung Liu and Kung-chia Yeh, but this does not go beyond 1959.[5] Special studies on the national income and the gross national product were undertaken by Alexander Eckstein[6] and by William Hollister[7] respectively. The energy resources[8] and the steel industry[9] were the subjects of two special studies by Yuan-li Wu. Food and agriculture have been reviewed for the years up to 1963 by Lossing Buck, Owen Dawson and Yuan-li Wu.[10] In addition to these historical studies there is China's press and radio, regularly abstracted in English by the US

[1] Yuan-li Wu, *An Economic Survey of Communist China* (Bookman Associates, New York, 1956).

[2] Choh-ming Li, *Economic Development of Communist China* (University of California Press, Berkeley, Cal., 1959).

[3] Yuan-li Wu, *The Economy of Communist China* (Pall Mall Press, London, 1965).

[4] Choh-ming Li (ed.), *Industrial Development in Communist China* (Praeger, New York, 1964).

[5] Ta-chiung Liu–Kung-chia Yeh, *The Economy of the Chinese Mainland* (University Press, Princeton, 1965).

[6] Alexander Eckstein, *The National Income of Communist China* (The Free Press, Glencoe, Ill., 1961).

[7] William W. Hollister, *China's Gross National Product and Social Accounts 1950–1957* (The Free Press, Glencoe, Ill., 1958).

[8] Yuan-li Wu, *Economic Development and the Use of Energy Resources in Communist China* (Hoover Institution, Stanford; Praeger, New York, 1963).

[9] Yuan-li Wu, *The Steel Industry in Communist China* (Hoover Institution, Stanford. Praeger, New York, 1965).

[10] John Lossing Buck, Owen L. Dawson, Yuan-li Wu, *Food and Agriculture in Communist China* (Hoover Institution, Stanford; Praeger, New York, 1966).

Consulate in Hong-Kong[1] and by the British Broadcasting Corporation in London[2] respectively. One more source deserves to be mentioned. *The Yearbook of the Great Soviet Encyclopedia*[3] published in 1965, contains some estimates of China's economic performance which, whilst similar to those published in Western journals, differ sufficiently to suggest that Soviet specialists have done their own independent work on the Chinese economy. While none of these sources provides ready answers to any questions on China's current or future performance, all of them deserve to be consulted in any attempt to answer these questions.

CHINA'S POPULATION

China's present population is unknown. For over five years official Chinese statements have quoted regularly the figure of 650 million – as if the population had remained stationary. In 1966 it was upgraded, in one leap, to 700 million. Some Western observers reckon it to be approximately 750 million, and some go as far as 800 million.[4] The estimated total is the sum of the assumed census result of 1953, increased by annual estimates of births over deaths in subsequent years.

Any error made in the annual projections is likely to be small by comparison with any possible error made in regard to the census of 1953. Several Western demographers have commented on this. John Aird of the US Bureau of the Census first reckoned with an undercount of at least 3% and at most 9%, but more recently he raised his range to 5 to 15%, implying a population in 1953 of at least 613 and at most 685 million.[5] Against this, Irene Taeuber found so many flaws in the census technique that she concluded her demographic review by saying that China remained a country without statistics.[6] Leo Orleans

---

[1] American Consulate General, Hong Kong, *Survey of the China Mainland Press;* also: Extracts from *Chinese Mainland Magazines.*

[2] British Broadcasting Corporation, *Survey of World Broadcasts*, Part 3, The Far East (Caversham Park, Reading, Berkshire).

[3] *Yearbook of the Great Soviet Encyclopedia* (Moscow, 1965).

[4] *Guardian*, London, 25 May 1966.

[5] John S. Aird, 'Population Growth in Mainland China' (unpublished, Berkeley, Cal., 1965).

[6] Irene B. Taeuber and Nai-chi Wang, 'Questions on Population Growth in China', in *Population Trends in Eastern Europe, the USSR and Mainland China* (Milbank Memorial Fund, New York, 1960).

summarized his demographic findings in these words: 'China's population will continue to be an enigma and a subject for academic guessing games for many decades to come.'[1]

One important aspect seems to have escaped Western demographers in their examination of Chinese official claims. The census followed a period during which some 100 million villagers (out of a total of 500 million) were said to be benefiting from the redistribution of land set in motion by the agrarian reform law of June 1950. It may well be, as Aird suggests, that certain evasions occurred during the year when the census was taken. Against this it seems probable that families eligible under the regulations of the land act overstated their numbers in the register of the village councils which first had a hand in the distribution of land and which were consulted in the summer of 1953 in communities where census counts proved unsatisfactory. The exaggeration of the rural population that could have resulted from such practices in the rural areas might well have exceeded the undercount due to evasions of registration in the urban areas.

The uncertainty as to the increase of the population since 1953 is just as great as that regarding the census itself. During the Great Leap Forward and the mass movement of population in the course of it, the register was apparently so dislocated that in 1964 re-registration became necessary in certain localities. However, the reports that a new nationwide census was taken at that time have not been confirmed. Projections of population changes ceased to be published after 1956. Official policies regarding birth control vacillated. In any event, they are unlikely to have had any effect outside the urban areas. The possibility of deliberate failure to report cases of death for the sake of receiving rationed foodstuffs and clothing cannot be ruled out. Other factors unknown to the Western world may also have played their part. If in 1953 the census understated the population, as Aird assumed, by anything of up to 15%, it might have grown by now to well over 800 million. If on the other hand the census overstated the true position by no more than 5%, the present population is unlikely to exceed 700 million; it might be less. In the light of what little is known

---

[1] Leo A. Orleans, 'China's Population Statistics: An Illusion?' *The China Quarterly*, no. 21 (London, January–March 1965).

about the current supply of foodstuffs and the state of nutrition as observed by foreign visitors and interviewers of refugees in Hong Kong, a population of 700 million seems the most likely figure. Any higher estimate does not appear to tally with estimated food supplies available during 1966/7.

FOOD AND FARMING

Foodstuffs and other farm products are hardly any better documented than the population. The last reasonably reliable estimate of grain production goes back to 1957, the last year before the Great Leap Forward, when it was officially given as 185 million tons. This figure can be taken as a yardstick by which to measure all later harvests, planned, claimed or achieved. The official record of the grain harvest of 1958 – by all accounts a bumper crop – was greatly exaggerated when, in the course of the Great Leap Forward, the statistical services lost all control to local officials and party enthusiasts. The impossibly high claim of 375 million tons was scaled down, after two recounts half-way through the season, to 250 million tons – in the light of later information still an improbably high figure. Since then no harvest estimates have been published, but at the end of 1964 Chou En-lai said that the grain crop that had just been gathered had reached the level of 'high yielding years of the past'. It was probably somewhat above that of 1957, but well below that of 1958, i.e. perhaps 190 million tons. The next year was less favourable and 1966 was less favourable still. The official claim of a bumper harvest in 1966 can be dismissed as unrealistic in view of prolonged droughts that, according to a report of the official Chinese news agency, NCNA, of 30 December 1966, hit many parts of the country 'with an intensity rarely seen in history'. The meteorological records that are compiled in Hong Kong tend to confirm this account. The grain crop of 1966 was then hardly more than 180 million tons.

Leaving the vagaries of nature aside, in 1967 the grain harvest is unlikely to yield more than in 1957, i.e. 185 million tons. Other crops will probably not do better than ten years ago either, with the possible exception of vegetables, pork and poultry, the foodstuffs produced on the cultivators' private plots and marketed outside the channels under government control. This means that within ten years China's farming has made practically no progress. As the input of labour and capital on the land has probably increased by a quarter since 1957, there must have been a significant decline in the productivity of labour on the farms.

In view of this state of affairs, the question of the size of the population is of more than purely academic interest. A discrepancy of 100 million mouths may mean the difference between meagre supplies and starvation. Allowing for seed, feed, waste and net trade, the present supply of grain and potatoes (given in Chinese statistics in terms of grain equivalent) is unlikely to provide more than 1,650 calories per head per day for a population of 700 million. If the nutritive value of non-grain foods is added, the total daily intake will hardly account for more than 2,100 calories. This is 5% less than was available at the time of the Japanese invasion of China in 1931. Barring major changes in the natural and political climate of the country, there is no reason to expect a significant change between 1967 and 1970, the last year of the current Five-Year-Plan period. If there were small improvements in domestic supplies, imports of grain would probably cease. While a diet of 2,100 calories is far from ample, it is sufficient to keep the population at work – provided, of course, that the distribution system continues to function normally. In the course of the Cultural Revolution it has been disrupted considerably in some of the deficit areas of the country.

In 1967 the defunct Twelve-Year Plan for agriculture was supposed to yield an output of almost 450 million tons of grain (against a probable crop of 185 million tons). This Plan was first introduced at a Supreme State Conference held in January 1956. It was later revised on points of detail. It was approved in its third draft by the National Congress of the CCP in May 1958 and eventually adopted by the National People's Congress in April 1960, when in view of the failures of the communes and the Great Leap Forward greater caution in forward planning might have seemed advisable. The ambitious targets of the plan were to be achieved as the result of simultaneous improvements over a wide field, resulting from the use of fertilizers and the control of irrigation water, from mechanization, land reclamation, high quality seeds, pest controls and from multiple cropping. The results were expected to accrue from the cumulative effects of these measures, whilst in fact they should have been treated as inter-dependent.

Early in 1960 Li Fu-chun, the chairman of the State Planning Commission, gave the farming industry pride of place in economic planning and in investment policy. Agriculture was to be treated as 'the foundation' of the economy, and thus to rank ahead of the industrial sectors concerned with the output of both consumer and producer goods. No information is available on the level of investment in agriculture, but the permission given to cultivators to engage in 'side-line production' on their private plots and to sell their produce in markets free from government control has had a salutary effect on the composition of the diet, though the impact on the volume of food produced has been small.

China's agriculture has, of course, some substantial untapped reserves, but as long as fertilizer supplies are only large enough to meet part of the needs of such commercial crops as oilseeds, cotton and tobacco, the shortages in basic foodstuffs are bound to remain. In 1966 approximately 8 kg. of plant nutrients contained in commercial fertilizers were available per hectare of arable land (7 lb. per acre). In Britain 25 times as much fertilizer was used, and in Japan as much as 40 times. No sizeable quantities of fertilizer and other farm requisites that are essential for raising crop yields are likely to be available for grain before 1970; present supplies are very low and fertilizer plants take five years to get into production – yet grains will continue to provide four-fifths of the diet. Farm mechanization is still in its infancy. Some 100,000 tractor units (in terms of 15 h.p.) equal to 50,000 actual tractors are now available in China. This compares with ten times the number of tractors available in Britain on an acreage which is approximately one-fifteenth of that in China. Mechanized irrigation facilities, though much improved since 1957, also fall much behind actual need. At present each h.p. of pumping equipment has to cope on average with 50 acres of cultivated land.

INDUSTRY AND OTHER NON-AGRICULTURAL ACTIVITIES

Information on China's industry, mining, handicraft and public utilities is no easier to come by than on farm production.

The main components of the country's industry are the modern industrial sector and the handicraft and cottage industries. Since 1958 it is no longer possible to separate the output of the modern sector from that of the traditional forms of production; nor have any production data or gross production indices been published since revised targets for 1962, the last year of the defunct second Five-Year Plan, were published in 1959. The Great Leap Forward played havoc with all forecasting, and actual results can only be gauged from occasional claims in the Chinese press and from Western and Soviet estimates. At the end of 1964 Chou En-lai claimed that the gross output of China's industry had grown at the rate of 15% within one year. The real rate must have been substantially less than this since (i) transfers from traditional to modern industry increased statistical coverage, (ii) new products were counted at cost prices of a later date and at prototype stage, (iii) increased subcontracting raised gross, or double counted, output more quickly than net. Due to the preference given to certain sectors of industry there were considerable variations in the growth rates of different commodities. Mineral oils, chemical fertilizers, cement and motor vehicles did better than other items. In 1965 industry was supposed to grow further by another 11%, but no plan results were published. The same is true of 1966. Performance probably lagged behind the plan.

In the absence of official data from Chinese sources, Western estimates have to suffice.[1] The latest available estimates are for 1964, but allowing for further growth until the Cultural Revolution began to interfere with industrial production at the end of 1966, some broad outline at the present level of output seems possible. Crude steel production was probably at a level of 12 million tons, i.e. still slightly less than in 1958. By common consent, at the end of 1964 China's industrial production, while larger than in 1957, had not yet reached the level attained in 1958, 1959 and 1960. On the whole the output of producer goods had increased more than that of most consumer goods, some of which had not yet regained the level attained in 1957. The position did not change materially in 1965 so that China in all probability started her third Five-Year Plan at production

---

[1] W. Klatt, 'China's Third Five-Year Plan', *The China Quarterly*, no. 25 (London, January–March 1966).

levels that were below those reached during the first few years of the second plan.

At the beginning of 1966 China's industrial base was still that of a pre-industrial society. Energy available per head of population equalled less than 300 kg. of coal or 6% of the energy available per capita in the United Kingdom. Worse still, in China some fifty persons have to make do with the electricity supply that one person has at his disposal in the United Kingdom. At 17 kg. per head China's steel consumption equals one-thirtieth and one-fortieth, respectively, of the levels attained in the United Kingdom and the United States. It is thus not surprising that, according to current official Chinese thinking, it will take twenty to thirty years before China will be able to catch up with Western industrial nations. In 1956 Liu Shao-chi in his political report to the Party's National Congress saw China transformed by 1967 from a backward agricultural country into an advanced industrialized nation. These expectations have proved to be over-optimistic.

Thanks to the highly selective nature of the industrial programme, remarkable achievements in some spheres have gone side by side with stagnation in others. The industries depending on the raw materials of the farm industry did particularly badly. Against this, China's nuclear programme, which by all accounts was given priority in the allocation of human, material and financial resources, progressed much faster than was generally expected. The first nuclear test explosion took place on 16 October 1964. Another atom bomb was tested on 14 May 1965. The third and fourth explosions occurred on 9 May and 27 October 1966. And the last explosion so far took place three days before the end of last year (1966). It coincided with the call for a new, all-round leap forward in industry and agriculture. The tests have revealed a high degree of sophistication in China's scientific and technological advance in this sphere, but there is no evidence yet of a similarly developed system for the delivery of nuclear weapons.

No information is available on the amount of private savings and public investments. In the course of the first Five-Year Plan gross investment increased from approximately 20% of gross domestic expenditure in 1952 to 25% in 1957. During the Great Leap Forward the investment ratio increased further, but a good deal of waste occurred within the communes and elsewhere. Currently the rate of investment is probably similar to that attained in 1957, though a slightly larger share probably goes nowadays into the industries which produce farm requisites. As in the past, almost half the total investment outlay is likely to provide for the capital and replacement needed in the modern industrial sector of the economy. Agriculture is unlikely to get more than a tenth of the total (it got less than that in the first Five-Year Plan).

Self-reliance continues to be one of the chief targets of Chinese planning. Foreign trade has grown faster than the domestic economy in recent years. Even so, it is unlikely to account for as much as 5% (one way) of the nation's economic activities. Whereas at the height of Sino-Soviet co-operation in 1959 Soviet trade accounted for almost one half of China's foreign trade turnover (imports plus exports), Russia's share has in the meantime declined to little more than one-tenth. The other countries of the European communist bloc have tended to follow a similar course in their trade with China. As a result, China's trade with non-communist countries now accounts for three-quarters of her total trade as against less than one-third in 1959. China's trade balance shows usually a surplus equivalent to $200 to $300 million a year. Overseas remittances, normally ranging from $50 to $100 million contribute to a favourable balance of payments, but in time of political stress, as during the Great Leap Forward and the Cultural Revolution, they tend to decline drastically. The need to spend up to $400 million a year on grain shipments from abroad is a heavy burden on the balance of payments and limits China's ability to buy foreign industrial equipment. Against this, the repayment of debts to Russia has freed some $250 million a year for purchases abroad. In 1964 China paid the remainder of the debts which had accrued in her trading accounts with the Soviet Union and owing to her having accepted Soviet long-term loans for civilian and military equipment. In the meantime China appears to have built up in Moscow a small balance of payments surplus of, say, $150 million.

NATIONAL AGGREGATES

Nothing is known from official sources about the current value of China's total national product and the size of its chief components. Up to 1957 reasonably consistent official estimates of national income and expenditure at market prices, exclusive of the so-called non-productive sectors, were published. Several Western calculations of gross and net national product and of net domestic product, based on official Chinese data, are available for the period up to the end of the first Five-Year Plan. From these it would appear that China's gross domestic product and expenditure increased (in 1957 prices) from approximately 75,000 million yuan in 1952 to 100,000 million yuan in 1957. This corresponds to an annual growth rate of approximately 6% (and it is slightly less than previously estimated).[1] After 1957 another year of good performance was followed by several years of severe retrenchment, caused by over-investment, errors in the allocation of scarce resources and lack of economic balance in the development programme as mapped out during the Great Leap Forward. The savings that had been forced on a population that was badly lacking some of its essential requirements and the insufficient use of industrial capacities facilitated the recovery that took place from 1963 onwards. Official claims for agricultural and industrial output seem to imply an increase by the end of 1966 of approximately one-third over and above the level which the gross domestic product had reached in 1957. This would be equal to an annual growth rate of approximately 3% during the nine years from the end of the first Five-Year Plan to the end of the first year of the current plan.

In spite of a shift of emphasis in favour of agriculture, the shares of the chief non-agricultural components in the gross domestic product have probably changed relatively little. The farming industry is likely to absorb two-thirds of the labour force, but to produce somewhat less than one-third of the total product of the nation. A similar amount is generated by the combined efforts of industry, mining, construction and handicraft which employ approximately one-sixth of the labour force.

[1] W. Klatt, 'The Economy of China', in Guy Wint (ed.), *Asia: A Handbook* (Blond, London, 1965).

The remainder of the total product and the labour force is accounted for by public activities, internal and external trade and other services. The use of the gross domestic product may well have undergone some changes. It seems probable that personal consumption has been curtailed during the years of the mad rush and the recovery that followed it, whilst the gross domestic expenditure devoted to government consumption and government controlled communal services is likely to have increased proportionately. No more than broad outlines can be given, but these may serve to indicate certain trends that seem to have emerged from the dislocations caused in past years.

OUTLOOK

As China is – once more – in the throes of an upheaval in the course of which, in the Chinese phrase, politics have taken command over economics, it would seem presumptuous to look beyond the most immediate future. If the *status quo ante* as it existed prior to the Cultural Revolution could be restored speedily, an increase of gross industrial production by 50% during the current Five-Year Plan might still be possible. This would imply an annual industrial growth rate of $8\frac{1}{2}\%$. As some of China's industrial capital is bound to be in need of repair, if not replacement, this rate might well be unattainable even under conditions of internal stability. Much would, of course, depend on the performance of the farming industry which has to supply not only food and agricultural raw materials for the rural and urban population, but also the financial means of 'primitive accumulation' without which industrialization cannot proceed. For the time being, nature rather than man determines the level of farm production. Few farm requisites that are capable of levelling out the effects of natural hazards and of levelling up the yields of the main crops are likely to become available before 1970. Thus the growth rate of the farming industry may not exceed that of the population; it may even lag behind it. In these circumstances gross domestic product and expenditure are unlikely to rise by more than one-third during the period of the current plan, or by an average of $5\frac{1}{2}$ to 6% per annum. This would correspond to the rate of performance attained during the first plan.

All this pre-supposes a speedy return to stability in domestic and foreign relations. At present China seems to be far removed from such a state of affairs. If the conditions of life and work remain disrupted for a year or more – as they were during and

Table 8.1   *Agricultural production* (in million physical units)

	Actual		Estimates		Forecasts	
	1952	1957	1964	1966	1967	1970
Crops (hectares):						
grains and potatoes	112·3	120·9	120·0	120·0	120·0	125·0
soyabeans	11·5	12·6	8·2	8·0	8·5	10·0
cotton	5·6	5·8	4·6	5·0	5·0	6·0
Crops (tons):						
grains and potatoes	154·5	185·0	190·0	180·0	185·0	200·0
soyabeans	9·5	10·0	7·0	7·0	7·5	9·0
cotton	1·3	1·6	1·5	1·5	1·5	2·0
Crops (tons/hectare)						
grains and potatoes	1·37	1·53	1·58	1·50	1·54	1·60
soyabeans	0·83	0·80	0·85	0·87	0·88	0·90
cotton	0·23	0·28	0·33	0·30	0·30	0·33
Livestock (no.):						
cattle and buffaloes	56·6	65·8	65·0	65·0	66·0	70·0
pigs	89·8	145·9	180·0	180·0	185·0	200·0
Net trade (tons):						
grains	−0·8	−0·5	+6·5	+5·5	+4·5	—
Available supplies (tons):						
grains	153·7	184·5	196·5	185·5	189·5	200·0

Table 8.2   *Industrial production* (in million physical units)

	Actual		Estimates		Forecasts	
	1952	1957	1964	1966	1967	1970
Electricity (000 kWh.)	7·3	19·3	33·0	50·0	55·0	70·0
Coal (tons)	66·5	130·7	220·0	250·0	275·0	350·0
Crude Oil (tons)	0·4	1·5	6·0	8·0	9·0	11·0
Crude steel (tons)	1·3	5·3	10·0	12·0	13·5	16·0
Cement (tons)	2·9	6·9	8·0	10·0	11·0	14·0
Fertilizers (tons)	0·2	0·8	4·5	5·5	6·0	7·5
Cotton cloth (000 metres)	3·8	5·0	3·5	4·0	4·5	6·0

Table 8.3 *Foreign trade* (in 000 million $ at current prices)[a]

	Actual		Estimates		Forecasts	
	1952	1957	1964	1965	1967	1970
Imports (from):						
Soviet bloc	0·8	0·9	0·4	0·4	0·3	?
non-bloc	0·3	0·4	1·0	1·3	1·5	?
Total world	1·1	1·3	1·4	1·7	1·8	?
Exports (to):						
Soviet bloc	0·6	1·1	0·7	0·5	0·4	?
non-bloc	0·4	0·5	1·1	1·4	1·7	?
Total world	1·0	1·6	1·8	1·9	2·1	?
Turnover:						
Soviet bloc	1·4	2·0	1·1	0·9	0·7	?
non-bloc	0·7	0·9	2·1	2·7	3·2	?
Total world	2·1	2·9	3·2	3·6	3·9	?
Balance:						
Soviet bloc	−0·2	+0·2	+0·3	+0·1	+0·1	?
non-bloc	+0·1	+0·1	+0·1	+0·1	+0·2	?
Total world	−0·1	+0·3	+0·4	+0·2	+0·3	?

[a] Trade with the Soviet bloc is valued at 1 yuan = 1 old rouble, which exaggerates its dollar value.

Table 8.4 *Overall economic indicators*

	Actual		Estimates		Forecasts	
	1952	1957	1964	1965	1967	1970
Rates of Growth						
(1957 = 100):						
gross agricultural output	85	100	100	100	105	110
gross industrial output	50	100	145	160	190	240
gross material output	65	100	125	135	155	190
gross domestic product	75	100	120	130	145	170
Rates of Growth						
(per cent per annum):	—	1957	1964	1965	1967	1970
		1952	1957	1957	1965	1965
gross agricultural output	—	3·0	0·0	0·0	2·5	2·0
gross industrial output	—	15·0	5·5	6·0	9·0	8·5
gross material output	—	9·0	3·0	4·0	7·0	6·0
gross domestic product	—	6·0	2·5	3·5	6·0	5·5

Table 8.5 *Domestic product and expenditure*

	Estimates		Estimates	Forecasts
	1952	1957	1965	1970

Domestic product (in 000 million yuan at 1957 prices)

	1952	1957	1965	1970
Agriculture	33·5	40·0	40·0	45·0
Industry				
mining, construction, handicraft	19·0	30·0	45·0	63·0
Trade, public utilities	22·5	30·0	45·0	62·0
Total	75·0	100·0	130·0	170·0

Rates of growth (indices)

	—	$\dfrac{1957}{1952}$	$\dfrac{1965}{1957}$	$\dfrac{1970}{1965}$
Agriculture	—	120	100	110
Industry, etc.	—	160	150	140
Trade, etc.	—	135	150	140
Total	—	135	130	130

Shares of components (per cent)

	1952	1957	1965	1970
Agriculture	45	40	30	27
Industry, etc.	25	30	35	37
Trade, etc.	30	30	35	36
Total	100	100	100	100

Domestic expenditure (in 000 million yuan at 1957 prices)

	1952	1957	1965	1970
Personal consumption	52·5	65·0	78·0	98·0
Government consumption, communal service and the investment of people's communes	7·5	10·0	19·5	22·0
Domestic investment	15·0	25·0	32·5	50·0
Total	75·0	100·0	130·0	170·0

Rates of growth (indices)

	—	$\dfrac{1957}{1952}$	$\dfrac{1965}{1957}$	$\dfrac{1970}{1965}$
Personal consumption	—	125	120	125
Government consumption, etc.	—	135	195	115
Domestic investment	—	165	130	155
Total	—	135	130	130

Shares of components (per cent)

	1952	1957	1965	1970
Personal consumption	70	65	60	58
Government consumption, etc.	10	10	15	13
Domestic investment	20	25	25	29
Total	100	100	100	100

Table 8.6 *Food balance 1966/67* (estimated population 700 millions)

Commodity	Acreage million ha.	Yield ton/ha.	Production million tons	million tons				per day		
				Net trade	Waste, seed, feed, ind. use	Gross supply	Net kg per head[c]	Calories	Prot. g.	Fat g.
Rice	30·0	2·85	85·0	—	7·5	77·5[b]	83·0	·	·	·
Wheat	25·0	0·80	20·0	+9·0[a]	4·5	24·5[b]	30·0	·	·	·
Other grains	55·0	1·00	55·0	—	22·0	33·0[b]	40·0	·	·	·
All grains	110·0	1·45	160·0	+9·0[a]	34·0	135·0	153·0	1,525	·	·
Potatoes (grains equiv.)	10·0	2·00	20·0	—	8·0	12·0	17·0	125	·	·
Grains and potatoes	120·0	1·50	180·0	+9·0[a]	42·0	147·0	170·0	1,650	40	7
Pulses and soya	20·0	1·00	20·0	-0·5	9·0	10·5	15·0	150	15	5
Sugar (refined)	·	·	·	·	·	1·5	2·0	20	—	—
Fruit and vegetables	·	·	·	·	·	50·0	70·0	60	4	—
Meat and poultry	—	—	7·5	—	0·5	7·0	10·0	80	5	7
Eggs and fish	—	—	7·5	—	1·5	6·0	9·0	20	1	1
Fats and oils	—	—	4·0	—	0·5	3·5	5·0	120	—	15
Grand Total								2,100	65	35

[a] Domestic prod. equiv. of 5·5–6·0 million tons.
[b] Extraction rates: rice 75%; wheat and other grains 85%.
[c] At retail level.

after the Great Leap Forward – the consequences might even be more serious than they were then. In that case, not only might China's industry lose the momentum regained recently; but the population might suffer even more serious hardships than eight years ago. It might even have to go to war. Periods of stagnation and retreat under conditions of internal and external warfare have not been unknown in the fifty years of communist history. If it were to be China's fate to experience what Russia had to endure in the years from 1928 to 1944, the increase of the population might provide the only growth rate of the nation, and even that might disappear. In that case China's leaders of 1970 might have to reflect on the effects of thirteen rather than eight years that were lost in the name of communist development.

9

CHINA ONE YEAR LATER

PETER WILES, 1968

China has recently been the classic example of the priority of politics over econometrics, even over linear extrapolation. It is the second of Dr Klatt's predictions that has been fulfilled: political chaos has continued and economic life has suffered. However, as he suggested, it has not hitherto done so badly, and even here prediction of a kind is possible.

First, mere political excitement and instability, of the kind witnessed at the beginning of the Cultural Revolution (August 1966), need not totally inhibit economic growth. A central plan, hammered out in Peking under such conditions, would have come out very late and been quite inconsistent with itself; but already since 1958 China has had a virtual market economy of the kind described on pp. 15–17. So long as the Cultural Revolution and the Red Guards confined themselves to the streets, the press, the wireless, the arts, the high schools, the universities and the organs of government, peasant, worker and even manager could *and did* get on with the job.

The costs of such a situation were not negligible. It is insufficiently appreciated how high the sheer direct economic cost of government by mile-long parade, mass meeting, permanent agitation and committees for all is. Even before 1960 private citizens were compelled to spend very approximately 300 million yuan a year on decorations for Labour Day and National Day alone.[1] This was about 0·3% of the national income. If we add government expenditures on these two major festivals, and all the expenses of the minor festivals, we may well arrive at not less than 1%. This estimate excludes, moreover, work-time lost. Every country has national holidays, but almost no other interrupts work for *ad hoc* political committee meetings and agitation. That such lost time was always very great by foreign standards is common knowledge.[2]

[1] Chow Ching-wen, *Ten Years of Storm* (New York, 1960), pp. 189–90.
[2] Just one reference will suffice: M. A. Klochko, *Soviet Scientist in China* (London, 1964), *passim*.

133

It is fair to assume that material expenditures on parades, wall newspapers, paint, train-trips for Red Guards, etc. doubled between 1965 and 1967. This will have taken, with extreme approximation, another 1% of the national income away from true consumption and productive investment, to spend it on objects more economically sterile even than defence. Secondly, more work-time was lost. This can scarcely have been under three more working days per man per year, thus knocking another 1% off the national product. Thirdly, higher education ceased, and most students went into political agitation full-time. This, like the first item, would have no immediate effect on economic performance, since according to ordinary definitions it was a switch from productive to unproductive investment. But in future years growth will of course fall.

Such temporary hindrances to economic performance are compatible with Mr Jan Prybyla's[1] general position, that July–December 1966, the first six months of the Cultural Revolution, was not a bad period. But then the movement went into the factories and farms, and simultaneously began to spill blood. There followed from January 1967 to July 1968, eighteen months of interference by young agitators with production of strikes by workers against this, of unauthorized travel to 'exchange revolutionary experience' by workers and peasants as well as Red Guards, of arms seizures and minor civil wars. Imports and exports have fallen.[2] Even the nuclear weapons effort has proved more susceptible to civil disorder than its French cousin,[3] and deliveries to Vietnam have been slowed by railway sabotage.[4] All in all, national income must have fallen, both in total and, more so, per head, between January 1967 and July 1968.

As this is written, this period is over, and some measure of order seems to have been established, though this may not apply to some of the outlying provinces. Higher education – technical only[5] – has been resumed. There are limits to

---

[1] In his 'The Economic Cost', in *Problems of Communism* (March–April 1968). I am also indebted to Mr Kevin Bucknall, the School of Oriental and African Studies, London, whose views are extremely similar.

[2] *New York Times*, 24 July 1968, p. 6.

[3] *New York Times*, 25 August 1969, p. 2.

[4] *New York Times*, 10 July 1968, p. 8.

[5] *New York Times*, 24 July 1968.

unreason, and it is safe to make the basic political prediction: whoever reigns, whoever wins, 1967–68 will not recur. I predict therefore that the rather healthy annual growth rates which Dr Klatt posited for an orderly China in 1965–70 will hold at least for 1969 and 1970, taking late 1968, rather than all 1968, as a base. For these rates correspond to the underlying capacity of the country, and world history shows that many economic institutions are efficient enough to exploit that.

Dr Klatt adds his own comment in the following chapter.

10

CHINA'S ECONOMY AFTER THE CULTURAL REVOLUTION

W. KLATT, 1969

ECONOMIC BALANCE SHEET

In view of the uncertainty which has prevailed in many of the urban and industrial areas of China for almost three years, it is exceedingly difficult to arrive at any national aggregates that have any meaning. It is even more difficult to look beyond 1970, the last year of the current plan period. Nothing is known about the current value of China's total national product and the size of its chief components – from either Chinese or Western sources. Economic development has been uneven in the last two years. Industry, transport, domestic and foreign trade have been disturbed more than agriculture as the result of the upheaval caused by the Cultural Revolution. Whereas the production of mineral oils, cement and fertilizers seems to have been reasonably satisfactory, the same cannot be said of fuel and power or of minerals and metals. Overall industrial production at the end of 1968 might well have been 10% or so below the level reached prior to the Cultural Revolution and foreign trade has contracted even more. In spite of a shift of emphasis in favour of agriculture, the shares of the chief non-agricultural components of the national economy have probably changed relatively little. The use of the gross domestic product, however, may well have undergone some changes. Personal consumption is bound to have been affected by the Cultural Revolution, though less so than during the Great Leap Forward.

If the *status quo ante* the Cultural Revolution can now be restored speedily, an increase of gross industrial production by some 30% during the period of the current Five Year Plan (1966–70) may still be possible (this is slightly less than was estimated in *Analyse et Prévision* in June 1967; see p. 127 above).

This would imply an annual industrial growth rate of 5·5–6·0%. As some of China's industrial equipment is bound to be in need of repair, if not replacement, this rate might well be unattainable even under conditions of internal stability. Much depends, of course, on the performance of the farming industry, where nature still determines the outcome rather than man. During the current plan period gross domestic product and expenditure are unlikely to rise by more than one quarter at the most, or by an average of 4·5% per annum (this, again, is slightly less than was suggested in *Analyse et Prévision* in June 1967). This growth rate would be a good deal less than the rate attained during the first plan, though more than during the interim period between the first and the third plan. A recovery of such magnitude presupposes a speedy return to stable government and administration. At this moment (autumn 1969) there is no certainty that law and order have been restored in all parts of China and that the rates of industrial output and of general economic growth which were achieved in the years before the Cultural Revolution can be resumed swiftly.

The long-term prospects of China's economy will depend first and foremost upon the political preference of the Party leadership that takes over when Mao's rule comes to an end. At this stage no prediction seems possible in this respect. If experiments such as the Great Leap Forward and the Cultural Revolution were banned from the political scene and continuity in economic planning and industrial performance was permitted, China might well advance significantly in the decade following Mao's death. The country's resources are larger and the means of mobilizing them are now more readily available than was once thought possible. If upheavals, such as those of the recent past, could be avoided, China should be able to become, before the end of the century, a major industrial nation. The weight of her presence is bound to be felt proportionally. As a major political factor China's predominance on the Asian continent will be checked only in so far as Japan and India become economically stronger and politically more influential in the area than they are today.

Table 10.1 *Domestic product and expenditure, 1965–70*

	forecast (000 million yuan of 1952)			forecast (1965 = 100)		
	1965 est.	1970 orig.	1970 rev.	1965 est.	1970 orig.	1970 rev.
Gross domestic product						
Agriculture	40·0	45	46	100	110	115
Industry, mining, construction	45·0	63	59	100	140	130
Trade, public utilities	45·0	62	55	100	140	120
Total	130·0	170	160	100	130	125
Gross domestic expenditure						
Personal consumption	78·0	98	95	100	125	120
Government consumption, commercial services	19·5	22	25	100	115	130
Domestic gross investment	32·5	50	40	100	155	125
Total	130·0	170	160	100	130	125

Table 10.2 *Agricultural and industrial production*

	forecast (million physical units)			forecast (1965 = 100)		
	1965 est.	1970 orig.	1970 rev.	1965 est.	1970 orig.	1970 rev.
Grains and potatoes (tons)	185·0	200·0	200·0	100	108	108
Vegetable oils (tons)	1·8	2·4	2·4	100	133	133
Cotton (tons)	1·5	2·0	2·0	100	133	133
Cotton cloth (000 metres)	5·2[a]	6·0	6·6	100	115	127
Coal (tons)	230·0	350·0	255·0	100	150	110
Electricity (000 kWh)	45·0	70·0	60·0	100	155	133
Crude oil (tons)	9·0[a]	11·0	12·5	100	122	139
Crude steel (tons)	11·0	16·0	15·0	100	145	136
Cement (tons)	10·5[a]	14·0	13·5	100	133	129
Fertilizers (tons)	4·5[a]	7·5	6·5	100	166	144

[a] Revised.

11

CZECHOSLOVAKIA

BORIS PESEK, 1967

Czechoslovakia entered this 1 January a new era: the 'New Economic Model'. What is the 'New Model' that is expected to have – and, in my opinion, is likely to have – such a revolutionary effect on the Czechoslovak economy? Basically, it constitutes a conversion of command enterprises into profit-maximizing enterprises. These enterprises are to buy factors so as to minimize their costs and produce and sell output so as to maximize their net revenue. Under what conditions this is to happen is – at present – still unclear. The rules are ambiguous, in certain key aspects contradictory, and all will depend on the way in which these rules are going to be converted into reality. Let me outline, before I go into the details of the New Model, some basic ambiguities and contradictions the resolution of which will make or break the New Model.

Enterprises are to determine freely their input mix and their output mix so as to maximize 'disposable net revenue' available for wage bonuses and reinvestment. They are to do so on the basis of prices of factors of inputs and outputs which originally were to be at least partially flexible but which the December 1966 decisions of the government froze for the next six months. At the same time, there is the fervent determination to make an end with surpluses and shortages and to have all markets, especially the labor market, cleared. Obviously, something here will have to give; my guess would be that the goal of clearing the markets will get the upper hand over the goal of fixing the prices and that price level stability will be pursued through macroeconomic tools rather than through attempts to fix individual prices.

Enterprises are to have incentives to maximize disposable net revenue; yet, they were formed into 85 trusts and the boards of directors of these trusts received the right to levy supplementary taxes on the disposable net revenue of successful enterprises with which to subsidize unsuccessful ones. Information about some of these trusts (which have wide autonomy) suggests that at least some key ones intend to use this power in an extremely responsible fashion. The metal working industry trust agreed on a program of supplementary taxes fixed in size for the next three years, some of which are to be merely long-term loans to be repaid starting in the year 1970.

Enterprises are to be competitive; yet, the trusts seem to provide a golden opportunity for the cartelization of the entire economy. Whether the effort by individual enterprises to maximize their disposable net revenue will overcome the temptation to run under the shelter of a cartel is to be seen. At present, there is fragmentary evidence that lack of 'discipline' within a trust is being solved by having a trust that supplies raw materials to do the policeman's work. A very aggressive co-operative producing readymade clothing just (in January) lost *all* its supplies of textiles and buttons; all the firms in the textiles and chemical trust utilized their new power to close or not to close delivery contracts by refusing to supply this co-operative. Yet, who can predict what will happen when markets are cleared and the suppliers are looking for customers rather than dispensing favors? Both American and European experience suggests that cartels containing numerous firms are not viable unless enforced by the use of state power. According to the present rules, anti-competitive agreements (including agreement about exclusive territories) will not be enforced; the trusts are not supposed to block competition among the member firms.

An admitted difficulty is that in the case of many products (TV sets, plastic powder used by the entire electrical industry, etc.) there is only one single producer; many other products are produced by two or three firms. Anywhere in the world, competition under these conditions is unthinkable; in a small country such as Czechoslovakia this problem is more pressing than in a big country since even one producer of many products may be facing a market too small for efficient production. However, the importance of this problem should not be over-stated. If the New Model succeeds in converting *all* command enterprises with their indifference to inputs and outputs into many competitive enterprises and some monopolies each of which will rationally organize its production, it will have done extremely well.

One of the major tasks which the enterprises are expected to accomplish is to reallocate the labor force. This is supposed to have two major effects: relieve the manpower shortage due mainly to gross overemployment of labor by enterprises indifferent to the size of the wage bill (since any deficit was covered out of the state budget) and by the very act of reduction of the labor force hired by individual enterprises to make the labor 'shape up'. Henceforth, jobs are not to be viewed as an inherent right that cannot be lost through persistent indifference and slackness but merely through gross and repeated breaks of basic discipline. Yet, only belatedly have the planners reached a decision, the details of which remain unpublished, not to impose the entire burden on those displaced, but to introduce provisions that are equivalent of the Western unemployment insurance. Also, the task of reallocation of labor both from overstaffed prosperous enterprises and from failing and to-be-closed enterprises to economic sectors short of labor (construction and services) is made inordinately difficult and painful by the fact that housing remains exempt from the scope of the New Model. No attempt is made to make labor mobility possible through the restoration of a free or reasonably free housing market. Since there is no inventory of free housing (akin to inventory of goods in retail stores), movement of labor from city to city is, and is likely to remain, a tortuous enterprise requiring clumsy barter or serious reduction in the standard of living.

Finally, when we move from microeconomics to macroeconomics there is the conflict – spurious, in my opinion – between those in Prague who insist on central planning and fear the New Model as the reintroduction of the competitive capitalistic anarchy and those who point out that rational national planning (as the past decade of stagnation has shown) is possible only through the use of macroeconomic tools of demand control and investment control; that rational regional planning (especially stimulation of some of the impoverished and backward parts of Czechoslovakia) is possible only through selective differentiation of the impact of some of these macroeconomic tools: taxes, investment credits, etc.

This brief enumeration of the contradictions contained in the New Model should suggest to the reader the tremendous uncertainties facing the Czechoslovak economy in the coming year. The temptation is great to conclude that in all these cases some compromise will be found by reasonable people. Yet, the New Model is so revolutionary that it appears that a compromise with its basic principles will simply represent a complete failure. For the old system is very deeply ingrained, and it tends to subsidize failure. Once this begins again on a large scale it will be impossible to stop an avalanche of it.

MICROECONOMICS: THE KEY ISSUE

The reader must have noticed that the bulk of my discussion was devoted to the problems facing the consumers, firms, and industries. The central planners, whether in the government in Prague or in the trust directorates, appeared only insofar as they are able to foster and hinder the reform that, if it can be won at all, must be won on the enterprise level. In contrast with the past two or three decades when the issues were such broad and impressive looking problems as whether to foster the steel industry at the expense of consumer good industries, or trade within the bloc rather than trade with the rest of the world, the issues are now less impressive in scope and yet, extremely significant in import.

Table 11.1 (p. 147) shows the basic entries in each enterprise's annual income statement. The performance of the enterprise is to be judged on the basis of item 15, which I translated as Disposable Income even though the official Czech term – probably selected to preserve terminological continuity with the Old Model – speaks about 'disposable gross revenue' (*pouzitelny hruby duchod*).

Needless to say, there are numerous modifications and exceptions which it is impossible to discuss in this limited space. However, it needs to be mentioned that the tax base for item 4 does not include capital sunk in enterprise-owned housing or cultural installations, nor will it contain capital purchased by the enterprises less than five years old.[1] Similarly, item 10

---

[1] This is in order not to penalize enterprises that have recently been successful. There is, by the way, a tax on land.

experienced numerous modifications even before it became operative; originally, it was much more punitive in nature. Recently, it has been reduced to $\frac{1}{2}\%$ and $\frac{1}{4}\%$ in numerous regions that the government declared as underdeveloped.

Investments are to be financed out of enterprises' own funds; the use of depreciation allowances is subject to the control of the trust and may be pooled with those of other enterprises to finance new projects. Finally, the banks are to lend to enterprises for the purpose of financing investment projects. While exceptions are foreseen, the financing of investment through budgetary allocations is to cease.

PRICES

Throughout 1966, the central authorities were working on a new set of wholesale prices which are to apply from 1 January 1967. While they increased by 6% in 1966, the revision increased them by another 3·3%. These prices were to be binding in 93% of the cases, with the remaining 7% subject to full enterprise control. Similarly, retail prices were split among fixed prices, free prices modified by floors and ceilings, and entirely free prices. However, in December 1966 the conservative element in the government won and *all* prices were frozen for the first half of 1967. It appears doubtful that this is of much significance since after two decades of experience enterprises seem, in many cases, to have little difficulty in changing market prices under the guise of special orders, emergency deliveries in extremely short time span, etc. Since after January of 1967 they also have the full incentive to do so, the price freeze is unlikely to be very effective.

FORECAST

After this description of the basic features of the New Model, our editor expects me to put my neck on the chopping block and make a prediction of the 1967 output and output five years from now. This year, however, this forecasting enterprise is – in my opinion – utterly impossible in the case of Czechoslovakia. The authorities were so busy with the preparation of the new model that data for 1966 are available only in the most rudimentary form – a hodge-podge of percentages, changes in money values of output, and changes in real values. The plan for 1967 has not been prepared as yet (i.e. 10 February). Finally, the government still does not have a budget and is operating under an emergency status (*stav rozpoctoveho provisoria*). With last year's figures not available, with this year's plan unknown, and with this year's budget unknown, and with the New Model just off the launching pad, no prediction of either 1967 performance or 1972 performance appears – at least to this writer – possible. While we frequently have to operate on the basis of very scanty evidence, in this case I would be operating on the basis of no evidence.

CONCLUSION

Economists studying Czechoslovak national income accounts for the past decade frequently wonder as to whether the relatively mild recession of 1962 merits the next to revolutionary response represented by the New Model. The answer, in my opinion, is that the reformers correctly perceive that national income accounts fail to register the basic malaise that engulfs the Czechoslovak economy. Objective as national income accounting appears to be, it is based entirely on the implicit assumption that the economy measured is reasonably competitive; when applied to a command economy it fails to register some crucial facts and thus persistently overstates the actual performance of such an economy.

It is fairly absurd to measure, as we do, the annual additions to the stock of consumer durables and to plant and equipment without measuring subtractions from this stock resulting from persistent shortages of spare parts. It is fairly absurd to measure additions to the society's stock of wealth when the existing economic organization rewards enterprises for tonnage produced; income accounts fail completely to distinguish between, say, two lighting fixtures satisfying the demand of two families and one fixture containing sufficiently more raw materials to make its value equal to the value of the two fixtures mentioned above. Starving distribution and services may show up as an increase in national income simply because these accounts do not measure the heavy non-market costs borne by households which waste several hours weekly in search of basic necessities and in unskilled repairs.

The New Model is explicitly designed to cure these fundamental ills; the 1962 recession is hardly more than a pretext, a convenient debating weapon. To a student of the Czechoslovak economy, the potential gains to be obtained as a result of the application of the New Model appear huge. Whether or not they will be realized depends to a great extent on the Czechoslovak policy makers. Will they be able to resist the tremendous pressures which they are now facing? Only time can tell.

Table 11.1   *From sales to net profits*

---

(1) *Gross sales.*
(2) Less: purchases of inputs other than labor.

(a) Capital cost

(3) Less: obligatory capital depreciation allowance.
(4) Less: fixed capital charge (6% of value).
(5) Less: inventory charge (2% of value).
(6) Less: interest on capital purchased on credit.
(7) Equals: value added.

(b) Labor cost

(8) Less: wage bill.

(c) Taxes

(9) Less: value added tax (18% of item 7).
(10) Less: excess use of labor tax (30% of item 8 in excess of 90% of its 1966 level).
(11) Less: local government tax (maximum: 2% of item 8).
(12) Less: air and water pollution taxes.
(13) Equals: net income.
(14) Less: repayment of credits.
(15) Equals: *disposable income* ('Disposable gross revenue').
(16) Allocated to: supplementary tax levied by the Trust.
(17) Allocated to: purchases of investment goods.
(18) Allocated to: incentive bonuses to employees.

12

CZECHOSLOVAKIA

BORIS PESEK, 1968

ECONOMIC PERFORMANCE, 1967

As I last year refused to make any quantitative predictions whatsoever about economic developments in the year 1967, self-criticism is impossible. According to the officially published figures (which after the exposé by Vice-Premier Sik must be taken with even greater scepticism than before) national income increased by ('roughly') 8%. Given the 1966 national income, that represents an increase by 15·8 billion[1] crowns. This would seem to be a highly encouraging result. However, inventories grew by 11–12 billion crowns rather than by the planned amount of 2 billion crowns. The evaluation of the true economic value of production that has not been sold is extremely difficult. Roughly one-third of the increase in inventories consisted of farm implements and subsequent reports indicate that one-third of *that* increase was of such low quality that it could not be sold at all and had to be scrapped. This makes it obvious that the reported increase in national income grossly exceeds the actual increase. When we count only the goods actually sold, the increase becomes much more modest: (15·8–11·5) or 2·2%. Since consumer prices are reported to have risen by 1·5%, the increase in national income was a modest one indeed. The first half of 1968 was even worse.

This suggests that my general expectations as to the ability of the New Economic Model to increase output remained unfulfilled and that Professor Wiles's dissent proved justified. I plead guilty, but with an explanation. In the course of 1967, the *ancien régime* of President Novotny imposed on the economy a policy of small steps, all leading back to the Old Model. One example will tell volumes: In January 1967 the economic plan binding enterprises was abolished so as to give enterprises

[1] 1 billion = 10⁹.

149

the chance to restructure their output. However, so as to give the bureaucrats in the central planning office something to do, they were permitted to work out not a plan but 'guide numbers' for the various sectors. Since enterprises were forced to become members of some 50 trusts, the Trust Directorates also had to have something to do and thus allocated these guide numbers to individual enterprises. And then came the New Model pay-off: in the fall it was decided that unless the enterprises fulfilled the quotas assigned by the advisory guide numbers, they might not pay all sorts of bonuses to management and employees. At least in one key aspect, by December 1967 the Czechoslovak economic organization was precisely where it had been during the past twenty years.

Second, partly because of the erroneous specification of the new wholesale prices (applicable from 1 January 1967) and partly because of reallocation of production and resource inputs, the profitability of enterprises increased from 9·6% to 12·3%. At the same time, there occurred – in the words of the official report – 'major and in many cases economically unjustified differences in the rentability of individual enterprises' (*Rude Pravo*, 30 January 1967). Needless to say, that was precisely what the New Model intended to accomplish so as to reallocate resources away from inefficient and towards efficient enterprises. However, once again the *ancien régime* of President Novotny either was unwilling to wait for equilibrium to be established or took this development as a pretext for leading the system back into the Old Model. In any case, despite all initial promises to the contrary, the rules of the game were changed in midstream and profitable enterprises became subjected by their Trust Directorates to extra levies designed to enrich the failing enterprises. This, in the long run, made it impossible for the equilibrating process to work itself out, since these excess profits were intended to permit increases in investment and output, and a movement downward along the demand function of the market prices of goods produced. In the short run, these extra levies took away any incentives from the enterprises to reorganize production, since the signal that they received was that any increase in profitability would be considered 'economically unjustified' and would be taxed away. So here was a second very important aspect, in which by

December 1967 the system was back where it had been during the past twenty years.

Under these conditions, economic performance in 1967 can hardly be considered a fair test. Even in the best of conditions one would have expected the first year of the New Model to be a shakedown cruise; a period of learning for both the captains of industry and the crew. In reality, the ship was inconspicuously dismantled during the year. It missed both the mediocre certainties of the Old Model and the stimulating features of the New. Indeed, if anything, I would say that the fact that the system continued to run at all under these conditions attests to the resilience of any economy when faced with tampering from all directions.

JANUARY–AUGUST 1967

While the press kept playing up the purely political issues, significant voices indicated that a major reason for the deposition of the *ancien régime*, led by President Novotny, was precisely the treatment given to the New Model. The public – permitted to travel in neighboring Western countries, especially Austria – became more and more dissatisfied with the economic performance of the system. At the same time, the experience of 1967 deprived the economic and intellectual leadership of all hope that any significant economic reform could be achieved. Economic and political discontent became unified in one single stream that proved overpowering. In December of 1967 Alexander Dubcek opened the question of leadership of the Communist Party and blocked an attempt to use the Czechoslovak Army for a *coup d'état*: the commander of tank units chosen for this task allegedly refused to move without written orders from the Central Committee of the Communist Party. This failure caused the escape of a key general (Sejna) to the United States and the suicide of another.

All this gave Dubcek a fillip that he lacked in December; in January he took over the Party, with the support of conservatives who were unable to face the prospect of continuing associations with a President who would send the Army to resolve a controversy in the Central Committee. The political upheaval made it impossible for the new leadership to pay any

6

attention to economic problems; it had to struggle for survival
since the President, in a last ditch stand, attempted to stir up
the workers against the new leadership. His tool was his own
speeches – and numerous articles written by his supporters –
asserting that the new leadership and the New Model planned
to sacrifice socialism, job security, and wage equality and intended to benefit the intellectuals, the technicians, and the
managers. His goal – this writer suspects – was a series of
strikes, possibly a general strike. Either would have made
continuation of Dubcek's leadership impossible. This attempt
failed and cost Novotny, in March 1968, his Presidency. Under
normal conditions, this is a ceremonial function and Dubcek
was willing to let the President – still powerful – keep it.
However, after the lion roared and in the process revealed his
impotency, his continuation in this function became simultaneously untenable and superfluous.

With the major internal power struggle out of the way,
Dubcek and his supporters could turn to the future. In April
they had an Action Program approved by the government
and the party containing a major statement on economic
policy. The principles of the New Model were re-affirmed and
even substantially strengthened. In the words of the program:

Reform of our economy ... cannot be undertaken on the basis of
traditional approaches and partial improvements of the planning
system, but only on the basis of a fundamental change in the
mechanism of the socialist economy. The new economic model
revives positive functions of a socialist market, undertakes indispensable structural changes...

Instead of a systematic effort to apply market criteria, which
would reveal economic backwardness and old deformations of our
economic structure, there are still efforts at work to deform these
criteria, to adjust them to existing conditions, and to create a
convenient situation in which backwardness and deformations
would survive in secret, and remain parasites at the expense
of all of us.

In economic policy there continues a system that protects
economic backwardness, supported by a price and subsidy policy
and by a system of taxes and subsidies on foreign trade. An in-
credibly complex net of protectionism creates conditions that lead
to survival of enterprises which are unprofitable, incompetently
managed, and backward. It is impossible, in the long run, to

practice an economic policy that takes away from those who work well and gives to those who work badly.

The Action Program promised freedom to enterprises in all economic decisions, unhampered by fear that profitable decisions would result in an increased tax burden. To assure enterprises of this, they were promised the right to join – or not to join – any of the Trust Directorates that proved to be the bastions of old type planning during the year 1967. The Action Program informed the workers that they would benefit or suffer with the enterprises in which they worked and, in return, promised the workers the right to organize 'democratic organs' which would appoint and control management and participate in decisions.

21 AUGUST 1968

However, the publication of the Action Program was followed by another fight for survival of the reform leadership; this time, the danger came from abroad. The Soviet government, until now faced by independent Yugoslavia and by domestically Stalinist but internationally highly independent Rumania, must have been gravely concerned about a new problem created by internationally orthodox but domestically liberal Czechoslovakia.

At first it was believed that heavy international pressure, aided by military exercises that brought the Soviet Army into Czechoslovakia, would shake the Czechs and Slovaks enough to cause them to recall the pre-January leadership. These efforts proved so counterproductive that the Soviets cut their losses and withdrew their procrastinating army. But a few weeks later somebody in the Kremlin pushed the panic button and the army marched back, this time uninvited and in force.

CZECHOSLOVAKIA'S ECONOMIC FUTURE

There is no doubt in my mind that the New Economic Model in Czechoslovakia is dead for a number of years to come. First of all, the Russians are explicitly hostile to it; their attacks against Professor and Vice-Premier Ota Sik, who originated this program, leave no doubt about that. At the same time, I have grave doubts that the present leadership would want to implement it. At the moment, the leadership has behind it a nation that is unified as it has not been since 1938, when Hitler and Munich performed the same organizing task. It would appear to me extremely doubtful that the existing leadership would be willing to risk this unity for the sake of an economic reform which, in the short run, is bound to be unpopular. Reorganization is always costly in the short run and is justified only by hopes of a long-run gain. For Dubcek and his colleagues, the Keynesian dictum about the long run has an almost literal validity.

Second, even before the Russian occupation, the Czech leadership realized that the economic reform would prove tolerable to the nation in the short run only if financed by sizeable foreign credits (a sum of $500 million has been mentioned frequently) and by a greatly intensified foreign trade with the Western countries. After the occupation, both the possibility of asking and the possibility of obtaining foreign credit appear to be gone; long-term economic agreements signed with the Russians seem to preclude any reorientation of foreign trade.

Third, as we in the United States are discovering to our sorrow, the public does not seem to have an attention span that would permit the introduction of more than one major public issue. It probably is not accidental that the population of Slovakia before 21 August was vitally interested in the issue of the proposed confederation and was quite indifferent to the issues of both personal freedom and economic reform. Given this limited attention span and the resulting monomania, it seems unlikely that, even if an attempt were made to revive the issue of the reform, the Czechs and Slovaks would pay any attention. Now and for some time to come, national independence is sure to be the only item on the national agenda.

For all these reasons I believe that the New Model proved to be a still-born child. After the passage of several years, or a decade or two, no doubt a new Model will make its appearance. In this madly changing world, it would require predictive powers which I do not possess to guess its outlines.

A short run prediction is no less difficult to make. The year 1968 contained so many diversions that output was bound to suffer, and seriously so. During the first three months, there was the Dubcek *vs.* Novotny struggle that was fought to a substantial extent in the nation's factories. Meeting followed meeting, resolutions were debated and passed, the daily press was read and discussed avidly. The international struggle in the summer caused another flurry of meetings protesting the delayed withdrawal of troops. Finally, the occupation caused serious economic damage to highways, interrupted both highway and railroad transport, affected summer receipts from tourism, and no doubt led to a serious loss in industrial output. It appears certain to me that the rate of economic growth this year will be a negative one. Whether the official statistics in January will show it, or be permitted to show it, remains to be seen.

POSTSCRIPT – SEPTEMBER 1970

Evaluation of past performance of the Czechoslovak economy remains impossible. Economists who support Premier Husak claim that in 1968 and in the first half of 1969 the economy has reached 'the edge of abyss'. The supporters of the deposed Dubcek argue that in 1968 the economic performance was the best one experienced during the sixties and, by achieving 8·4 rate of growth in national income, surpassed the rates of growth experienced during the same year by East Germany, Hungary, and Poland. Since both sides are motivated by an obvious self-interest, I feel completely unable to decide whose figures one should trust.

The future seems easier to fathom. There was practically a unanimous agreement among economists that the directed economy preceding the New Model proved to be unworkable. After Marshall Grechko deposed Dubcek and imposed Husak in 1969, the New Model has been dismantled. Workers' Councils were disbanded, labor union leadership elected in 1968 has been purged both on the local level and on the national level. The managers of industrial enterprises who cooperated with the workers, or supported Dubcek, or opposed Soviet occupation likewise had to go. In view of a twenty per cent inflation that occurred in 1968 all prices were frozen. Commercial relationship between enterprises has been, once again, replaced by a binding economic plan prepared in Prague and in Bratislava. To this writer it seems most doubtful that this restoration of the *ancien régime* by Husak in 1969 will prove any more successful than the one undertaken by Novotny in 1967. Indeed, I would expect it to be less successful since in the more recent case the dead hand of lack of economic incentives becomes greatly reinforced by nationwide opposition to the Soviet-imposed leadership.

13

EAST GERMANY

HORST SEIDLER, 1967

I THE BASIS OF THE FORECAST

At the time of preparation of this projection of East Germany's economic performance, there is no medium range economic plan available to the general public. There are only a few approximate target figures known for 1970, these being mentioned in the prime minister's speech to the annual SED party congress in April of this year. Nevertheless, the author considers it feasible to forecast the main economic aggregates: the medium-range economic plan – to be published next month – only runs to 1970. Some of the targets in this still uncompleted plan could be considered unrealistic.

Moreover, the importance of this second point has lessened in the past few years. This is shown by a comparison of plan targets and actual fulfilment in recent years. The quality of East German economic planning has improved a lot since widespread under-fulfilment of the Seven-Year Plan (1959 to 1965) forced its abandonment about 1963. But over and above the real there is also an apparent improvement, in that, during recent years, the annual economic plans have published less detailed information, thus diminishing the possibility of checking plan fulfilment from outside. However it is possible to say that general fulfilment of planned economic development has been rather satisfactory, although differences between detailed targets and actual results may have and probably still do happen.

The overall, long-term goals of economic planning are easily discernible in the annual economic plans and were also reflected in the figures recently revealed by the prime minister. The planners' long-run view of the economy is as follows:

(a) Target growth of national income is moderate, compared with former years, at about 4 to 5%.

(b) Target growth in manufacturing is above average; the priority growth sector is metalworking (electrical engineering, machinery, precision engineering and optics).

(c) Expansion of distribution (transportation, wholesaling and retailing) is below average.

(d) In agriculture, livestock output is to grow faster than arable farming production; long-term growth of arable production is about 3% annually, subject to weather conditions.

(e) Building and civil engineering output is to expand more than the average. In the past, plan targets have mostly proved to be over-optimistic and under-fulfilment has often been widespread. A recurrence of this cannot be excluded.

(f) In allocation, gross fixed capital formation is to be given priority; growth targets for private consumption are very moderate.

(g) It seems that there has been considerable change in target for external trade recently. In the past, target growth of foreign-trade turnover has been about 5%, close to overall economic growth. The rise in 1966 seems to have been much higher and targets known for 1970 show that higher growth is intended.

Table 13.1 *Data on economic development 1961 to 1966* (annual growth in per cent[a])

Sector	1961	1962	1963	1964	1965[b]	1966[e]
National income produced	3·3	2·2	3·1	4·8	3·4[c]	5
Gross industrial production	5·9	6·2	4·3	6·6	6·2	6·5
Building and civil engineering production	2·5	7·2	1·4	6·2	7·7	3
Retail turnover	5·8	−0·7	0·3	3·3	4·1	4·1
Gross fixed capital formation[d]	.	1·8	5·4	8·7	7·7	6
Turnover in foreign trade[e]	2·9	5·7	5·4	10·4	5·6	9

[a] At current prices, excepting gross industrial production.
[b] Preliminary.
[c] The growth rate does not reflect that of value added because of price increases of intermediate products and higher prices for depreciation.
[d] Including major overhauls.
[e] Total exports plus total imports and including interzonal trade.

In this forecast, it was assumed that these general goals would be adhered to. They are in accordance with the aim of securing successful economic growth in East Germany; i.e. in a country with a relatively low gross investment ratio and still extremely backward in international specialization, compared with the industrialized countries of the West.

The forecast for 1967 mainly follows the targets of the current annual plan. Gaps in the published figures have been filled by the author's own estimates.

II DEVELOPMENT IN 1967 AND UP TO 1971
(a) 1967

Overall growth has been quite stable in recent years. Allowing for the adjustment of prices in the recent industrial price reform, real net material product rose at an annual rate of between 4 and 5% during 1964 and 1965. Preliminary results for 1966 put annual growth at 5%. The current annual plan also includes a net growth rate of 5% for the material production sectors of the economy. This growth rate is certainly realistic. The slack capacity, which accumulated in the years of economic stagnation (1962 to mid-1964), has not yet been fully taken up. It is now hoped that such excess capacity as still exists will be brought into production by the reforms included in the New Economic System and mainly introduced with the finalization of the price reform on 1 January 1967. These stimuli should guarantee repetition of last year's growth, for this year at least, even disregarding any increase in labour input or the stock of capital. The author is a little more optimistic, estimating growth at 5.5% for 1967.

Growth of industrial production is estimated at 7%. Effort will be concentrated on heavy manufacturing production (+ 8%), with electrical engineering enjoying top priority (+ 9%). Heavy engineering, machinery, building, optics, and chemicals will also be leading growth industries. Mining will again show zero or negative growth, because lignite mining is yielding to substitutes in overall energy consumption, and there is a fall in energy consumption per unit of product. The remaining industries of the primary metals and basic products sector will experience growth between the above extremes, averaging out about 6%.

Consumer goods industries (including small industries, i.e. *Handwerk*) will grow about 5%, with little serious deviation from the average. Growth of consumer goods industries will be somewhat higher than of food, beverages, and tobacco. In 1967, the harvest could turn out especially good, making the two growth rates equal.

In agriculture, crops suffered badly from the weather last year; arable production was only the same as in the previous year. Total production rose 2%, due to higher livestock production. This year, arable production, particularly grain, will be higher than last year. Growth is assumed to be 4 to 5%. Total gross agricultural production can be expected to expand by up to 5%.

A similar effect to the one in agriculture is expected to happen in building and civil engineering. Output was hindered by unfavourable weather last year, pushing the actual growth rate (3%) well below target. The contractors will be obliged to make good their losses this year and so far the weather has proved helpful. Growth can be expected to reach 10% in 1967.

In recent years, expansion in transportation and communication has been surprisingly low, lagging behind the material producing sector. The reason lies in the change in structure of demand for transportation (a fall in lignite output); but better organization has also contributed. These trends will persist in 1967 and the following years. For 1967, growth is assumed at 3%.

Expansion in wholesaling and retailing depends largely on the movement of private consumption. The plan allows for growth of 4.5% during 1967, little more than last year.

The aggregation of these individual forecasts means that global gross material production (global social product) will increase about 6.5% at constant 1966 prices. Faster growth of intermediate consumption and depreciation connect this rate to growth of net material product at 5.5%.

Allocation of the national product will favour gross fixed capital formation. An increase of 9% (from 20.8 billion MDN[1] to 22.7 billion MDN) is anticipated. Depreciation will rise from 10.5 billion MDN to 11.2 billion MDN; net investment will therefore rise 11.5%. There will also be a pronounced shift in the composition. Investment in rationalization will increase while investment in extensions decreases. This will be especially so in sectors where the capital stock has a high average age (agriculture, transport); but in manufacturing also, half of

---

[1] Mark of the German Central Bank. 1 billion = 10^9.

gross investment will be for rationalization. There is no break-down of gross investment by sector. However, it is likely that recent high growth of investment in industries such as mining will decelerate, in favour of metal working. Housing investment is also to increase more than the average, after several years of stagnation or even decline. The expected acceleration of growth in building production will make this possible. On the other hand, private consumption (goods only) will grow less than the average at 4·5%. The consumption ratio is to decline again.

There is no information available on the other sectors of allocation (public consumption, exports, imports): neither plan fulfilment in 1966 nor targets for this year. Targets and fulfilment have, so far, only been made known for turnover in foreign trade. The data in Tables 13.4–13.5 (pp. 163–4) are the author's estimates. Public consumption growth is to be above average at 6·5% this year, in accordance with the trend.

Table 13.2   *Table on economic development 1966, 1967 and 1971*

	Unit	1966	1967	1971	Annual rate of increase, per cent	
					1967	1971[a]
Population and labour force						
Total population	1,000	17,080	17,102	17,180	—	—
Population of working age	1,000	9,793	9,773	9,740	—	—
Total employment	1,000	8,550	8,550	8,550	—	—
Population of working age	per cent of total population	57·4	57·1	56·7	—	—
Total employment	per cent of total population	50·1	50·0	49·8	—	—
Gross fixed capital formation (at constant (1966) prices)						
Gross fixed investment	bill. MDN	20·8	22·7	30·9	9	8
Depreciation	,,	10·5	11·2	14·1	7	6
Net fixed investment	,,	10·3	11·5	16·8	11·5	10
Capital stock	—	—	—	—	7	6
Capital intensity of labour	—	—	—	—	7	6
Labour productivity	—	—	—	—	5·5	5
Net material product	bill. MDN	87·2	91·5	112·4	5·5	5

[a] Average of 1968 to 1971.

East Germany's foreign trade data are also rather special: the official trade statistics report in *Valuta–Mark* (VM). This currency unit is independent of the domestic currency (MDN) and of domestic prices. The government makes deficiency payments for differences between export receipts and exported

Table 13.3   *Table on economic development 1966, 1967 and 1971*

	Unit	1966	1967	1971	Annual rate of increase per cent 1967	1971
Total social product						
Agriculture, forestry	bill. MDN[a]	19·6	20·5	24·5	4·5	4·5
Manufacturing:[b]	,,	143·3	153·2	195·0	7	6
heavy	,,	81·2	88·0	116·0	8	7
light	,,	62·1	65·2	79·0	5	5
Building, construction	,,	12·1	13·3	16·8	10	6
Transports, communication	,,	9·2	9·5	11·0	3	4
Retailing and wholesaling	,,	18·6	19·4	22·7	4·5	4
Other sectors[c]	,,	2·4	2·6	3·0	—	—
Total social product	,,	205·2	218·5	273·0	6·5	5·5
National income						
Total social product	bill. MDN	205·2	218·5	273·0	6·5	5·5
Minus:						
depreciation	,,	10·5	11·2	14·1	7	6
intermediate products	,,	107·5	115·4	146·5	7·5	6
Net material product	,,	87·2	91·9	112·4	5·5	5

[a] At constant (1966) prices.
[b] Including *Handwerk*.
[c] Of material production only.

goods at domestic prices. This is also done for imports. Consequently the export surpluses of the foreign-trade statistics do not imply much about the value of this surplus at domestic prices. The amount of these subsidies is kept secret. Tables 13.4–13.5 include an estimate of the trade balance at domestic prices, calculated as the residual allocation sector of the social product.

Turnover in foreign trade rose 9% in 1966 and is planned to rise 7% in 1967. In recent years, the USSR and other Comecon countries have been taking an ever smaller share of foreign trade; the latest announcements indicate a reversal of this trend. Therefore, it must be assumed that the Western industrial countries' share of East Germany's foreign trade will cease to grow, as also that of German interzonal trade. Constant shares can be assumed for 1967; this is certainly so in exports. The development of imports and changes in shares of foreign trade will largely depend on the availability of credit from the West.

Table 13.4   *Table of economic development 1966, 1967 and 1971*

| | | | | | Annual rate of increase per cent | |
	Unit	1966	1967	1971	1967	1971
National income (allocation)						
Individual consumption	bill. MDN[a]	63·1	65·9	77·1	4·5	4
Social consumption	,,	6·2	6·6	8·8	6·5	7·5
Net fixed investment	,,	10·3	11·5	16·8	11·5	10
Inventories	,,	+3·4	+3·6	+4·2	—	—
Trade surplus[b]	,,	4·2	4·3	5·5	—	—
Net material product	,,	87·2	91·9	112·4	5·5	5
Allocation quotas of national income						
Individual consumption	per cent	72·4	71·7	68·6	—	—
Social consumption	,,	7·1	7·2	7·8	—	—
Net fixed investment	,,	11·8	12·5	15·0	—	—
Inventories	,,	3·9	3·9	3·7	—	—
Trade surplus	,,	4·8	4·7	4·9	—	—
Net material product	,,	100·0	100·0	100·0	—	—

[a] At constant (1966) prices.
[b] Residual; at domestic prices.

(b) 1971

This assessment of medium term developments is based on projections of the labour force and the capital stock, these being the determinants of future production capacity. There will be some growth of the total population up to 1971, but the number of persons of working age will decrease, owing to the age structure. These movements will compensate each other and total employment is therefore assumed to remain constant at 8·55 million.[1] Provision is made for a further increase in age-specific employment quotas, by raising the participation rate of women and keeping old age pensioners at work. This

Table 13.5　*Table on economic development 1966, 1967 and 1971*

	Unit	1966	1967	1971	Annual rate of increase per cent	
					1967	1971
External trade						
Total turnover	bill. VM[a]	26·5	28·4	36·0	7	6
Imports	,,	12·7	13·5	17·0	6	6
Exports	,,	13·8	14·9	19·0	8	6
Surplus[c]	,,	1·1	1·4	2·0	—	—
Surplus	bill. MDN[b]	4·2	4·3	5·5	—	—
Foreign trade subsidies[c]	bill. MDN	3·1	2·9	3·5	—	—
Ratio of subsidies to trade turnover[c]	per cent	11·7	10·2	9·7	—	—
External trade turnover by groups of countries						
Total turnover	bill. VM[a]	26·5	28·4	36·0	7	6
Comecon countries	,,	18·6	20·0	25·5	7·5	6·5
USSR	,,	11·4	12·3	16·5	8	7·5
Other comecon	,,	7·2	7·7	9·0	6·5	4·0
Other countries[d]	,,	7·9	8·4	10·5	6·5	5·5
Total turnover	per cent	100·0	100·0	100·0	—	—
Comecon countries	,,	70·2	70·4	70·8	—	—
USSR	,,	43·0	43·3	45·8	—	—
Other Comecon	,,	27·2	27·1	25·0	—	—
Other countries[d]	,,	29·8	29·6	29·2	—	—

[a] Valuta Mark, the East German foreign-trade currency.
[b] See Table 13.4 above.
[c] Subject to changes in terms of trade.
[d] Including German interzonal trade.

way of expanding the labour force tends to depress the average quality of labour, but this will be more than compensated by better training and education. No growth of labour input, then, is allowed for as contributory to production growth.

[1] Including employees omitted from the official statistics, e.g. employees in uranium mining, special government services, and armament plants.

East Germany's national income data refer only to the sectors of material production. The labour force in the service industries is expected to increase; this will be the only way of satisfying future demand for services, which rises faster than the average. However, there are unmistakable signs that these needs are being neglected. It is therefore doubtful whether there will be any sizeable shift in the distribution of labour between material production and services.

Growth of material production will have to come from a rise in labour productivity. There are reasons to hope for great progress in productivity. Annual gross investment in manufacturing has been high in the past, in spite of a low gross investment ratio overall. The gross investment ratio is to be raised in all sectors, including manufacturing, in the next few years; growth of the capital stock will be faster than in the early sixties. Capital intensity will rise at the same rate.

It is doubtful whether progress in productivity will equal the rise in capital intensity; but it is certain that the two rates will not be far apart. Rationalization has become a priority of gross investment. The comparatively high level of labour productivity in West Germany indicates the scope for increasing productivity by modernizing.

For the economy as a whole, annual growth of gross investment is estimated at 8%. The capital stock will then be rising at about 6% per year. The capital-labour ratio will rise at this rate also. On this basis, annual growth of real national income of 5% between 1968 and 1971 should be feasible.

Tables 13.2–13.5 include a breakdown of growth by sector. Growth in manufacturing is estimated at 6%; heavy industry (7%) growing faster than light industry (5%). Annual growth of 6% is assumed for building and civil engineering. Gross production of the remaining sectors of material production is forecast to grow by 4% annually. In agriculture, livestock production will increase slightly faster than total agricultural production, arable farming output will grow slower than the average.

These growth prospects are by no means exaggerated, and the annual growth rate estimated for total social product is 5·5%, slightly higher than that of national income.

There will be substantial changes in the allocation of national income. Private consumption is forecast as dropping from 71·5% in 1967 to 68·5% in 1971. It will be necessary to enforce a stringent incomes policy to keep growth of this sector below the average.

Wages per person will not even be able to rise as fast as consumption per person, as transfer incomes (old age pensions) are to shoot up because of the age structure of the population. There have also been recent announcements of rises in existing pension rates. After this, there is only 3% per year left for growth of wages per employee.

Public (social) consumption will continue to rise at a rate of 7% per year, i.e. faster than private consumption. Public consumption will rise to 8% of national income. This is due to both civil and military expenditure on goods. It is doubtful whether this amount includes all expenditure on military hardware; there could be up to 2 billion MDN more, tucked away in various other items of goods consumption. This makes it difficult to estimate growth of public consumption accurately.

Growth of net investment is dependent on the gross growth rate. As mentioned above, the aim is that the latter should be 8%. In terms of net investment, annual growth will be more than 10%. By 1971, net investment will have risen to 15% of national income, compared with the present less than 12%. The East German economic authorities have been aiming for such a rise for several years. It was not until the last couple of years that it became a feasible goal in a medium term plan.

Known plan targets for external trade to 1970 only relate to turnover. Up to 1970, turnover is to rise to 33 to 35 billion VM; after 24·3 billion VM in 1965. This would give average annual growth of 6·5 to 7·5%. Considering 1966 results and the above estimates for 1967 and stretching the period under review to 1971, foreign trade turnover can be expected to rise to around 36 billion VM. The long-term trade agreements with the other Comecon countries, made at the end of 1965, provided only under-average growth of this sector of external trade, particularly the Soviet Union. However, since then, the agreement with the USSR has been extended and now trade with the Soviet Union is to rise faster than the average (by 7·5 to 8·5% per year from 1965 to 1970). In this case, the Soviet Union's share of foreign trade will rise from 43% in 1966 to

46% in 1971 (i.e. by 5 billion VM to 16·5 billion VM). All Comecon countries' share of external trade would then be 71% in 1971, one point higher than in 1966. Trade with the rest of the world will then grow 5·5% annually between 1967 and 1971.

East Germany's visible trade balance is in structural surplus to equal a (secret) deficit in the services and capital accounts. Presumably, this surplus (1·1 billion VM) will have to be increased. A surplus of 2 billion VM was estimated for 1971. The figures of Tables 13·2–13·5, showing the allocation of national income, do not indicate an even change in the foreign trade surplus between 1967 and 1971 (at domestic prices). The reason for this disparity lies in reduced subsidies for foreign transactions, i.e. the higher foreign trade surplus for 1971 is mainly due to expectation of better terms of trade. One of the main aims of the recent New Economic System is to reduce these subsidies.

III ⸢ CONCLUSION

The general prospects for economic growth in East Germany are pretty good; growth in the past two years has been strong and is continuing in the current year. Economic development has been set clear lines in the annual plans and fulfilment has been satisfactory.

Nevertheless, there are some sources of uncertainty which cast shadows on this fair picture. First, the labour scarcity will prevent sufficient growth of the service industries. The rising standard of living will produce higher consumer demand for services. The sectors outside 'material production' at present employ about 20% of the labour force. The slight rise of this in recent years is mainly due to higher employment in the government sector. It is possible that consumer service industries will not profit from future changes. However, the economic planning authorities will, now and in the future, have to take more account of current development of consumer demand than they have done in the past. Therefore, it is possible that present economic goals will have to be adjusted in the coming years, leading to slower growth in the material production sector.

Secondly, the forecasts of foreign trade are uncertain. Among other things, more and better machinery will have to be imported if industrial modernization and rationalization are to progress. The obvious source of these imports is the West, if currency is available. The shift shown in the structure of foreign trade may handicap the fulfilment of modernization needs; it may be necessary to export more than desirable to the East.

Thirdly, there is still the problem of improving the infrastructure. Failure to realize adequate growth in the building and civil engineering sector would render a solution more difficult and damage prospects of overall growth.

Fourthly, it is impossible to forecast government budgets reliably. The current budget was only finalized with a clause allowing for adjustments during implementation. The introduction of the New Economic System has brought a large degree of uncertainty.

Most uncertain are the budget estimates for amounts of investment finance, for foreign trade subsidies, and for subsidies to hold consumer prices constant. There will be considerable changes in government receipts and expenditure, both in total and in composition; we must await actual developments in order to make realistic forecasts.

14

CRITICAL REMARKS ON FORECASTS OF THE ECONOMY OF THE GERMAN DEMOCRATIC REPUBLIC IN 1967 AND 1971

GERT LEPTIN, 1968

GENERAL PRELIMINARY REMARKS

The desirability of accurate forecasting is indisputable, although it may not be considered a necessary part of any science, or even as an indicator of the stage of development of that science. Examples from many fields of research show that the ability to forecast is no measure of the quality of a scientific approach; thousands of years ago, astronomy was able to forecast eclipses of the moon and sun with great accuracy; today, meteorology can still only forecast tomorrow's weather with unsatisfactory precision. Nevertheless, no reasonable person would consider ancient astronomy to be more highly developed than modern meteorology. Also, if a shepherd forecasts the next day's weather correctly, whereas official forecasts were again proved wrong, the resulting disappointment would not be sufficient justification for maintaining that the official forecasts were less scientific.

These two examples illustrate the general difficulties involved in forecasting. The difficulties of forecasting the East German economy are much the same. On the one hand, there is the problem of exogenous variables. These are factors which affect developments and whose interdependence is unknown or cannot be assessed on well-based assumptions. A forecast is based on estimates of the development of exogenous variables and on consideration of the consistency of all partial forecasts. However, the certainty that consistency is achieved in a forecast decreases as the number of exogenous variables grows. The possibility of confronting forecasts with reality changes little in this situation, as is shown by the second example (meteorology). Correct forecasting can be accidental in individual cases and the number of cases observed is often insufficient for stochastic verification.

Nevertheless, there is no doubt that the development of adequate forecasting methods is important. This applies to economics generally and to the study of planned European economies in particular. The problems raised here recommend more strict observation of certain requirements in future forecasts. These requirements are: full description of all sources of information used in the calculations; clear indication of all own estimates; and a summary of the assumptions under which the forecast is supposed to be true. In addition there should be an explanation of the model connections assumed to exist between the individual values to be interpreted. Finally, the author should indicate the degree of accuracy attached to his forecasts. This manner of presentation for forecasts is important so that all, or at least the main, steps can be checked. At the present stage of development of forecasts for East-European economies, methodological problems should be given priority over actual results – especially with regard to the restrictive and selective publication of data from these countries.

FORECASTS FOR EAST GERMANY IN 1967

The main difficulty in forecasting the East German economy in 1967 was that, at the time of preparation, there was neither the long term economic plan nor the actual results for 1966 available as a basis for forecasting. The forecaster therefore had to rely mainly on the annual plan, which had been published. Much the same is true of these critical remarks: they are based on the report on plan fulfilment and preliminary results for 1967.

On the whole, the East German economy developed according to plan in 1967. In so far as the forecasts were agreed with the economic plan, there were, therefore, no great deviations between the forecast and actual developments. However, there are some special points worthy of note.

The forecast estimated growth of the national income at 5·5% and was somewhat more optimistic than the plan which was based on growth of 5%. Now it seems that the plan was correct:[1] the report on plan fulfilment says that real growth of the national income was 5%. Incidentally the official statistics[2] show nominal growth of 5·7%. If both reports are correct, then price increases seem to have been in the region of 0·5%.

The forecasts of growth in construction and transportation turned out especially well. The forecast growth rate of 10% in construction is nearer the actual growth rate of 9·1% than the plan's expectation of 8%. More important than the accuracy of the percentage rates was the fact that overfulfilment of the plan was correctly foretold. The case was similar in transportation where underfulfilment was correctly forecast. The annual plan foresaw growth of 6% whereas the forecast gave 2%. This result is indirectly confirmed by inferences from the plan targets and expected growth rates for 1968.

The difficulties for forecasting – and for a critical appraisal of the forecasts – resulting from the industrial price reform finalized in 1967, are clearly shown in investment. Both the plan and forecast estimated investment growth at 9%. This rate was confirmed by the report on plan fulfilment. However, the official statistics[3] show growth at current prices from 18·9 billion M.[4] to 23·9 billion M., i.e. a growth rate of 26·2%. If all the values are correct then prices for installed investment goods must have risen around 16% overall.

The information given on foreign trade seems to be of doubtful merit. This is not so much due to the deviation of expected turnover growth of 7% from the actual rate of 4·9% (because of relatively slow growth of imports), as to the methods used to convert the foreign trade balance from valuta marks to domestic marks and to assess foreign trade subsidies. It is somewhat heroic to calculate the foreign trade balance in domestic marks as the residual in the allocation of the social product (p. 163). This method means that all errors and omissions in other components are concentrated in the trade balance. The conversion coefficients from valuta to domestic marks, resulting from a comparison of the published valuta

[1] *Neues Deutschland* on 27 January 1967.
[2] *Statistisches Taschenbuch* (1968) (East Berlin, 1968), p. 22.
[3] *Statistisches Taschenbuch* (1968), p. 25.
[4] M. = Mark (replacing MDN): the official currency unit since 1 January 1968. 1 billion = 10^9.

balance with the domestic balance thus calculated, vary between
2·7 in 1966 and 3·8 in 1971 (3·80 M. = 1 VM.). These results
are all too high. From information supplied on the foreign
trade turnover for 1965, we know that the coefficient is in the
region of 1·58 M. = 1 VM.[1] *Also*, it is doubtful whether
foreign trade subsidies can be derived as the difference between
the M. trade balance and the VM. trade balance. For the
results contain in addition all the sources of error involved in
calculating balances from the social accounts. Finally, presentation of the foreign trade subsidy in marks as a percentage of the
foreign trade turnover in valuta marks is inappropriate because
of the difference in dimensions. The subsidy should be compared with foreign trade turnover calculated also in marks.
Assuming the conversion coefficient for 1965 to be valid for
1966 and 1967, then foreign trade turnover was about 42·6
milliard M. in 1966, and about 44·7 milliard M. in 1967.[2]
This gives subsidy ratios[3] in the two years of 7·3% and 6·5%
respectively. Of course all these calculations have a wide
margin of error.

THE FORECAST FOR EAST GERMANY IN 1971

The forecast for 1971 cannot yet be compared with results.
It is only possible to check the assumptions made on developments to 1971 by comparing them with the figures in the
perspective plan to 1970, which has been published in the
meantime, and with growth achievements in 1967. The general
considerations, which form the basis of the forecast, must also
be re-thought in this light.

It is still acceptable to emphasize the dependence of growth
on the development of the labor force and the increase in
capital stocks. Regarding labor, it must be considered whether
the use of foreign labor, started in 1967 by the employment of
between 10,000 and 20,000 Hungarians, could not mean a
noticeable increase in the total labor force.

If not, then growth can only come from increasing labor

[1] The foreign trade volume was about 59 milliard domestic marks in 1965 (the
official statistics show 24·7 milliard valuta marks): Wilfried Maier, *Preis und
Rentabilität im Aussenhandel* (East Berlin, 1967), p. 5.

[2] Using the latest *Statistisches Taschenbuch*.

[3] Net subsidies in M, ÷ trade turnover in VM.

productivity. The forecast is quite conservative in its assumption of future progress in productivity at around 5%; at least more conservative than the perspective plan which works with rates between 6·2% and 7·7% in the non-farm sector. The amount of investment required in 'non-productive' sectors may justify this conservatism.

The forecast's assumption of investment growth at 8% is also at the lower limit of the perspective plan's expectations (8·2% to 8·7%). Past experience indicates that growth over 8% can hardly be maintained over long periods. Certain difficulties must be expected from postponements of building and equipment investment, which have become necessary.

The more conservative estimates of progress in labor productivity and of investment growth are the reason why the forecast expects less growth of the national income than the national plan. The forecast provides for an annual rate of 5% which is beneath the lower limit in the perspective plan which provides for growth between 5·1 and 5·7%. Even if only 5% is maintained up to 1971, the achievement will be exceptional. The forecast's views as to the future development of the social product, the consumption ratio, public consumption and individual incomes meet with my full agreement. There are only doubts as regards the foreign trade balance of 2 billion VM. and the assumed development of the terms of trade. There is not sufficient information available to justify any estimates.

All in all this review shows that both the forecasts for 1967 and up to 1971 can be accepted in their main points. There are many unsolved problems and numerous uncertainties. This justifies the opening tenet that methodological problems should be given priority over forecast contents at the present stage of development.

15

HUNGARY:
Perspectives up to 1970

ALAN BROWN, 1967

I LONG-TERM PLANNING IN HUNGARY

Its foundations

When the second Five-Year Plan (1961–65) was being prepared, rapid industrialization was the main end, but it was still
not the same as in previous years, for this end had to be attained
without outside help and without radical political change.
The plan emphasized reducing the foreign debt, and a relatively slow growth of the national income – indeed the slowest
to be fixed by a Communist country for this period. But the
targets were not met, except in industrial production. Instead
of the annual rate of growth predicted at 6·3% (36% over the
five years), gross domestic product only grew at 4·6% (25%).
In agriculture, where the Plan sought an increase of 22–23%
between the 1961–65 average and that for 1956–60, global
production rose only 10% and net production remained
practically constant. Only global industrial production, with
an annual average growth of 8% (say 47% in the five years)
practically attained the Plan target.[1]

The balance of payments did not improve. Although the
current account was nearly in balance in the first and second
years of the plan, in the course of five years visible exports
exceeded imports by only about $300 million. Given that the
invisible account is generally negative, the external debt has
continued to rise. It is above all with Western countries that the
plan targets have not been achieved: Hungary is still in deficit
with them. Instead of ending with a visible export surplus of
about $60 million as planned, the annual average deficit is of
this order of magnitude.

[1] See Table 15.7, p. 186.

The targets of the third Five-Year Plan

The third Five-Year Plan (1966–70) appears to be a continuation of the second and rests on the same economic and political principles. But it takes account of the economic reforms which are to come into force in the first two or three years. Rapid industrialization remains the principal aim, but its pursuit is less doctrinaire. The accent is placed upon organizational improvements in, and the rationalization of, production, and also in making an industrial structure appropriate to the needs of Hungary and her trading partners. The contrast with previous developments is striking: instead of trying only to produce more steel, coal, cement and machine tools, the government is trying to modernize industry and agriculture, to develop export markets and to improve the standard of life. The planners have learned from the experience of the fifties: they cannot without adaptation transplant either the Soviet planning strategy or Soviet economic priorities to a small country which has only a few natural resources and is very dependent on foreigners.

The principal industrial objectives are the rapid development of skill-intensive sectors which use few raw materials, and the rationalization of the supply of basic products. The favoured industries are chemistry and precision engineering. To reduce energy costs, coal is to be replaced by natural gas and oil, which will have to be in part imported. In ferrous metallurgy the accent is on profitability and adapting the quality of output to the needs of engineering. In machine building the planners will emphasize the construction of high quality goods in order to raise value added per unit of raw materials and to develop exports. These changes should be helped by greater co-operation within the CMEA in matters of raw materials. For instance the Friendship Pipeline will assist the development of energy consumption. The CMEA will also help to specialize production among its members. All this, coupled with a moderate rate of growth of output, should permit Hungary to equilibrate better the supply of raw materials with her production capacity, while reducing pressure on her balance of payments.

Agriculture seems to have been given greater priority. In

Hungary agriculture is still fundamental to the growth of consumption, and agricultural exports are necessary for the foreign trade targets. Better supplies of fertilizer and insecticides should assist production, but they imply considerable investment in the chemical industry. There is greater tolerance of the private plots retained within collective farms, if we may believe recent official declarations.

As to foreign trade, the principal concern is to improve the balance of payments. This will not be done by lowering imports but by increasing exports more rapidly than them. There will be no change in the geographical distribution of trade; established after the events of 1956 at 70% with Communist countries, 30% with the rest, this distribution will remain almost constant.

Only a small improvement in the standard of living is expected. The plan foresees a growth of less than 2% per annum in real wages, and in real incomes, which include certain social services, about 3%. The housing shortage should ease, but two thirds of new housing is to be financed by private savings.

II CONTENT ANALYSIS OF THE THIRD FIVE-YEAR PLAN[1]

The growth and the distribution of the national income

The net domestic material product[2] is to rise by 19–21% in five years, or at 3·7% per annum as opposed to 4·6% in the previous five years. Global industrial production is to grow by 32–36%, construction by 24–28% and agriculture by 13–15% (in agriculture, the average of these five years over the average of the last five). Distributed income will grow less than produced income (the weighted average of the growth of productive sectors), because subsidies for the purpose of equalizing prices, which are deducted from the totals of production in the national accounts, are to grow more rapidly than production. This is because foreign trade will outstrip the national income and, within this sector, the more heavily subsidized exports will outstrip imports.

The composition of national income by sectors of origin will favour industry as follows: industry will pass from 72·8% in

[1] See Table 15.8, p. 188.
[2] From 1959 this Marxist concept is widened to include passenger travel.

1965 to 75–76% in 1970, and agriculture from 21·4% to 17–19%. 'Others' will move from 5·8% to about 6%.

These figures are founded on the constant prices of 1965. But the proportion for industry is lower if we take account of the exaggeration of relative prices in that sector. An idea of the order of magnitude of this exaggeration is given in the official economic weekly: 'According to the statistics for 1963, industry represented 61·5% of national income and agriculture 20·5%. But the proportions are very different if we reckon the national income in terms of market prices. In this case the proportion for agriculture is about 35% [... so ...] the proportion for agriculture is comparable to that for industry.'[1]

The new price system, which should become valid on 1 January 1968, will reflect costs more accurately. It will raise agricultural and diminish industrial prices so that the results of the third Five-Year Plan will make the relation between agriculture and industry look more balanced than the projection in the initial version of the Plan.

Data on the distribution of national income among final uses are incomplete. But it is improbable that the ratio between consumption and investment or between socialist and private ownership will change markedly. Consumption is to account for 76–78% and net investment for 22–24% of national income. Gross fixed capital formation is to be 15–17%.

The factors of growth

We shall examine here the supply, the distribution and the productivity of two quantifiable factors: labour and capital. Other factors like technology, incentives, enterprise organization, etc., will be analysed in the sections on industry and agriculture.

The increase of national income forecast for the third plan is very moderate. It even appears rather pessimistic, whether in relation to previous Hungarian targets or to the norms of other Communist countries. Barring particularly unfortunate events (a series of bad harvests or unforeseeable balance of payments crisis), the plan targets will be amply surpassed.

(1) *Labour* is a bottleneck in Hungary. The growth of population

---

[1] *Figyelö*, 29 June 1966.

has been very slow since the beginning of the fifties, one of the slowest in Europe, because the birth-rate is not only low but falling. Between 1958 and 1965, during the second Three-Year Plan and the second Five-Year Plan, population grew by 4% and this rate is forecast for 1966–70. The active population is to grow 0·5% faster. The labour force will rise by 160,000–200,000, in proportion to the rise of the active population. This phenomenon is based on the continual increase of the proportion of active to total population, which is now about 47%. These forecasts are more realistic than those in the second Five-Year Plan, which foresaw an increase in the labour force of 289,000 people, while the result was lower by a half.[1]

Non-agricultural employment. About 68% of the labour force was in the non-agricultural sector in 1965, or 3,227,000 people. Although the plan does not give a complete breakdown by sectors one can estimate from the planned increases of production and productivity that non-agricultural employment is to rise by 6–8% in the five years, to reach 3,448,000 people or about 70% of the labour force in 1970. The industrial labour force is to grow by 107,000 from 1,572,000 in 1965, and the rest of the non-agricultural labour force by 114,000. Only 18–19% of this increase will be due to rural migration; the increase will essentially arise from the influx of young townsmen and of female labour. This rise of 6–8% is very moderate even for Hungary. The second Five-Year Plan foresaw an increase of 12·3%, while the actual figure was 15·5%. A certain flexibility is imparted by the fact that rural migration can exceed the plan. In any case the major consideration seems to be less an absolute increase in the labour force (for the plan foresees a diminution in hours of work) than an increase in productivity. This should account for at least 80% of the increase in production (we have figures only for industry) and is to be obtained by modernization, technical progress, an improvement in the supply system and a reform of incentives (essentially a readjustment of the norms to correspond with the marginal productivity of labour). The targets for productivity are ambitious but not overestimates to judge by the past. The rise during this Five-Year Plan of 24–27% is hardly greater than the 26% obtained during the last five years.

[1] See Table 15.1, p. 180.

Table 15.1 *Labour force*

| | | | Population active (in millions) | | |
| | | | | Non-agriculture | |
	Total	Agriculture	Sub-total	Industry	Other
Annual values					
1960	4,710	1,925 (40·9%)	2,786 (59·1%)	1,291 (27·4%)	1,495 (31·7%)
1965	4,738	1,511 (31·9%)	3,227 (68·1%)	1,527 (32·2%)	1,700 (35·9%)
1970 (plan)	4,918	1,470 (29·9%)	3,448 (70·1%)	1,634 (33·2%)	1,814 (36·9%)
Absolute changes					
1961–65	28	−414	441	236	205
1966–70 (plan)	180	−41	221	107	114
Percentage changes					
1965 (1960 = 100)	0·6	−21·5	15·8	18·3	13·7
1970 (1965 = 100)	3·8	−2·7	6·8	7·0	6·7

Sources: Statisztikai Évkönyv 1965, pp. 50–51; 'Law no. 2/1966', *Magyar Közlöny*, 3 July 1966.

Agricultural employment. The Hungarians have shown a certain concern about the manpower problems which arose in agriculture after the fifties; as a result of collectivization rural emigration became very great. Increased mechanization should reduce these tensions but during this third Five-Year Plan (and this is clearly laid down) migration has to fall. Nevertheless

Table 15.2   *Productivity of the industrial labour force, 1960, 1965, 1970* (including construction)

	Global production (milliard forints)	Labour force ('000)	Production per head ('000 forints)	Indices (given year minus five = 100) Global production	Labour force	Production per head
1960	80·5	1,291	62			
1965	116·0	1,521	76	144	118	126
1970 (plan)	155·4	1,631	95	134	107	125·5

Sources: as in Table 15.1.

Table 15.3   *Productivity of the agricultural labour force, 1956–60, 1961–65, 1966–70* (Plan).

	Global production (milliard forints)	Labour force ('000)	Production per head ('000 forints)	Indices (Last five years = 100) Global production	Labour force	Production per head
Average 1956–60	60·6	1,985	30·5			
Average 1961–65	66·8	1,630	41·0	110	82	134
Average 1966–70						
(Plan)[a]	76·0	1,590	47·8	114	97·5	117
Estimate[b]	76·0	1,360	55·9	114	83·4	136
Estimate[c]	73·5	1,360	54·0	110	83·4	132

[a] is the official plan figures.   [b] and [c] suppose a more rapid rural exodus, i.e. 80,000 people a year (see *Délmagyarorszag*, 9 March 1966).   [c] further supposes that agricultural output grows 10% less than in the plan.
Sources: see Table 15.1.

we must point out that even in the absence of such migration the agricultural labour force would diminish because the number of young people of working age is so small owing to the lower birth-rate of the recent past, and the average age of the population is rising with a resulting increase in deaths and retirements. A supplementary factor is the high number of collective farmers retiring as a result of recent measures.[1]

From the targets published, one can estimate the fall in the agricultural labour force during the five years at about 41,000 people or 3%. This target is probably optimistic: if one considers the reports published after the approval of the plan it appears that the fall might attain 400,000 people by 1970.[2]

The growth in the productivity of the agricultural labour force, calculated from the data in the plan, should be 17%, or only half the gain registered in the previous five years. If the rate of migration from the countryside should rise to its recent level, productivity would continue to rise at about 32–37% over five years, a rate very close to the 34% registered in the previous period.

(2) *Investments*. The goal of the third Plan for gross fixed investment is 250–60 milliard forints.[3] This is an average increase of 26% compared with that of the last five years; this goal should be reached without much difficulty given that the national income has risen by 25% during the last five years. Although the data available do not permit sector-by-sector comparisons, the published summary of the Plan indicates that investment should grow more rapidly in industry and construction than in agriculture and the so-called unproductive sectors. It is planned that the share of industrial investment shall grow from 44·5% in the last plan to 46·5% in this one, the share of 'unproductive' sectors shall fall from 21·7% to 16–20%, and that of agriculture

---

[1] The plan says: 'Over and above the development of co-operatives the economic measures taken by the central power should slow down the fall of agricultural employment. We must take into consideration that young people in the countryside are looking for a permanent, properly remunerated job with career perspectives. The co-operative can contribute to this.' *Magyar Közlöny*, 3 July 1965.

[2] *Délmagyarorszag*, 9 March 1966.

[3] The value of the forint varies with the nature of the product. The exchange rate of 30 forints = $1, which has been used since the mid-fifties to set domestic prices for imports, must be increased according to recent input–output calculations. An average rate of 50 to 1 would be a more realistic estimate for producer goods.

from 18–19% to 16–18%. As Table 15.4 below shows, this is a prolongation of previous tendencies.

Table 15.4   *Distribution of gross investment, 1958–60, 1961–65 and 1966–70* (Plan)[a]

	(in milliards of forints at 1960 prices)						
	Second Three-Year Plan (1958–60)	Second Five-Year Plan (1961–65)	Third Five-Year Plan		(in percentages)		
			Range	Mean	1958–60	1961–65	1966–70
Industry (including construction)	40·0	89·8	117–128	123	43·7	44·5	45–50
Agriculture	16·3	38·7	41–46	43	17·8	18·9	16–18
Transport and trade	14·1	30·2	36–41	39	15·6	14·9	14–16
'Unproductive' sector	20·9	44·1	41–51	46	22·9	21·7	16–20
Total	91·3	202·8	255		100·0	100·0	100

[a] Failure of sub-totals to add up is due to rounding.
Source: 1966–70, 'Law no. 2/1966', *Magyar Közlöny*, 3 July 1966; *Statisztikai Évkönyv 1965*.

The forecast relation between the growth of production and the value of investments is lower than in the previous five years: a 26% growth in investment but a 20% growth in national income. The reasons for this diminished 'productivity of capital' cannot be identified precisely in the absence of a sectoral breakdown. In the light of information available we can suggest that the marginal output/capital ratio in industry and construction, which is higher than the total ratio, is to fall to 36% while that of agriculture is to rise to 21% (see Table 15.5, p. 184). Since industrial investment is about one half of the total, the fall in this sub-ratio explains the moderate forecast for the growth of the overall ratio in the period.

To a certain extent the rise may be only temporary, the result of high investment costs incurred to increase the production of fuel, energy and chemicals, not to mention heavy investment in transport and means of communication. Much is expected of the dieselization and electrification of the railways (a programme begun in the fifties and not yet finished), in the matter of cost reduction. The expenses of modernization, while increasing total capacity, guarantee only a slow growth in production

Table 15.5 *Productivity of investments, 1961–65 and 1966–70* (Plan)

	Second Five-Year Plan (1961–65)	Third Five-Year Plan (1966–70)	Percentage growth between the two Plans
Both sectors			
growth of global value added (milliard forints)[a]	35·2	35·0	0
gross investment (milliard forints)	202·8	255	26
marginal output/capital ratio	0·17	0·14	−19
Industry (including construction)			
growth of global production (milliard forints)[a]	38·7	44·4	15
gross investment (milliard forints)[a]	89·8	123	37
marginal output/capital ratio	0·43	0·36	−16
Agriculture			
growth of global production (milliard forints)[a]	6·2	9·2	48
gross investment (milliard forints)[a]	38·7	43·3	12
marginal output/capital ratio	0·16	0·21	31

[a] Constant prices.
Sources: 1961–65, *Statisztikai Évkönyv*, 1965; 1966–70, *Magyar Közlöny*, 3 July 1966.

in the immediate future. Moreover it is planned to relieve the housing shortage, which will tend to raise the overall ratio because housing, like transport and communications, is very capital-intensive. Even if these factors are partly temporary, the present level of the capital/output ratio may be a better long-term indicator than the ratio of the preceding Five-Year Plan; this was raised by the existence of unemployed capacity at the beginning of the period.

Although the Hungarians have reckoned with a decreasing overall ratio, it is possible that the planned investments should

Table 15.6   *Certain industrial products, 1960, 1965, 1970* (Plan)

Products	1960	1965	1970	1970 as index (1960 = 100)[a]
Chemicals				
fertilizers (1,000 tons)[b]		265	550–600	217
imports		92	130–150	150
consumption[b]	168	357	700–730	200
consumption[c]	748	1,454	3,315	230
plastics (1,000 tons)	9·9	26·7	95–100	375
synthetic fibres (1,000 tons)	4·2	6·3	11–12	182
Minerals and metals				
pig-iron (million tons)	1·25	1·58	1·8–1·9	117
crude steel (million tons)	1·89	2·52	2·9–3·0	117
rolled steel (million tons)	1·23	1·72	2·80	162
bauxite (million tons)	1·19	1·48	3·10	121
alumina (1,000 tons)	218	267	450–470	117
crude aluminium (1,000 tons)	50	58	60–65	108
Fuel and energy				
coal (million tons)	26·5	31·4	32	102
natural gas (million cubic metres)	342	1,107	3,300	300
oil (million tons)	1·22	1·80	1·80	100
imports	1·46	2·25	3·50	155
consumption	2·88	4·05	5·30	131
share of natural gas and petroleum in fuel	23%	30%	38%	
Electricity				
capacity (mw)	1,400	2,000	3,000	150
production (milliard kwh)	7·6	11·2	18·5	165
share of imports	7%	12%	17%	
Building materials				
cement (million tons)	1·57	2·38	2·7–2·8	115
brick (milliard)	1·77	1·85	2·7–2·8	148

[a] Taking mean value of range in 1970.
[b] Effective weight.
[c] Gross weight.
Sources: 1960 and 1965, *Statisztikai Évkönyv 1965*: 1970, *Magyar Közlöny*, 3 July 1966.

not be enough for the production targets. This is particularly true for net output, which will probably grow less quickly than global output. Agriculture in the last Five-Year Plan is the best instance: net output did not rise at all while global output rose by 10%. The same may in future apply to industry because of structural changes (switch from coal, where net output is a large percentage of global, to oil and natural gas, where it is a

Table 15.7   *Foreign trade, 1960–65* (million dollars)[a]

	1960	1961	1962	1963	1964	1965	1961–65
Imports							
socialist countries	687	704	821	900	996	1,018	4,440
capitalist countries:							
developed	252	272	270	332	403	407	1,686
under-developed	37	49	54	73	95	95	366
Total	976	1,026	1,149	1,304	1,495	1,520	6,492
Exports							
socialist countries	623	756	810	849	963	1,058	4,436
capitalist countries:							
developed	199	205	225	289	311	351	1,382
under-developed	51	68	64	67	78	101	378
Total	874	1,029	1,099	1,206	1,352	1,509	6,196
Trade balance							
socialist countries	−64	52	−10	−51	−33	40	3
capitalist countries:							
developed	−53	−67	−45	−43	−92	−56	−302
under-developed	15	19	9	−6	−18	6	20
Total	−102	3	−49	−100	−143	−11	−299

[a] Imports, c.i.f.; exports, f.o.b. Failure of sub-totals to add up is due to rounding.
Source: *Statisztikai Évkönyv 1965*.

small one). It is possible to introduce a certain flexibility. Investments could be increased if it were possible to slow up the amortization of external loans. Even without recourse to foreign aid, investment could exceed the plan in branches of low capital intensity while reducing them in sectors where investment is unprofitable. This could be done, for example, by raising the national output of fuel less quickly than imports.

Industrial production[1]

According to the Plan, industrial production is to grow by 32–36% in the course of the period, or at 5·7–6·3% per annum. The plan emphasizes the principal options: (1) to rationalize industry (technical progress in particular in the mass production industries so as to raise labour productivity); (2) the actual fulfilment of the targets, and (3) priority for certain sectors (more particularly chemicals, electric generators and certain branches of engineering).

(1) *Chemicals*. The third Five-Year Plan gives absolute priority to chemicals. Continuing the tendency of the second Plan, chemical production should rise by 55–60% – the highest in industry. The emphasis is on fertilizers and synthetics. Fertilizers (net weight) are to rise by 117% (149% for nitrates, 76% for phosphates) from 265,000 tons in 1965 to 550,000–600,000 tons in 1970. Given that production is to outstrip consumption (which will rise by 100% over 1965), it will be possible to restrain the growth of imports to only 50% (from 92,000 tons to 130,000–150,000 tons).

Synthetics are to be developed as substitutes for other raw materials, to increase the efficiency of industry, to improve the quality of consumer goods and to reduce imports. In 1965 the consumption of plastics was four kilograms a head, of which one quarter had to be imported. In 1970 imports are to be about zero. Production is to triple while consumption will only rise 2½ times. The production of synthetic fibres, still very low, is to rise 2½–3 times to increase the supply of raw materials to light industry. This, too, should reduce the pressure on the balance of payments, especially in convertible currencies, since the West is the principal supplier.

(2) *Metallurgy*. The plan says that 'the most important task . . . is the full utilization of production capacity, modernization and a greater diversification of products. The production of alloys, sheet and forgings should outstrip the average'.[2] While the

---

[1] For sectoral increases see Table 15.8 (p. 188). The increases of certain industrial products are given in Table 15.6 (p. 185).
[2] 'Law No. 2/1966', *Magyar Közlöny*, 3 July 1966, 457.

production of casting and ingots is only to grow by 17% in the five years, rolled steel is to grow by 62%. More elaborate products (steel wire, tubes and sheets) should outstrip the

Table 15.8 *Principal indicators of the Hungarian economy*

	Percentage growth within period			Annual percentage rates[b]		
	1961–65		1970	1961–65		1970
	Plan	Actual	Plan	Plan	Actual	Plan
National income	36	25	19–21	6·3	4·6	3·7
consumption	22	20	14–16	4·1	3·7	2·8
investment	50	68	25	8·5	11·0	4·6
Labour force						
total	1·2	0·6	3·8	0·2	0·1	0·7
non-agricultural	12	16	6·8	2·3	3·0	1·3
agricultural	−4·3	−21	−2·7	−0·9	−4·5	−0·6
Global industrial						
production	48–50	47	32–36	8·3	8·0	6·0
heavy industry	56	51	37–40	9·3	8·6	6·7
light industry	35	38	20–24	6·2	6·6	4·1
food industry	41	43	28–32	7·1	7·4	5·4
chemical industry	75	90	55–60	11·8	13·7	9·5
engineering	64	57	40–45	10·4	9·4	7·3
building materials	44	36	25–30	7·6	6·3	5·0
Agriculture[a]						
global production	22–23	10	13–15	4·2	1·9	2·7
crops	24	6	11–13	4·4	1·2	2·3
livestock	20	13	15–17	3·7	2·5	3·0
Visible foreign trade						
total	46	60		7·9	9·9	
exports	61	73	46	10·0	11·6	7·9
imports	33	56		5·9	9·3	
Wages and prices						
real wages	not	{ 9	9–10	not	{ 1·8	1·9
prices	published	{ 3	0	published	{ 0·6	0

[a] Growth between five-year averages.
[b] Certain figures are means of ranges.
Sources: 1961–65: *Magyar Közlöny*, 17 October 1961; *Népszabadság*, 4 October 1966; 1966–70: *Magyar Közlöny*, 3 July 1966.

simpler ones. The aim is to develop an export of quality steel from the total of 368,000 tons in 1965. The planned increase in steel production of 200,000–300,000 tons is the smallest for Eastern Europe, except Albania, and it is probable that it will be attained without great difficulty. But in the case of rolled products the fulfilment of the plan is more doubtful and will depend upon investment.

The development of aluminium is one of the most significant elements in the plan. A greater increase is provided for the production of bauxite and alumina than for aluminium; i.e.

Table 15.9   *Global agricultural production* (milliard 1959 forints)

	Global production			Estimates of global production	
	Actual	Adjusted[a]	Percentage deviations from mean	Mean[b]	Dispersion[c]
1956	52·4	57·8	−9·8		
1957	59·4	69·3	8·1		
1958	62·7	66·3	3·4		
1959	66·2	68·5	6·8		
1960	62·9	63·6	−0·8		
Average 1956–60	60·6	65·1	7·6		
1961	63·3	62·5	−2·5		
1962	64·4	62·1	−3·1		
1963	67·6	64·0	−0·2	68·8	63·6–70·2
1964	71·0	65·5	2·2	68·7	65·4–72·2
1965	67·9	61·5	−4·0	70·6	67·2–74·2
Average 1961–65	66·7	63·1	−7·6		
1966				72·5	69·0–76·2
1967				74·4	70·9–78·3
1968				76·3	72·9–80·3
1969				78·3	74·5–82·3
1970				80·3	76·4–84·4
Average 1966–70				76·4	72·7–80·3

[a] The decennial trend, evaluated by the method of least squares, is not included in the annual figures of the first column.

[b] Based on the forecast annual growth of 2·7% p.a. between the quinquennial means, 1961–65 and 1966–70.

[c] Confidence intervals of 10%.

Sources: 1956–65, *Statisztikai Évkönyv 1965*; the estimates are based on the third Five-Year Plan in *Magyar Közlöny*, 3 July 1966.

the structure of production will be adjusted to comparative advantage. Having regard to the small amount of electricity available and to its high cost, Hungarian economists have always insisted that the country should abstain from producing aluminium ingots, and rather export bauxite and alumina; and then reimport the metal to supply the industries working it up. By recent agreements Hungary will export in 1970 120,000 tons of alumina to USSR, or two thirds of the planned increase in production, as opposed to 60,000 tons of aluminium. In 1970, assuming that there will be no net exports, Hungary should be able to double her consumption of aluminium.

(3) *Energy.* The proportion of petroleum and natural gas should rise: from 23% in 1960 and about 30% in 1965 to 38% in 1970. Although the plan emphasizes these two commodities, one can estimate that in absolute value the production of petroleum will actually fall a little. The prospecting undertaken during the third Five-Year Plan will not affect production until 1970. In terms of calories, coal will remain the principal source of energy, but its relative importance and, according to recent information, the absolute quantities produced, will diminish in order to limit the fall in quality of domestic coal. It will be replaced gradually by petroleum products, both for the production of electricity and for the chemical industry.

To satisfy a growing demand for petroleum products, refinery capacity will be considerably increased. The plan tells us that the productive capacity of the refinery of Szászhalom-batta, built during the second Five-Year Plan, will be raised to 3 million tons in 1970. Imports, which grew from 1·45 million tons in 1960 to 2·25 million in 1965, should reach at least 3·5 million by 1970, partly by reason of the new pipeline which unites Hungary to the southern branch of the Friendship Pipeline running between the Ukraine and Bratislava.

Electricity capacity, which rose from 1,400 mw. in 1960 to 2,000 mw. at the end of 1965, will continue to grow at this rate, adding 1,000 mw. by 1970. Actual production is to grow more rapidly than capacity, from 11·2 to 68·5 milliard kWh. during the plan. Given that imports will increase 2·6 times, they will be 17% of production in 1970, as opposed to 12% in 1965 and 7% in 1960.

(4) *Other heavy industry.* Engineering is to grow very quickly. It was a quarter of global industrial production and 33% of exports in 1965, and production is to grow by 40–45%, exports by 50–55%. In correspondence with the comparative advantage of the country and CMEA agreements, the most rapidly developing branches will be: machinery and equipment for chemical and food products, diesel locomotives, buses, office machinery, ball bearings, telecommunications equipment, precision instruments, high tension electrical machinery and certain machine tools. Some of these branches, especially the last four, have already grown rapidly; others, like diesel loco-motives, buses and chemical materials, face their greatest development in the future. Bus output is to rise from 2,779 units in 1965 to 7,000 in 1970; that of ball bearings, where co-operation within the CMEA has been a success, from 85,000 units to 130,000.

The building material industry is to raise its output by 25–30% (cement by 15% and bricks by 48%).

(5) *Processing and food industries.* The plan reveals only few details on the evolution of this sector, probably because the new economic system, particularly the determination of goals by consumer demand rather than central directive, will be put into practice here. The global production of light industry should rise by 20–24%; that of food industry by 28–33%. The table below shows the principal structural changes envisaged:

Industrial production by sectors (%)

Sectors	1960	1965	1970 (plan)
Heavy industry	61.6	64.5	66.6
Light industry	20.4	18.5	16.9
Food industry	18.0	17.0	16.5

Nevertheless the plan does not envisage any substantial increase in investments in order to obtain these results. This sector will receive 14–16% of total investment, while in the previous five years, when it was thought to be neglected, it received 14.9%.

Transport and means of communication

In this sector the plan is particularly ambitious. Hungary has always insisted on its importance. In a recent article the minister of Transport and Communications said: 'In these last years it has been proved again that if the speed of development of transport lags behind that of other sectors, the economy as a whole suffers. The transportation of certain products has been subject to delays, enterprises have registered losses and delays in the execution of projects owing to the lack of raw materials.'[1] The shares of dieselization and electrification are to pass from 45% in 1965 to 75–80% in 1970. Almost 400 km of track are to be electrified. Almost 350 km of secondary lines are to be built, and 2,400–2,600 km of existing track entirely relaid.

In 1965 there were 80,000 motor cars belonging either to the state or to enterprises, and 20,000 private cars. The total number is to rise by 90% in the five years.[2]

Agriculture

The third Five-Year Plan foresees an increase of 13–15% in global agricultural production on average, compared with the average of 1961–65. If at first glance this is only a moderate growth compared with that of industry, when we look at the experience of the past it is not an unambitious goal. Thus between 1956–60 and 1961–65 global production rose by 10%, but net production not at all. The growth of livestock products is to be 11–13%; taking account of this target and of the general growth of agriculture, grain products are to rise by 15–17%.[3]

Between 1966 and 1970 agriculture is to receive 44–45 milliard forints, a total 16% greater than that of the last five years, but implying that the capital coefficient will continue to grow, as opposed to its decline in industry. This presupposes that the rate of decline of the agricultural labour force will be slower than before. However if the most recent forecasts are correct (fall of 400,000 people), the production target will

[1] György Csanádi, 'Transport and Communications in the Third Five-Year Plan', *Népszabadság*, 24 July 1966.

[2] *Esti Hirlap*, 23 July 1966.

[3] *Figyelö*, 29 June 1966.

require a still greater agricultural investment. In any case the supply of agricultural machinery will be an important issue. For instance the third Five-Year Plan makes no provision for the growth of tractors and harvesters; and although it provides for more lorries and half tracks, their number seems much inferior to the goals set by the Ministry of Agriculture.[1] In the past the slow pace of mechanization has revealed shortages of manpower at certain periods; even during mediocre harvests it has been necessary to call in the army, students and industrial workers.

The use of mineral fertilizers will increase rapidly. Consumption, which nearly doubled during the second Five-Year Plan (from 748,000 tons to 1,454,000 tons), is to more than double during this Plan, attaining 3,315,000 tons in 1970. Improvements of agricultural technology are also emphasized: better seeds and a more rational use of insecticides.

These improvements should raise average yields and permit the development of horticulture. The plan foresees a need for 2·1–2·3 million tons of vegetables in 1970: 0·9 million for individual consumption, 1 million for industry and 0·2 million for export in a raw state. For this reason the output of vegetables (1·5 million tons in 1965, of which 43% from private plots) is to rise by about 50%.[2]

The yields of wheat and corn are to be raised to reduce imports. The plan particularly hopes to reduce fodder imports and eliminate those of flour.[3] The table on p. 194 shows how low yields will remain in Hungary, despite an upward tendency.

The plan gives no information on animal products, but according to a report of the Agricultural Commission of Parliament, the annual production of milk per cow is to rise from 2,100–2,200 litres in 1965 to 2,500–2,600 in 1970, while the output of eggs rises from 2·3 milliard to 2·9 milliard. To realize the targets in the livestock sector, Hungary will have to import 45–50% more protein fodder in the course of the period.[4]

---

[1] The Ministry estimates that 45,000 half tracks and 10,000 lorries will be necessary to secure transportation within agriculture. The plan is for 35,000–36,000 half tracks and 4,400 lorries: *Magyar Nemzet*, 18 July 1966.

[2] *Tudomány és Mezőgazdaság*, July 1966.

[3] During the second Five-Year Plan a good deal of grain was imported: from 548 to 816,000 tons: *Statisztikai Havi Közlemények*, May 1966.

[4] *Figyelő*, 29 June 1966.

The procurement of agricultural products is to rise by 28–32%; this means that the state will buy about 80% of net agricultural production where it only bought 70% during the five previous years. The plan insists quite particularly on horticultural products; the export of these is to grow by 50% (over 60% to socialist countries and 40% to the West).[1]

Average yields of wheat and corn (quintals per hectare)

| | Hungary | | | Austria |
	1961–65	1965	1970	1964
wheat	18·6	21·7	20·8	26·5
corn	26·3	29·3	31·3	42·4

Sources: *Statiszikai Évkönyv*, 1964; *Statisztikai Havi Közlemények*, August 1966; *Esti Hirlap*, 23 July 1966.

New stimuli will bring about this increased procurement. Compulsory deliveries at low prices have been suppressed since 1956 and agricultural income has risen considerably, even though it remains lower than urban income. Since 1960 the system of 'labour units' (which reflect the number of days of work and the type of work) has yielded to that of payment in cash on collective farms; even in certain cases regular monthly payments have been produced. A certain number of collective farms have adopted the system of participation in the harvest of secondary cereals, assigning parcels of land to each member after having recovered the principal crop. In this system members can keep 50–70% of their production. Nonetheless collective farmers think that their share in marginal product is higher on their private plots, given that the size of these plots has not fallen. A large proportion of livestock is raised on these plots, about one half of cows and pigs, 15% of sheep and 90% of poultry. If production outside private plots is to be raised there must be considerable investment in stables, scientific breeding and veterinary services.

[1] *Népszabadság*, 26 July 1966.

Foreign trade

Hungary's foreign trade is to rise by 46% in value or at an annual rate of 7·9%. This is double the rate of growth of national income, but it is not especially rapid in relation to the past. Trade rose more rapidly during the last Five-Year Plan, both in absolute value and in relation to national income. In fact ever since the beginning of detailed planning in Hungary the marginal ratio between foreign trade and national income has been about 2·0% as the table below shows.

Growth of foreign trade and national income (percentages)

	Exports	Imports	National income	Marginal foreign-trade– national- income ratio[a]
1951–55	13·1	9·1	4·9	2·5
1956–60	10·0	12·2	6·5	1·7
1961–65	11·6	9·3	4·6	2·4
1966–70 (forecasts)	7·9	7·9	3·7	2·1

[a] The average growth of exports and imports, divided by the growth of the national income.

Note: For an analysis of the figures up to 1960, see my *The Economics of Centrally Planned Foreign Trade: the Hungarian Experience* (doctoral thesis, Harvard University, 1966). The methods of allowing for changes in price and of calculating national income at factor costs are analysed in chapter 4. There also I justify the use of the marginal FTNI ratio rather than of the income-elasticity of trade, which implies a functional relation between income and foreign trade–a doubtful hypothesis in a planned economy.

Sources: Calculations based on *Statisztikai Évkönyv* (different years); *Statisztikai Havi Közlemények*, 1966; *Külkereskedelem*, July 1966.

The official résumé gives no details on foreign trade. It rehearses the habitual recommendations on efficiency which 'is to be increased ... in exports ... and in imports'.[1] Also a positive balance of trade is required. Pressure on the balance of payments is a theme which appears in all the commentaries on foreign trade. An article in the review of foreign trade, for

[1] *Magyar Közlöny*, 3 July 1966, p. 455.

example, states: 'During the elaboration of the options for the
1966–70 plan, one of the principal points was the search for
an improvement of foreign trade [and] the re-establishment of
equilibrium in the balance of payments.'[1] The statistics in the
same article show nevertheless that, according to the forecasts,
exports will not rise more rapidly than imports, but both at the
rates quoted above; this contradicts the plan when it states:
'Exports are to outstrip imports.'[2] The second Five-Year Plan
on the contrary tried to raise exports by 61% and imports by
only 33%, so that Hungary could repay punctually what she
had borrowed from Communist countries, raise her offers of
credit to underdeveloped countries, and cover her invisible
deficit.

Hungary is heavily indebted abroad: this began in 1952 and
has got worse. During the first half of the fifties, the difficulties
arose from invisibles (debt service, reparations), which raised
borrowing at short term although the commercial balance was
positive.[3]

After the events of 1956, Hungary received large loans from
the other Communist countries: c. $300 million, the majority
of which was used to raise imports ($260 million). These
borrowings should have been repaid during the sixties, but
instead of the export surplus of several million dollars forecast,
the second Five-Year Plan ended with a cumulative deficit in
visible trade of $300 million (see Table 15.7, p. 186).[4]

Having regard to Hungary's international obligations, her
foreign trade targets are rather astonishing. In 1965 the short
term foreign debt was at least $730[5] million. In the absence of

[1] *Külkereskedelem*, July 1966, p. 193.
[2] *Magyar Közlöny*, 3 July 1966, p. 460.
[3] Although the commercial balance resulted in a cumulative surplus of $38
million in 1950–55, the balance of payments deficit rose to about $130 million
(1·5 milliard devisa forints). See *Adatok és adalékok* (Budapest, 1956), pp. 310–11.
[4] The second plan forecast a visible export surplus of $110 million in 1965 alone,
but in fact the deficit exceeded $10 million (*Közgazdasági Szemle*, November 1961;
and *Statisztikai Évkönyv*, 1965).
[5] Hungary, like all other Communist countries, publishes no balance of payments
figures. The figures for foreign debt are extracted from my forthcoming article,
'The Hungarian Balance of Payments.' Briefly if we add to the short term debt
contracted during the fifties (about $130 million up to 1955 and $300 million in
1956–60) the visible deficit in the course of the second Five-Year Plan we arrive
at $730 million. The actual figure must be greater since the invisible balance
is negative.

precise indications one can only guess as to what the planners can do within the framework of the plan. USSR and the other Communist countries could aid the economy, if the situation worsens, by granting a moratorium or an annulment of certain of the debts contracted since 1956. But Hungary is more and more indebted towards the West as well, and granted that she can hardly pay this debt back with long-term Communist loans, one may imagine that the foreign trade plan will be realized thanks to the renewal of these Western credits. Hungary has been trying to obtain such credits at long term for several years. Apart from the political aspects of the question, the attempt can only succeed if her economy grows successfully. If serious difficulties supervene, the country would be more dependent on foreign aid than ever but the possibility of long-term credit, and even of renewal of short-term credit, would be greatly reduced.

One might think, having regard to the pressure on the balance of payments, that unless Hungary obtains considerable loans from the West, her exports to underdeveloped countries (which themselves depend on the credit that she can provide) will not grow as quickly as before. This will obstruct the expected changes in the distribution of foreign trade: 'To improve our foreign trade, its development will have to follow different directions according to whether it is with socialist or capitalist countries. In comparison with 1965, our imports in 1970 from socialist countries will outstrip our exports, whereas exports towards capitalist countries will outstrip imports'.[1]

Taking account of the new economic mechanisms, the foreign trade plan approved by Parliament was called a 'minimum plan', particularly with regard to capitalist countries.[2] This fact shows that the way of formulating the plan has been greatly changed, because in the past the output targets were established at higher levels than those indicated by the best forecasts available (the targets were determined by the method of 'taut planning'). There is no certainty that the 1967 Plan is a 'minimum plan'. On the one hand the new economic mechanism will not begin to apply until 1968, and on the other, experience teaches us that the planners' reach exceeds their grasp.

[1] *Külkereskedelem*, July 1966, p. 193.   [2] *Ibid.*

To what extent is the Five-Year Plan 'taut'? On the side of imports, given the dependence of Hungary on foreign machines and raw materials, flexibility must be low. The Plan may be too optimistic here, since it supposes that industry can econo-mize in inputs. But on the export side there is greater flexibility. The over-fulfilment of the targets depends largely on agri-culture, a sector full of uncertainties. But even if we rule out the possibility of a series of bad harvests, we can at best expect that the agricultural export forecast will not be attained; this will be largely offset by industry which will profit by an unplanned access of labour. In any case, whether in the industrial sector or in the marketing of exports, there remain 'unutilized reserves', which could be put to work by the appropriate measures. During the debate on the plan a number of problems were discussed and remedies proposed, but accord-ing to reports the potential advantages resulting from these measures were not included in the targets. For example the refrain was taken up again that 'the stocks of disposable goods do not always correspond to foreign demand': there should be an improvement because the plan has taken for one of the success indicators for industrial enterprises precisely sales abroad.[1] To introduce more flexibility into exports the plan for the first time 'contains no specifications by product, but determines the principal targets for each sector – as for foreign trade ...'.[2]

III   THE TWO FIRST YEARS OF THE SECOND FIVE-YEAR PLAN: ACHIEVEMENTS[3]

When we turn to foreign trade the 1967 plan has its mysterious side, and the rare details revealed are contradictory. The official résumé states that imports and exports are to grow by 6 to 7%.[4] Although this target was confirmed in an editorial of the Hungarian foreign trade periodical,[5] one month later,

---

[1] Külkereskedelem, July 1966, p. 193.   [2] Ibid., p. 194.

[3] We omit at this late date of reprinting the passage, containing no predictions, on 1966, and the description of most of the 1967 plan. But the 1967 foreign-trade plan contained discrepancies, and here Professor Brown could adumbrate a forecast.

[4] Népszabadság, 18 December 1966.

[5] Külkereskedelem, January 1967, p. 1.

in the same journal, the director indicates that only imports are to grow by 6%, while exports are to remain at the 1966 level.[1] This source gives a geographical distribution, which shows that the plan forecasts a rise of 5% in exports to and of 3·5% in imports from capitalist countries. We can deduce that imports from socialist countries are to rise by more than 6%, while exports to them are to fall slightly.

These contradictions lead us to suppose that the foreign-trade plan has been discreetly revised. In any case there is a certain disquiet about 'the geographical distribution of the plan targets, which creates certain tensions' (*ibid.*). These tensions are to some extent due to the excess of detail in the plan: 'We have met difficulties with practically every type of good offered by enterprises and destined for export to capitalist countries' (*ibid.*). This excessive care for detail creates problems 'at the same time as the tension of the plans, even though a part [of this tension] can be relieved during the year and the targets show themselves to admit of overfulfilment' (*ibid.*). The national planning office has tried to solve the problem, in formulating the 1967 plan, 'by reducing the number of obligatory indicators and outputs decided by the central planners' (*ibid.*), in anticipation of the new economic system. Over and above these difficulties, the foreign trade plan must be revised within the framework of the other planned economies. In this connexion, quite explicit allusion is made to the unforeseen disequilibrium between exports and imports. It seems that 'the experience of 1966' necessitated a last minute change in the foreign trade targets for 1967 (*ibid.*, pp. 33–4).

[1] *Külkereskedelem*, February 1967, p. 33.

16

THE HUNGARIAN ECONOMY 1966-70

R. D. PORTES, 1968

Barring political upheaval, economic regularities should tell us something about the future, in communist and non-communist economies alike. Some of the functional relationships obtaining in the latter will not hold in the former, because of the absence of certain markets, different types of connexions between real and monetary phenomena, or the profoundly different role of expectation. But other regularities should take their place, and we may overlook some which remain common to both systems. Even before the economic reforms, some markets operated in Eastern Europe, and now the scope for market behaviour is widening. Incentives are incentives – however distorted their structure, we must believe that economic man reacts to them in some sort of predictable way. Demography is totally unaffected, and here easily measurable causes precede easily predictable effects, giving us a great advantage, at least for short- and medium-term forecasting. Even politics is not a totally exogenous field, and economic policy much less so.

Hungarian politics have been remarkably stable during the past decade and are likely to continue on the same gradualist lines for some time, assuming the events in Czechoslovakia (whose outcome is quite obscure at the time of writing, July 1968) will be for the most part 'contained'. Hence one ought to be able to say something about the future. Fortunately, my feeling that Professor Brown was too cautious does not, under the terms of my own assignment, require that I come out with a full range of predictions. My task is to comment on his paper of last year, not to write his next one; and limitations of space preclude my going into the detail necessary to back up any firm quantitative predictions. What I shall do is to try to show why one of his forecasts was probably erroneous, and then to illustrate how what one did know and could infer might have been used to predict events of 1967. Naturally, both these efforts will benefit substantially from hindsight and the year which has elapsed since he wrote. Finally, I cannot resist the temptation to make a few broad and qualified guesses of my own, especially in regard to the economic reforms and their effects.

In his exposition of the third Five-Year Plan, Professor Brown chose to question its basic hypotheses in only two respects: the balance of payments and labor supply estimates. I shall return to the former at various points below; here I want to question his predictions about the labor force.

Professor Brown cites an article in a provincial newspaper (published before the Plan itself appeared) [1] to suggest that over the five-year period, agricultural employment would fall by 400,000. He then calculates (from output and productivity data in the Plan) that the Plan assumed a fall of only 41,000; [2] with a rise of 180,000 in total employment (the midpoint of the Plan's 160,000–200,000 estimate), this implies a rise of 221,000 in non-agricultural employment, of whom 107,000 would go into industry. [3] Accepting the rise in total employment (180,000), he posits his own figure for agricultural employment and derives very different subtotals for other sectors (see Table 16.1 below). He uses these discrepancies to draw important conclusions about possible shortfalls with respect to the agricultural output and productivity hypotheses of the Plan, and the table for Hungary in the Appendix to this book (p. 376) modifies this assumption to predict a lower rate of growth of industrial productivity (3.7%) than that in the Plan (5%).

In fact, however, two months after the plan came out, the head of the manpower division of the National Planning Office said it had supposed a fall of 80,000 in agricultural employment, a rise of 180,000 in total employment, and thus a

---

[1] *Délmagyarország*, 9 March 1966; the Plan was published in *Magyar Közlöny*, 3 July 1966.

[2] No figure for the change in agricultural employment was given in the Plan itself.

[3] These data are in his Table 15.1 (p. 180). Unfortunately, the data for 1960 and 1965 in this Table are data as of the beginning of the year cited (and so inappropriate for dealing with the 1961–65 and 1966–70 Five-Year Plans) and relate to 'active earners', a category which differs in certain respects from actual employment. Thus they cannot be directly compared with the figures cited below in the text giving changes in employment in 1966 and 1967.

rise of 260,000 in non-agricultural employment, of whom 118,000 would go into industry.[1]
The divergent estimates can be summed up as follows:

Table 16.1   (*'000 workers, end–1965 to end–1970*)

	Appendix	Plan according to Brown	Plan official	Official estimates early 1968
Fall in agricultural employment	241 (400)[a]	41	80	80
Rise in total employment	180	180	180	210–20
Rise in non-agricultural employment	421	221	260	290–300
of which, rise in industrial employment	207	107	118	

[a] See above p. 202 and Table 15.3 (p. 181).
Sources: Brown, pp. 179 ff. and see note 1, p. 202 and notes 1 and 2, p. 203.

Moreover, subsequent events indicate that the Plan goal for agricultural employment is not unrealistic and that the rise in industrial employment will not significantly exceed the Plan's assumption. Estimates made at the beginning of 1968 suggest an increase in total employment of 210,000–220,000 during the period, this being 30,000–40,000 more than the Plan, and no change in the Plan's 80,000 drop in agriculture.[2] The estimated fall in agricultural employment in the first two years of the Plan is only 25,000–30,000, precisely in line with the Plan. Industrial employment has grown somewhat faster than planned: 20,000 in 1966 and 50,000 in 1967.[3] But 1967 was a year of exceedingly rapid demand-induced industrial growth (to be discussed below), which is most unlikely to be repeated; and it is revealing that this did *not* pull workers out of agriculture in excessive numbers, and the jump in industrial employment went with an abnormally high increase in output

[1] J. Timár, *Népszabadság*, 12 September 1966. These figures were confirmed by the Deputy Prime Minister, M. Timár, in *Pártélet* October 1967.
[2] See *Népszava*, 28 January 1968 and I. Pál in *Közgazdasági Szemle*, xv/2 (February 1968). The latter periodical will be cited below as *KSz*.
[3] *Statisztikai Hávi Közlemények*, 1968/2–3, p. 98. Hereafter cited as *SHK*.

per worker (shades of Verdoorn's Law!).[1] It is therefore unlikely that the total increase in industrial employment during the Plan period will exceed 140,000–150,000, this being only 20,000–30,000 more than the Plan goal; and the industrial productivity target is still feasible.

Why was the estimate of a drop of 400,000 in agriculture so far off the mark? At the outset it was clear that the planned increase in total employment was on the low side, as were all the growth objectives of the Plan (as Professor Brown indicated). Professor Brown said that labor supply was a tight constraint on Hungarian growth, because of a low and 'still falling' birth-rate. But the birth-rate, though indeed still low, in fact began to rise in 1966, and there is good reason to expect this to continue;[2] and of course this is irrelevant to the short-run picture, which is dominated by the anti-abortion law in force from February 1953 to June 1956. To deal with its effects, the planners have expanded vocational education, moved to pension off partially disabled workers, planned a reduction of the work week, introduced new child-care arrangements to limit the rise in female participation rates,[3] and begun a program to train young workers in East Germany.[4] There may nevertheless be difficulties in employing all school-leavers, especially young girls. In any case, labor resources are more than ample to meet the planned increase in non-agricultural employment without drawing excessively on agriculture.

In agriculture, on the other hand, the planners have finally begun to recognize the power of economic motives. The recollectivization of 1959–62 naturally caused a substantial outflow, but this was a one-shot affair. Incentives in agriculture have improved substantially with recent measures to ameliorate

[1] This 'law' states that in advanced industrial countries the rate of growth of industrial productivity is an increasing function of the rate of growth of industrial employment.

[2] Births per 1,000 were 12·9 in 1962, 13·1 in 1965, 13·6 in 1966, and 14·5 in 1967. 1968 shows a further increase. This can only in part be attributed to the effects of the new child-care arrangements (giving special benefits to working women who want to stop temporarily to have a child), since these were introduced at the end of 1966. Reckoning with this incentive, one might anticipate a rise to 16 per 1,000, which is almost respectable. See *SHK*, 1968/5, p. 9, and Pál, *KSz*, xv/2.

[3] It is hoped that up to 100,000 women will ultimately take advantage of this.

[4] 4,000–5,000 per annum are going for two to three year periods, thus taking 10,000–15,000 when the program is in full swing; see *Népszabadság*, 4 May 1968.

the financial status of the collective farms; these have included a rise of 17% in the average level of agricultural producer prices, in two installments, with a third of 3% to come by 1970.[1] The provisions of the economic reforms which allow collectives to set up a wide range of ancillary industrial-type activities should be a strong further inducement to keep people on the farms. It seems, then, that both demographic and economic forces have been working to support the planners' hypotheses, and there was no reason to believe they were far wrong. Indeed, Professor Brown himself cited the Plan's intention to make agricultural employment more attractive, and he gives no indication as to why he accepted the estimate of a 400,000 fall.

Let us now turn to a question of short-run prediction: the significant acceleration of economic expansion which took place in 1967, contrary to the intention of the Plan. Professor Brown's discussion of the 1967 Plan contained no predictions on a matter which was, I think, eminently predictable. One had no need of a full-scale econometric model, nor even of an investment equation, to do it.[2] Observable data, together with our knowledge of the past and the way in which the economy operates, should have been sufficient.

The problem of investment 'cycles' in Eastern Europe has recently been widely discussed.[3] I prefer the term 'fluctuations', because they have relatively little effect on output or employment, which do not fluctuate. Whatever the name, they do have certain cumulative features, and they *are* closely related to

[1] B. Csikós-Nagy, *Népszabadság*, 23 July 1967. The first increase was 9% in January 1966.

[2] This is not to say that one should refrain from constructing either. The Hungarians themselves have research groups in the Central Statistical Office working on both a small simultaneous equations macro model and industrial production functions. And rightly so. Despite the shortcomings of the data, they are at least as good as those in many countries for which such work has been done. As we have argued, command economies exhibit economic regularities and functional relationships; and as the importance of markets increases, these will be replaced or modified by other functional relationships. The change in structure will make the exercise more difficult, but no less worthwhile.

[3] See J. Goldmann in *Economics of Planning* 1964 and 1965; the discussion on socialist countries in the proceedings (to appear shortly) of an SSRC conference in London, April 1967, on 'Is the Business Cycle Obsolete?'; the study in *Economic Bulletin for Europe*, vol. 18, no. 1; and the references in Mieczkowski's footnote 1, p. 250.

at least one other economic variable: the balance of trade.[1] In Hungary since 1957, there has been a regular one-year lag of investment (gross fixed capital formation) behind the foreign balance. A good year in foreign trade allows an investment splurge in the following year, and a bad year forces retrenchment. And conversely: an investment boom usually brings a balance of trade deficit, again sometimes with a lag. The subsidiary relation between investment in machinery and equipment and the balance of trade with socialist countries shows this same pattern even more clearly. All this is hardly surprising for a country which is highly trade-dependent and holds limited reserves.

Thus the switch from a trade deficit in 1965 to surplus in 1966 should immediately have suggested the possibility of a greater than planned increase in investment in 1967. Each investment boom has involved two successive big years, so the fact that 1966 was the first year of recovery from the investment plateau of 1965, and as the first year of a Five-Year Plan saw a large number of new starts, should have pointed further in this direction. The approaching reforms were also clearly stimuli: not merely the gradual expansion of 'decentralized' investment, the effects of which can easily be overestimated; more important were uncertainty about capital goods price changes and availability (especially of imported machines) in 1968, and an easily foreseeable effort by enterprises to get in under the wire, while investment was still a free good. The regulation governing the financing of 'above-limit' investments in process at the time of the changeover was published shortly after Professor Brown wrote, but it took a predictable form: the State would finance the remainder of all projects beyond a certain degree (80%) of completion by 31 December 1967, and the enterprise would have to contribute to financing all other projects underway.[2] As if this were not enough, ministries were allowed to regroup their allocations of dollars between materials and machines; since everyone knew that Western machines would be very hard to get after 1967, and prices of some of the major

---

[1] See my comment in the conference proceedings cited in the preceding footnote; and an interesting paper by J. Zala in *Gazdaság*, 1/1 (November 1967).

[2] 18/1967 GB hat., in *Pénzügyi Közlöny*, 1967/17 (31 May 1967). Hereafter cited as *PK*.

raw materials Hungary buys in the West were falling, the response was obvious.[1] Finally, the large export surplus with socialist countries in 1966 required (because of bilateral balancing) some direct measures to stimulate socialist imports in 1967; among these was the provision of special credit preferences to enterprises which asked by 31 August 1967 for credit to finance machine imports from socialist countries.[2]

Thus many factors, most of them observable past events or predictable reactions, led to the increase in fixed investment of 21% in 1967 (the Plan said 6–7%). It was accompanied by 23% and 31% increases in imports of machines from dollar and rouble markets respectively. Construction investment rose 18%, while machinery investment rose 26%.[3] Meanwhile, exports were rising more than anticipated, in part because of an upsurge of investment in other Eastern European countries. These influences were reinforced by a rapid expansion in consumption demand, originating from both higher peasant incomes from the good 1966 harvest and higher wage incomes from the rise in industrial employment, and spurred by uncertainty about 1968 consumer price changes. The planners made special efforts to allow this demand to be realized without shortages, in accordance with their repeated attempts to reassure consumers about prices and supplies for the economic reforms. They were aided by the good 1966 harvest and consequent better raw material supplies to the consumer goods industries, which increased their output by 10%; and by special imports of consumer goods, in part meeting existing shortages[4] and in part stocking up for the beginning of 1968, so the changeover to the new system would be accompanied by equilibrium in the consumer goods market. Thus industrial consumer goods imports rose by 27% from rouble markets and 23% from dollar markets.[5]

Summing up, these details of 1967 should suggest that the rapid expansion and certain of its features might have been foreseen at the time Professor Brown wrote. Among the signs

[1] See S. Czeitler, *Figyelö*, xii/7 (14 February 1968).
[2] *Népszabadság*, 8 August 1967.
[3] *SHK*, 1968/2–3, p. 86, and Czeitler, *Figyelö*, xii/7.
[4] E.g. in furniture and meat – like most planners the Hungarians seem consistently to underestimate the income – elasticity of demand for meat!
[5] Czeitler, *Figyelö*, xii/7.

were the following: observed past regularities (the investment cycle and investment–trade balance relationship) and events (the good harvest and trade balance of 1966); stimuli arising from (known) features of the reforms and working in the context of behavioral patterns established in the past (the rush for 'free' investment, the anticipation of producer and consumer price changes in 1968); straightforward economic relationships (a rapid rise in industrial output requires an increase in industrial employment and thus in consumer incomes); institutional constants (the desire of socialist trade partners to redress the previous year's imbalances); and known overall policies, in this case the desire of the reformers to have an equilibrated consumer goods market and ample stocks for the transition period of the reforms. Professor Brown's résumé of the plan for 1967 did not consider these factors, and consequently his suspicions about the Plan for foreign trade did not lead him to question the other Plan data he presented.

What about 1968 and longer-term perspectives, both for specific economic variables and the reforms as a whole? Some general remarks on the reforms and their effects may be in order, and they will relate to Professor Brown's survey of the third Five-Year Plan.

Annual plans now have a different character, of course, being much closer to 'indicative' than 'command' planning. Detailed central allocation is limited to a small number of commodities, although there are export and import quotas for others, and more are subject to certain restrictions on distribution or obligations on producers to sign contracts. Thus trade in both producer and consumer goods is relatively but not absolutely free. Prices have changed, and many can henceforth change freely or within limits. Profit is now the basis of incentives, as modified by an exceedingly complex set of taxes. Foreign prices and their variations are now directly transmitted to the domestic market (except for certain fixed import prices) by a system of 'conversion factors', uniform for each of the two main currency blocs.[1] There is, however, an extensive system of differentiated export subsidies, since these 'conversion factors' still overvalue the forint. Investment decisions have in principle been substantially decentralized.

[1] Though with a cross rate differing from the official dollar/rouble rate.

Without going into further detail, it should be clear that these reforms make a sharp break with the past. There are still significant and powerful central controls, more than were originally envisioned, but in my view most are necessary. The reforms go further than in any other Eastern European country, save perhaps Czechoslovakia, and they are surely much better prepared than those in that rather confused country. Indeed, with a bit of luck, it seems to me quite possible that they will create a workable system, one which will naturally be modified in the light of events, but which may escape recentralization while not courting the problems besetting Yugoslavia.

In this context, and with the background of 1967, the comparatively modest 1968 plan[1] seems quite sensible. Although its projected industrial growth rate of 6–7% is still above that specified for 1968 by the Five-Year Plan, the Central Committee was probably correct in its reported view that any further slowdown would be an excessive contrast with 1967 and lead to disruptions.[2] The real retrenchment is in – predictably – investment. A minimal (1%) increase over 1967 is planned, with only 16 new starts on large state-financed projects.[3] After two years of investment expansion, and following a large balance of trade deficit in 1967, the pattern discussed earlier continues its normal course.

On this ground alone, I should expect the actual performance in 1968 to exceed the Plan by very little, if at all, especially in machinery (construction may be somewhat more buoyant). But there are further reasons for confidence in this forecast. The apparently greater freedom of enterprises to indulge their always strong desires for new plant and equipment will be curbed in the short run, since a substantial portion of the 'decentralized' funds is tied up in financing investments in process.[4] The Investment Bank has been slow in processing enterprise requests for credit; despite the resulting complaints, this delay is probably good, insofar as it gives breathing space. The requirement of 150% prior import deposits (non-interest-bearing, to remain blocked for two years), in addition to

[1] See the plan outline in *Népszabadság*, 24 December 1967.
[2] L. Rév, *Társadalmi Szemle*, XXIII/1 (January 1968). Cited below as *TSz*.
[3] I. Dobos, *KSz*, XV/1 (January 1968).
[4] A. Balassa, *Figyelö*, XI/52 (28 December 1967).

payment, on imports of machines from dollar markets should restrict this activity,[1] although there are no restrictions on such imports from rouble markets. The 'development funds' to be formed from 1968 profits will not be available to enterprises until 1969.

Several of these factors, however, could mean a strong expansion of investment in 1969–70, despite remarks by some economic leaders which would indicate a continuing tightness.[2] And there should be room for new starts by then, as most of the projects begun in 1966 were meant to be completed within two years.[3] The major question is of course the balance of payments. The CC expects the dollar deficit to continue this year, and when the Plan was being drawn up, it asked only that it should be kept to the 1967 level.[4] And although early figures show a sharp improvement, one cannot expect this to continue. The fair 1967 harvest, with poor yields of root crops and a shortfall in fodder (necessitating substantial fodder imports in 1968), has been followed by a severe drought in spring of this year. This will hurt both bread grains and fodder, and although the record grain harvest of 1967 eases the situation somewhat, the prospects at the time of writing are at best uncertain, and agricultural problems could accentuate balance of payments tensions. Thus it is only with some diffidence that I would suggest the possibility of a significant increase in investment in the last two years of the Five-Year Plan.

In regard to employment, it should be noted that one cannot expect the reforms to result in substantial dismissals of labor in the short run. Quite the contrary: the construction of the new enterprise incentive system retains an element of the 'average wage control' of the old system, and with it a tendency toward keeping employment up.[5] The increased freedom for enter-

---

[1] See 2/1968 MNB körl., in PK, 1968/3 (31 January 1968). A subsequent Economic Committee resolution excludes investment financed by medium-term credits from this regulation; see Magyar Hirlap, 2 June 1968.

[2] J. Fock, TSz, xxii/11 (November 1967); M. Timár, TSz, xxiii/1 (January 1968). One might guess that these remarks were meant primarily to justify the 1968 slowdown.

[3] L. Molnár, Figyelö, xi/7 (15 February 1967); I. Dobos, Figyelö, x/52 (28 December 1966).

[4] Rév, TSz, xxiii/1. This deficit was $58 million (SHK, 1967/2–3, p. 50).

[5] Average wage increases are limited to 4% in 1968 over the 'base level' of 1967,

prises to lay off workers and for workers to change jobs will primarily increase labor force turnover. Yugoslav-style unemployment is a long way off, and if it comes, it will be a macroeconomic rather than a microeconomic phenomenon. Of course average wage control will also play an important role in limiting cost-inflationary pressures.

The fundamental issue raised by the reforms is whether the increase in allocative efficiency they should eventually engender will be outweighed by countervailing forces: a loss of impetus arising from a diminution of planners' tension, an inability of the new system of decentralized investment to internalize externalities as did the planners, and macroeconomic difficulties, especially in regard to inflation and the balance of payments. And if such problems arose, might they result in recentralization, of the creeping or galloping variety? The broadest prediction in this comment is one of qualified optimism. Cost inflation will ultimately appear, and the balance of payments problem will continue to be severe, but my present guess is that these problems can be handled and will not cause recentralization. The beneficial effects of the reforms will appear only slowly, but there is no strong group of conservatives waiting to say 'We told you so' and to cut off the experiment before it can prove itself. The reformers themselves have recovered a little from their initial *naïveté* about the market, and the further disillusionment to be expected should not be crushing. Thus it seems to me that the Hungarian reforms have at least as good a chance of success as any in Eastern Europe. They will not bring remarkable changes in the economy, but then it has not been doing all that badly up to now; and over a period of time, they should substantially improve the effectiveness of both investment and foreign trade.[1]

---

and any increase in total wages resulting from an increase in the average wage over the base level must be met out of the (post-tax) 'sharing fund' coming from profits. This is a strong inducement to retain unskilled labor, and there is no surplus of skilled workers. For details of these regulations, see 11/1967, PM rend., 122/1967 (17) MüM ut., in *PK*, 1967/33 (29 November 1967). [In the event, this incentive operated even more strongly than I had expected. Employment in industry rose quite rapidly in 1968-9; this was *not*, however, at the expense of agriculture. – Note added January 1970.]

[1] Deals like the recent $50 million agreement to send machinery to Iran for oil are a sign of sensible overall foreign trade policy, as is the current emphasis on co-operation agreements with Western enterprises (J. Biró, *Magyar Hírlap*, 26 June

To return to the premise with which we began, however, all this assumes no fundamental political changes. The present situation in Czechoslovakia, with the exceedingly ambiguous Hungarian attitude to it, makes this *caveat* a more important one in regard to Hungary than at any time since 1956.[1]

1968). But there will be no significant change in the present geographical distribution of trade: one-third with the USSR, one-third with other CMEA countries, and one-third in dollar markets (this itself is a slight change from the past 70–30 policy); see J. Fock, *Népszabadság*, 24 April 1968.

[1] For a more recent discussion of the effects of the economic reforms and their future prospects, see the present author's paper, 'Economic Reforms in Hungary', *American Economic Review* (May 1970).

17

POLAND

MICHAEL GAMARNIKOW, 1967

It is often said that the state of the Polish economy is the Achilles heel of the Gomulka regime. Indeed, the snail pace of the economic progress, especially in respect of the living standards, is the main reason for the widespread feeling of frustration which prevails in Poland ten years after the memorable events of October 1956.

This subjective feeling of stagnation prevailing among the great masses of population is apparently contradicted by the official statistics. During the five-year period 1961–65 the national income (Marxist concept) has been growing at a healthy average rate of about 7% per year[1] and another 6% increase was chalked up in 1966,[2] while public consumption maintained a fairly steady increase in the range of 4–6%.[3] At the same time employment in the socialized economy (outside agriculture and forestry) increased from 7.3 million in 1961[4] to 8.5 million in 1966.[5] On the surface, those figures and percentages would seem to support the official claim about a healthy and relatively dynamic growth of Polish economy.

However there are other figures (also the régime's), which shed a different light on the economic situation of the country.

Such huge discrepancies between the planned-for targets and actual fulfilment in the key sectors of the economy are obviously a manifestation of some serious economic disproportions, which might well materially affect the performance of Polish economy in the forthcoming five-year period. Thus their detailed

[1] *Rocznik Statystyczny (Statistical Yearbook)*, 1966, p. 77 (in 1961 prices).
[2] *Trybuna Ludu* (Warsaw), 8 February 1967. Communiqué on the National Economic Plan fulfilment in 1966.
[3] *Rocznik Statystyczny (Statistical Yearbook)*, 1966, p. 80 (in 1961 prices).
[4] *Biuletyn Statystyczny*, 1/67 (Warsaw), 10.
[5] *Trybuna Ludu* (Warsaw), 8 February 1967. Communiqué on the National Economic Plan fulfilment in 1966.

analysis is highly pertinent, as far as any predictions of the future developments are concerned.

Among the o bjective dfficulties, as opposed to those of the régime's own making, thei chief is the huge disproportion between the labour resources which would become available in the current five-year period and the investment means which the Polish planners have at their disposal. Indeed the situation is so grave that a serious unemployment problem is the main shadow hanging over Poland's economic future. At the end of 1966 unemployment in Poland was reliably estimated at about 300,000 people,[1] and was expected to grow seasonally, before the winter was over. The presence of a tremendous labour surplus is also shown by the gross over-fulfilment of the employment plan. Thus in the 1961–65 period employment in socialized industry grew by 1,244,000 people, as against the planned increase of only 734,000.[2] This means that the expected employment limit was exceeded by about 510,000 people, or by some 70%. In the long run the situation may well become much worse, for reasons which I shall explain below.

The real point is that the whole employment issue is more complicated than a mere imbalance between available manpower and capital resources. They claim that by using all available investment means they would be able to provide some 1·5 million new places of work by 1970[3] to absorb the whole net increase in the *urban* labour force and a small spill-over from the countryside after the total manpower in agriculture is frozen at the present level. But in this case they may well have no resources left to increase real wages. This dilemma was put in a nutshell by the régime's own weekly *Polityka* in which it was

[1] According to official figures there were 58,422 registered unemployed persons in Poland on 1 December 1966 (cf. *Biuletyn Statystyczny*, 1/67, 14). However *Życie Gospodarcze*, 7/57, has estimated that this official figure has to be multiplied by five to arrive at the actual unemployment. Thus a realistic estimate of the current unemployment figure is about 290,000–300,000. The discrepancy between the official figures and the actual number of jobless is due to the fact that most unemployed do not bother to register since there are no unemployment benefits in Poland, barring exceptional circumstances. Remarks at the bottom of the unemployment tables in *Biuletyn Statystyczny* underline the fact that official figures are incomplete.

[2] *Trybuna Ludu* (Warsaw), 11 February 1966. Communiqué on the National Economic Plan fulfilment in 1965.

[3] *Życie Gospodarcze* (Warsaw), 12 April 1964.

stated about a year ago: 'One thing is certain and we must all realize that. The population must choose: either additional, significant growth of employment, or *limited employment* and *a better growth of real wages*. There is no third way.'[1] In the past the régime has chosen to increase employment (as we have seen) at the cost of real wages. For instance during the whole five-year period 1961–65, the average real wage increased by only 8%[2] as against the planned target of 23–25%,[3] and a rise in income per head of about 25%. (Incidentally in 1966 the real wage increased by 3%[4] and is expected to grow by another 2% in 1967.[5] In other words, either full employment and stagnation of the living standards of the employed, or some rise in the standards for these latter, at the price of a fairly substantial unemployment.

Neither solution is politically acceptable for the Polish régime. And the central planners in Warsaw assert that by 1970 they can both provide enough new jobs (1,562,000 to be exact)[6] to ensure work for everybody *and* raise real wages by some 10%.[7]

But this assertion is based on several assumptions, none of which can be considered realistic in the light of the past performance of the Polish economy and to prevailing social and economic trends.

First of all it is assumed that during the 1966–70 period there will be no significant migration of the *present* surplus labour from the countryside to the towns. In other words it is hoped that the 1·5 million new jobs will all be available to the new entrants into the labour market and that the manpower in agriculture will remain unchanged at the 1965 level.[8] This

[1] Cf. *Polityka* (Warsaw), 26 February 1966 (emphasis supplied).

[2] *Trybuna Ludu* (Warsaw), 11 February 1966. Communiqué on the National Economic Plan fulfilment in 1965 and preliminary assessments of the 1961–65 results.

[3] Cf. Jedrychowski, speech at the III Party Congress, *Nowe Drogi*, 4/59 (Warsaw), 130.

[4] *Trybuna Ludu* (Warsaw), 8 February 1967. Communiqué on National Economic Plan fulfilment in 1966.

[5] Unsigned editorial, 'Basic Tasks of the National Economic Plan for 1967', *Gospodarka Planowa*, 1/67 (Warsaw), 4.

[6] Unsigned editorial, 'The Program for a Universal Development of our Country' *Nowe Drogi*, 12/66 (Warsaw), 7.   [7] *Ibid.*

[8] Cf. *Życie Gospodarcze*, 12 April 1964. This periodical reports on the meeting of the Polish Economic Society (PTE). During the proceedings this learned gremium

8

assumption is not only contrary to past experience in Poland, but to the generally prevailing attitude of rural youth, which as elsewhere in the world tends to migrate to the cities in search of better paid jobs, better working conditions, shorter hours and more attractive social life. The Polish countryside is still very much overcrowded and labour productivity on the farms is low. The introduction of more machines and other labour-saving equipment will inevitably decrease demand for man-power. Significant migration to the towns would thus hardly be prevented.

The second optimistic assumption is that in the course of implementing the 1966–70 plan, no major difficulties will arise which would necessitate switching investment means and concentrating them on those sectors of the economy which are in serious trouble. Such an assumption is again contradicted by past experience. In all previous Five-Year Plans in Poland (as well as in the Six-Year Plan 1949–55), after the initial period of intensive over-investment, there came the inevitable years of retrenchment and belt-tightening. The story is always the same. Investment schedules tend to drag on. Cost estimates are exceeded and in the middle of the five-year period a major rearrangement of the investment plan becomes necessary.

The most recent example of this specific form of a Com-munist trade cycle was the breakdown of the Polish 1960–65 Plan in the winter of 1962/63.[1] But the same pattern was clearly discernible in the previous five-year periods. The usual result is that some investment projects have to be abandoned or curtailed and the planned investment expenditure in the so-called 'productive' sector has to be raised at the expense of the funds earmarked originally for the increase in the living standards and for investments in the 'unproductive' sector. The net effect is that (because of unrealistic cost estimates) the implementation of the investment projects falls below the planned target, while the intended increase in real wages fails

---

expressed grave doubts whether employment plans can be based on the assumption that during the 1966–70 period the labour force in agriculture would remain unchanged. The meeting expressed the view that the 1·5 million increase in em-ployment should be considered a minimum.

[1] Cf. Politbureau Report submitted to the XIV Plenum of Polish CC, 'An analysis of the economic situation on the basis of the first three years of the Five-Year Plan', *Nowe Drogi*, 12/63 (Warsaw), 3–30.

to materialize. During the 1961–65 period for instance the investment plan was fulfilled only 98·4%[1] (despite a substantial switch-over of funds from the so-called 'unproductive' to 'productive' investments) and instead of a 23% increase in real wages a (highly disputable) 8% growth was officially registered.[2]

Finally the central planners in Warsaw apparently failed to take into account a very real possibility that the introduction of a more strict cost accounting method and the adoption of profit, as the main measuring rod of economic performance at the enterprise level, may well result in substantial lay-offs of the existing manpower in the profit minded undertakings (as well as wholesale dismissals of labour due to closing down of uneconomic enterprises). This is not only possible, but highly probable. Both the experience of other Communist-bloc countries, where economic reform is more advanced[3] and the initial effects of the application of the new system in Poland[4] are certainly pointing in that direction. To realize what savings in labour costs are possible in Poland one has only to point out that a firm of Western efficiency experts, invited to assess the performance of 'Ursus Mechanical Works' near Warsaw, has advised the management of that tractor-producing enterprise that, with a better organization of work and with the application of modern time-and-motion-study techniques, the production tasks assigned to this factory in the 1966–70 plan could be fulfilled with a labour force of only 12,400, instead of one of 22,500 provided for by the plan.[5]

Should the optimistic assumptions of the Polish planners prove false, as they are almost certainly bound to do, then the

[1] *Trybuna Ludu* (Warsaw), 11 February 1966. Communiqué on National Economic Plan fulfilment in 1966.

[2] *Ibid.*

[3] Within the framework of the New Economic Model, both Czechoslovakia and Hungary have begun to close down uneconomic mines and enterprises, as well as cutting down the labour force in the remaining factories. In Czechoslovakia it is estimated that some 105,000 workers would lose their jobs as the result of these efficiency measures (Cf. *Rude Pravo*, 24 March 1965). Some efficiency promoting layoffs were also reported from the Soviet Union (cf. *Ekonomicheska Gazieta*, 13 October 1965).

[4] Cf. Resolution of the October 1966 Polish Central Committee Plenum, 'Concerning the tasks in respect of improving the organization of work and management in the enterprises', *Trybuna Ludu* (Warsaw), 1 November 1966.

[5] J. Redlich, 'Vitamin O', *Życie Warszawy* (Warsaw), 16 September 1966.

influx of surplus manpower from the countryside would prove much greater than expected; despite a switch-over from 'unproductive to productive' investments the underestimation of costs in the plan would turn out to be so great that fewer new work places will be available by 1970; and mass lay-offs due to the drive for greater efficiency, will further increase the existing pool of unemployed. This would make the employment dilemma far more complex than it already is. And it certainly is difficult enough.

The post-war population bulge came in Poland a bit later than in most Western countries. But between 1950 and 1955 a peak birth-rate in the range of 763,000–794,000 per year was registered.[1] This population bulge will be entering the labour market during the 1966–70 period at a rate of some 620,000 in the first two years and at about 670,000 beginning with 1968.[2] Thus, even with the normal retirements and deaths, the Polish planners would find it rather difficult to keep the net increase in labour force (outside agriculture) at the level of some 300,000 per year.[3] The only real solution of the problem posed by the population bulge would be to make full employment rather than growth of national income (let alone real wages) the objective number one of the national economic policy.[4] But the Polish planners flatly refuse to change their standard order of priorities.

The situation on the labour market in Poland will not become really acute until after the usual initial construction boom of a new Five-Year Plan period is over, say by the second half of 1968. I would say therefore that the 1967 employment target of a 303,000 net increase in the labour force (outside agriculture)[5] is again likely to be exceeded by some 10–15% (mainly in distribution and in the services). The situation would probably be similar to that in 1966, when the planned net increase in work force (274,000) was exceeded by some 27,000

[1] *Rocznik Statystyczny (Statistical Yearbook)*, 1966, p. 51.

[2] E. Rosset, '1965–70 In the eyes of a demograph', *Trybuna Ludu* (Warsaw), 7 March 1964.

[3] Unsigned editorial, 'The Program for a Universal Development of our Country', *Nowe Drogi*, 12/66 (Warsaw), 6–7.

[4] Such full-employment oriented policy was indeed advocated by some Polish economists – for instance: 'Employment 1966–1970' – a series of two articles by B. Fick, *Życie Gospodarcze*, 13/66 and 14/66 (Warsaw).

[5] Op. cit., *Nowe Drogi*, 12/66 (Warsaw), 7.

people.[1] By contemporary Polish standards such a 10% discrepancy between the employment target and the actual implementation is by no means substantial.

However, by 1970 the situation may well become much worse. Even if half a million new work places are created by then, which I doubt, this will not, in my opinion, provide sufficient employment opportunities for the then available manpower reserves. We have already seen the general reasons for this. But also in particular the 1970 employment target (9·7 million) is based on a purely mechanical balance of net increase in labour force (after the unrealistic assumption about rural manpower) with the expected supply of new work places resulting from the investment effort. No account has been taken of the normal difficulty of matching jobs with qualifications and of problems of labour mobility.

I would say therefore that despite the fact that the 1970 employment target of 9·7 million people[2] (outside agriculture) is likely to be quite substantially exceeded, global unemployment in Poland is bound to increase – perhaps to the level of 600,000–750,000. The actual level of unemployment would, of course, depend on what the Party authorities would consider politically tolerable. They may insist on strict cost accounting procedure in the enterprises and swell the number of the jobless. Or they may return to past practices of turning a blind eye to the economic evils of over-employment for the sake of political and ideological, perhaps also social, expediency. But with the fixed limits of the so-called 'wage fund' this can only be done at the expense of average earnings and the planned growth in the value of average real wage.

As already noted, the average real wage is expected to increase by 10% during the five-year period 1966–70. This is mainly a statistical growth, which does not take much account of the actual cost of living increase as reflected in the so-called 'unofficial' price hikes. These are a common practice in Poland, the essence of it being that a cheaper brand of, say, washing powder (or any other staple commodity) disappears from the

[1] *Życie Gospodarcze* (Warsaw), 19 February 1967, an editorial note 'Employment in 1966'. Incidentally it is disclosed in that note that the employment target in the socialized sector was exceeded by 43,000 people. (The plan: 8,519,000 – actual employment at the end of the year 8,562,000.)

[2] Op. cit., *Nowe Drogi*, 12/66 (Warsaw), 7.

shops and a new 'luxury' brand (much more expensive, but hardly different in quality) is offered instead. The price of the cheaper brand (which is unobtainable) is still used, however, in evaluating the cost of living index.[1]

Thus the value of real wage is over-estimated to start with. But the pressure exerted on the labour market may well make it impossible to attain even this problematic growth of real wage. This may not yet be the case in 1967, when the modest planned increase of 2%[2] may well be reached. But by 1970 other factors may well intervene. First of all, excessive employment may slow down the expected growth of nominal wages. Secondly the implementation of economic reforms and the pursuance of the profit motive may well result in some unanticipated *official* price increases. Czechoslovak and Hungarian experience certainly points in that direction. Finally any serious difficulty in implementing the investment plan may well force the authorities to dip into the reserves earmarked originally for the increase in living standards. After all this did happen in the past with monotonous regularity.

On the other hand, the 10% increase in the average real wage planned for 1970 is the most modest one in the history of the Polish Five-Year Plans. If no serious problems should arise in the course of implementing the Plan (both on the investment sector and on agriculture) it may well be reached (if only in terms of official statistics). The 1970 target is this time near enough the 8% growth actually achieved (again in statistical terms) in the 1961–65 period.[3]

Another weak spot of the Polish economy is foreign trade. The basic problem here can be defined quite simply: how to earn enough foreign exchange (both exchange roubles and hard currency) to pay for the essential imports. This is a problem which every underdeveloped and swiftly industrializing country has inevitably to face. But in Poland the problem is made more difficult by several factors.

[1] Several of the régime's own papers have protested against such practices, but in vain. See: A. Bober, 'The button hole in a shirt is no novelty', *Życie Warszawy* (Warsaw), 14 December 1965, or unsigned editorial 'When would the secret price increases end?', *Życie Warszawy* (Warsaw), 3 February 1960.

[2] Unsigned editorial, 'The main task of the National Economic Plan in 1967', *Gospodarka Planova*, 1/57 (Warsaw), 3–4

[3] *Trybuna Ludu* (Warsaw), 11 February 1966. Communiqué on the National Economic Plan Fulfilment in 1965 and the preliminary results of 1961–65.

One of them is the planner's insistence on a high rate of industrial growth to be achieved almost exclusively by new investments. This burdens the import side of the trade balance with a huge bill for imported capital equipment. Another factor is the irrational structure of Polish industry, much of which was built according to purely doctrinal considerations without any regard for the existing raw material base. In consequence, whole branches of Polish industry depend on imports for their supply of raw materials. The third factor (until now) was the huge expenditure on grain imports.

To those basic burdens one may add several more recent negative developments. One is the sharp decline in the demand for coal (a staple export product of Polish economy) and growing imports of oil. The second is the restrictive practices of the Common Market, which hinder the export potentials of Polish agricultural surpluses. Finally there is the downward trend in the dynamics of Comecon trade[1] and the growing buyers' resistance within this community. All those factors are bound to affect adversely the export side of Poland's foreign trade.

Already the results of 1966 reflect these problems and diffi- culties. The total value of exports, excluding shipping and transit rail fares, was 9,088 million exchange zlotys (2,274 million dollars) while that of imports was 9,970 million exchange zlotys (2,492·5 million dollars).[2] Thus there was a visible trade deficit amounting to some 218·5 million dollars. That there was a true payments deficit outside the Comecon we may well infer, but presumably invisible exports as usual brought about a payments surplus within the Comecon. But this was not the whole story. The 1966 results reflect first of all the much slower growth of inter-Comecon exchanges. While in the period 1963–65 Poland's trade turnover with other 'socialist countries' was growing at an average annual rate of 9·1%,[3] in 1966 this increase fell to 1·6%.[4] True, some of this

[1] The actual figures are: In the period 1951–5 the inter-Comecon trade grew by 95%, in the period 1956–60 by 71%, in 1961–65 by 55% and the expected increase in 1966–70 is estimated at 40–50%. Cit., S. Albinowski, 'There is no smoke without fire', *Życie Warszawy* (Warsaw), 19 February 1967.

[2] *Trybuna Ludu* (Warsaw), 8 February 1967. Communiqué on the National Economic Plan Fulfilment in 1966. (The exchange zloty is a fictitious unit calculated at 4 zlotys to US dollar.)

[3] J. Niegowski, 'Foreign Trade in 1966 – a difficult beginning', *Życie Gospodarcze*, 8/67 (Warsaw), 19 February 1967.   [4] *Ibid.*

decrease was due to the introduction (as of 1 January 1966) of new agreed prices in inter-Comecon exchanges, which on the average were somewhat lower than those in force during the 1963–65 period.[1] But the main reason was simply a slower growth of interbloc trade, especially in respect of raw materials, source of energy, agricultural produce and capital goods.[2] In short, the inherent contradictions of the Comecon trade structure have come home to roost.

The slump in inter-Comecon exchanges (which is a bloc-wide phenomenon) was by no means compensated by an increase in trade with the so-called 'capitalist countries', although here the results of 1966 were relatively better. In the outside-the-bloc exchanges the total trade turnover increased by $9 \cdot 3\%$[3] – but here again the increase in imports ($14 \cdot 1\%$) was higher than that in exports. The net effect of all this was that in contrast to the previous five-year period, the percentage increase in foreign trade turnover was lower than the percentage growth of national income.[4]

Those unfavourable results reflect the specific problems of Polish foreign trade. Apart from the slump in inter-Comecon exchanges, the central planners in Warsaw are also faced with the necessity of adapting the structure of Polish exports to the rapidly changing conditions of extra-bloc trade. In 1965 about 90% of Polish exports to EEC and EFTA countries consisted of raw materials, coal and agricultural produce.[5] But in the current Five-Year Plan, this export structure would have to undergo a radical change if the relatively high growth-rate of trade with Western Europe is to be maintained. The exports of raw materials are bound to fall off because of the growing demand on the home market.[6] The prospects for increasing coal exports are hopeless and the restrictive practices of the EEC in respect of agricultural produce from third countries (the so-called 'price equalizers') are bound to affect negatively the profitability of agricultural exports.[7]

---

[1] S. Brzoska, 'Polish Foreign Trade Turnover in 1966', *Rynki Zagraniczne* (Warsaw), 4 February 1967, p. 3.
[2] J. Niegowski, 'Foreign Trade in 1966 – a difficult beginning,' *Życie Gospodarcze*, 8/67 (Warsaw), 19 February 1967.
[3] *Ibid.*   [4] *Ibid.*
[5] S. Albinowski, 'Two sides of the Coin', *Życie Warszawy* (Warsaw), 28 February 1967.   [6] *Ibid.*   [7] *Ibid.*

The consequent gap in the export revenue can be only filled by a substantial increase in exports of industrial products (both capital equipment and consumer goods). But this is easier said than done. First of all (both in respect of the EEC and of EFTA), Polish products are liable to higher import duties than those paid by their competitors. Secondly – and this is perhaps more important – with very few exceptions Polish goods cannot compete in respect of design, quality and finish with Western products. There remains always the alternative of dumping, but this is never a rational long term solution.

For all those reasons, the future prospects of Polish foreign trade are rather bleak. True, the 1970 goals are modest. It is foreseen that during the 1966–70 period the foreign trade turnover will increase by 30·6% (imports by 33%, exports by 28%).[1] This compares with a 62% growth of trade exchanges in the years 1961–65.[2] However, taking into account the unfavourable results of 1966 and their long-term implications, it seems rather doubtful to me if even this modest growth rate can be reached. The objective difficulties in both intra and extra-Comecon trade are just too great. The 1970 Plan targets are based on the assumption that the structure of visible exports would change considerably. The share of coal and raw materials is to decrease from 35% in 1965 to 28% in 1970 and that of agricultural produce from 18% in 1965 to 11% in 1970.[3] On the other hand the share of capital goods is to increase from 35% in 1965 to 44% in 1970 and a substantial growth in exports of consumer goods is also anticipated.[4] I just don't believe that it can be done.

During 1967 the Polish planners want to increase their visible foreign trade turnover by 8·1%.[5] The 1966 proportions are to be reversed: imports are to grow by only 4·3%, and exports by a substantial 12·4%.[6] My estimate is that the

---

[1] Cf. Jedrychowski's Exposé in Polish Parliament – 'The main assumptions concerning the development of the national economy in 1966–70', *Trybuna Ludu* (Warsaw), 22 September 1966.

[2] *Trybuna Ludu* (Warsaw), 11 February 1966. Communiqué on the National Economic Plan fulfilment in 1965 and the preliminary results of 1961–65.

[3] Jedrychowski's Exposé, op. cit., *Trybuna Ludu* (Warsaw), 22 September 1966.

[4] *Ibid.*

[5] Unsigned editorial, 'The basic tasks of the National Economic Plan for 1967', *Gospodarka Planowa*, 1/67 (Warsaw), 1.   [6] *Ibid.*

increase in visible trade turnover at the end of the year will be below the 8·1% target, that the expected growth rate of imports will be exceeded, while the assumed increase in exports will not materialize. The same is true, to a still greater extent, as far as the 1970 targets are concerned. Incidentally the non-fulfilment of the export plan, especially to the hard currency areas, may well create additional balance of payments difficulties, since a significant amount of foreign credits is due for repayment both in 1967 and in the remainder of the current Five-Year Plan period.[1]

During the 1956–60 period and, to a lesser degree, during the 1961–65 one (especially until 1963) the success of the export plan depended to a considerable extent on the results of agricultural production. In the current five-year period the size of agricultural surpluses will not materially affect the income from exports. The limiting factors are now rather 'price equalizers', quotas and other trade barriers. However, good agricultural results may still help to ameliorate the balance of trade position, if grain imports could be reduced, or better still dispensed with altogether. This is why self-sufficiency in grain output is the main objective of the 1966–70 plan on agriculture.[2]

Can this aim be realized? Any predictions in respect of future agricultural output are notoriously risky. In 1965–66 Poland had two consecutive good harvests, with the grain output exceeding 15 million tons – 15·7 million tons in 1965[3] and 15·5 million tons in 1966.[4]

The main question is, can this luck be maintained? The Five-Year Plan targets in agriculture anticipate increases of 15·8–18·1% in crop production and 14·1–17·3% in livestock.[5] This relationship is aimed at achieving the planned increase

---

[1] During the 1966–70 period a substantial part of the US agricultural credits granted in the years 1957–60 is due for repayment. There is always a possibility, however, that the US government will accept part payment in zlotys. A concrete proposal concerning the amount due in 1967 was already made by Washington.

[2] PAP release: 'The Five-Year Plan in Agriculture', *Trybuna Ludu* (Warsaw), 1 October 1966.

[3] *Trybuna Ludu* (Warsaw), 11 February 1966. Communiqué on the National Plan fulfilment in 1965.

[4] *Trybuna Ludu* (Warsaw), 8 February 1967. Communiqué on the National Plan fulfilment in 1966.

[5] Jedrychowski's Exposé, op. cit., *Trybuna Ludu* (Warsaw), 22 September 1966.

in livestock mainly on the basis of domestically produced grain fodder. The expected increase in grain output is to be realized almost exclusively by intensive methods. The average yield per hectare is to grow from 17·1 cwt. in the 1962–66 period to 20–21 cwt. in 1970.[1]

These may seem rather optimistic estimates, but – barring a series of bad harvests – I consider these targets quite realistic. First of all they are near enough the actual average growth rates achieved in the recent years. Secondly, the current Five-Year Plan allocates much larger resources for the development of agriculture than any previous plan. The share of agricultural investment in the total is to increase from 14% in the 1961–65 period to 18% in the 1966–70.[2]

But there are also other factors which would tend to promote higher agricultural output. First of all, the régime now offers the individual farmers (who after all are the decisive element since they own 85·3% of all arable land[3]) much better prices for agricultural produce and additional material incentives. Secondly, the supply of fertilizers is to increase considerably. And finally, after many years of hesitation, the government has decided to proceed with the process of amalgamation of individual peasant holdings. Polish agricultural economists have calculated that only by eliminating the problem of scattered strips of land, can the grain production in Poland be increased by an additional 1·5 million tons or 75% of the present grain deficit.[4]

1965 was an exceptionally good agricultural year and grain output increased some 13% over the average global yield of 1961–64.[5] 1966 was also an above average year, with a grain output only slightly lower than in 1965. In their 1967 estimates the Polish planners played it safe and budgeted for only 1·8% increase in the crop output in relation to 1963–66 average, which in real terms actually means that they expect the grain output to decline slightly from the 1966 level.[6] I

---

[1] Jedrychowski's Exposé, op. cit., *Trybuna Ludu* (Warsaw), 22 September 1966.
[2] *Ibid.*   [3] *Rocznik Statystyczny (Statistical Yearbook)*, 1966, p. 229.
[4] Prof. R. Manteuffel, 'Cumbersome Checkerboard', *Życie Warszawy* (Warsaw), 13 January 1967.
[5] *Trybuna Ludu* (Warsaw), 11 February 1966. Communiqué on the National Economic Plan fulfilment in 1965.
[6] Unsigned editorial; 'The basic tasks of the National Economic Plan for 1967', *Gospodarka Planowa*, 1/57 (Warsaw), 2.

would say that this cautious estimate will be exceeded, as will the planned 8% increase in livestock (again in relation to 1963–66 average). The available stocks of fodder grain due to two consecutive good harvests should permit a more substantial increase in the number of both cattle and pigs.

I am equally optimistic about the 1970 prospects. Barring a series of bad harvests, the grain output should reach 17–17·5 million tons, which would be more than enough to eliminate the problem of grain imports and to provide a sound fodder basis for the expected increase in livestock.

The final agricultural results (whatever they are) will have a definite bearing on the level of mass consumption and the standard of living as well as on the general economic conditions in the country. After all in Poland some 49·4% of the average working-class family budget is still being spent on food.[1] A relatively plentiful supply of food tends always to correct the imbalance between the total purchasing power and the available market supplies. Conversely, food shortages tend to increase inflationary pressures within the Polish economy and often push the régime to adopt retrenchment measures. This makes the performance of agriculture far more significant than it may seem. For better or for worse, the fluctuations in food supplies have a much greater influence on the general economic situation in Poland than the fulfilment or non-fulfilment of the industrial production targets by a couple of per cent.

Employment, foreign trade and agriculture are the most neuralgic sectors of Polish economy. But the actual performance of this economy in the forthcoming years is likely to be affected by two other factors of a more subjective nature. Both belong to the realm of politics rather than economics. One is the peculiar way in which the Gomulka régime is running the economy, the other is the inconsistencies of the Polish economic model.

One of the great shortcomings of the present rulers of Poland is that they are seemingly unable to evolve a clear-cut and consistent long-term economic policy, with firmly established objectives. Their methods of planning are purely mechanical and are limited, as a rule, to an attempt to achieve a purely

[1] *Biuletyn Statystyczny*, 1/67 (Warsaw), 46, Table 60 (this percentage includes alcohol, but not tobacco).

formal and temporary balance between available resources and the ideologically oriented policy aims. Their approach to the crucial issue of employment is a typical example of this method of planning.

The result is that when something goes wrong, as has happened many times in the past, economic decisions are usually made on day-to-day basis and *ad hoc* measures are adopted to deal with a particular contingency. Due regard is not paid to the likely side-effects of those measures in other sectors of economy. The best example here is the periodic mass lay-offs of workers to boost the falling labour productivity indices and to keep the wage fund expenditure within the limits prescribed by the plan.[1] These measures usually bring some temporary relief in the endangered sectors, but the subsequent dislocation of production targets sooner or later forces the enterprise managers to rehire approximately the same number of workers they dismissed previously.

One has to remember also that within the leadership of the Polish Communist Party (PUWP) there are at least two groups advocating different economic policies. Practical decisions usually represent some sort of compromise. The final arbiter in determining economic policy is Gomulka, who has little understanding of economic problems and usually tries to maintain a balance between the 'pragmatists' and the 'hard-liners' within the party leadership and the conflicting policies they advise him to follow.

Another complicating factor is Poland's half-way system of planning and management. Here again Gomulka's compromise approach to economic problems is at fault. Under the pressure of 'pragmatists' the Party leadership has twice embarked upon a program of economic reforms.[2] But both times it has clearly shown that it lacks the political will to carry the reformist measures to their logical conclusion. The result was that the 'dogmatist' wing was able to reassert its influence and every

[1] Within the last ten years three major lay-off actions were initiated by the Party leadership in Poland: one in the spring of 1958, another in the winter of 1964, and still another at the end of 1966. In all cases employment in socialized industry returned to 'normal' after an interval of a few months.

[2] Once in the 1956/57 period, when the much bolder version of the 'Polish Economic Model' was worked out, and again in mid-1964 when the IV Congress of PUWP approved a mini-program of economic reforms.

pragmatic measure was hedged with bureaucratic safeguards, which tend to perpetuate the basic elements of arbitrary decision making and direct administrative control.

In consequence what has evolved in Poland is an unworkable system of planning and management, in which elements of the 'new economic model' and pragmatic approach are mixed with elements of ultra-centralist planning and administrative control in a way that permits neither of them to work effectively. For those reasons the Polish Party was unable to create an efficient machinery of economic management which would make it possible to put a consistent long-term economic policy into effect, if such a policy existed. And these are the additional complicating factors which make it more difficult to implement the National Economic Plan.

APPENDIX

(1) *National Income*. The FYP 1966–70 assumes that the national income (in constant 1965 prices) will increase by some 34%[1] over the 1965 level. This means an annual average growth of 5·9–6%. An increase of 'about 6%' was in fact registered in 1966,[2] but only a 3·4% rise in the national income is predicted for 1967.[3] Since the value of the national income in 1965 (in the current 1965 prices) was 563·8 billion[4] zlotys,[5] its 1967 value should reach some 590 billion zlotys and its 1970 value 716–718 billion zlotys (in constant 1965 prices). I consider that both estimates are realistic (within the limits set by the vagaries of agricultural output). First of all, they are well within the limits of growth achieved in the previous (rather difficult) 1961–65 period. Secondly, a larger percentage of new products (the national constant prices of which are as a rule relatively high) is bound to swell the value of national income by 1970.

(2) *Consumption*. The FYP assumes a 27% increase in total consumption (the so called consumption fund), or 20% per head of population, and a 25% growth of private consumption (18% per head):[6] both in 1965 constant prices. This amounts

---

[1] Jedrychowski's Exposé, op. cit., *Trybuna Ludu* (Warsaw), 22 September 1966.
[2] *Trybuna Ludu* (Warsaw) 8 February 1967 (1966 plan results).
[3] *Gospodarka Planowa*, 1/67 (1967 plan targets).   [4] 1 billion = 10^9.
[5] *Rocznik Statystyczny (Statistical Yearbook)*, 1966, p. 76.
[6] Jedrychowski's Exposé, op. cit., *Trybuna Ludu* (Warsaw), 22 September 1966.

to an average annual increase of 5%. In 1966 an increase of 'about 6%' was actually registered[1] mainly thanks to exceptionally good agricultural results of 1965 and the consequent above-normal growth of food supplies. For 1967 a modest 2·6% increase in private consumption is foreseen.[2] Predictions are difficult, because of vagaries of agricultural output and changing consumption patterns (especially noticeable in Poland). But I would say that the 1967 estimate would be exceeded (good agricultural results in 1966). On the other hand, I have some doubts about the 1970 target, mainly because by then the cost of housing construction will be passed on almost *in toto* to the population, which will reduce income available for other things.[3] The growth of consumption would be also unevenly distributed. Because of a mainly statistical growth of real wages (explained in my main contribution), the main beneficiaries of increased private consumption would be the families with new wage earners.[4] On the basis of all this, as well as the past performances, I would say that the 1970 target of a 25% growth in private consumption will not be reached. A further reason is that the Polish economy (because of its inefficient model) shows a constant tendency for the dynamics of growth of production to be exceeded by that of the stocks.[5]

(3) *Investments.* The FYP 1966–70 provides for an expenditure of 840 billion zlotys (in constant 1965 prices) for investment purposes.[6] This is about 37·5% more than in the 1961–65 period.[7] The share of net investments in national income will increase from 17·1% in 1965 to 18·7% in 1970.[8] (The share of total accumulation is, of course, much bigger.) In 1966 net

[1] *Trybuna Ludu* (Warsaw), 8 February 1967 (1966 plan results).

[2] *Gospodarka Planowa*, 1/67, (1967 plan targets).

[3] The now existing housing allowance, which covers a part of the increased rents of public housing (but not the payments for co-operative housing), will probably be consumed by the wage increases. For the provision is that one-half of the value of the wage increase is deducted from the housing allowance received by the head of the family.

[4] This is frankly admitted by régime's own sources, cf. G. Pisarski 'Consumption 1966–70', *Życie Gospodarcze*, 29 May 1966.

[5] For instance in 1966 for every 1% growth of industrial output there was a 1·65% increase in stocks. Cf. *Życie Gospodarcze* 5 March 1967.

[6] Jedrychowski's Exposé, op. cit., *Trybuna Ludu* (Warsaw), 22 September 1966.

[7] *Ibid.*   [8] *Ibid.*

investment expenditure was 132·4 billion zlotys – an increase of 7·6% over the 1965 figure[1] and another 8% increase is foreseen for 1967.[2]

Investment expenditure estimates in Poland can never be considered realistic because of the notorious practice of deliberately under-estimating the cost of the new investment projects. Also the construction periods tend to drag on. This time however the situation is somewhat better than in previous plans, since for the first time a central investment reserve is now available. Of the 840 billion zlotys earmarked for investment purposes only 816 billions were actually allocated, while 24 billions are held in reserve at the disposal of the central planners.[3] Of the reserve only 6 billion zlotys may be used in the first three years of the FYP, i.e. until 1968, 5 billion in 1969 and 13 billion in 1970.[4] This gives the planners the necessary means to prop up investment plans on the danger sectors. Besides this time the implementation of investment plans is a condition *sine qua non* of avoiding a substantial growth of unemployment (as explained in my contribution). I am willing to risk the prediction that the investment targets may well be reached, if only in terms of global expenditure. (I doubt if all the investment projects will be completed.)

(4) *Sectoral composition of investment.* Out of the 816 billion zlotys of allocated investment expenditure some 626·8 billion are earmarked for 'productive investments' (343·6 billion in industry, 147·9 in agriculture, 85·5 transport, etc.).[5] The main position in 'unproductive investments' (189·2 billion zlotys) is housing construction – 115·7 billion, education – 30·5 billion and health and social insurance – 12·4 billion.[6] On the basis of what I said already in section (3) and the past experiences I would estimate that the 'productive investment' targets will be reached, even if at the expense of 'unproductive' ones and the living standards. The only doubtful quantity is the investments on agriculture (147·9 billion zlotys), since this figure

---

[1] *Trybuna Ludu* (Warsaw), 8 February 1967 (1966 plan results).
[2] *Gospodarka Planowa*, 1/67 (1967 plan targets).
[3] Z. Szeliga, 'How shall we spend the 840 billion?', *Polityka* (Warsaw), 10 December 1966.
[4] *Ibid.*   [5] *Ibid.*   [6] *Ibid.*

includes a substantial estimate of the private peasants' own investments. In the private sector investment decisions depend only partly on purely economic considerations and psychological factors are perhaps more important – (such as the feeling of security of tenure). But as the matters stand now I would presume that the peasants are going to invest (private peasant investment increased by 6% in 1966).[1]

(5) *Defence*. No adequate and reliable data are available.

(6) *Industrial production*. The planned growth of industrial production foreseen in the 1966–70 FYP is generally lower than that achieved in the 1961–65 period. The relevant percentage increases are 43·6% for the current FYP,[2] as compared with 51% actually achieved in the 1961–65 period.[3] The main difference between the two plans, however, is a substantial decrease in the disparity between the growth rates foreseen for group A and group B. In the 1961–65 FYP this disparity amounted to 21·2 points, in the current one it is reduced to 11·2 points.[4]

A particularly high growth-rate has been planned for the following industries: chemicals (80%), electrical (68%), machine and metal construction (60%), and especially for those manufacturing industries which are working for export (92%).[5] Roughly the same proportions are retained in the plan for 1967.[6] I would predict that the 43·6% growth rate for the global industrial production would be easily implemented and perhaps quite substantially exceeded. After all the 7·5% average annual growth assumed is lower than the average of all previous plans (8·1%).[7] More important still are two other factors. Namely that the output of harvest-related industries which was planned very conservatively (24% increase)[8] is likely to be substantially increased if the expected growth of

---

[1] Editorial note 'Increases in the countryside and in the towns', *Życie Gospodarcze*, 19 February 1967.

[2] Jedrychowski's Exposé, op. cit., *Trybuna Ludu* (Warsaw), 22 September 1966.

[3] *Trybuna Ludu* (Warsaw), 11 February 1966 (the results of 1961–65).

[4] *Trybuna Ludu* (Warsaw), 10 November 1966 (final report on the 1966–70 Plan).

[5] *Ibid.*

[6] *Gospodarka Planowa*, 1/57 (1967 planned targets).

[7] *Trybuna Ludu* (Warsaw), 10 November 1966 (final report on the 1966–70 Plan).

[8] *Ibid.*

agricultural production is realized, and that the global production of 1970 is likely to include a great proportion of new and more sophisticated products, the higher prices of which are bound to swell the value of global industrial output. The now available central investment reserve will also (hopefully) prevent the delays in the construction time of the new investment projects. I would say therefore that in the 1966–70 period the disparity between the growth of output of group A and group B will decrease substantially, that metal-working industries will undergo a process of sophistication, which is bound to be reflected in a more highly priced output and that the harvest-related industries will easily exceed their planned targets (particularly in 1967, but possibly in the whole FYP period as well). The only critical area is fuel and power industry, where the switch over from (home produced) coal to (imported) oil may well create severe difficulties, while electric energy supplies are notoriously in short supply.

(7) *Agricultural production.* See pp. 224–6.

(8) *Construction volume.* Only the data pertaining to housing are adequate and reliable. The 1966–70 plan provides for a 115·7 billion zlotys expenditure on housing construction,[1] which is less than the actual expenditure for this purpose in the 1961–65 period. This is explained by the fact that a much larger percentage of the total cost of financing the housing construction is to be borne by the population. The bulk of the new apartments (55–60%) is to be made available by the housing co-operatives, and not by the subsidized state-owned housing. The plan calls for some 975,000 urban apartments to be constructed during the 1966–70 period and foresees a slight reduction of density per room from 1·40 persons in 1965 to 1·37 in 1970.[2] But otherwise the actual apartment construction plans are not very precise.

In 1966 174,500 new urban apartments were built[3] as against 169,000 in 1965.[4] I would say that another 175,000–

[1] Op. cit. *Polityka* (Warsaw), 10 December 1966, urban housing plus rural housing paid for by the state. Subsequent figures are urban only.
[2] Jedrychowski's Exposé, op. cit., *Trybuna Ludu* (Warsaw), 22 September 1966.
[3] *Trybuna Ludu* (Warsaw), 8 February 1967 (1966 plan results).
[4] *Gospodarka Planowa*, 2/67.

180,000 will be constructed in 1967. At this rate the target of 975,000 new apartments by 1970 may well be reached, but only just. However in all previous FYPs the housing construction targets were always reduced in the course of the plan implementation and the investment means earmarked for this purpose were systematically raided to fill the gaps elsewhere. I am inclined to say therefore that the housing construction plan will not be fulfilled either in 1967 or in the whole 1966–70 period. Industrial investment – because of the employment situation – is bound to have an absolute priority.

(9) *Exports*. See pp. 220–4. In addition I would only say that the present percentage of turnover with Communist bloc countries (60%) is likely to be further reduced.

18

POLAND

BOGDAN MIECZKOWSKI, 1968

Having been asked by the Editor to make comments on Michael Gamarnikow's paper of last year I find myself in the unenviable position of trying to better one of the expert observers of the current economic scene in Poland. Even with the benefit of the hindsight this is a difficult task in view of Gamarnikow's thorough analysis. I will proceed step by step, covering the same points which Gamarnikow did last year, and then adding some new ones. My emphasis will be on change, rather than on static description.

EMPLOYMENT

Employment rose in 1967 by 3·9% to an average for the year of 8,890,000.[1] The rate of increase was higher than in 1966, when it was 3·7%,[2] and it was higher than the planned increase, as forecast by Gamarnikow. This over-fulfilment of the Plan was a continuation of the 1961–65 trend established by the preceding Five-Year Plan, when employment rose by 17·5% as against the planned rise of 8·6%, while labor productivity rose by 28·3%, against the 40·1% planned rise.[3] In 1966 labor productivity rose again less than planned,[4] while in 1967 it grew at a rate of 3·5%, as against the 4·6% average rate planned for the current 1966–70 Five-Year Plan.[5] 1967 saw a decline of work discipline. For instance, total unexcused absences rose by 6% in industry and by 8·6% in construction,[6] which in itself tends to hold down the rise in labor productivity,

---

[1] 'Economic results in 1967', *Nowe Drogi* (Warsaw), 3/68.

[2] *Rocznik Statystyczny*, 1967, p. 69.

[3] A. Karpinski, 'Employment and labor productivity in industry during 1961–65 period', *Gospodarka Planowa*, 1/67.

[4] W. Fronczak, 'Problems of employment and wages in 1966', *Gospodarka Planowa*, 11/67.

[5] 'Economic results in 1967', loc. cit.

[6] *Ibid.*

measured in terms of global production per worker. Lack of labor discipline, together with faulty organization of production processes were already in 1966 responsible for the loss of 334–482 million hours in industry, made up partly by 173 million overtime hours worked.[1] The deterioration of labor discipline in 1967 is likely to result in a reimposition of the stricter labor policies which in the late 1950s brought some tightening of the labor discipline.[2] For the time being, however, employment is being expanded unduly, at least as compared with effective job openings. Gamarnikow pointed out that actually there is overemployment in the sense that more workers than technologically needed are performing productive tasks. Such overemployment continues, and only more thorough reforms in the management of enterprises may eliminate it in the future. For the time being, Polish economists complain about unduly high employment,[3] stating that this is partly due to demographic pressures, and partly due to the pressures on enterprise managers to fulfill the Plan.

The postwar demographic wave has now just started to reach the labor market, with the crest of the wave expected during the next Five-Year Plan, 1971–75.[4] There will be more than twice as many new entrants into the labor force as during the 1950s. At a time when opening a new job requires an investment of about half-a-million zlotys[5] this poses a prodigious problem. In addition, however, there exists a large army of presently unemployed or underemployed. Here I take issue with Gamarnikow who reports the 1966 unemployment at about 300,000. I have estimated this number to be more than two million persons, including those currently underemployed.[6]

[1] W. Fronczak, 'Problems of employment and wages in 1966'.

[2] Stricter labor discipline has been introduced during the first half of 1968. See I. Wolberg, 'Changes in the code of labor discipline', Praca i Zabezpieczenie Społeczne, 5/68.

[3] E.g., G. Pisarski, 'Among problems of market equilibrium', Nowe Drogi, 8/67 and A. Gutowski, 'Modernization: Increase in labor productivity', Życie Gospodarcze, 29/67.

[4] W. Szyndler-Głowacki, 'Demographic dilemmas', Życie Gospodarcze, 6/68.

[5] M. Kabaj, 'Rational employment', Polityka Gospodarcza Polski Ludowej, part I (3rd ed., Warsaw, 1965), p. 161.

[6] B. Mieczkowski, 'Poland: More Workers than Jobs?', East Europe, 3/66, p. 22. Gamarnikow gave a figure based on estimated under-registering in employment offices. My estimate, which like his covered only the socialized sector and, consequently, excluded almost all of the hidden agricultural unemployment, took

An excellent recent article in the leading Polish journal devoted to planning estimates excess labor supply during the current Five-Year Plan, without new entrants and without under-employment, at almost one million.[1] This would appear to be the same thing as estimating present rural and urban un-employment at one million. On top of this comes hidden agricultural and industrial under-employment, the latter reported by Gamarnikow to amount in one factory on the periphery of Warsaw (which is not considered a labor-surplus area) to 45%. With a socialized industry and construction employment of almost 4·5 million in 1966[2] such percentage, if representative, would amount to two million persons! Whatever then our method of estimation, the officially published figures (57,500 out of a labor force outside agriculture of about $8\frac{1}{2}$ million in 1966, or just two-thirds of one per cent) seem grossly inadequate.[3] It is paradoxical that in this situation official spokesmen deride the notion of unemployment in a planned economy, while at the same time arguing in favor of limiting additions to employment. During the 1961–65 Five-Year Plan employment in the socialized sector rose over half a million above the planned increase.[4] If just the planned employment targets were achieved, no communist economist would talk about unemployment either.

The plan for 1968 determines a rise in employment of only 3·1% (as against an actual 3·9% rise in 1967), despite rising

account of estimated over-employment due to which there is not enough work to go around with resulting idleness on the job. Under-employment may be equated with unemployment insofar as, given a state of technology, a certain output can be produced, say, either with 75% of the labor force while 25% is unemployed, or with 100% of the labor force, the marginal output of the last 25% being zero. The communist systems tend to approximate to the latter example.

[1] W. Przelaskowski, 'Demographic aspects of economic planning', *Gospodarka Planowa*, 12/67, p. 28. The Soviet Union also experiences some unemployment problems, as stated by a Soviet economist, M. S. Sonin, in *Zycie Gospodarcze*, 43/67.

[2] *Rocznik Statystyczny*, 1967, p. 69.

[3] For a defense of official figures, see T. Kochanowicz, 'Employment and the demographic situation', *Nowe Drogi*, 5/67; for their criticism, see M. Kabaj, 'Rational Employment', p. 182. After showing the existence of industrial under-employment (pp. 173–4), Kabaj states: 'Experience teaches that not all of those who are looking for work register at employment offices. ... The worse the situation is, and thus the harder it is to obtain work that way, the fewer people probably register at employment offices.' (p. 182).

[4] *Polityka Gospodarcza Polski Ludowej*, op. cit., part I, p. 111.

numbers of new entrants into the labor force. A reasonable forecast would then envisage rising unemployment, most of it hidden, as at present. Three alleviating elements, however, are present in this situation. One is that at the end of 1967 much of industry was freed from maximum employment quotas,[1] which will tend in the future to raise the actual rate of additions to employment still more above the planned one than was true in the past. Unless, that is, a clear break takes place away from the usual communist practice of stressing gross production achievements, about which more will be said below. Incidentally, some pronouncements indicate a tightening-up of the employment limits, which would in itself tend to worsen the employment situation.[2]

Another alleviating element is the fostered growth of private handicraft. The current Five-Year Plan envisages a 64·5% growth in the services of private handicraft, which during the 1965–66 period achieved 18·7% of the 1965–70 rise. In order to achieve the full goal of the Five-Year Plan the rise of production in that sector would have to be accelerated during the 1968–70 period.[3] To be sure, private handicraft is like a drop in the bucket, employing at the end of 1966 only 278,000 persons, barely 22·7% above the 1958 level,[4] but it is a tinted drop, the pigmentation from which colors a larger part of the contents of the bucket. Under the demographic pressure and as the result of widespread dissatisfaction with the level of state-provided services the central planners decided to encourage the growth of private handicraft. Already during 1966 the revenues of private handicraft rose by 20%, as compared with a 9–10% rise during the preceding period[5] as a result of earlier tax concessions. At the beginning of 1967 several, on the face of it, far-reaching fiscal measures were adopted further to promote handicraft development: (1) the handicraft income tax was lowered; (2) the handicraft turnover tax was lowered;

---

[1] According to the Chairman of the Planning Commission, Stefan Jedrychowski, as broadcast by Radio Warsaw, 20 December 1967. Radio Free Europe monitoring release, 21 December 1967.

[2] W. Dudzinski, 'In the third year . . .', *Życie Gospodarcze*, 2/68.

[3] J. Libhard, 'About the development of services for the population during the period 1966–70', *Wiadomosci Statystyczne*, 10/67.

[4] *Rocznik Statystyczny*, 1967, p. 597.

[5] *Życie Gospodarcze*, 22/67, p. 8, and J. Gabjan, 'Old and new problems in the development of handicraft', *ibid.*, 49/67.

(3) the scope of these reductions was increased and the stability of handicraft was raised due to the introduction of the so-called handicraft card; (4) the right to obtain the handicraft card was broadened, in some cases including establishments with up to seven employees – a rather substantial formal increase of 'capitalistic' activity; (5) the degree of previous administrative arbitrariness was reduced by allowing the craftsman to have his tax liability fixed for a period of three years in advance, as against frequent past assessments *ex post facto*, and by allowing him to keep his card even if caught not reporting some of his income, in which case only stated penalty fees are to be imposed. The planners have obviously at last realized that the growth of private handicraft raises national income without imposing any financial demands on the state, and that handicraft production is more responsive to market expectations than the centrally directed industry. However, in view of past unpleasant experiences of craftsmen at the hands of the administration[1] it is doubtful that *temporarily* raising the profitability of handicrafts will attract sufficient numbers of new entrants to reduce visibly the pressure of unemployment in Poland. As shown below, the case of Polish agriculture proves that the communists have not reconciled themselves to a permanent presence of the private sector in their economy. Be that as it may, March 1968 saw employment in handicraft rise to about 310,000, or almost the level of end of 1947, after which there was a decline.[2]

The third element which may alleviate somewhat the unemployment problem is the new stress on labor-intensive production. Quality production is being stressed, as well as introduction of new, 'modern' products.[3] Better use is also made of industrial scrap. All this leads to a tendency to use more labor per unit of capital, thus increasing employment. How far this tendency will be allowed to go depends again on the enterprise success indicators selected by central planners. So far, the indicators have led to the saving of human labor, inter alia because of a rule that the wage fund should not

[1] See B. Mieczkowski, 'An assessment of the Polish economy', *Kultura*, 7–8/61 (Paris), 140–1.
[2] *Życie Gospodarcze*, 22/68, p. 12.
[3] A. Karpinski, 'After two years of the realization of the current Five-Year Plan', *Gospodarka Planowa*, 12/67.

exceed a certain percentage of the value of planned and realized production.[1] What is proposed now is to use, instead of the net and gross rentability indicators and instead of the indicator of the rentability of manufacture, the indicator of the rate of profit, defined as

$$w_s = \frac{z}{i+o}$$

where w_s is the indicator of the rate of profit, z is the book-keeping profit, i is the value of fixed capital, and o is the value of inventories.[2] The use of such a success indicator would promote economies in scarce capital resources, and would rather lead to an expansion of production through higher employment and better organization of production.

Even if the last source of improvement in the employment situation has the greatest potential, all three of them do not amount to much. It is my contention, therefore, that the employment situation, aggravated by the demographic wave and by a shift of the population from agriculture into urban areas, will continue to plague the Polish economy.

The palliatives sometimes advocated in Poland do not concentrate on maximization of national income and of the rate of economic growth, but on 'optimal rather than maximal employment', on longer education for youth, lesser labor force participation rates on the part of younger women to offset the trend to steeply falling fertility rates, etc.[3] Such advocacy contents itself with hiding rather than solving the employment problem. I do, therefore, agree with Gamarnikow's conclusion that 'in the long run the [employment] situation may well become much worse ...'. We differ, however, in the quantitative assessment of the gravity of the unemployment problem. To my mind the basic reason for the perseverance of this problem, in contrast with the experiences of West European economies, is not the demographic wave, but the gross inability of doctrinaire planners to utilize the economic initiative of the population, including both the private and socialized sectors. Symptomatically, one of the chief planners, Jozef Pajestka,

[1] M. Kabaj, 'Rational employment', p. 173.
[2] E. Winter, 'Directive financial indicators', *Finanse*, 2/67.
[3] W. Szyndler-Glowacki, 'Demographic dilemmas'.

wrote recently about 'freeing the creative activity of enterprises', rather than about freeing their initiative.[1] The problem
of the utilization of initiative hinges on the discussion of the
role of the market which I will cover separately.

WAGES AND LIVING STANDARDS

Gamarnikow expected that in 1967 'the modest planned increase
[in the real wage] of 2% may well be reached'. The nominal
average monthly wage rose in 1967 by 5·1% (as compared
with the 2·5% planned rise),[2] while prices of goods bought by
consumers rose according to my estimate by between 1·5% and
4%, more likely nearer to the latter figure.

I quite agree with Gamarnikow that many price hikes remain
hidden in communist countries, and that, therefore, the movement of real wages is overstated in official statistics. The same
holds true of the average standard of living, as measured by
the consumption index. True, such an index tends to rise
faster in Poland due to rising labor force participation rates,
but as my own research has demonstrated, the official index
of consumption is overstated.[3] A recently published book on
consumption problems in Poland[4] notes 'the permanent non-
fulfilment of plans for raising consumption, and in particular
for raising real wages'.[5] The post-war rise in consumption has
been much less than that of national income, and has been
very uneven between years and periods. The author concludes
that consumption was not allowed to act properly as an
incentive to economic growth. The growth of consumption is
retarded by the slow growth of agricultural production, even
despite its very satisfactory recent performance. Consumption
in Poland depends to a larger extent than in most other
European countries on its food component, which accounts
for 46·9% of household expenditures.[6] This, naturally, makes

[1] J. Pajestka, 'Perfecting the planning system: the enterprise and the association',
Życie Gospodarcze, 4/68.

[2] Gospodarka Planowa, 3/68, p. 38.

[3] B. Mieczkowski, 'Changes in the standard of living in Poland', Kultura, 9/66
(Paris).

[4] A. Hodoly, Problemy spożycia w Polsce (Warsaw, 1966).

[5] L. Beskid, book review, Ekonomista 5/67, p. 1310.

[6] Trybuna Ludu, 15 March 1968, based on a 1966 study by the Main Statistical
Office.

it more dependent on the slow rise of agricultural production. Additionally, however, the production of industrial consumption goods has been lagging, mainly as the result of a relatively slow planned and realized development of that sector. During the 1961–67 period the real income of the non-agricultural population is supposed to have risen by 48%, that of the agricultural population by 63%, while sales of industrial consumption goods rose by only 35%, despite all experiences in other countries with Engel's law, according to which as income increases its proportion spent on food decreases, and the proportion spent on 'non-necessities', represented partly by industrial consumption goods, increases. There are, therefore, substantial unfilled needs for such goods.[1]

I doubt, incidentally, whether the consumption of foodstuffs really rose by more than 48%, despite all the complaints in Poland about 'an unduly high' increase. The consumption of services rose probably less than that of durable consumers' goods.

An argument may be made that the consumption mix in Poland is irrational because of irrational prices which are kept relatively low for necessities, while other consumer goods are burdened with high prices. Consequently, the consumption of food is artificially encouraged, and that of industrial goods discouraged. As a result the state collects almost no revenues on the sale of foodstuffs, their sale is encouraged, and in order to raise their production the state has to sink large funds in agriculture and agriculture-supporting industries, where the capital/output ratio is high. This state of affairs gave rise to the advocacy of more price flexibility in consumer goods, in particular with the view of raising the relative consumption of goods which have high marginal social profitability.[2] Much attention is devoted also to improving the shoddy quality of consumer goods and to checking the 'compulsory prosperity' introduced through hidden price raises when low cost products are withdrawn and higher-priced but not necessarily better or proportionately better brands become available.[3]

[1] W. Dudzinski, 'In the third year ...'.
[2] S. Markowski, 'Economic rationalization and the structure of consumption and of incomes of the population', *Życie Gospodarcze*, 14/68. An independent check of the assertion that the capital/output ratio is higher in agriculture-supporting industries than in other industries seems highly desirable.
[3] *Ibid.*

The prospects for 1968–70 are of increasing efforts to narrow the gap between the growth of national income and the growth of consumption. Early reports for 1968 indicate increasing supply of machinery for consumption industries. That the gap will continue to exist, however, seems safe to expect. The most that can be hoped for is that it will decrease, bringing with it a faster rise in consumer wellbeing.

One factor in the possible slowing down of the rise in monthly wages and of the standard of living, however, is the possible reduction of the work week from the present 46 hours to 41 hours as in the Soviet Union, or to some other lower level, as is apparently being done in Czechoslovakia.[1]

FOREIGN TRADE

I agree with the general assessment by Gamarnikow of the basic Polish foreign trade difficulties, stemming from high import needs, particularly needs for some essential raw materials (e.g. oil, iron ore), for grain and machinery; from close ties with the Comecon which is at present characterized by slow growth of intra-bloc foreign trade; and from uncompetitive exports. Efforts are made to diversify exports and to improve their quality. Probably as the result, exports of industrial consumption goods in 1967 scored the highest increase (by 23·3%) over 1966, higher than envisaged in the export plan. Exports of machinery and equipment rose less than planned, apparently because Polish products are still of not adequately attractive quality. The total of exports rose by 2·1% above the plan, rising to 11·3% above the preceding year. Imports showed a smaller, 5·6% increase, with the group of machinery and equipment rising fastest, to indicate a modernization effort. Table 18.1 shows the changes which took place between 1966 and 1967:[2]

Aggregate foreign trade turnover rose in 1967 by 8·3% over its 1966 level. Its main territorial direction is shown in Table 18.2 in millions of devisa zlotys (which are a special accounting unit for international transactions), expressed in current prices.[3]

[1] H. Otto, 'The economics of workweek reduction', *Życie Gospodarcze*, 38/67.
[2] *Biuletyn Statystyczny*, 2/68, Annex.   [3] *Ibid.*, p. 57.

Trade with other communist countries rose in 1967 by 11·1%, while trade with capitalist countries increased by 3·5%. Imports from other communist countries rose by 8·3%, while imports from capitalist countries increased by 1·9%. Exports to other communist countries rose by 15·1%, while exports to capitalist countries increased by 5·0%. Consequently, the relative dependence of Poland in its foreign trade on other communist countries increased during 1967.

Table 18.1

	1967 actual, million devisa zlotys	1967 % of plan fulfillment	1967 volume, 1966 = 100	Structure in % 1966	1967
Exports					
Total	10,111·8	102·1	111·3	100	100
Machinery and equipment	3,663·9	93·6	113·6	35·5	36·2
Fuel and raw materials	3,305·5	105·9	107·6	33·8	32·7
Agricultural products and food	1,590·9	111·6	103·8	16·8	15·7
Industrial consumption goods	1,551·5	107·8	123·3	13·9	15·4
Imports					
Total	10,531·8	103·5	105·6	100	100
Machinery and equipment	3,833·1	106·6	109·3	35·2	36·4
Fuel and raw materials	4,795·3	98·5	104·5	46·0	45·5
Agricultural products and food	1,268·7	110·0	100·4	12·7	12·1
Industrial consumption goods	634·7	112·5	103·2	6·1	6·0

The earliest indications for 1968 are that in the first quarter exports of machinery to capitalist countries increased by 40%, as compared with the plan for the year of a 24% rise, but that they rose by only 6·5% to communist countries, as compared with the planned increase for the year of 11%.[1]

There has been, apparently, some improvement in the Polish balance of payments during 1967. This improvement may not continue into 1968 because imports are planned to rise in that

[1] G. Pisarski, 'Our economy after first quarter', *Zagadnienia i Materialy*, 10/68.

year at a faster rate than in 1967, and because the Soviet Union seems to be dissatisfied with the prices it is getting for its exports of raw materials and fuels to its East European part-ners,[1] even though such prices are apparently by some 10–15% higher than the prices it is receiving for the same raw materials in the West. Consequently, there is a possibility of higher import prices for raw materials imported from the Soviet Union.

Table 18.2

| | Turnover | | Imports | | Exports | |
	1966	1967	1966	1967	1966	1967
Total	19,064·6	20,685·3	9,976·2	10,579·1	9,088·4	10,106·2
Socialist bloc	12,016·0	13,392·5	6,415·4	6,947·6	5,600·6	6,444·9
Other	7,048·6	7,292·8	3,560·8	3,631·5	3,487·8	3,661·3

Additionally, during the first quarter of 1968, while exports rose by 13·6%, imports rose faster yet, thus causing a deterioration of the balance of payments.[2] However the Polish balance of shipping services is likely to improve in view of the temporarily high world demand for shipping.

AGRICULTURE

The Polish national income still consists in 20% of agricultural production, some 50% of the population lives in villages, and 33·5% of the population maintains itself from agriculture.[3] No wonder then that agriculture constitutes an important sector in the Polish economy. The last three years, 1965–67 have been very successful in agriculture, contributing in an important way to the generally satisfactory performance of the economy.

---

[1] M. Deniszczuk, 'Factors and conditions of the development of the Polish foreign trade in the perspective of 1970's', *Gospodarka Planowa*, 4/68.

[2] *Trybuna Ludu*, 23 April 1968.

[3] *Rocznik Statystyczny 1967*, pp. 82, 22, 43. The share of agricultural production in national income depends on the definition of the latter and on valuation of the former. See T. P. Alton and Associates, *Polish National Income and Product in 1954, 1955 and 1956* (New York, Columbia University Press, 1965), ch. IV.

Global agricultural production, the preceding year taken as
100, grew in the recent past as follows:

1963	104·1	1966	105·4
1964	101·2	1967	102·3
1965	107·7	1968	98·5 (plan)[1]

Gamarnikow's expectation for 1967 has been fulfilled, output
for that year having held up very well. Interestingly enough, to
be on the safe side Polish planners plan for a decrease in agricultural output in 1968, hoping at the same time that they will
be proven overcautious. Some criticism has been raised in this
connection in Poland, based on the observation that agricultural expectations of the current Five-Year Plan are too pessimistic since they assume increasing input/output relations.[2]

Like Gamarnikow, I expect agricultural production to reach
its target by 1970. I do see, however, some clouds in the longer
run. Voices have been heard for some time in Poland advocating
the socialization of agriculture, which in 1966 was about
87·5% in private hands, as measured in terms of global
production.[3] Party Secretary Gomulka said in a speech to the
Central Committee in March of 1964: 'We will develop and
strengthen all elements of socialism in the villages and the
forms of socialist economy in agriculture. ...' One prolific
economic writer has been waging a campaign for socialization
of agriculture at least since 1965 in *Życie Gospodarcze*, *Ekonomista*
and the Party organ *Nowe Drogi*. He maintained recently that
the only adequate road of agricultural development is through
slow socialization.[4] These voices may be straws in the wind,
foretelling future developments. Agricultural circles, which are
farm machinery co-operatives regarded as a step toward
socialization of land, are spreading widely in the countryside
under strong governmental support. And the 'soil fund' of the
state annually absorbs thousands of acres of land from peasant
farmers for different reasons: (1) non-payment of taxes;
(2) inadequate production record (defined as yields which

[1] K. Secomski, 'The biennium 1968–69', *Gospodarka Planowa*, 2/68, p.3, and
S. Markowski, 'The basic tasks of agriculture in 1968', *ibid.*, 4/68.

[2] M. Rakowski, 'A little optimism', *Życie Gospodarcze*, 15/67.

[3] *Rocznik Statystyczny*, 1967, p. 224.

[4] M. Mieszczankowski, 'The system of gradual socialization', *Życie Gospodarcze*,
15/67.

over the past three years were by more than one-third lower than average in a given village), on the basis of an Act passed early in 1968; (3) ceding to the state in exchange for old age pension privileges (2·8% of farmers planned to do so in 1967); (4) demise of the owner without a successor for the farm being present. It is estimated, on the basis of a Ministry of Agriculture census conducted early in 1967, that peasant farms without successors occupy about 8·7% of the individual farm land, and constitute about 7·9% of the farms.[1]

In this way a steady erosion takes place in private agricultural proprietorship. The larger the extent of that erosion, the easier it may be in the future to socialize the rest of the land by administrative measures. While such a development depends ultimately on the political situation in Poland, its feasibility seems progressively greater. Since before 1956 socialized agriculture, at least in the form of agricultural collectives, proved relatively inefficient, a consummation of such an eventuality would conceivably spell a setback for agricultural productivity.

Despite the generally good agricultural performance, due mainly to a 3·2% rise in crop production, there were sectional setbacks in 1967. Fruits and vegetables showed a decline, and animal husbandry was weak, leading to an acute meat shortage, as the result of which the end of the year witnessed a raising of meat prices. In order to promote further agricultural growth the plan for 1968–69 stresses provision of industrial supplies to agriculture, especially of fertilizers and machinery, the latter to help displace the high density of horse population.[2] During 1967 the stock of tractors (expressed in uniform units) increased from 183,000 to 214,000, as the result of which cultivated land area per tractor declined from 108 ha. to 93 ha.[3] During the first quarter of 1968 the sales of agricultural machinery and of fertilizers grew briskly, the former by 50% over the first quarter of 1967.[4]

[1] A. Szemberg, 'The old man and the farmstead', Życie Gospodarcze, 17/67.

[2] K. Secomski, 'The biennium 1968–69'. Polish density of horses is the highest in Europe, amounting to 15·1 per 100 ha. in 1965. See R. Bachanska and L. Wisniewski, 'The horse and the tractor on peasant farms', Życie Gospodarcze, 11/67.

[3] S. Markowski, 'The basic tasks of agriculture in 1968', Gospodarka Planowa, 4/68.

[4] Życie Gospodarcze, 18/68, p. 12, and 19/68, p. 1.

9

STRUCTURE OF INDUSTRY

While it is common knowledge that communist planners stress the development of 'group A', or producers' goods industry, Polish planners seem to have gone one step farther in achieving more favoritism than planned. During the first two years of the present Five-Year Plan the plan for growth of capital and intermediate goods production was 14·5%, while the actual record was 18%. Over the same period the plan for growth of consumers' goods production was 11%, while the actual record was 11·5%. During 1967 the plan was actually not reached in the growth of the underprivileged 'sector B'.[1]

To put this problem in perspective, the growth of production of consumers' goods is shown below, assuming the growth of production of capital and intermediate goods over the relevant period as 100:[2]

1947–49	102	1956–58	110
1950–53	79	1959–60	49
1954–55	85	1961–63	58

There is an obvious downward relative trend in these figures, halted only temporarily during the period of political turmoil 1956–58, at the end of which the political screw had been tightened again. The average growth of 'group B' during the current Five-Year Plan is expected to be 6%, while the Plan envisaged a growth rate for that sector of 6·5%.[3] For the first four years of the present plan period, realized and planned rates of growth were as shown in the table on p. 249 (in terms of annual increments of global production, preceding year taken as 100).[4]

Thus the gap between the two sectors began narrower than in 1961–63, but within the Five-Year Plan period it has tended to widen again. If we add to this the tendency to over-fulfill the plans for the production of capital and intermediate goods,

[1] A. Karpinski, 'After two years of the realization of the current Five-Year Plan', *Gospodarka Planowa*, 12/67.
[2] A. Karpinski and J. Pajestka, 'General problems of the policy of economic development', *Polityka Gospodarcza Polski Ludowej*, part I, op. cit., p. 76.
[3] A. Karpinski, 'After two years of the realization of the current Five-Year Plan'.
[4] K. Secomski, 'The biennium 1968–69', p. 3.

and to keep the production of consumption goods at the planned level or below it, the discrepancy between the growth rates of both sectors appears considerable.

Of course department A must also provide inputs for agriculture, construction and exports, as well as merely feeding B and itself. Of these non-industrial sectors exports and construction are outstripping B, and so provide substantial external

	A Capital and intermediate goods	B Consumption goods	Growth of A as percentage of growth of B
1966	108	106·4	80
1967 (preliminary)	109	105	56
1968 (plan)	108·2	105·1	62
1969 (plan)	109	105·6	62

justification for A to outstrip B. But there is one more factor: the state budget for 1968 envisages a growth of *defense* outlays by 10%,[1] as compared with the planned growth of national income of 4·8%. Thus the relative importance of defense production in the economy increases, and this explains at least some part of the growing relative importance of capital and intermediate goods (for all arms count as department A). Anyhow the consumer seems to be left with the short end of the stick. It may be only hoped that future political changes will lead to lesser emphasis on producers' goods and armaments, but it is wellnigh impossible to forecast developments in the political situation.

One can expect a continuation of the trend toward industrial concentration. In 1965 the socialized industrial plants employing over 200 workers constituted only 5·9% of the total, but they employed 73·7% of all workers. Their share in total production was higher yet. Similarly, there was a concentration of fixed capital in few plants, 2·4% of which had 73·5% of the total value of fixed capital.[2] Concentration brings about

[1] J. Albrecht, 'The 1968 state budget', *Finanse*, 1/68.
[2] S. Paradysz, 'Experiences and results of the 1966 industrial census', *Wiadomosci Statystyczne*, 4/68, p. 26.

economies of scale, and consequently it should be regarded as desirable, at least up to a point.

INDUSTRIAL PERFORMANCE

One of the stated aims of the new financial system has been the eradication of the cyclical fluctuations which have plagued the communist systems.[1] Fluctuations were discovered within the daily rhythm of work, as between individual decades of a month, between quarters and years. Their comparison with the short-term fluctuations in capitalist countries revealed an inferiority of communist countries, where many articles, especially during the 1965–67 period, were devoted to this problem. At the beginning of 1967, pursuant to the Seventh Plenum of October 1966 during which fluctuations were 'discovered', efforts were made to improve the organization of production, with a view to dampening the cycles. The result has been an improvement in the production rhythm, although not an overwhelmingly satisfactory one. In January 1967 global industrial production constituted 8·3% of planned annual production, while the same period in 1966 accounted for only 7·7% of the annual production. The first-quarter figures for 1967 and 1966 on the same basis were 24·8% and 23·7% respectively. A comparison of the percentage share of the three first months in the quarterly output of the machine industry revealed the improvement in the monthly cycle (actual production as percent of quarterly plan), shown in the table below.

| | 1966 | | 1967 | |
	Global production	Material production	Global production	Material production
January	31·5	29·0	33·6	31·5
February	31·7	30·2	32·0	31·8
March	37·3	42·2	34·7	37·5

[1] See B. Mieczkowski in *East Europe*, 11/1967, and G. Staller, 'Fluctuations in Economic Activity: Planned and Free-Market Economies, 1950–60', *The American Economic Review*, June 1964.

The share of decades (ten-day periods) in the global production plan fulfillment in machine industry in 1967 also showed an improvement (percentages of plan total in decades):

	I	II	III	Total
January	26·7	33·2	40·7	100·6
February	31·4	34·5	34·3	100·2
March	31·6	30·6	38·0	100·2

A similar improvement of monthly and decadal rhythm was shown in the chemical industry. The degree of plan fulfillment by enterprises and associations also increased dramatically. The author of the study showing the above results concludes, however, that 'Despite a general improvement in many associations and plants, the fluctuations in production did not improve, and in places a deterioration can be even noticed.'[1]

Another author, while noting the steps taken by enterprises to protect themselves from fluctuations in production, complains that there has been a tendency to change planned tasks during the year,[2] although it has to be noted that he utilizes pre-financial-reform data of 1966. In that year, among 114 enterprises only 4 did not change their plans [!], 74 changed them 1–5 times, 24 changed them 6–10 times, 10 changed them 11–20 times, and 2 managed to change their plans over 20 times! The author ascribes this proclivity to changes in the product-mix in response to the market (especially in production for export), to delays in the exploitation of new investments, to changes in organization, to difficulties with subcontractors and to inability to sell the product. He concludes that the real reason for such changes is 'probably the tendency of enterprises and associations to insure themselves against lack of fulfillment of command tasks, and especially of the rentability indicator' because this determines the size of the enterprise fund.[3]

A central planner makes also a reference to the need to 'actualize' periodically the Five-Year Plans and the perspective plans.[4] Such revisions originate probably both from the

[1] J. Niedzwiecki, 'Toward a systematic improvement in the organization of production and administration', *Nowe Drogi*, 5/67, p. 8.
[2] E. Winter, 'Directive financial indicators', parts II and III.
[3] *Ibid.*, part III, p. 14.
[4] J. Pajestka, 'Perfecting the planning system', part III.

pressures imposed by plan changes made by enterprises, and from political as well as international changes.

An editorial in *Życie Gospodarcze*[1] flatly states, in contrast with the conclusion quoted above, that fluctuations in production have decreased. Thus no unanimity of opinion exists, though some improvement seems probable, and more can be expected in the future.

It is difficult to show any direct connection between economic performance and the decentralization of industrial management, or indeed the newly proposed recentralization (see elsewhere in this chapter). But one interesting direct result has been that although inventories held by enterprises have risen, the rise 'took place exclusively in the group of half-finished goods and production-in-process',[2] which indicates the presence of a conscious effort to avoid fluctuations in production. In the first quarter of 1968 inventories grew by about 4%, i.e. less than the growth of production, which rose by 10·4% over the first quarter of 1967.[3] This is a remarkable result since inventories usually tended to rise faster than production. The decentralization has also, apparently, helped to promote a long-range outlook in enterprise managements.

Global industrial production increased by 7·5% during 1967, production in the producers' goods sector rising by 9·0%, that in the consumers' goods sector rising by 4·8%. Industrial labor productivity rose by 3·5%, a larger part of the increase in production being due to an increase in industrial employment.[4] The same trend continued into the first quarter of 1968.[5]

GENERAL INDICATORS OF CHANGE

The net material product in 1967 reached in current prices the level of 614 billion zlotys, indicating a 7% real growth over 1966. The rate of growth of domestic product declined somewhat due to a fall in the rate of increase in net agricultural production to 2% (compared with 4% growth in 1966). Net

[1] 'The laws of intensification', *Życie Gospodarcze*, 32/67.
[2] E. Winter, 'Directive financial indicators', part II, p. 37.
[3] *Trybuna Ludu*, 23 April 1968.
[4] *Biuletyn Statystyczny*, 2/68, Annex.
[5] G. Pisarski, 'Our economy after first quarter'.

industrial production rose by 8% (compared with a 7% growth in 1966), construction increased by 13% (compared with a 9% growth in 1966). The share of industry in national income, including the turnover tax, which it bears almost alone, increased from 51·8% in 1966 to 52·6% in 1967, the share of construction rose from 9·1% to 9·7%, while the share of agriculture declined from 21·4% to 20·1%.

Consumption increased by 6% (same increase as scored in 1966), while individual consumption of goods rose by 5% (compared with a 6% growth in 1966). Investment ('accumulation') increased by 2% (compared with an 11% growth in 1966), but net investment in fixed capital increased by 15% (compared with a 12% growth in 1966), indicating a substantially slower rate of growth of working capital.[1]

During the first quarter of 1968 global industrial production rose by 10·4% above the first quarter production of 1967 (compared with the planned increase of 7·1%), investment in fixed capital increased by 15·2% (compared with the planned 5·6% increase), while the rise of inventories for the first time in four years was slower than the rise in production.[2]

On the whole, the economic performance in Poland during the first period of the current Five-Year Plan has to be regarded as satisfactory, laying the foundations for mature industrialization and improvements in the standard of living. How these economic gains will be actually utilized is another question, hinging mainly on political changes and objectives.

PREDICTION

I expect a continuation of the rise in economic indicators, including that of national income, albeit at a slower pace. Bumper agricultural harvests are unlikely to continue uninterrupted, and peasants may show some socialization jitters. Polish intra-bloc foreign trade is likely to show in the future the pattern of Czechoslovakia, with its problems and difficulties. And unless a more far-reaching reform is instituted in industry, with its demands for greater flexibility, industrial production seems unlikely to hold up its rate of growth.

[1] *Wiadomosci Statystyczne,* 4/68, pp. 46–8.
[2] *Zycie Gospodarcze,* 19/68, p. 1.

The 1966–70 period has been also called 'the quality Five-Year Plan', owing to its emphasis on raising the quality of production. Better quality of products should help solve two key economic problems of contemporary Poland, namely, the problem of the domestic market and the problem of the foreign market. The latter requires more exports, which can be increased through raising the attractiveness of Polish products. The former has witnessed increasing purchasing power in the hands of the population and new demands for better products. In the late 1960s, unlike in Marxist writings, quantity does not change by itself into quality, to the distress of both Marxist theoreticians and practitioners.

THE RELIABILITY OF OFFICIAL INDICATORS

As has been reiterated many times, Communist official statistics are not reliable. For one thing, the use of global concepts leads to double counting, which in turn causes a tendency to overstate the rates of growth. For another thing, some areas of communist systems are shrouded in secrecy, making it possible to attribute to them almost any growth rates. Finally, the system puts a premium on statistical achievement, encouraging optimistic reporting, an exaggerated example of which took place in China during the Great Leap Forward.

Some recently published indices of growth for several East European countries, prepared under the editorship of Thad P. Alton by the Research Project on National Income of East Central Europe at Columbia University, have arrived at the following conclusions: 'The growth rates on both the old and the new official index [of transport and communications in Poland] considerably exceed those obtained in [independent] calculations, but the difference is very much reduced in the new index.'[1] And again: 'All three [Polish] official measures show considerably more rapid growth over the period 1950–65 than the [construction] materials consumption measure computed [independently].'[2] Curiously enough, in the consumption of construction materials there was a greater discrepancy during more recent periods between official and independently calculated indices. This result is contrary to usual

[1] Occasional Paper, 19 (1967), p. 16.   [2] Occasional Paper, 22 (1968), p. 7.

observations. The project arrives at the more usual result for Czechoslovak industrial output: 'There is a significant divergence in the measured rate of growth between the [independent] and the official gross value indexes throughout the entire period [1948–65], although most of the divergence occurred in the late forties and early fifties.'[1]

While, on the whole, official statistics seem to improve in reliability and comprehensiveness as time goes on, giving them currently full credence may be unwarranted. In sectors like agriculture or industry, where the basic calculations are made in physical terms, the reliability seems generally fairly satisfactory. Statistics on price movements, defense, consumption, investment and foreign trade, on the other hand, can be regarded only as at best indicative of the direction of changes. And where official dogma is at stake, as in the case of Marxist assertions about 'full employment under socialism', strong *caveats* have to be invoked. Therefore, although the preceding pages use official statistics, and although qualifying remarks were not made with each datum presented, some reservations should be kept in mind when evaluating the information reproduced above.

[1] Occasional Paper, 24 (1968), p. 19. Compare Appendix, line 20.

19

POLAND AND CZECHOSLOVAKIA: THE PITFALLS OF ECONOMIC PROPHECY IN THE COMMUNIST WORLD

MICHAEL GAMARNIKOW, 1969

The practitioners of the tender art of economic forecasting are always faced with considerable odds. Quite apart from the normal vagaries of human behavior and the unpredictability of cumulative effects of individual economic decisions, they must also take into account a number of political factors, some of which cannot be really foreseen. And yet these unexpected political events may well have a profound impact which is likely to change the economic situation almost overnight. The revolt of French students and workers in May–June 1968, is here a classic example. Who could have foreseen, say in February or in March, when the dollar scare was still the top news and when France was still riding the crest of the gold-speculation wave, that barely three months later the French economy would be in shambles, and de Gaulle's pride of a gold hoard almost half gone and the franc itself under severe pressure?

There are many people who claim that the odds of this type are much bigger when one is dealing with a free market economy, where the central authorities have far less control over the actual course of events and where the process of economic decision-making is infinitely more decentralized. In fact, the very opposite is often the case. For while the centralistic system of arbitrary economic planning may well tend to minimize the vagaries of human behavior (by simply ignoring effective demand) and to reduce the unpredictable effects of economic decision-making (although not those of normal human error), it is far more vulnerable to the impact of political factors. And this can hardly be otherwise in a system that openly preaches the priority of politics over economics.

Moreover, quite often those political factors are not only impossible to foresee, but are (in many cases) totally unrelated (at least in terms of normal logic) to their ultimate effects.

Let me explain briefly what I have in mind. In the Western world, the economic forecaster is also faced with many unknown political quantities. But most of those factors can be easily recognized as such and their probable impact on the economic situation of the country in question may well be calculated, within the acceptable limits of probability. Or, to put it in another way, there is always some predictable logical relationship between the cause and effect. One knows for instance that in the United States presidential elections are held every four years (although one cannot foresee their outcome). One is also fully aware of the fact that a change in the Administration (to use the American colloquialism) may well bring about radical changes in economic policy. But, although all those political factors do increase the normal hazards of economic forecasting, at least one is dealing here with predictable quantities. Thus, the alternative trends of economic development in the USA can be prophesied with tolerable accuracy by inserting the political factors into the straight economic analysis and by applying the logical norms of cause and effect.

True, even in the West, there are certain political events, the effects of which cannot be predicted with any exactitude (even in terms of alternatives) and there are some which cannot be foreseen at all. Here again one may give the example of the near-revolution in France in May and June 1968. But, although the revolt itself was unexpected, the makings of a powerful social conflict were quite clear to every serious student of the French economy. While the actual date of the showdown and its intensity could not be foreseen at all, the political factor of the social ferment in France was certainly a known quantity, and as such it could be logically fitted into the analytical projection of the economic future.

The Arab–Israeli war was also a largely unforeseeable political event. As in the case of France, the makings of the conflict were there for everybody to see, although nobody could have predicted either the exact date, or the intensity of the confrontation, or, for that matter, its outcome. But here the similarity ends. For no process of normal logical reasoning could have ever led an economic analyst to a conclusion that the war between the Israelis and the Arabs might have a serious impact on the economic development of such a remote and totally uninvolved country as Poland. And yet this is precisely what has happened.

The chain reaction involved here makes a sheer mockery out of any attempt at serious economic forecasting. For the connecting links between the primary cause and ultimate effect consisted of entirely unrelated political factors, which not only do not fit into the normal process of (logical) economic reasoning, but also (when put into their proper order) show conclusively that (Marxist–Leninist theory notwithstanding) the odds due to the vagaries of irrational human behavior are infinitely greater, when one is dealing with a system of mono-party oligarchy.

Early in June Israel routed the Arab countries in a six-days' war. Up to 6 June 1968, the relations between Poland and Israel were reasonably friendly. But six days later the same Israel had become a 'fascist aggressor' and 'the evil tool of American imperialism'. This ideological metamorphosis was still innocuous enough, as far as Poland's economic development was concerned. And it would have quite likely remained so, if not for the fact that a number of Polish Jews yielded to their inner sentiment, by openly celebrating the Israeli victory. This enraged the Communist oligarchy and on 19 June Gomulka (who never previously has shown any anti-Semitic tendencies whatsoever) made a violently anti-Jewish speech, castigating the 'Zionist agents in our midst'.[1]

All this (however regrettable) was still completely unrelated to the problems of economic development in Poland. But it so happened that an intensive power struggle was raging at that very time within the top hierarchy of the Polish Communist Party and, since many members of the Establishment were of Jewish origin, one of the factions has decided to exploit Gomulka's emotional 'anti-Zionist' outburst in order to use anti-Semitism as a political weapon in the inter-party struggle for power. This weapon, used at first against some minor fry in the mass communication media, was wielded with greater force some eight months later, after the student revolt had

[1] Cf. *Trybuna Ludu* (Warsaw), 20 June 1967.

shaken the Communist regime in Poland (March 1968). The main blame for this wave of political dissent was attributed to a score or so of university professors and other intellectuals – mostly of Jewish origin. Again it so happened that some of those professors were not only Jewish, but also very prominent reform economists. In fact, they were the moving spirits behind Poland's modest economic reforms and the main protagonists of economic pragmatism.

So far, this purely haphazard chain reaction has led from the Israeli victory over the Arabs, to the dismissal of prominent professors of political economy. But economic policy, as such, was not yet directly involved. Now, however, we are beginning to enter the proper sphere of economic forecasting. The dismissal of the prominent scholars and the outright condemnation of their reformist theories were perceived by Poland's hardliners as a green light for an all-out attack on every single manifestation of economic pragmatism. And not only in the field of economic policies: the net result of this offensive of economic obscurantism has been a considerable roll-back and a significant strengthening of the prerogatives of central planners.

Here we are no longer dealing with the problems of the theory of planning or those of an economic *modus operandi*. In the specific conditions of the Polish economy (which are discussed elsewhere in this volume by Professor Mieczkowski) the degree of permissible pragmatism in the practical implementation of concrete economic policies is literally a bread-and-butter issue. Neither the key problems of the balance of payments deficit, of the unfavorable structure of Polish exports and of improving the effectiveness of investment outlays, nor the perennial troubles on the sector of labor productivity and rational use of manpower resources can ever be solved within the framework of a purely dogmatic approach. Some fairly optimistic predictions (including my own, reprinted on pp. 213–33), concerning the fulfillment of the (admittedly rather modest) goals of the Polish 1966–70 national plan, were based – among other things – on the assumption of a gradual (though still very inadequate) rationalization of economic practices, which was indicated in the resolutions of the IVth Party Congress in 1964 and in the July 1965 Central Committee Plenum. But half-way through the plan (and apparently as a result of a totally irrational chain reaction, sparked by the Israeli victory over the Arabs) this trend toward economic rationalism has been reversed.

This roll-back in the sphere of economic management was due to purely political factors. The dogmatic retreat in the sphere of practical economic policy came with the first symptoms of dogmatic ascendancy over the more liberal elements, just after the Arab–Israeli war. Nor is it only the future economic development of Poland which has been adversely affected. Indeed, the first negative effects of the more centralistic and arbitrary approach to the problems of planning and management have been already clearly discernible. In his keynote speech at the Vth Party Congress (in November 1968), Gomulka admitted quite frankly that there were serious shortcomings in the fulfillment of some essential targets of the current Five-Year Plan. Thus – for instance – the effectiveness of investment outlays was lagging behind the estimates in the Plan, labor productivity was well below the expected level and the desired ratio between the industrial outputs of industrial groups 'A' and 'B' had not been achieved.[1]

It could be argued, of course, that all these shortcomings, as well as over-employment (in relation to the planned for targets in this sector) and the lack of any meaningful improvements in the structure of exports have been for years the perennial headaches of Polish planners and thus could not be directly attributed to the more centralistic and arbitrary methods of planning and management. But even if all those shortcomings were indeed of a chronic nature, there was no escaping the fact that the 1968 performance in these key sectors was far worse than in the preceding years. And this decline was most noticeable in those areas which are especially sensitive to the effects of arbitrary decisions on a macroeconomic scale. Thus, the least one can say is that the dogmatic comeback in the sphere of economic practices has made the situation worse than it could have been otherwise.

This was particularly the case in the investment sector. In Poland, the global investment outlays throughout the economy

[1] Cf. Gomulka's Report to the Vth Party Congress, *Trybuna Ludu* (Warsaw), 12 October 1968.

notoriously exceed the annual targets of the National Plan.[1] So the real issue is not over-investment as such, but the extent of it. As long as there existed a sort of power equilibrium between the dogmatic and the pragmatic wings in the Party establishment, over-investment in Poland was kept within tolerable limits. Thus, in 1965 (the last year of the previous Five-Year Plan) there was a 10·1% increase in global investment outlays (over the 1964 level), as against the 9·0% growth foreseen in the National Plan.[2] In 1966 the respective figures were 7·6% realized against 5·8% planned, but in 1968 investment expenditure jumped to 9% over the 1967 level, as against a planned increase of only 5·9%.[3]

Now, new investment is the standard extensive method by which the champions of the command economy tend to promote economic growth. The essence of the current Five-Year Plan in Poland was the declared intent of the central planners to substitute intensive methods of promoting economic growth for the standard tools of centralistic and arbitrary planning. Within the framework of the half-way system of planning and management (which conforms to Gomulka's own concept of economic reforms), this basic objective never had much chance to be realized in full. But one could well expect some degree of improvement. Instead of this, ever since mid-1967 there has been a definite retrogression.

This expansion of investment demand has produced adverse effects on other key sectors of the Polish economy. First of all, there was a substantial increase in imports of machinery and other industrial equipment (as compared with the original targets of the current Five-Year Plan), and this in turn increased the balance of payments deficit. Secondly, it induced a much bigger disproportion between the output of group 'A' and group 'B' than in the previous years, with the inevitable adverse effects on market equilibrium and on the standard of living.

[1] This is essentially due to deliberate underestimation of the construction costs in respect of various pet investment projects promoted by provincial Party bosses. The idea is to produce low estimates in order to have the project included in the National Plan. Once the construction is well advanced the estimates are revised, on the assumption that the central authorities would not want to waste the initial outlay and will provide the additional means to finish the project.

[2] Cf. the monthly table 'Some Data About the Current Economic Situation and the Realization of the National Plan', *Gospodarka Planowa*, October 1968.

[3] *Ibid.*

Finally, the expanded investment demand (as well as the overall tendency to use extensive methods of promoting economic growth) has aggravated the employment situation, where the 1970 target figure of 10 million people was already reached by the second half of 1968,[1] with not the slightest sign that its dynamics would tend to decrease.

All these negative effects of arbitrary and centralistic methods of planning and management have already forced the Polish planners to undertake a series of major revisions of the current Five-Year Plan. Indeed, the Resolution of the Vth Congress called for 'a concentration of investment effort in the remaining two years (of the Plan) on selected key sectors of the National Economy'.[2] This is but another way of saying that the original investment plan has to be revised and that some secondary investment projects have to be frozen or abandoned. Similar revision is apparently necessary in respect of the output of the groups 'A' and 'B', in order to restore (at least to some extent) the original proportions of the national plan.[3]

What is really significant, however, are not all those difficulties and disproportions (which as far as the fulfillment of the National Plan in Poland is concerned must – to some extent – be regarded as a routine), but the fact that (in my opinion) there exists a definite cause and effect relationship between the much higher degree, with which these negative phenomena have manifested themselves throughout 1968 and the dogmatic ascendancy within the Polish Party establishment. If one looks back at the seemingly irrational chain reaction, which leads to the virtual political annihilation of the progressive and pragmatic wing of the Polish Party, one can see quite clearly that Poland's economic development in the second half of 1967 and throughout 1968 would have most probably followed a different (and a more positive) course, were it not for a totally irrelevant fact that the Israeli army humiliated the Arabs in a six-day war. From the point of view of serious economic forecasting, this is – needless to say – a very disturbing and thought-provoking conclusion.

---

[1] Cf. *Biuletyn Statystyczny*, 9/68 (Warsaw), 11.
[2] Cf. The Resolution of the Vth Party Congress, *Trybuna Ludu* (Warsaw), 21 October 1968.　　　　　[3] *Ibid.*

Incidentally, early in 1969 Poland has again entered a period of economic reforms, which are apparently intended to be quite substantive and far-reaching. This sudden change of heart, which again has found a positive reflection in the field of practical economic policy, fully conforms to the general pattern of unpredictability. The real purpose of the anti-Semitic hue and cry was not, after all, to oust the Party dignitaries of Jewish origin from the corridors of power, but to put hardline appointees in their place. But the Czechoslovak crisis made the Kremlin leaders very wary of all changes in top leadership. For this reason – at the Vth Party Congress in November 1968 – Moscow gave its full political backing to Gomulka, who was thus able to stop the hardliners' drive for power and regain the supremacy within the Polish Communist Party.

But while the anti-Semitic hue and cry failed in its primary political objective it did create at the level just below the top a great many opportunities for rapid promotion. The massive purges of alleged 'Zionists' and all kinds of 'revisionists' created many vacancies in the apparatus of power. Apart from that, the Gomulka group felt an urgent need to refurbish its image and to deny the claim of their adversaries that political power in Poland has been usurped by 'tired old men'. The net effect was that a large number of well-qualified people in their late thirties and early forties have advanced to the positions where they could exert real political power.

In political terms, all those new entrants into the corridors of power could hardly be classified as liberals. But they were definitely far less dogmatic than their predecessors, much better educated and much more conscious of the pressing need for a more pragmatic approach to economic issues. Thus, the shift in the power structure within the ruling élite – a shift which objectively speaking was the net effect of the anti-Semitic purges – coupled with a rapidly worsening economic situation of the country, created a more favorable climate for a new dose of economic pragmatism. This was precisely the opposite effect from that which the hardliners intended to achieve when they instigated the anti-Semitic hue and cry.

The invasion of Czechoslovakia provides yet another example of the pitfalls of economic prophecy in the Communist World, although in this case the logical relationship between the cause and the effect has been, perhaps, a little less irrational. Armed aggression and a prolonged period of foreign occupation are some of the extreme political risks which an economic analyst must always bear in mind, provided that such an invasion lies within the sphere of normal (or even abnormal) political probabilities. Thus – for instance – back in the late nineteen thirties, any long-term economic prognosis concerning the Austrian Republic had obviously to take into account (as one of the alternatives) the effects of a possible *Anschluss* with the Third Reich. For such an *Anschluss* was then the openly declared political objective of Austria's aggressive and much more powerful neighbor. In this case therefore, foreign aggression had to be regarded as a potential political factor, which must be realistically reckoned with.

But in the case of Czechoslovakia, very few reputable political analysts and experienced statesmen were ready to accept the possibility that Moscow would indeed resort to military force, in order to bring the Czechoslovak reformers to the heel. After all, the Brezhnev doctrine (unlike the relevant portions of *Mein Kampf*) was not publicly spelled out until after the event. Thus, there were no valid rational grounds for taking the possibility of a Soviet armed intervention into account when forecasting the future economic trends in Czechoslovakia. And yet the Soviet tanks did roll in and the adverse effects of this invasion are likely to change the basic trends of Czechoslovakia's economic development for years to come.

One could argue, of course, that, objectively speaking, it was the ouster of Novotny and the sudden break with political and economic orthodoxy, which was the unpredictable political factor and that the Soviet invasion, regardless of the admitted moral (and political) evil involved in this brutal act, merely restored the status quo. But this type of argument disregards the essential trend of political (and economic) development in Czechoslovakia ever since the mid-nineteen sixties.[1] The bitter

[1] There is no space in this short essay to substantiate this assertion. But the fact remains that, long before the ouster of Novotny, both the Czechoslovak social scientists and the more progressive elements in the Party establishment were working for the transformation of Czechoslovakia into a participatory and pluralistic socialist democracy. A detailed analysis of this general political trend can be found in my article 'Political patterns and economic reforms', published in the March–April issue of *Problems of Communism*.

political infighting, which culminated in the downfall of Novotny, accelerated, no doubt, the process of political change, which – at a later stage – acquired a specific momentum of its own. But this does not change the fact that the post-January 1968 course of events did tend to follow (by and large) the path, which has been clearly outlined ever since the XIIIth Party Congress. True, the Dubcek era brought with it some really qualitative changes in the order of basic priorities (such as the formal acceptance of the doctrine that meaningful political reforms are an indispensable precondition for an effective implementation of the new economic model). But the over-all direction of the process of changes (although certainly not its momentum) remained essentially the same as it was in the closing months of the Novotny's era.

There is little doubt that the real motive of Soviet aggression was to reverse this process of political and economic change, before it reached the point of no return. Whether such a reversal can – in fact – be effectively imposed (except in the short run), is another matter. But it is already quite clear that the Soviet military occupation (i.e. a major political factor, which could not be reasonably foreseen) is bound to have a number of far-reaching economic repercussions.

One of the areas where the impact of the Soviet political hegemony is already being felt in a really meaningful manner is economic relations with the West. The problem involved here is a much larger one than that of a mere direction of foreign trade, or even of restoring the imposed trade patterns. The real issues are a major structural change in industrial output and a basic reorientation of the whole of economic activity. For one of the things the Czechoslovak reformers were essentially aiming at was a return to the pre-1948 pattern of the structure of industrial production, with the main emphasis on the output of a short series of highly sophisticated goods, especially adapted to the requirements of the traditional pre-war markets.

One can also express this policy objective in another way. Namely, that it was a deliberate attempt to break away from the repetitive and technologically backward production patterns imposed on Czechoslovakia by its Comecon obligations. Ever since 1965, when the economic reform program was adopted as an official Party policy, the Czechoslovak pragmatists insisted on their *ceterum censeo* that there is no other way to break out from the vicious circle of economic stagnation (which held the country in its grip ever since the early sixties), except by a return to the pre-1948 production patterns, which meant a basic reorientation of the whole Czechoslovak economy and a substantial loosening of Comecon ties.

The essential validity of this argument was tacitly accepted by the Czechoslovak ruling élite long before the ouster of Novotny, despite all the lip service which was still being paid to the alleged advantages of the Comecon membership. Realizing that the technological gap was a major obstacle to a meaningful reorientation of the trading patterns, the Czechs took the necessary steps to acquire the latest technological know-how, either by an outright purchase, or through co-production agreements concluded with the more advanced Western industrial concerns. By the time of Novotny's ouster the trend toward closer economic relations with the West was already fairly well established (and as such constituted an important element in any long range economic forecast). After the Czechoslovak pragmatists gained the upper hand in the political power struggle, this trend toward the reorientation of foreign trade inevitably gathered momentum. So much so that, in the first nine months of 1968, the volume of trade with the non-Communist countries grew by 11·8%, while that with Czechoslovakia's Comecon partners grew by only 6.3%.[1] But that was just a foretaste of the things to come. It is no secret that the Czechoslovak reformers were urgently seeking a huge investment credit of some half a billion dollars in convertible currencies,[2] weeks before the invasion. This credit was to be used to modernize the industrial plant of Bohemia and Moravia, as well as to acquire the latest know-how, with the express purpose of making Czechoslovak exports fully competitive on Western markets. The contemplated changes in the organizational

[1] Those figures were reported in the November issue of *Noviny Zahranicniho Obchodu*, which is the official organ of the Ministry of Foreign Trade.

[2] Cf. *New York Times*, 8 August 1968. This report was confirmed by premier Cernik in an interview broadcast over Austrian Radio on 17 August 1968. Earlier the official government spokesman F. Kouril indicated at a press conference in Prague (16 May 1968) that the Czechoslovak government was seeking a loan of about 450–550 million dollars in convertible currency. But he did attempt to give the impression that this credit had been requested from the Soviet Union.

structure of industry and in foreign trade practices were also geared to promote this Westward oriented export offensive. The state monopoly of foreign trade was to be abolished and individual enterprises were to be permitted to deal with their foreign customers either directly, or through specialized export–import agencies (which were themselves supposed to operate according to purely commercial principles). It was also planned to achieve a full convertibility of the Czech crown within five to seven years.[1] Finally, the activity of all Czechoslovak enterprises was to be based on objective business considerations, with no nonsense about the priority (cost what it may) of the Comecon's obligations. By the late spring of 1968 all those pragmatic measures had reached the implementation stage and any long-term economic prognosis of the economic development of Czechoslovakia, made at that time, would have to take as its starting point the major reorientation of the trading patterns. But the Soviet invasion changed the situation in a very drastic manner.

A careful study of the basic political documents of the pre- and post-invasion period, such as the Bratislava Declaration, or the preliminary agreement signed by Svoboda, Dubcek and Smrkovsky in Moscow at the end of August, discloses that, apart from reestablishing such ideological imponderabilia as the leading role of the Party and the ideological control over the mass communication media, the Soviet side was mainly concerned with restoring Czechoslovakia's economic commitments toward the bloc and her imposed trading patterns. This was done in such a way as to preclude any meaningful reorientation of the Czechoslovak foreign trade. Thus, it was no coincidence that the very first economic agreement between Moscow and Prague, concluded just after the Soviet military intervention, involved future deliveries of Soviet raw materials and fuel in exchange for direct Czechoslovak capital.[2] All the subsequent trade and economic co-operation agreements signed

[1] The intention to achieve full convertibility of the Czech crown within five to seven years was fully confirmed by Ota Sik during his press conference in Basle on 28 November 1968.

[2] This agreement was signed in Moscow on 10 September 1968. In exchange for increased supplies of the Soviet natural gas in the nineteen seventies, Czechoslovakia was forced to invest her capital in the construction of a gas pipeline on Soviet territory.

in 1968 and 1969 were geared to the same basic objective, namely the strengthening of economic ties between Czechoslovakia and the Comecon. Thus, not only were the Czechoslovaks forcibly prevented from seeking investment credits in the West, but also their own investment potential was to be drained off, lest it would be used in a way which did not fit with the imposed trade patterns.

Apart from restoring orthodoxy in the sector of foreign trade relations, the Soviet invasion has had many other direct economic consequences, which are likely to have a lasting impact on the future economic trends in Czechoslovakia. First of all, both the invasion itself and the subsequent mass occupation of the country resulted in heavy material damage (as well as the loss of output), the total amount of which it is quite impossible to assess objectively.[1] Then the invasion itself created a sort of 'purchasing psychosis' or a buying spree, combined with a run on savings. This was due both to the fear of future shortages, resulting from the re-imposed foreign trade patterns, and to loss of confidence in the value of money.[2] As a result of this retail turnover grew by 18·6% in August, by 19% in September and by 17% in October. At the same time saving deposits dropped by 2·8% between 15 August and 15 September.[3] Needless to say this 'purchasing psychosis' destroyed market equilibrium and intensified inflationary pressures. The subsequent disintegration of the Czechoslovak economy and the conscious go-slow in the factories resulted in persistent shortages of most staples, very low labor productivity, non-fulfilment of contracts, etc. Economic crisis in Czechoslovakia is now an officially acknowledged fact.[4]

[1] The actual extent of this damage is very difficult to estimate since within the framework of 'the policy of normalization' a strict censorship has been imposed on all pertinent information. The only figures one has at one's disposal are the (obviously exaggerated) claims made in the very early post-invasion period. Thus, Finance Minister Sucharda estimated the loss of production during the first three weeks of Soviet occupation at 2 billion crowns (280 million dollars), *Radio Prague*, 11 September 1968. Damage to roads and transport facilities was put at 5 billion crowns (700 million dollars) and property damage at 3 billion crowns (420 million dollars), Radio Prague, 4 September 1968. These figures are of the order of 1% of national income and national capital respectively.

[2] *Radio Bratislava*, 3 December 1968.

[3] *Rude Pravo* (Prague), 20 November 1968.

[4] Husak's speech to People's Militia. *Rude Pravo*, 13 September 1969.

Indeed, *Rude Pravo* warned in September 1969 that 'the economic situation of our country might soon become critical'.[1]

In the longer run, however, the most significant negative effects of the Soviet invasion are likely to be felt on the sector of economic reform. The political framework of a participatory, pluralistic democracy, which the Czechoslovak reformers deemed to be absolutely necessary for the successful operation of their new economic model, was effectively destroyed in the post-invasion political retrogression. And while the vestiges of the economic reform blueprint itself may well be saved, the very cohesiveness of Sik's original concept is likely to be greatly impaired by the reimposed trade patterns. Thus (contrary to the situation which prevailed before the invasion), one can hardly expect that the implementation of the pragmatic reforms (if any) would influence the economic development of Czechoslovakia in any meaningful manner. For any reforms, which are still likely to be put into effect, are bound to bear the patchwork mark of the inevitable political compromise.[2] And yet the probable effect of the comprehensive economic reform scheme, as envisaged in the original Sik's blueprint, was certain to be regarded as the key element in any long-term economic forecast made prior to the Soviet invasion. Which all goes to show how big are the pitfalls of economic forecasting in the Communist world.

[1] *Rude Pravo*, 18 September 1969.
[2] A. Lantay, 'What next in the economic reform?', *Nove Slovo* (Bratislava), 11 September 1969.

20

RUMANIA

MICHAEL KASER, 1967

As already stated (p. 87), no link appears to be possible with earlier estimates of GNP, or NMP. So little has been revealed on current or plan aggregates, that the forward estimates presented in Table 20.1 (below), are highly tentative. The only components of national income by origin published in value terms for 1966 are global outputs of industry and agriculture; the ratio of gross to net must be assumed from 1965 returns. For the 1967 and 1970 plans only global industrial

Table 20.1 *Forward estimates of Rumanian national accounts* (billions of lei at 1966 prices)

	1967		1970	
Net material product 'disposable'	178·7		207	
of which:				
consumption of goods		125·1		147
accumulation (net of depreciation)		53·6		60
Depreciation	24·2		33	
Consumption of services (incl. rent)	51·8		60	
Expenditure on gross national product	254·7		300	
of which:				
personal consumption	145·2		164	
– by retail sales		81·0		106
defence expenditure	5·0		8	
other public consumption	26·7		35	
gross capital formation	77·8		93	

Note: As the Five-Year Plan quoted no target for net material product 'produced' or its distribution by industrial origin, no estimates were made for the trade balance or for the foreign-price differential. It is estimated that in US dollars GNP in 1967 was approximately $13·8 billion, viz. (at 19·25 million population) $720 per capita. If the volume of exports originally planned (7·6 billion lei in the text of the Five-Year Plan) has been sufficiently over-fulfilled to represent the revised import plan and if, as estimated for the present study, the lei is 3·2 times overvalued, import dependence (as per cent of GNP) in 1967 would be just under 18%. The tourist rate for the lei is three times the official rate (100 lei = $16.50).

Table 20.2   *Main published indicators of the Rumanian Five-Year Plan (1966–70) and for certain years (prices of 1963, unless otherwise stated. Table brought up to date in 1969).*

	1965 actual	1966 actual		1966–70 Plan		1967 Plan		1967 actual		1968 Plan	
	Bn. lei	Bn. lei	Index 1965 = 100	Bn. lei	Index 1965 = 100	Bn. lei	Index 1966 = 100	Bn. lei	Index 1966 = 100	Bn. lei	Index 1967 = 100
Net material product	—	—	107.9	—	—	—	108.5	—	109.5	—	—
Global industrial production (socialist sector)[a]	168.2	188.2	111.7	280.0–291.8	166–173	209.6	111.3	221.1	113.5	235.5	106.1
– Group A, index	114.2	—	112.3	193.8[h]	170–177	—	(112[b])	—	112.8	—	—
– percentage of global output	62.8%[c]	63.6%	—	—	—	—	—	—	—	—	—
– Group B, index	54.0	—	109.9	86.2[h]	160–165	—	—	—	112.3	—	—
– percentage	37.2%[c]	36.4%	—	—	—	—	—	—	—	—	—
– metal working, index[b]	—	—	112.9	62.8–68.1	—	—	111.7	—	117	—	113.0
– percentage	21.2%[c]	21.6%	—	—	—	—	—	—	—	—	—
– harvest-related, index[b]	—	—	110.4	55.0–56.0	—	—	—	—	109	—	—
– percentage	22.0%[c]	21.4%	—	—	—	—	—	—	—	—	—
– import-related, index[b]	—	—	111.7	36.9–38.7	—	—	—	—	115	—	—
– percentage	14.0%	14.1%	—	—	—	—	—	—	—	—	—
– ferrous metals, index	—	—	109.1	26.5–26.9	—	17.9	—	—	101.0	—	—
– percentage	8.3%	8.1%	—	—	(126–132[d])	—	—	—	—	—	—
Global agricultural production	61.5	70.4	114.4	64.6	160	52.0	117	52.2	117.1	58.0	111.1
– (per cent crop origin)	63.2%[c]	64.1%	—	—	—	—	—	—	—	—	—
– (per cent animal origin)	36.8%[c]	35.9%	—	—	—	—	—	—	—	—	—
Centralized investment from state resources	40.3	44.5	110.7	—	—	—	—	—	—	—	—
Construction volume	—	—	112.3	—	—	—	—	—	120.6	—	—
Export volume: 1966 prices	6.79[e]	—	—	10.3–10.4	150–155	—	—	—	—	9.34	—

	1965	1966	Index	1970 Plan						
Exports: current prices	6·61	7·11	107·7	—	—	—	—	7·98	112·4	109·0
Imports: current prices	6·46	7·27	112·6	—	—	—	—	8·9	122·4	107·0
Turnover of foreign trade: 1965 or 1966 prices	—	—	110·1	—	120	—	—	—	—	—
Retail sales (state and co-operative shops): 1966 prices	67·3	74·3	110·4	104·3–107·0	155–159	81·0	109	109·8	84	108
current prices	67·6	74·3	109·9	—	—	81·4	—	—	—	—
Price index investment goods	—	Index	97·3[f]	—	—	—	—	97·9[f]	—	—
retail goods	100	—	99·5	—	—	—	—	—	—	103
Real income: workers	100	100	105·7	125	—	—	—	—	—	105·5
peasants	100	100	—	120–125	—	—	—	—	—	—
Farmers' money incomes	100	—	108·8	—	—	—	—	109·8	—	—
Workers' and employees' money incomes	100	—	112·4	—	—	—	—	108·9	—	—
Workers and employees in socialist sector	4305 *Thousands*	4496·7	104·4	5200 *Thousands*	120·8	—	—	4678	104·0	—

[a] In 1955 prices the socialist sector was 99·7% of total industrial production.

[b] Output of relevant ministry (respectively engineering, food, light industry).

[c] At 1955 prices 28·3, 14·8, 14·2, 5·6, 65·3, 34·7, reading downwards.

[d] 1966–70 mean (1961–65 = 100) in 1955 prices.

[e] Derived from mid-points of ranges of value and index number given for 1970 Plan: error margin too large to derive price index for 1965 and 1966.

[f] 1959 = 100: derived from 1965 investment valued at 1959 prices (41·3 billion lei according to *Anuarul statistic 1966*, p. 377) and at 1963 prices (40·30 billion lei according to *Scînteia*, 31 January 1967, p. 3).

[g] All this row is calculated enterprise by enterprise, on the basis of the enterprise's global production. In 1965, calculating product by product, on the basis of the preponderant destination of the product, read 65·2% and 34·8% downwards.

[h] Calculated enterprise by enterprise: see note [g]. On a product basis, read 202·6 and 89·2 downwards.

Sources: 1965, *Anuarul statistics al RSR, 1966*; 1966, *Scînteia*, 31 January 1967 (real wages from *ibid.*, 27 December 1966); 1967, *Scînteia*, 28 January 1967; 1970 Plan, *Probleme economice*, No. 7, 1966, pp. 158–63; 1967 Plan, *Scînteia*, 27 December 1966; 1968 Plan, *Scînteia*, 27 and 28 December 1967; foreign trade: 1966, Gh. Surpat and H. Ionel, *Probleme Ecomnice*, 2/1968, p. 82; 1967, *The Economist*, 14 September 1968, p. 79.

Note: In Tables 20.3 and here — means 'not available'.

production has been stated; the sole figure for agriculture is the average increment for the plan period 1966–70 as percentage of the mean for 1961–65 (see Table 20.2, pp. 272–3). No comprehensive aggregate is available for the use of national income: centralized investment from state funds covers only part of gross capital formation and the volume of retail sales in state and co-operative shops relates to only part of personal consumption. The Rumanian Central Directorate of Statistics has not published for any recent year the distribution of NMP between accumulation and consumption, two ratios commonly available for other Eastern European countries. The estimates prepared for this study imply a ratio of just under 30% for accumulation to NMP during 1967, falling very slightly by 1970. If, as is assumed in this paper, the Rumanian government is determined to expand the wage-labour force[1] from 4·5 to 5·2 millions between 1966 and 1970, to raise the real wage of those workers by 18%, and to raise the real income of peasants by between 20 and 25% by 1970 in comparison with 1965, the relaxation of the present rather high rate of accumulation is understandable. The substantial increase in state pensions and the start of a pension scheme for collective farmers, both effective from the beginning of 1967, contribute to the Rumanian government's need to assure a significant expansion of consumer-good supplies if inflation is to be avoided. A cognate consideration is the government's stated policy to reduce the deficit in the balance of trade. The very large rise planned for retail sales implies that there is to be a relatively small direction of new resources into consumer services. The planned increase in turnover embraces a replacement of auto-consumption and household processing in line with rural migration to towns (or other wage-earning occupations) and the secular rise in the value of processing and of distribution costs of the goods sold. It is believed that the consumption of services will increase by only a modest excess over the rate of demographic growth: education and public health will certainly do more than keep up with population expansion but a significant part of the outlays on education will not appear as consumption of services, since they will be on the job training in production:

[1] 'Workers and employees in the national economy', viz. excluding members of co-operatives and workers on own account.

the opening of certain skill bottle-necks in industry seems to be more important than general educational expenditure. Although the level of personal services per capita in constant prices may not diminish, one would imagine that at Rumania's present level of development little expansion is either expected or warranted until 1970. The development of the tertiary sector could well come in the seventies.

It has already been emphasized that the projections assume no major change in planning and management methods. The Central Committee of the Rumanian Communist party in its session of 27–8 March 1967 took a decision on the improvement of state farm management which could be the forerunner of changes in the management of other sectors: it is possible, though unlikely, that the personal service sector could be thrown open to private enterprise on a large scale. Some such move seems to be under consideration in the Soviet Union and is already emerging in other countries of Eastern Europe; this could throw out the present projection of the service sector. The estimates for other government services and for defence are inevitably very uncertain.

ECONOMIC ACTIVITY 1960–66

Development to 1960 in Rumania has been covered in an article published in the *Economic Bulletin for Europe*, vol. 13, pp. 54–107 (November 1961). The Six-Year Plan which began in 1960 was executed under conditions of some external economic stress, though in nothing like the severity that Albania experienced. Rumania's dissatisfaction with Comecon led to an export drive in Western markets and the consequential incurring of compensation settlements for the post-war nationalizations (still not all settled: Dutch claims were agreed in January 1967.

The most notable feature of the implementation of the Six-Year Plan was the vast failure of the agricultural programme. A planned rise of global agricultural production of 70–80% above the 1959 level was matched by an actual rise of only 13%.[1] The article in the *Economic Bulletin for Europe* already cited called

[1] According to the communiqué on the plan results; 15% according to the 1966 statistical year book.

The extraordinarily ambitious plans for farm output ... a severe test not only of the ability of the Rumanian planners to provide the necessary material inputs and incentives but also of the efficiency of the institutional pattern now established. Underlying the plan are assumptions that rural labour will be better utilized and that any farms receiving about the same inputs as state farms do now will achieve the same yields (p. 99).

The unreality of these assumptions and the poor response of peasants after a collectivization campaign (linked with farm amalgamation) which was at its peak between 1958 and 1961 seem to have been the main constituents of failure. On the positive side the enlargement of farms from the small peasant holdings to large collective units, and the supply of fertilizer etc. have stabilized output to a degree that is startling in comparison even with the preceding six years.

Because the food supply fell much below the planned level, the real-wage target of an increase of 40–45% was under-fulfilled: the actual rise was 35%. An increase of 40% in the real income of the peasants was planned but neither the statistical year book for 1966 nor the official report on plan fulfilment published on 13 February 1966 quoted an index for this magnitude. It is safe to say that little change in peasant real incomes could have taken place. The plan for retail sales was also under-fulfilled.

Industrial expansion, on the other hand, proceeded faster than the plan envisaged, and the pride of the new industrial base, the chemicals industry, increased at the quite remarkable rate of 24% *annually*, against a planned increment of 22%: the volume of chemicals, cellulose and paper produced in 1965 was no less than 3·6 times that of 1959. The other major growth sector, engineering, planned to expand by 16·5% per year in fact rose by 17·6% a year, i.e. an overall rise of 165%. The Rumanian government had hoped not only to support its investment programme with home-made manufactures, but also to sell its engineering products abroad. In the event the export drive was constrained partly by the unwillingness of Comecon partners to take Rumanian machinery (Rumania having queered its pitch by failure to fulfil some of its Comecon specialization agreements), and partly by the difficulty of entering Western European markets protected behind the barriers of EEC and EFTA. The percentage of engineering goods in total exports rose from 15·0% in 1959 (and 16·9% in 1960) to 18·5% in 1965 but imports rose from 32·4% in 1959 (32·5% in 1960) to 39·0% in 1965. A speech by the Secretary General of the Rumanian Communist Party, Mr Ceausescu,[1] complained that the 1966 percentage (19%) of engineering goods in export was a poor showing in comparison with that of its neighbours (24% in both Bulgaria and Yugoslavia). Rumanian trade dependence, long close to the Soviet and Albanian as the lowest in Eastern Europe, had risen during the Six-Year Plan, but Rumania is still being held back by inadequate exports. In 1965 its exports were $68 per head of population compared with $144 in Bulgaria.

It would be reasonable to expect that the severe under-fulfilment by agriculture and a moderate over-fulfilment by industry (a 2·2-fold increase instead of 2·1 as planned) would result in a considerable shortfall of net material product. According to the official estimates, agriculture contributed, at current prices, 29·3% to NMP in 1965 (37·8% in 1959) and industry 48·9% (40·9% in 1959); other sectors thus contributed virtually the same share in each year (between 21 and 22%). Yet the official statistics claim that net material product rose by 70·7% (from 1966 statistical year book: the plan result communiqué stated 68%) between 1959 and 1965. The plan increment for NMP had been 70 to 80%. Considerable changes in prices could reconcile the declared increments at constant prices with the stated shares at current prices, but little use can be made of such index numbers for analytical purposes.

In 1966 both industry and agriculture did rather well. As Table 20.2 shows, the global output of industry rose by nearly 12% and of agriculture by just over 14%; foreign-trade turnover rose a little more slowly – by 10% as a combined aggregate, comprising 8% for exports and nearly 13% for imports. Once again the chemicals industry was the most dynamic, global output of Ministry of the Chemicals Industry increasing by 24%; the Ministry for Engineering showed a corresponding rise of almost 13%. The first major production of aluminium – begun in a small way before the war by a

[1] *Scinteia*, 25 February 1967.

Swiss firm – epitomized during 1966 a new branch of industry, nearly 47,000 tons of pure and alloy metal being produced.

PROJECTION FOR 1967 AND 1970

The agricultural target for 1970, insofar as it can be deduced from the quinquennial average cited in the plan, is clearly more modest than that of the last plan and realistic in the light of the rises shown in each of the three years 1964, 1965, and 1966. The association of collective farmers with the organs of local government managing agriculture – the one reform in which Rumania is ahead of the other countries of Eastern Europe with co-operative farming – seems to be paying dividends, but the policy of further dispersing industry into the predominantly agrarian regions may enlarge the phenomenon of 'worker peasants' with resultant declines in peasant incentives.[1] The industrial worker who maintains his links with a farm tends to neglect the agricultural side of his activities as non-farm opportunities present themselves within easy travelling distance. In the new Five-Year Plan the share, for example, of the predominantly agricultural region of Argeş (hitherto famous only for its fruit and ţuica plum brandy) in industrial production will rise from 3·2% in 1965 to 5·3% in 1970. The Five-Year Plan requires explicitly the location of new industrial projects in seventy of the hundred or so districts which hitherto have no such plant.

Rumania can draw particular advantage in growth from its low rate of defence expenditure (although, as in all Eastern European countries and the Soviet Union, the budget item 'defence' does not cover all outlays which would be classified as military in a western budget). It seems likely that expenditure made to and on behalf of the armed forces is especially low in Rumania in comparison with other Eastern European countries. In the first place Rumania cut its period of military service (and hence its spending on pay, subsistence, and equipment) in order to show its allies in the Warsaw Treaty

---

[1] The estimates for 1970 in Table 5.1 of my chapter on Albania (p. 93) imply an absolute decline in auto-consumption on farms, consistent with the heavy migration to towns: a relative decline in per capita auto-consumption of those remaining is not to be inferred.

Organization that it did not accept the role of a supplier of conventional forces envisaged for it when the USSR moved towards the integration of Warsaw-Treaty forces – with increasing Soviet concentration on strategic forces, and correspondingly more reliance on theatre forces from Eastern Europe. Rumania's geographical position does not encourage heavy spending on the research and development of sophisticated weapons, and the recent disputes between it and other members of the Warsaw-Treaty Organization would not lead one to believe that other members would be selling it costly equipment of this nature. Rumania has been adamant in its opposition to contributing to the foreign-exchange costs of Soviet forces stationed in other Treaty-member territories. Finally Rumania is not apparently undertaking any significant training or supply functions for 'neutral' countries (i.e. members neither of WTO nor of NATO) which would come out of the domestic budget.

The two crucial problems which Rumania has to face during the current Five-Year Plan are those of the efficiency of investment and of the gain from trade. The Plan appears to envisage a fairly constant incremental capital-to-output ratio in industry and an increasing ratio in agriculture. Within industry it is presumably expected that the decline in capital efficiency which would be associated with the further dispersal of industrial location will be offset by the enhanced productivity of the now-established new industries.

But it seems also to be hoped that some of the new industrial capacity to be installed during the plan period will embody more advanced technology than that built into Rumanian equipment. The need for imports of technologically-advanced equipment is a strategic element of the Plan, an aspect highlighted by the visit to the United Kingdom in March 1967 of a Rumanian technological delegation led by Mr R. Moldovan, chairman of the State Committee on Science and Research and a former vice-chairman of the State Planning Commission. The expansion of exports to cover such purchases is one facet of the planned increment (50–55%) of export volume over the five years. The other facet is Rumania's need to gain the economies of scale desired in industry by foreign sales: the home market is already too small for its metallurgical, chemical and engineering production.

10

Table 20.3 *Quinquennial volumes (at 1963 prices) of gross centralized investment from state funds in Rumania; also 1966 annual (table updated in 1969)*

| | 1961–65 | 1965 | 1966 | | 1967 | | 1966–70 Plan | |
	Billion lei	Billion lei	Billion lei	Index 1965 = 100	Billion lei	Index 1966 = 100	Billion lei	Index 1961–65 = 100
	(1)	(2)	(3)	(4)	(5)	(6)	(7)	(8)
Industry	95·5	22·5	24·2	108	30·1	123·8	156·6	164
Construction	—	1·8	(2·1)	117	2·3	112·1	—	—
Agriculture	21·5	4·9	5·3	108	6·0	113·8	35·7	166
Transport	17·0	4·0	5·3	124	5·4	107·1	32·2	189
Municipal economy	—	1·1	(1·2)	110	1·2	96·7	—	—
Education, health, etc.	0·6	—	1·4	—	—	—	9·3	164
Education and culture	—	1·1	(1·7)	147	1·7	102·0	—	—
Housing	1·7	—	3·3	107	—	—	23·8	139
Health, science and housing	—	3·1	(3·2)	—	3·3	101·7	—	—
Other	32·7	(1·8)	4·9	—	(2·2)	—	55·6	170
Total	169·0	40·3	44·4	111	52·2	117·1	280·5	166

Source: as for Table 20.2; column (1) is derived from columns (7) and (8). Columns (5) and (6), and an index of 1967 on 1965 not shown here, are from *Scînteia*, 28 January 1968: columns (2) and (4), and the bracketed items in column (3), are derived from these. Where the item 'Other' appears in brackets it is a residual.

A host of trade agreements with Western European countries bear testimony to Rumanian anxiety to gain openings in, and supplies from, the highly-industrialized countries of Western Europe. Rumania was willing to incur the opprobrium of the 'northern tier' of the Warsaw Treaty organization (the German

Table 20.4 *Rumanian public accounts 1965–67* (billions of lei. Table updated in 1969)

	1965	1966	1967
Current prices			
Expenditure:			
national economy	62·1	71·5	86·6
social–cultural	22·4	24·1	27·7
defence	4·7	4·9	5·1
administration	2·3	2·8	2·9
other	1·6	2·1	0·8
Total expenditure	93·1	105·4	124·3
Surplus	3·9	3·5	5·0
Revenue:			
turnover tax	28·7	31·4	34·3
profit tax	20·7	22·5	30·4
from persons	5·7	6·5	7·3
social-insurance premia	5·9	6·6	7·0
Total revenue	97·0	108·9	129·3
1963 prices			
Investment in state enterprises and institutions (from budget grants, retained profits and depreciation)	44·4	49·0	57·5
of which:			
industry	22·9	24·8	30·9
agriculture	7·5	7·7	8·6
housing	3·1	3·4	3·7

Source: Anuarul statistic al RSR, 1969.

Democratic Republic, Poland and Czechoslovakia) by the establishment of diplomatic relations with the Federal Republic of Germany as the price of improved commerce. Besides Western Germany and the United Kingdom, Rumania is placing considerable hope on trade with France and Benelux.

In January the Minister of Foreign Trade, Mr Gh. Cioara, signed an agreement on economic and industrial co-operation in Paris: Franco-Rumanian trade has been rapidly expanding and seems already to be near the upper limit envisaged by the earlier agreement covering 1965–69. The 1967 agreement significantly provided for the establishment of special committees of co-operation in chemicals, and engineering. Rumanian trade with Benelux in 1966 was no less than 50% greater than in 1965 and high-level visits on each side this year (the Rumanian Foreign Minister visiting Belgium and Holland and the Dutch Foreign Minister visiting Rumania) have been particularly concerned with trade expansion. Rumania also is looking for markets in the moderately-developed European economies. A consular and commercial agreement with Spain was signed early this year (representing a major change of policy on both sides) and a new trade agreement with Finland, which followed shortly afterwards, envisaged a substantial increase in mutual trade during 1967–70.

The speech by Mr Ceausescu, to which reference has already been made, emphasized that 'dollars at any cost' was not a sound policy. Rumanian economists and foreign-trade officials have hitherto lagged far behind their colleagues in other Eastern European countries (Albania only excepted) in assessing the efficiency of foreign trade. Reforms can confidently be expected in foreign-trade organization, certainly by permitting ministries and enterprises to engage in direct negotiation with foreign firms, possibly by liquidating the foreign trade corporation and probably by a further wholesale-price revision. The 1963 wholesale price list has begun to draw criticism (e.g. in *Scinteia*, 19 March 1967) and there are numerous signs that the authorities are now prepared to accept a charge on capital: again in company with Albania Rumania is still operating on budget grants for investment in state enterprises.

A final bottleneck which threatens the Rumanian economic expansion forecast in the plan is that of railway transport. The park of goods waggons is only 40% greater than in 1938 and the state railways have long been starved of investment funds. Outlays on signalling, double-tracking and the modernization of stations and marshalling yards are urgently needed. Because much of the increment in new industrial capacity is located in regions ill-served by rail, an extension of the network is needed at the same time as intensification.

After a decade of amazing industrial growth, Rumania has come to the testing point at which capital deepening cannot be avoided.

21

RUMANIA: AFTERTHOUGHTS

MICHAEL KASER, 1969

National accounts statistics remain shrouded in secrecy and no real verification of the forecasts can be made. A reference, not seen by the present writer at the time (*Revistă de statistică*, vol. 14, no. 3 (1965), pp. 3–14), contained, however, a figure for net material product in a table described as of 'conventional' figures. NMP was given as 74·3 billion lei[1] in 1957 and 119·5 billion lei in 1963. If the figures are not 'conventional', but actual, application of the officially announced annual increments would indicate a 1967 NMP of 172 billion lei (against the 178·7 billion lei in the projection for that year).

The expected maintenance of the very high rate of accumulation of NMP at 30% has been confirmed – it is to remain at the figure in the 1969 Plan and for the 1971–5 Five-Year Plan, and the increase in farm output was in the event 'modest': in 1967 global agricultural production rose by only 1·0 and the serious drought in 1968 reduced it by 3·6%. The belief that marginal capital efficiency in industry would be fairly constant seems to have been borne out – the evidence is that it has slightly declined.

It was assumed in the article that 'no major change in planning and management methods' would emerge. The Party decision of October 1967 was no 'major' change in new enterprise rules, and began to be implemented experimentally in 71 enterprises the following year and 'central offices', to which a number of ministerial planning powers were devolved, began to be established in April 1969. The changes, overall, are the least radical of any in east Europe.

On the other hand the 'confidently expected' liquidation of the foreign-trade monopolies, wholesale-price reform and charge on capital have obstinately not been embraced. The only aspect to which the article looked with 'certainty' which

---

[1] 1 billion = 10^9.

has emerged is direct negotiation by enterprises (and 'central offices') with foreign firms; such contacts are nevertheless subject to Ministry of Foreign Trade supervision and one can only hope that the optimism then expressed will eventually be justified.

22

SOVIET INDUSTRY

FRANCIS SETON, 1967

When the Party Plenum of February 1966 passed the Draft Resolution on the current quinquennium (1966–70) – later to be re-named the 'Eighth Five-Year Plan' – its program appeared to most observers as a model of cautious realism. Some of the targets looked almost pusillanimous compared with earlier Plans, and most of Khruschev's visions for 1970, endorsed by the 22nd Party Congress as recently as October 1961, were ruthlessly cut down to size or consigned to oblivion. If the Five-Year Plan as it now stands is fulfilled, the 1970 output performance will fall short of Khruschev's Party Program by about 15% in industry as a whole, with a shortfall of 8% in producer goods branches and of 30% in consumer industries. For individual products the sights have been lowered

by 10–15% for oil, electricity, steel, and household goods,
by 15–20% for mineral fertilizers and cement,
by 20–30% for gas, textiles, and leather footwear, and
by over 50% for new-type chemicals (plastics, synthetic resins, and fibre).

Even allowing for some exaggerated optimism in the original Party Program, the cuts are certainly of sufficient size to make the new targets plausible, – though, clearly, some will be much more difficult to attain than others.

Table 22·1 (p. 288) is designed to test the degree of realism of various planned growth-rates when seen against the performance of the last two quinquennia, and the extent to which fulfilment will come within reach if the current year (1967) measures up to planners' expectations.

OVERALL PERFORMANCE

In basing our appraisals on the Draft Resolution of February 1966 we must firmly bear in mind that the implied 'Eighth

Table 22.1 *Annual growth rates* (% p.a.)

	Quinquennial 1956-60	Quinquennial 1961-65	Averages 1966-70 Plan	1966 Plan	1966 fulfilment	1967 Plan	First quarter 1967[a]	Average required for 1968-70[b]	Soviet per capita output as (%) of US output[e] (mid-sixties)
National income (Marxist concept)	9·2	6·3	7·0	6·4	7·4	6·6	—	6·8	52
Gross industrial output	10·4	8·6	8·2	6·7	8·6	7·3	10·9	8·4	55
Of which:									
producer goods	11·3	9·6	8·5	6·9	9·0	7·5	—	8·6	—
consumer goods	8·5	6·3	7·6	6·0	7·0	6·6	—	8·2	—
Labour productivity	6·3	4·7	6·1	4·7	5·0	5·5	6·7	6·7	40-50
Output of:									
1. Oil	15·9	10·4	7·6	8·6	9·0	7·9	8	7·0	50
2. Rolled metal	7·6	6·8	6·5	6·6	8·4	5·2	8	6·3	—
3. Forge-presses	11·8	2·8	8·2	—	11·0	—	8	6·4[d]	88
4. Cement	15·1	9·7	7·2	7·7	10·0	—	7	5·3[d]	66
5. Leather footwear	9·1	3·0	5·0	4·9	7·4		10	3·4[d]	—
6. Television sets	28·4[e]	16·5	15·5	17·0	20·4	12·0	9	15·1	—
7. Furniture	21·5	10·0	8·4	—	11·1	10·0	9	7·1	—
8. Mineral fertilizer	7·4	17·6	15·2	14·0	16·1	8·3	16	17·3	50
9. Gas	35·4	22·4	13·0	14·6	12·4	10·3	11	14·0	21
10. Coal	5·5	2·5	2·9	3·5	1·2	1·0	1	4·3	103

11. Steel	7·6	5·8	6·8	6·3	6·6	5·2	6	7·4	61
12. Machine tools	5·9	3·5	4·0	—	3·2	—	6	4·5[a]	—
13. Oil equipment	13·8	8·5	10·0	3·6	8·3	—	−1	11·1	106
14. Timber	4·3	5·2	1·2	—	0·2	2·0	7	1·6	158
15. Fish catch	5·3	10·4	8·6	7·9	3·4	8·6	4	10·4	158
16. Textiles	3·0	3·0	5·2	7·9	7·7	—	7	3·5	50
17. Radio sets	3·3	4·5	8·3	—	11·5	—	23	6·3[a]	—
18. Electric power	11·5	11·6	10·8	10·6	7·5	9·7	10	12·2	34
19. Pig iron	7·0	7·2	7·6	6·4	6·2	6·0	5	8·5[a]	67
20. Steel tubes	10·4	9·2	10·0	9·8	9·9	—	9	11·4	—
21. Motor vehicles	3·3	3·3	18·4	—	9·6	—	12	24[a]	—
22. Tractors	7·9	8·3	11·5	8·0	7·6	—	8	14·2[a]	76
23. Knitwear	6·2	9·2	13·4	29·0	9·2	—	10	16·3[a]	—
24. Plastics, etc.[f]	13·4	19·8	21·8	—	21·2	18·0	25	23·3	24
25. Chemical fibres	13·8	14·1	14·6	—	12·5	9·2	9	17·2	—
26. Tinned goods	8·6	7·6	13·6	—	5·7	—	10	19·2[a]	—
27. Motor cycles, etc.	7·7	5·5	7·8	—	4·4	—	4	10·1[a]	—

[a] As percentage of first quarter 1966 (*Pravda*, 16 April 1967).

[b] Assuming 1967 Plan fulfilled.

[c] Soviet claims, mostly for 1964, computed from *Narodnoe khozyaystvo SSSR v 1964 g.*, pp. 87 et seq.

[d] Assuming 1966 growth-rate maintained.

[e] 1959–60.

[f] Including synthetic resins.

Sources: 1956 and 1960 from *Narodnoe khozyaystvo SSSR v 1960 godu* (Moscow, 1961), pp. 237 et seq., and *Pravda*, 19 October 1961; 1965 and 1970 Plan from *Pravda*, 20 February 1966; 1966 Plan from *Pravda*, 8 December 1965; 1966 Fulfilment from *Pravda*, 29 January 1967; 1967 Plan from *Pravda*, 16 December 1966.

Five-Year Plan' has not as yet been worked out in definitive form. It was meant to be completed by December 1966, but various factors which can only be guessed at have enforced a delay of unspecified length. Among the most plausible explanations are the continuing uncertainty about the military situation (the efforts to be put into ABMs and the commitment to Vietnam), and the somewhat unpredictable effects of the large-scale economic reforms now under way. It would be unwise to assume, therefore, that the targets of the Draft Resolutions were necessarily the last word on Soviet intentions for the next four years. Nor is it clear to what extent the annual plans for 1966 and 1967 were conceived as stages on the road to an already discernible goal and to what extent they were mere stopgaps while that goal was still in gestation. Nevertheless the Draft Resolution is all we have to go on for the moment, and at the time of writing we have no choice but to accept it at face value – always mindful of the fact that the publication of new targets, possibly in the summer of 1967, might make a drastic revision necessary.

Looking first at the upper portion of Table 22.1 we note that the recent decline in the growth-rate of national income is to be halted and reversed. In this matter both disappointment of the past and hopes for the future must clearly hinge on the performance of agriculture, and this is, strictly speaking, outside the scope of this article. Suffice it to say that the target of 7% annual growth on average for 1966–70 seems not unreasonable in view of the 1965 recession in the grain harvest and the massive investments planned for agriculture. The planners were evidently hoping for a modest start of the recovery in 1966 and 1967 with a rapid acceleration in the late sixties when the increased agricultural investment had borne fruit. The record harvest of 1966, however, greatly exceeded all expectations and helped to boost the growth-rate of national income well above what was planned for the quinquennium as a whole. As a consequence the growth-rates which remain to be achieved do not greatly exceed the performance of the depressing first half of the sixties and would appear to be attainable on past showing. Indeed, some degree of over-fulfilment seems quite possible, unless there are two or more really bad harvests in the next four years, and provided the 'metal eaters' do not succeed in diverting to their own ends the resources already earmarked for agricultural investment and incentives.

In the matter of industrial development the planners were wise enough not to seek a forced reversal of the declining trend in overall growth rates. Indeed, the industrial expansion planned for 1966 and 1967 seems unambitious by past standards. No doubt allowance was made for considerable diversion of resources to agriculture, substantial shifts in industrial structure, re-tooling problems, and possibly some unsettling effects of the new reforms of management and incentive in its initial stages. In the past year this modesty has been rewarded by spectacular over-fulfilment, particularly in producer goods industries. This seems to have taken the form of improved product-mix and shifts to better quality rather than over-fulfilment in the physical output of standard products (as a glance at the lower portion of the Table will show), but this is probably just what was needed. If the lower targets for 1967 are no more than fulfilled industry will have to perform somewhat better in the last three years of the quinquennium than was planned for the period as a whole. However, there is some hope of repeated over-fulfilment – particularly in the development of consumer industries in the wake of a record harvest – and if this comes about, industry as a whole should be well abreast of its quinquennial task in 1968 in spite of the relatively modest plans for 1967.

Matters stand quite differently in the field of industrial productivity. Here the planners were seeking a sharp reversal of the past decline in growth rates and hoped to approach the performance of the 'roaring fifties' after the severe relapse of the intervening years. Again the recovery was to be very gradual, leaving most of the work to be done in the late sixties. Even with the over-fulfilment claimed for 1966 and the slightly raised target for 1967, the tempo implied for 1968–70 exceeds anything achieved for more than two years at a stretch since the early fifties. Past experience by itself would accordingly suggest that this target may be underfulfilled. Much hope is evidently being pinned on new technological processes, automation, and the reformed system of management and incentives but the speed with which workers can be 'shaken out' of technologically obsolescent enterprises and transferred to new occupations may well have been over-estimated. Moreover, as we see below the influx from collective farms has probably been under-estimated.

The performance of the first quarter however, suggests that the targets for industrial output and labour productivity are well on the way to fulfilment this year.

INDIVIDUAL PRODUCTS

The lower part of Table 22.1 lists the main products for which comparable plan- and fulfilment-data covering all or most of the years under review were found to be available. The products are arranged in four groups corresponding to four different ratings of the likelihood of plan-fulfilment by 1970, so far as this can be judged from the performance of the recent past: products 1 to 7 will be ahead of schedule if the 1967 plan is fulfilled or if last year's performance is repeated (column 8 < column 3); moreover the growth rates which will then remain to be achieved are well within the capabilities already demonstrated in the last decade (column 8 < column 1 or 2). Accordingly, it seems likely that the relevant 1970 targets will be met.

The second group of products (8–15) will be behind schedule even if this year's targets are reached, but the growth-rates which will then remain to be achieved do not exceed what has already been shown to be possible in the last decade. Fulfilment of the Five-Year Plan by this group is therefore somewhat more doubtful, but if the planners' intentions remain unaltered, the evidence does not suggest that there will be any particular difficulty in realizing them.

For the remaining two groups plan-fulfilment during 1968–70 is likely to require growth-rates unprecedented in the pre-plan decade. On present showing, however, industries 16 and 18 will be ahead of schedule by the end of 1967 while the fourth group (18–27) will have fallen behind in varying degrees. Accordingly, it is the last ten targets which would seem to be the least likely to be reached in the current five-year period.

We must, however, beware of accepting the verdict of the past as the sole guide to the future. The strategy and tactics of policy makers may change: resources may be thrown from one sector to another or additional efforts made in investment policy and modernization which can bring unprecedented growth-rates within the reach of any selected branch. The production of pig iron and steel tubes may catch up with the plan thanks to increased investment allocations announced this year, while the performance of the car industry will be vitally affected by the activities of foreign firms (especially Fiat) in putting newly constructed plant into commission. It may be doubted, however, whether the announced intention of almost quadrupling car production in five years will be maintained in view of the large road-building program which this would eventually entail and the competing claims of the space program and defence.

Special efforts may be made to speed the advance of power generation, as the program for rural electrification (trebling electricity consumption per farm-worker in 5 years) is obviously central to the long-delayed revival of agriculture, and the planned saving of 6–8% in electric power per unit of industrial output still takes the eye of faith to see.

The targets for new-type chemicals (plastics, synthetic resins, and artificial fibres) are obviously motivated by the need to save metal and primary products. They still look very high in spite of the severe pruning which followed Khrushchev's fall from power. Quite possibly the renewed attention now being paid to the basic metal industries will permit some further lowering of sights in this exacting field.

By contrast some other targets which have come to look rather small in the light of recent developments in demand may well be stepped up. This could apply to timber, oil, and gas – and possibly to coal as an interim measure. The planners are hoping for a substantial rise in the share of oil and gas in the country's fuel balance by the end of the decade, but additional commitments to supply European countries with gas have since been undertaken. To the extent that these will cut into domestic consumption, somewhat greater reliance on coal may still be necessary.

The performance in January and February 1967 suggests that all the industries whose 1967 targets have been published were on schedule or somewhat ahead of it. Assuming a steady growth rate for six bi-monthly periods throughout the year, the percentage of the annual output required in the first two months is approximately 14·8% if the total is to be met. Apart from the production of television sets, where only 14·9% of the annual target was attained in January and February, all the branches listed are substantially ahead of this figure. The production of electric power, oil, steel, and furniture amounted to 15–16% of the annual task, that of coal, gas, rolled metal and steel pipes to 16–17%. The fishing industry is well ahead of schedule (with over 17%) and timber-hauling in the vanguard (over 20%).

For industries whose annual targets were not announced in the 1967 plan, the January–February performance allows only hypothetical conclusions. For all of them, except cement, however, the assumption that they were no more than on schedule would imply unusually high growth targets for the year as a whole.

THE MANPOWER POSITION

After five years of virtual stagnation the Soviet working-age population is now entering an expansionary phase due to the post-war 'baby boom'.[1] This will bring important changes, not all of them conducive to an easing of the planners' burdens. Above all the influx into urban employment during the next four years may well exceed the level which can be absorbed without large diversions of investment and other resources into comparatively unproductive uses.

Throughout the past decade the number of 'workers and employees' (a category that excludes collective farmers) has grown at an average rate of just under 4·5% p.a.[2] While a small portion of this may have been due to the changed status of *kolkhozniks* whose collectives had been turned into state farms, the bulk of it certainly reflected a true addition to urban

[1] The Russian Republic which accounts for well over half the total population suffered an actual decline in working population during 1959–61 and in the early sixties its labour force increased at barely half the rate of population growth. In the late sixties, however, the working population is expected to grow some 40% faster than the population as a whole – quite possibly at the rate of 1½% p.a. One would not be surprised if the growth rate of urban employment turned out to be twice or three times as high.

[2] Discounting the statistical effects of the 'nationalization' of producer co-operatives in the late fifties.

employment (4·35% p.a. during 1961–65). It is clear that this greatly exceeded the planners' expectations, since the 1965 employment level (76·9 million) was no less than 16% above the target of the Seven-Year Plan. There can be no doubt that much of the excess was due to a flight of younger age-groups – particularly skilled workers – from the collective farms where material rewards had failed to expand at a sufficient rate and the régime had shown itself unable to implement the welfare and incentive measures initiated under Khruschev.

It has been recognized for some time now that a movement of this sort creates serious obstacles to progress in both agriculture and the urban economy. Now that the most obvious slack of agricultural over-population has been removed, all further rural labour leaving the land must be replaced by agricultural machinery, mechanical transport, and fertilizer in large and apparently ever-increasing proportions. This requires a diversion of resources from industrial and other urban investment substantial enough to whittle down or outweigh the gains normally accruing to industry from an inflow of rural labour. At the same time the departure of young and relatively skilled men from agriculture has a depressing effect on farm production which even an adequate inflow of tractors and fertilizer cannot outweigh in the short run, particularly if there is barely enough skilled labour left to put these to proper use.

In the towns the rapid increase in population demands a program of housing and municipal development which seriously impedes the investment effort in other, more immediately 'productive' directions, particularly as it is super-imposed on an already heavy commitment to make good some of the perennial backlog in these fields. Last, but not least, an influx of labour into urban areas poses a serious threat to full employment. This is greatly aggravated by the larger age cohorts now entering the labour market and by the 'spontaneous' geographic shifts of the working population from East to West. Further, the manager is now receiving far greater rights to fire uneconomic labour, as we see below and technological progress increasingly takes the form of automation and other labour-saving innovations. There is no doubt that Soviet society possesses, or can develop, institutional arrangements to cope with this situation, but it is equally clear that this can only be done at considerable cost to economic growth and development as measured by the traditional criteria to which the régime is still committed. The need to provide labour-intensive rather than capital-intensive forms of employment, the necessity of building new factories in small and medium-size towns rather than in the larger centers where overhead facilities and external economies are available, the need to expand 'non-productive' services – all these must be felt to be a drag on expansion.

It is not surprising therefore that the régime is trying to stem the tide of excessive emigration from the countryside. The Five-Year Plan foresees an average annual growth in urban employment[1] of only 3·6% p.a. compared with 4·4% p.a. in

Table 22.2 *Number and growth of employed workers, including members of urban co-operatives*[a]

	Overall total	Of which: agriculture and forestry	In urban occupations		
			Total	Industry and con- struction	Trade, transport, services
Number (million):					
1958	55·9	6·6	49·3	25·3	24·0
1960	62·0	7·5	54·5	27·4	27·1
1965	76·9	9·4	67·5	32·7	34·8
1966	79·7	—	—	—	—
1970 Plan	91–92	—	—	—	—
Annual growth rate (%):					
1959–60	5·3	6·8	5·2	4·1	6·2
1961–65	4·4	4·7	4·3	3·6	5·1
1966	3·6	—	—	—	—
1966–70 Plan	3·55	—	—	—	—

[a] Excluding collective farmers and family workers on private plots whose total may be estimated at approximately 26 million in 1964.

Sources: 1958, 1960 from *Narodnoe khozyaystvo SSSR v 1960 godu*, pp. 545 et seq.; 1965 from *SSSR v tsifrakh v 1965 godu*, p. 121; 1966, 1970 Plan, see Sources to Table 22.1 (p. 288).

[1] This refers to the number of 'workers and employees', which includes about 25% of those occupied in non-urban pursuits (Stat e farm and forestry workers but not collective farmers or private plot-holders).

the previous quinquennium (1961–65). It may be doubted, however, if the level and character of agricultural incentives is even now sufficient to reduce the trend. Experience has taught us that the Soviet system is apt to throw up pressures that can whittle down the best-intentioned welfare- and incentive-measures in agriculture. This happened in the last years of Khrushchev's term of office and could easily happen again, particularly after a reassuring harvest.[1] If it is allowed to happen, all industrial targets (as well as the agricultural ones) will be severely threatened, and even if it is not, the trend may continue with sufficient force to put the productivity target in doubt.

The recently announced growth target of 4.14% for employment in 1967 suggests that the planners may already be reconciled to a substantial over-fulfilment of the Five-Year Plan as far as the number of 'workers and employees' is concerned.

CAPITAL CONSTRUCTION AND EQUIPMENT

One of the salient features of recent economic development which has caused Soviet planners most concern has been the pronounced fall in the return to capital investment in terms of physical output. A Western estimate of the marginal capital-output ratio (based on net capital stock and gross national income in 1937 prices) shows an increase from 2.2 to nearly 3.2 between the first and the second half of the fifties,[2] and a Soviet source states that between 1958 and 1963 the 'co-efficient of capital absorption' has risen by 17.6 percentage points.[3] There is every reason to suppose that the trend will continue and certain Soviet pronouncements clearly imply the expectation – no doubt a highly optimistic one – of a further 6–7% fall in the yield of investment by 1970. Capital investment, the traditional fuel of the Soviet engine of growth, is evidently losing its potency and stands in need of replacement by innovation and streamlining (both technological and organizational) if growth is to continue.

[1] Cf. D. Polyanski in *Pravda*, 3 March 1967.
[2] Richard Moorsteen and Raymond P. Powell, *The Soviet Capital Stock 1928–1962* (Homewood, Ill., 1966), p. 368.
[3] P. Malyshev in *Voprosy Ekonomiki*, no. 6 (1965), p. 40.

Some Soviet economists appear to have accepted this as a law of nature in a maturing economy, working through the exhaustion of readily available natural resources, the accelerated growth of capital-intensive industries, and the lengthening age-structure of the capital stock. Others are not so easily reconciled and point to specific and remediable features of the Soviet system. The traditional disincentive to capital saving, excessive emphasis on building as opposed to equipment, laxity in design and project making, and above all the 'frittering' of the investment effort among too many projects which freezes resources in uncompleted projects and makes for premature obsolescence. Much of the success of the Five-Year Plan will evidently depend on the extent to which these failings can be corrected, but at the same time the need to 'bring up' the backward agricultural – and housing – sectors imposes an investment structure which is anything but conducive to a lowering of capital-output ratios. The temptation to divert resources back to urban industries in the course of plan fulfilment will be great; it must be resisted if the long-run balance and growth-prospects of the economy are not to suffer.

Within urban industries themselves, however, the planned investment pattern shifts away from the most capital-absorbing branches (transport, fuel, power, metals, and engineering) to the relatively less demanding sectors, such as chemicals and light industry. With a 45% increase in allocations to all these branches, investment in transport is to increase by 18% only, while light industry is to get 133% more than in the last quinquennium; fuel, power, and metal-based industries are to get 50–60% more – chemicals as much as 88%. Here there may have been a tendency to sacrifice balance to the goal of lower capital-output ratios from the start. The niggardliness towards transport may result in costly delays in supplies, and the rush from metals into chemicals in shortage of key products such as steel tubes and rolled metal.

As will be evident from Table 22.3 (p. 299), the fulfilment record in the field of capital investment is not good. Last year the plan was again under-fulfilled by some 5%. The growth rates in the lower part of Table 22.3 suggest that the greatest spurt in investment effort in both agriculture and urban industries will have to come in the last three years of the decade if the plan is to be fulfilled. There is a good chance, however, that greater attention to completion dates and deliveries of complementary sets of sub-assemblies and equipment may

Table 22.3 *Volume and growth of fixed capital investment*

| | Total fixed capital investment | | | | Of which: centralized[c] | | |
	Total	Industry, etc.[a]	Agriculture	Residual[b]	Actual	Plan	Fulfilment (%)
Billion roubles at constant prices:							
1961–65	211	105	38[h]	68[h]	—	—	—
1966–70 Plan	310	152	71	87	—	—	—
1960	35.9	17.3	6.2	12.4	24.8	24.6	96.9
1961	37.5	18.0[j]	6.9	12.6[j]	28.0	29.0	96.6
1962	39.3	19.1	7.4	12.8	30.5	30.6	99.7
1963	41.3	20.5	8.2	12.6	32.3	33.5	96.4
1964	45.0	22.7	9.7	12.6	34.8	36.0	96.7
1965	48.3	23.8[f,i]	10.8	12.7	37.2	39.5	94.2
1966	52.0	26.1[f,i]	11.5	14.4	38.7	40.4	95.8
1967 Plan	55.8	27.5[g]	12.2[g]	16.1	—	41.2	—
required average							
1968–70[d]	69.0	32.8	15.8	18.5	—	—	—
Average annual growth-rate (%)							
1961–65	6.1	7.5	11.7	0.5	—	—	—
1966–70[e]	9.3	7.6	16.5	9.8	—	—	—
1968–70 required[d]	11.0	9.1	17.8	8.0	—	—	—

[a] Including construction, transport, and communications.

[b] Comprising housing, municipal services, schools, hospitals, trade and other services. It is not clear into which category defence durables come.

[c] Subject to planning and detailed financial control by the centre.

[d] Required to fulfil Five-Year Plan, assuming 1967 performance as planned or growing at 1966 rate.

[e] Implied steady growth-rate.

[f] Planned.

[g] Assuming 1966 growth-rate continues in 1967.

[h] The coverage and/or pricing of the quinquennial totals does not apparently correspond to the annual data.

[i] Figure for industry alone, scaled up in 1966 proportion.

[j] Estimated as residual of 1961–65 period.

Sources: Narodnoe khozyaystvo SSSR v 1963 g. (p. 452) and *v 1964 g.* (p. 513–14); *SSSR v tsifrakh v 1965 g.*, pp. 112–13; *Pravda* 3 February and 8 December 1965, 20 February 1966, and 29 January 1967.

speed the new capacity actually put into operation, even when the investment plan as such is under-fulfilled. The recent over-haul of administrative structure in the construction industry (which is now under one of seven specialized ministries) could do much to improve technological performance provided incentives do not suffer.

ECONOMIC REFORM

The transfer of industrial enterprises to the new system of management and incentives is now well under way. By the end of 1966 over 700 enterprises accounting for 12% of production and 10% of the labour force in industry had been converted; by early March this year another 1,800 had joined them, and in 1967 as a whole enterprises and branches employing a total of nine million workers will make the transition. By the end of the year more than one third of the country's industrial labour force will work in 'new-style' enterprises.

It seems likely that in the longer run, and possibly by 1970, the new system will have a decidedly beneficial effect on industrial efficiency. The greater freedom from centralized targets, the switch from gross output to actual sales as the main success indicator, the new system of capital charges, investment finance, and incentive funds – all these will make direct appeals to powerful economic motives which have for long been spurned: adaptation to market demand, modernization, cost-reduction, and input-saving. At the same time the return from a pseudo-regional to the 'branch' principle in economic administration should play its part in improving co-ordination in research and development and promoting technological advance. Accordingly, one would like to add this factor to labour and capital investment as a third 'input' into the production function and hazard the guess that its influence will be at least as strong, and likely to increase within the next four years, while that of the other two will be stable or declining.

In the shorter run, however, the effects of the new system are much more problematic. As long as it encompasses only a select band of enterprises, as it is likely to do in the early part of this year, there should be morale-boosting effects from the special attention being paid to the experiment and from the enterprises' own feeling of being in the vanguard. Moreover it is likely that the first enterprises to come under the new dispensation will be those whose performance records were good in the past.[1] At a later stage, however, when less favoured enterprises will be swept into the net, the unsettling effects of the change are likely to make themselves felt – as they are already beginning to do where financially weak establishments are prematurely forced into the transition for the sake of completing the transfer of whole 'branches'. At the same time the welcome opportunities for saving labour which become available can hardly pass without embarrassing effects on the urban employment situation. Redundancy in certain branches and areas is already making its appearance, and the redirection of the investment effort which it will enjoin must eventually result in some impairment of the growth performance which would otherwise be possible.

On the whole, however, the outlook may be described as 'bracing'.

[1] The fact that in the first 11 months of 1966 the new-style enterprises increased their output nearly 1·5 percentage points faster than the industrial average (and their labour productivity 2·8 percentage points faster) does not necessarily establish the superiority of the new system, since nothing is known of their performance under previous conditions.

23

THE SOVIET ECONOMY IN 1967: FORECASTS AND REALITY

FRANCIS SETON, 1968

Now that my previous contribution to this series can be examined in the harsh light of subsequent events I must not flinch from the task of being my own 'just and stern' critic.

To begin with let me recall that I had to use the Draft Resolutions leading up to the 23rd Party Congress as the only available benchmarks against which the chances of success or failure could be measured. I did, however, sound a warning against accepting them as the last word on Soviet intentions for the next three years. My reticence soon turned out to be justified; for barely six months later we were presented with a new blueprint in the shape of Baybakov's report to the October session of the Supreme Soviet.[1] This makes no mention of the still unratified 'eighth Five-Year Plan' (1966–70), but reveals in rough outline how the earlier pronouncements which might have coalesced in such a document have had to be modified in the subsequent eighteen months.

While the total growth target (national income) is only marginally revised (from 40 to 39% for the five-year period), there is to be noticeably greater concentration on industry (53% growth instead of 47–50% in the five years ending 1970). Since no change in the agricultural target is envisaged, this will presumably be achieved by a curtailment of the targets for building construction and the tertiary sectors (transport, trade, etc.). Construction plans will clearly be trimmed in the wake of what is perhaps the most striking change in announced intentions – a swingeing cut in fixed capital investment (from a projected 47% to 43% above the level of the preceding quinquennium) whose chief victims are the investment targets for iron and steel, chemical works, and urban housing. A large part of this is no doubt intended to benefit current consumption,

[1] *Pravda*, 11 October 1967.

as evidenced by the fact that consumer industries had their targets raised somewhat more than producer branches. Another portion, however, may simply betoken higher priorities for defence spending – the closest rival of capital investment – or increased reliance on technical and managerial improve- ments – its closest substitute in the drive for higher produc- tivity. Both these hypotheses may of course be true. The first supported by the raising of output targets for engineering and metal industries unmatched by similar boosts for their chief non-military consumers (civilian construction, motor vehicles, etc.); the second appears plausible in the light of the widespread disillusionment with the ever diminishing effectiveness of physical capital in raising output.

The targets for nearly all individual commodities are slightly cut back or consigned to the lower end of the previously projected range, with the most sizeable curtailments (10–20%) reserved for plastics and artificial fibres. This, in conjunction with the raising of the *global* targets for industry, reinforces the impression that improvement in *quality* and *product-mix* – in a word in technical efficiency – is to be given even higher priority over the mere accumulation of tonnages than was at first supposed. Significantly enough, agriculture is totally exempted from the downward revisions; indeed, its centralized investment target is slightly raised and the plan for rural housing confirmed at the top end of the projected range. It would appear, then, that the revisions can be chalked up as a further advance towards rationality in the setting of targets, the timing of invest- ment effort, and the distribution of incentives, motivated partly by the internal logic of economic development and partly by the supposed need to husband resources for greater military preparedness.

A glance at Table 23.1 below (p. 305) will convince us that the bulk of the revised targets (column 3) are now within reach, and that the further growth performance required to achieve them (column 7) is well within the capabilities already demonstrated in the not very brilliant first half of the decade (column 1). In fact, thanks to these second thoughts by the planners nearly all the targets listed would now shift into what I had identified as the most 'realistic' groups in my previous article (Table 22.1, items 1–15, p. 288); indeed, only the targets

Table 23.1 *Annual growth rates* (%)

	Average 1961–65 actual	Average 1966–70 draft[a]	(Plan) revised[b]	1966 actual	1967 Plan	1967 Actual	Average required for 1968–70[c]	1968 Plan
National income	6·3	7·0	6·8	7·4	6·6	6·7	6·6	6·8
Industrial output	8·6	8·2	8·9	8·6	7·3	10·0	8·6	8·1
Of which:								
producer goods	9·6	8·5	9·2	9·0	7·5	10·2	8·9	7·9
consumer goods	6·3	7·6	8·3	7·0	6·6	9	8·6	8·6
Labour productivity (industry)	4·7	6·1	—	5·0	5·5	7	6·1[a]	6·0
Output of:								
1. Oil	10·4	7·6	7·6	9·0	7·9	9·0	6·6	7·3
2. Rolled metal	6·8	6·5	6·3	8·4	5·2	7·0	5·2	4·2
3. Gas	22·4	13·0	10·7	12·4	10·3	10·0	10·4	8·8
4. Steel	5·8	6·8	6·3	6·6	5·2	6·0	6·3	4·7
5. Chemical fibres	14·1	14·6	11·5	12·5	9·2	11·0	11·3	—
6. Plastics, etc.[b]	19·8	21·8	17·0	21·2	18·0	14·0	16·5	—
7. Electric power	11·6	10·8	9·6	7·5	9·7	8·0	10·8	10·4
8. Mineral fertilizer	17·6	15·2	14·7	16·1	8·3	12·0	15·1	4·7
9. Motor vehicles	3·3	18·4	17·2	9·6	—	8·0	23·2	—

[a] Directives of 23rd Party Congress, April 1966.
[b] Baybakov's report to Supreme Soviet, October 1967.
[c] Required to fulfil the revised targets.
[d] Assuming no revision of draft target.
[e] Including synthetic resins.

Sources: 1966–70 Draft and Revised targets from *Pravda*, 10 April 1966 and 10 October 1967; 1966 *Pravda*, 29 January 1967; 1967 *Pravda*, 16 December 1966 and 25 January 1968; 1968 Plan, *Pravda*, 11 October 1967.

for electricity and fertilizer would fail to make the very top grade (like items 1–7 in that table), by virtue of being still somewhat behind schedule (column 7 > column 3 here).[1] Should I congratulate myself on this implicit recognition that my grouping was right? I hardly think so, for the only exceptions to the massive shift into the 'realistic' groups – the targets for consumer goods and industrial labour productivity[2] – are very crucial ones indeed. The former depends largely on the performance of agriculture (which is outside my terms of reference), and of the latter we shall hear more anon. Both, however, by the exigencies of their fulfilment, may well affect the readiness and success with which all the other targets will be maintained and pursued.

Let me now engage in a more systematic *post mortem* on my conjectures of over eighteen months ago. To take the credits first: I had expressed doubts on the fulfilment of the centralized investment target and on the wisdom of placing so much reliance on investment in general. The target was under-fulfilled and the future program materially cut. I had expressed confidence in the realism of the national income target. It was slightly over-fulfilled and left substantially unchanged for the next three years. I had described the global targets for industry as 'unambitious by past standards'. They were over-fulfilled by ample margins and substantially scaled up for the remainder of the quinquennium. I was also proved right in my conjecture that the global target for consumer industries would be exceeded by a greater margin than that for producer branches. As for the individual output-targets listed above (confining the selection to those for which both fulfilment and revised plan figures were available), there should be few surprises for those who have read my previous contribution: Oil and rolled metal were forecast as easily attainable targets – they were amply exceeded. For gas and steel I had slightly more misgivings – there was a shortfall in the former and over-fulfilment of the latter, but the longer-term program for both was substantially curtailed. I had more serious doubts about the

---

[1] The target for motor vehicles ought to be excluded from such comparisons since there are special expansion plans for this industry with the aid of foreign firms.

[2] Since Dr Seton is seriously wrong only in 1967 I think he is too self-critical – P. J. D. W.

remaining five targets. All of them were severely cut in the longer-term projections, and two of them (electric power and plastics) were also gravely under-fulfilled. The over-fulfilment of the fertilizer and artificial fibre targets, however, is not what I had foreseen.

In general, as I had anticipated, the year 1967 turned out to be a good one for the Soviet economy – due largely to the new-found realism in target-setting, the continuing diffusion of economic reform measures, and the delayed effects of the previous year's bumper harvest. My diagnosis – admittedly not a very original one – that the economy stood in need of greater efficiency rather than large investments, greater incentives rather than higher targets, and further increases in the rewards to agriculture relatively to those in urban industries is certainly not belied by the policy changes implicit in the revised targets.

Where I went wrong quite seriously – at least in the short run – was in my rating of the outlook for manpower and productivity in industry. It is true that I had allowed for the possibility of fulfilment of the productivity target (in the light of the report for the first two months of 1967), but I certainly had not expec-ted the degree of *over*-fulfilment which was in fact achieved (7% as against 5·5% as planned). Most probably this must be linked to the unexpectedly small increase in industrial employ-ment – only 3·3% – where a growth by nearly 4·2% had been envisaged. I had made rather heavy weather with the danger of an excessive migration from the countryside to the towns, both for its effects on agriculture and for the demands it would make on the urban economy, and I had anticipated that rural living standards would still be insufficient to stem this tide. It now appears that, at least in 1967, there was some let-up in this respect, and authoritative voices even complain of incipient labour shortages in industry. I was clearly wrong to disregard them. In mitigation, however, it should be noted that the situation is one of great complexity. While the largest towns of the country had obviously experienced labour shortages for some time, particularly in the service industries, it was also clear that the great mass of small and medium-sized urban centres were trying to cope with a sizeable surplus recently arrived from the countryside which they did not have the resources to employ. Moreover, the abrupt raising of agricultural incentives – almost exclusively benefiting young and skilled workers – might well have no more than a once-for-all effect in persuading likely migrants to stay on the land. Once the first flush of satisfaction with this material advance is over it may require *continued* and *increasing* doses of it to prevent a renewed acceleration of the rural outflow. We know that the régime has been (at least temporarily) alerted to these needs. But is it permanently converted, and will it be able to enforce the new priorities sufficiently against the formidably entrenched lobbies of super-industrializers, militarists, metal-eaters, and what have you? It is much to be hoped, but only time will tell. Meanwhile, as far as my own conjectures are concerned, it may yet be too early for sackcloth and ashes.

24

SOVIET AGRICULTURE

W. KLATT, 1967

When the present series of analysis and prediction was designed, a paper on 'Soviet Farm Output and Food Supply in 1970' was already in the press. It was presented originally at the Conference on Soviet and East European Agriculture held at Santa Barbara, California, in August 1965. Text and statistical tables were amended slightly in the light of information that became available before the paper appeared a year later in the *St. Antony's Papers* (No. 19).[1] As not enough has happened in the six months since publication to justify another article of analysis and prediction, it will be one of the purposes of this note to bring up to date last year's account. But more important, the publication of the present series of papers provides the opportunity, in this particular instance, of engaging in the exercise of self-criticism.

It would be presumptuous to suggest that the assessment of Soviet farm output and food supply has 'passed from the stage of craftsmanship and chronicling to that of becoming a science'. This stage may have been reached in other areas of economic research: not so here. Analysis and projection is more difficult in the case of agricultural processes than it is in other sectors of Soviet society. The reason for this lies partly in the particular way in which this all-important area of national endeavour has been treated by the Soviet Union ever since the revolution fifty years ago. The approach to the farming industry has been marked by a lack of rationality which has not affected other sectors to anything like the same degree.

MARXIST MISUNDERSTANDINGS

This lack of rationality may be explained to some extent by the very nature of agriculture which the Marxist school and its

[1] W. Klatt, 'Soviet Farm Output and Food Supply in 1970', *St. Antony's Papers*, no. 19 (Oxford, 1966).

followers have never handled very happily. It would be wrong
to suggest that agriculture follows patterns of behaviour that
are different from those observed in other spheres of human
endeavour (in fact, the Marxist school committed this very
error when using as a measure of its agricultural concept the
size of the farm instead of its capital input and its output per
man). Yet, agriculture has certain specific characteristics that
are absent from the environment of other industries.[1]

Farming, unlike industry, has to take into account space and
weather as limiting factors. In normal conditions the cost of
haulage is more decisive in determining farm sizes than certain
economies of scale frequently quoted. In Soviet Russia the
amalgamation of farms has been carried out without regard
to the cost of transportation. As to the effect of weather and
distance on labour, the farm-hand who mostly works without
a roof over his head and without a superior at close quarters,
operates with a measure of freedom of decision that is most
unusual in the case of the industrial worker of corresponding
grade. The larger the farm, the greater the need to delegate
decisions to the individual. Under communist conditions the
tendency is generally to do the opposite. In agriculture too –
unlike industry – the producer, besides being a consumer of
his own product, is mostly also a processer of finished foodstuffs.
He is therefore able to alter the pattern of production, utilization and marketing in many ways and thus to evade public
controls far more effectively than the industrial producer who
rarely is a consumer of his product. Thus in agriculture, far
more than in industry, a relationship of mutual trust is needed
between the producer and the State. None of these characteristics of the farming industry has been taken properly into account
during the last fifty years of Soviet agricultural history. It seems
doubtful whether they are fully understood in Russia even
today. If they were, the conclusion would be inescapable that
the existing system has to be dismantled rather than amended.
The political consequences of such a recognition would be
momentous indeed.

Projections are not necessarily predictions; much less
prophecies. They merely provide indications of the direction
in which production and consumption are likely to move. One

---

[1] W. Klatt, 'Fifty Years of Soviet Agriculture', *Survey*, no. 64 (London, 1967).

does not have to be a good prophet to recognize that in the *terra incognita* of Soviet agriculture the rate of fallacy is high and the degree of accuracy is open to chance, to say the least. In this situation it is fortuitous that the Soviet authorities, whilst still unnecessarily secretive on such matters as farm and food prices, have recently revealed some data that are of assistance in the process of self-criticism. Last year, for the first time in a quarter of a century, the Soviet government issued industrial wage data[1] without which it is difficult to estimate the portion of the industrial worker's income that is spent on food. This ratio serves as a useful rod against which to measure the likelihood of any improvement in the diet during the period under review. It so happens that the published data, though slightly different from those used in the first version of 'Soviet Farm Output and Food Supply in 1970', fully confirmed the original calculation, i.e. that approximately one half of the average industrial working family's income is spent on food. This sets a rather severe limit to the prospect of a substantially improved diet at a time when the propensity to purchase industrial durables is great and the likelihood of retail prices and retail price ratios changing in favour of foodstuffs is minimal.

The latest information that has become available relates to the level of consumption of certain selected foodstuffs. The last firm information on the food consumption of the non-farm population could be gleaned from Gosplan's project of the first Five-Year Plan.[2] This was forty years ago. Now per capita consumption figures are given for five foodstuffs, i.e. grains and pulses; potatoes; meat and animal fats; milk and milk products; and eggs.[3] No information is given on the level of consumption of sugar, fish, fruit and vegetables, and vegetable fats. Thus some of the most valuable items of the diet have been ignored by the compilers of last year's statistical yearbook. The items listed account only for approximately 80% of the total daily food intake. The available information is most welcome none the

[1] *Narkhoz 1964* (Moscow, 1965), p. 554.
[2] *Gosplan, I* (Moscow, 1928), 106.
[3] *Narkhoz 1965* (Moscow, 1966), p. 597.

11

less. It permits a check on views expressed previously on the level and composition of the Soviet diet. As the items listed account for approximately 2,400 calories of the daily food intake and the missing items can be estimated with a reasonable degree of certainty, the total nutritive value of the Soviet diet would seem to amount at present to no more than 3,000 calories (against 3,100 calories previously estimated). As to the composition of the diet, grains and potatoes, the two main sources of carbohydrates, seem to supply only 60% of the total intake (as compared with 65% previously estimated).

Whilst these amendments of previously held views may appear to be rather trifling, the information released contains, in fact, some important revelations. The level of consumption of grains and pulses (in terms of flour) is given at 156 kg., or less than 350 lb., per head per annum (against 180 kg., or almost 400 lb., previously estimated – about 15% too much). Even allowing for as high an extraction rate as 80%, the total consumption of grains would be less than 200 kg. (as compared with 220 kg. previously estimated). Total human requirements would thus amount to approximately 45 million tons (or 5 million tons less than was assumed in the food balance for 1965/66). Almost half the total amount is, of course, needed in the rural areas rather than by urban consumers. Even allowing for the additional requirements of industry and of the food deficit countries of the communist bloc, it is difficult to see for what reasons the Soviet authorities insist on an annual procurement and delivery target of over 55 million tons. A goal of this order of magnitude implies that all grain, including the amount consumed by the farm population, passes through State-controlled channels. This hardly seems a necessary procedure; nor would it seem desirable in a country that is still short of country roads, storage space and administrative skill. There is reason to suspect that at least some of the grain recorded as procured merely moves on paper and not in reality. Even so, the actual movements seem unnecessarily great.

Some part of the apparent saving in grain supplies is made up by a larger consumption of potatoes than previously estimated, i.e. 141 kg., or over 300 lb., as compared with 125 kg., or 275 lb. – an under-estimate of 10%. This error suggests that either more potatoes are produced on the private plots than is actually reflected in the national production figures or that less potatoes are fed to pigs in the rural areas than would seem sensible. Considering the poor conditions of the roads it hardly seems prudent to transport 4 million tons of potatoes instead of 1 million tons of grains.

Compared with the figures for grain and potatoes, the two chief items of the diet, the discrepancies revealed by the official statistics with regard to the two animal products, meat and eggs, though far from trifling, have a less serious impact on the overall picture. The consumption of meat (including animal fats) is given officially at 41 kg. (or 90 lb.)[1] against 36 kg. (or 80 lb.) previously estimated – 15% too little. The corresponding figures for the consumption of eggs are 124 (about 6 kg.) and 100 (5 kg.) respectively – an under-estimate of almost 25%. If less grain is needed to meet human requirements and more grain is available for feeding purposes, the output of animal products must be assumed to be higher and the element of exaggeration to be lower than in my original estimates. Even so, there can be no doubt that not only does the official grain record have to be deflated by approximately 20%, but correspondingly the official production figures for meat and eggs need scaling down by approximately 15% (against 20% assumed previously: see Table 1 and 2 of *St. Antony's Papers*, no. 19). They cannot in any other way be brought into line with the consumption data now available. This applies equally to the official production estimate for milk which has to be deflated by 15% so as to be brought into line with the official consumption estimate for milk and milk products on which there is no discrepancy between the official data and the estimates made previously.

FOOD BALANCE 1966/67

An all-time record grain harvest was reported at the end of 1966. The Soviet Union thus enters its fiftieth year in a comfortable position with regard to both the rural producer and the

[1] Shortly after this figure was published in the *Soviet Statistical Yearbook for 1965*, Vladimir Matskevich, the Minister of Agriculture, stated at a press conference on 27 December 1966, that the Soviet consumption of meat (including animal fats) was now 44 kg. (97 lb.) – as against 41 kg. (90 lb.) given in the yearbook. He compared this with 100 kg. (220 lb.) of meat consumed in the United States.

urban consumer. Even if the official crop estimate has to be deflated by 20%, reducing the total from 171 to approximately 135 million tons, there is enough grain in the country to put 15 million tons into reserve after all normal domestic needs and export commitments have been met. This satisfactory result is partly due to the exceptionally favourable weather conditions that prevailed throughout the season in all the main grain-growing areas – a situation that rarely occurs more than once or twice in a decade. Besides, the farm policy that has been followed since Khrushchev's fall from power in October 1964 has borne its first fruits.

The 'urgent measures for the further development of Soviet agriculture', introduced by Brezhnev since the plenary meeting of the Central Committee held in March 1965 have not been without effect. The announcement of fixed grain delivery quotas for a period of six years, the payment of a bonus of 50% for above-quota deliveries, the increase in purchase prices for livestock and animal products, the increase in farm invest-ment, the restoration to their former size of the private plots, the promise of a guaranteed monthly pay for members of collectives, and the creation of a moderate pension for their retired members are bound to have created an atmosphere in the countryside more favourable than has existed since col-lectivization was introduced 40 years ago.

On the technical side, for the first time in Russian history substantial amounts of commercial fertilizers have fallen on grain other than maize – the only grain that used to be so treated when it was Khrushchev's favoured crop. Some 2·5 million tons of plant nutrients may have been applied on 125 million hectares of grain. The application, in a year of favour-able weather, of 20 kg. of nutrients per hectare (18 lb. per acre) of grain might well have been responsible for the bulk of the 25 million tons (dry grain equivalent) that were harvested in 1966 over and above the crop of 1965. In a bad year the fertilizers allocated to grain would have to be supplemented by corresponding efforts in the control of soil moisture, plant diseases and weeds to secure a similarly favourable result. A bumper crop of cotton was also harvested, but the yields of sugar beet, potatoes, vegetables and sunflower seeds were lower than in 1964, the last good year on record.

In animal farming, a decline in pig numbers, both for the pig industry as a whole and in the private sector in particular, deserves to be recorded. On 1 January 1966, the pig population was registered at 18·2 million, or one quarter larger than twelve months earlier. The members of collectives and other private pig breeders had clearly drawn their own conclusions from Brezhnev's announcements of March 1965. Instead of taking advantage of the bonus paid for grain deliveries above the target quota, they had chosen to retain as much grain as possible. Thus in a year in which the grain harvest was low, farm retentions increased whilst deliveries declined drastically from 68·3 million tons in 1964 to 36·3 million tons in 1965, thus forcing the Government to augment domestic supplies through grain purchases abroad. The farmers' reaction to the price changes of 1965 was not dissimilar to that observed twelve years earlier when the increase in October 1953 of meat prices caused a run on the country's grain supplies and thus a shortage that led to the virgin land campaign. The situation was less serious in 1965, and the bumper crop of 1966 removed all possible cause for anxiety. Yet, the decline on 1 January 1967 in total pig numbers by 3% and by 9% in the private sector suggests that local authorities persuaded farmers in 1966 to accept the above-quota grain bonus to collective farms in place of the private income, earned in 1965 from turning grain into pork.

THE PROSPECTS FOR 1967 AND 1970

The bumper crop of grain has relieved the Soviet leaders of the need for imports which in the two bad seasons of 1963/64 and 1965/66 cost the country a total outlay of almost $2,000 million in foreign exchange. Against this, the purchase – at special prices – of 20 million tons of grain over and above the obligatory delivery target is likely to cost the exchequer in 1966/67 over R. 2,000 million, equivalent to 2% of the national budget. In the interest of reducing the calls on public funds, the official procurement policy may well have to be amended once again. In the immediate future, in an attempt to recoup some of the cost of the grain bonus, the exchequer is likely to urge state farms and collectives to increase their own contributions

to the farm investment programme. Last year actual investment fell behind the plan by R. 1,000 million or 10%; whilst
the shortfall of the collectives was only 5%, the State investment plan was under-fulfilled by 13%. The plan for 1967
provides for farm investment of R. 11,300 million, split evenly
between the budget and the collectives. It thus falls somewhat
behind the targets originally set. The input of farm requisites
is likely to be affected by these economies in the investment
programme.

In view of this, the planned increase in gross farm output by
4% in 1967 seems the most that can be expected in normal
conditions. The rate of growth may in fact be less since winter
grains suffered from lack of soil moisture in the autumn. It is
too early, however, to be definite on the prospects for the season
that lies immediately ahead. Looking further into the future,
the prospects of fulfilling by 1970 the moderate farm targets of
the current Five-Year Plan have improved as a result of the
good head start in 1966, the first year of the plan period. The
present Soviet leadership has wisely based its plan targets in
agriculture on five-year averages. Khrushchev, having based
his Seven-Year Plan (1959 to 1965) on the exceptionally good
harvest of 1958, faced embarrassment when later on poor crops
were related to the base year. In spite of the good start on this
occasion, setbacks cannot be ruled out since the input of farm
requisites is not yet large and varied enough to counter-balance
the great fluctuations in yields which are still a mark of the
farm industry in the Soviet Union – as in other agriculturally
neglected parts of the world. The growth rate of 10% in gross
agricultural output in 1966 was superimposed on a rate of 2%
in 1965. In fact, there was probably a decline of farm output in
the year.[1] The statistical manipulation in the first year of rule
by the new leadership may well prove a disservice to their
ultimate record of achievements in this sphere.

Whilst the harvest estimate of 1966 and the release of official

[1] At the end of 1965 Polyansky, the Party's agricultural specialist, estimated a
decline of gross agricultural production of 2–3% compared with 1964. This estimate
was changed in the plan fulfilment report to a rise of 1%, and it was changed again
in the statistical yearbook to an increase of 2%. Nothing is known to have happened
in the farm industry of the Soviet Union following Poliansky's statement that
would justify the statistical changes.

In the Report of the Joint Economic Committee of the US Congress, an increase consumption data have necessitated some amendments, there does not yet appear to be any need to alter the forecast presented for 1970. The only foreseeable cause for a further reassessment might be any far-reaching resolutions of the forthcoming Third Kolkhoz Congress. This was first scheduled to take place early in 1959, but it has been repeatedly – and even recently – postponed for reasons not stated. As the commission charged with drafting a new agricultural model charter has not yet released its findings, the results of this conference cannot be anticipated with any degree of certainty. If the liberal critics of present farm politics were to gain ground, substantial improvements in the structure and performance of agriculture could result. If the traditionalists hold their ground – and this seems more probable in present conditions – no startling changes are likely to occur. In that case the fulfilment of the plan targets for 1970 is the best that can be hoped for. Even an increase, in five years, of 25% over the level achieved in 1965 would be no mean achievement. The output of the farm industry could increase by as much as 30% in the case of exceptionally favourable weather, but the increase could be as little as 15% in adverse circumstances. This was the forecast in *St. Antony's Papers* No. 19, and it thus stands in spite of the adjustments that have been made in this paper and in the following statistical tables.

---

of 1% in gross garm production is set against an estimated decline of 4% in net (value added) farm production (*New Directions in the Soviet Economy* (Washington, 1966) p. 493).

Table 24.1 *Revised estimates of gross and net output of farm products in the Soviet Union, 1965/66, 1966/67 and 1970/71 (million tons, roubles per ton, and thousand million roubles at 1958 prices)*

Commodities	Quantities (million tons)			Farm prices (roubles per ton)		Output (thousand million roubles at 1958 prices)		
	1965/66	1966/67	1970/71	1958	1965	1965/66	1966/67	1970/71[c]
Gross output:[a]								
grains	120·50	170·80	180·00	75	85	9·05	12·80	13·50
potatoes	88·00	87·20	100·00	40	70	3·50	3·50	4·00
vegetables	17·00	17·20	24·00	90	75	1·55	1·55	2·15
sugarbeet	71·50	73·88	80·00	23	28	1·65	1·75	1·90
sunflower seed	5·40	6·14	6·50	172	180	0·95	1·05	1·10
flax	0·45	0·50	0·55	2,300	2,300	1·05	1·15	1·25
cotton	5·75	6·00	6·50	340	383	1·95	2·05	2·20
wool	0·35	0·37	0·40	3,500	3,500	1·25	1·30	1·40
milk	72·50	76·10	82·50	115	150	8·35	8·75	9·50
meat (live weight)	16·00	17·50	20·50	685	890	10·95	12·00	14·05
eggs	1·45	1·57	2·00	1,200	1,400	1·75	1·90	2·40
Total	—	—	—	—	—	42·00 =100	47·80[d] =114[d]	53·45 =127

Net output:[b]

grains	51·50	70·00	68·00	75	85	3·85	5·25	5·10
potatoes	36·50	38·00	37·00	40	70	1·45	1·50	1·50
vegetables	15·50	15·50	21·50	90	75	1·40	1·40	1·95
sugarbeet	65·00	70·00	75·00	23	28	1·50	1·65	1·75
sunflower seed	5·00	6·00	6·50	172	180	0·85	1·05	1·10
flax	0·45	0·50	0·55	2,300	2,300	1·05	1·15	1·25
cotton	5·75	6·00	6·50	340	383	1·95	2·05	2·20
wool	0·35	0·37	0·40	3,500	3,500	1·25	1·30	1·40
milk	55·00	58·50	63·00	115	150	6·35	6·70	7·25
meat (live weight)	13·50	15·00	17·50	685	890	9·25	10·25	12·00
eggs	1·25	1·35	1·70	1,200	1,400	1·50	1·60	2·05
Total	—	—	—	—	—	30·40 = 100	33·90 = 111	37·55 = 123

[a] Based on production levels officially claimed or likely to be claimed.

[b] Net of waste, seed, feed and statistical exaggeration.

[c] Assuming 1965 farm prices.

[d] The gross output is claimed to have exceeded 61·000 million roubles in 1966 and to have been approximately 10% more than in 1965 (Pravda, 29 January 1967). This suggests that prices higher than those used here have been applied and that commodities not listed here, e.g. fruits and oilseeds other than sunflower seeds, have been included. This difference may also account for the different rate of growth in 1966 compared with 1965.

Table 24.2 *Revised estimates of food balances for the Soviet Union in 1966/67 and 1970/71 (million tons, kg. per head, and calories per day)*

Commodities	Domestic production[a]	Net trade net reserves	Domestic supply	Waste, seed, feed	Industrial use	Human consumption Total	Human consumption kg. per head	Human consumption Calories per day
			1966/67 (Population: 235 million)					
Grains and pulses (as such)	135·00	−20·00	115·00	65·00	4·50	45·50	195·00	—
(as flour)	—	—	—	—	—	36·50	155·00	1,535
Potatoes (fresh)	90·00	—	90·00	52·00	5·00	33·00	140·00	260
Sugar (refined)	9·50	−1·25	8·25	0·25	0·50	7·50	33·50	350
Fruit and vegetables	26·00	—	26·00	2·50	—	23·50	100·00	90
Meat (dressed)	9·25	—	9·25	—	0·50	8·75	37·00	220
Fish (landed)	5·00	—	5·00	1·50	—	3·50	15·00	25
Milk (liquid)	64·50	—	64·50	6·00	30·50	28·00	120·00	215
Cheese	0·75	—	0·75	—	—	0·75	3·00	20
Eggs	1·35	+0·05	1·40	—	—	1·40	6·00	30
Fats and oils (as such)	3·75	—	3·75	—	0·75	3·00	12·50	—
(pure)	—	—	—	—	—	—	11·00	255
Total	—	—	—	—	—	—	—	3,000

1970/71 (Population: 250 million)

Grains and pulses (as such)	145·00	−15·00	130·00	77·00	5·50	47·50	190·00	—
(as flour)	—	—	—	—	—	37·50	150·00	1,495
Potatoes (fresh)	100·00	—	100·00	63·00	4·50	32·50	130·00	235
Sugar (refined)	9·50	+0·50	10·00	0·50	0·75	8·75	35·00	370
Fruit and vegetables	33·00	—	33·00	3·00	—	30·00	120·00	100
Meat (dressed)	11·00	—	11·00	—	1·00	10·00	40·00	240
Fish (landed)	6·00	—	6·00	2·00	—	4·00	16·00	30
Milk (liquid)	70·00	—	70·00	7·00	31·75	31·25	125·00	225
Cheese	1·00	—	1·00	—	—	1·00	4·00	25
Eggs	1·60	+0·15	1·75	—	—	1·75	7·00	35
Fats and oils (as such)	5·00	—	5·00	—	0·75	4·25	16·50	—
(pure)	—	—	—	—	—	—	15·00	345
Total	—	—	—	—	—	—	—	3,100

a Deflated so as to eliminate statistical exaggerations and components of production not included in Western definitions.

Table 24.3 *Revised estimates of cost of food supplies in the Soviet Union, 1966/67 and 1970/71 (kg. per head, roubles per kg, and roubles at 1958 and 1965 prices)*

Commodities	Kg. per head		Roubles per kg.		Roubles at 1958 prices		Roubles at 1965 prices	
	1966/67	1970/71	1958	1965	1966/67	1970/71	1966/67	1970/71
Bread	125·0	125·0	0·15	0·16	18·75	18·75	20·00	20·00
Flour	55·0	50·0	0·30	0·30	16·50	15·00	16·00	15·00
Potatoes	140·0	130·0	0·08	0·08	11·20	10·40	11·20	10·40
Sugar	33·5	35·0	0·94	0·94	31·50	32·90	31·50	32·90
Fruit and vegetables	100·0	120·0	0·50	0·50	50·00	60·00	50·00	60·00
Meat	37·0	40·0	1·40	1·80	51·50	56·00	66·60	72·00
Fish	15·0	16·0	1·20	0·75	18·00	19·20	11·25	12·00
Milk	120·0	125·0	0·20	0·26	24·00	25·00	31·20	32·50
Cheese	3·0	4·0	3·20	3·20	9·60	12·80	9·60	12·80
Eggs	6·0	7·0	1·40	1·80	8·40	9·80	10·80	12·60
Fats and oils	12·5	16·5	2·10[c]	2·20[d]	26·35	34·60	27·95	36·40
Total per head	—	—	—	—	265·80	294·45	286·60	316·60
Total per family (of 3·5 persons)[a]	—	—	—	—	—	—	1,003·00	1,108·00
Earnings per worker	—	—	—	—	—	—	1,200·00	1,310·00
Earnings per family (of 1·6 workers)[b]	—	—	—	—	—	—	1,920·00	2,109·60
Cost of food supplies (in per cent of family earnings)	—	—	—	—	—	—	52·2	52·5

[a] M. Sonin, *Current Problems of the Use of the Labour Force in the USSR* (Moscow, 1965).
[b] *Narkhoz 1964* (Moscow, 1965), p. 554.
[c] Butter 2·70; margarine 1·50; cooking fat 2·20.
[d] Butter 3·50; margarine 1·50; cooking fat 1·80.

25

SOVIET FARM OUTPUT AND FOOD SUPPLY AT THE END OF THE EIGHTH FIVE-YEAR PLAN

W. KLATT, 1970

The eighth Five-Year Plan got off to a good start. Brezhnev's 'urgent measures for the further development of Soviet agriculture' were more balanced, if less daring, than those of his predecessor. It was thus understandable if some Western observers expressed confidence that this time – for the first time in Soviet history – the agricultural plan would be fully met. There was even a certain amount of speculation that by the end of the current plan in 1970 Russia might enter the world market as a grain supplier rather than as the large-scale buyer of the recent past.[1]

A mere marginal change for the better or for the worse can, of course, turn a national deficit into a surplus and vice versa. Even so, steps taken during and after the Party's Central Committee meeting of March 1965 never seemed sufficient to secure in full the growth of Soviet agriculture by 25% during the eighth Five-Year Plan – equal to an average annual compound rate of $4\frac{1}{2}\%$ – or by twice as much as had been possible in the preceding five years. Whereas an increase of that magnitude over 1965, a year of poor performance, seemed within reach, the same could not be said with certainty when the Soviet leaders took the more favourable five-year average 1961–65 as their reference for the current plan. On this basis a growth rate of 20% over five years, or a little over $3\frac{1}{2}\%$ a year, seemed the most that could be expected.

The chief reasons underlying this view were threefold: (1) The targets for farm investment from public and collective funds as well as those for essential farm inputs seemed unduly optimistic; (2) the probability of annual fluctuations in grain output, due to the continued reliance on marginal lands in

[1] K. Bush, Radio Liberty, CRD 403 and 405 of 8 and 11 November 1968.

Central Asia, and thus in the supply of concentrated feedstuffs for the livestock industry seemed to have been ignored; and (3) a fundamental change of approach to the structural weaknesses of Soviet agriculture, due to doctrinal preconceptions, seemed as unlikely under the new Soviet leadership as it had been under its predecessors. In the event the assumptions underlying this prognosis have proved correct and the conclusions drawn are likely to be as close to reality at the end of 1970 as will ever be possible in a sector of the national economy which is still subject as much to the whims of nature as to the commands of man.

Just the same, the achievements of the current plan period must not be belittled. Although the planners had overestimated the productive capacities of the equipment and fertilizer industries as well as the absorptive capacity of the agricultural sector, barring unfavourable growing and harvesting conditions the physical and financial returns of 1970 will be fairly satisfactory, even though somewhat below target in certain areas, such as commercial and fodder crops and in livestock farming. Progress has been made in both the application of agricultural technology and the techniques of farm management. This success can be attributed chiefly to the material inducements granted under Brezhnev's 'urgent measures', in particular the increase in financial returns from grains and livestock products and the monthly guaranteed minimum pay to members of collectives. As a result, the purchasing power of the kolkhozniks has improved significantly and the income differential between urban and rural society has declined markedly.

Farm output cannot be expected to progress as predictably as industrial production. Even so, the annual fluctuations of gross agricultural production rates (1966: 8·7; 1967: 1·5) and of crop production in particular (1966: 12·7; 1967: 0·1) have been surprisingly severe. 1967 and 1969 have been disappointing years. The large long-term investment in land improvement and the annual outlay on current account, designed not only to raise output but also to reduce annual fluctuations, have largely failed; only in the livestock sector has a reasonable degree of stability been reached. Livestock herds have increased though, by a mere 8% (measured in livestock units) and milk

yields and carcass weights by approximately 15%. Deliveries
of livestock products have increased faster than production –
a sign of improved market facilities.

The price of what has been achieved has been high. Farm
investment has increased at twice the rate of farm output.
At an average annual increase of R. 4,000 million in investment the volume of gross farm production is likely to have
grown on average by less than R. 15,000 million. The annual
farm support bill surpasses R. 7,000 million by now. The
success of the current plan might well have been greater and
less costly, if the drafters of the new Kolkhoz Charter, belatedly
approved at the Third All-Union Congress of Kolkhozniks in
November 1969, had been half as daring as some of their
critics. In the event the Charter turned out to be a singularly
uninspiring document which merely institutionalized existing
practices and confirmed doctrinal prejudices. Brezhnev admitted certain mistakes committed in the course of Stalin's
collectivization campaign, but he disowned those who, he
held, exaggerated the cost of a great revolutionary event.[1]

As an exercise in prognostication, the preparation of the
original paper presented at the Conference on Soviet and
East European Agriculture (Santa Barbara, California, August
1965), the amended version published in *St. Antony's Papers*,
no. 19 (Oxford, 1966) and the agricultural section of Professor
de Jouvenel's *Analyse et Prévision*, III, no. 6 (Paris, June 1967),
which in turn forms the basis of the postscript, has been highly
worthwhile. Although the forecast of 1965 and the (partly
unpublished) statistics underlying it have stood the test of the
subsequent five years, there have been errors. The most serious
of them has been the overestimate of pig numbers and pork
production – a notoriously difficult subject, as anyone concerned with pig cycles knows all too well. In the public sector
pig numbers increased by a mere 10% in five years, and in the
private sector they declined slightly. On 1 January 1970, the
overall total was 56 million as against the all-time record of
70 million in 1963 (and an estimated end of plan figure of
75 million). The effect of growing pressure on collectives to

---

[1] The issue on which, before the end of the Congress, Polyansky, the Party's
spokesman on agricultural matters, came into conflict with his superiors has not
yet been divulged. Hence this affair cannot be assessed at this juncture.

Table 25.1 *Soviet Union. Agricultural indicators*

Five-Year Plan periods (calendar years)	Agricultural gross production			Agricultural gross investment		
	Million roubles (constant)	Roubles per ha. arable land	Roubles per employed agricultural person	State farms million roubles	Collectives million roubles	Total million roubles
Average 1961–65 (actual)	66·3	290	2,140	5·0	3·6	8·6
Average 1966–70 (provisional)	80·0	354	2,665	6·6	5·9	12·5
Average 1961–65 = 100	121	122	124	132	164	145

Five-Year Plan period (calendar years)	Agricultural production			Agricultural production		
	Grains million tons	Potatoes million tons	Sugarbeet million tons	Meat million tons	Milk million tons	Eggs million tons
Average 1961–65 (actual)	130·5	81·6	59·2	9·3	64·7	1·43
Average 1966–70 (provisional)	163·8	95·4	82·3	11·5	80·7	1·76
Average 1961–65 = 100	125	117	140	124	125	123

	Crop and livestock yields			Farm deliveries		
Five-Year Plan period (calendar years)	Grains tons per ha.	Meat kg. per livestock units	Milk tons per cow	Grains million tons	Meat million tons	Milk million tons
Average 1961–65 (actual)	1·02	98	1·69	51·6	5·3	31·1
Average 1966–70 (provisional)	1·33	113	1·97	65·3	7·2	42·8
Average 1961–65 = 100	130	115	117	126	136	138

	Farm requisites			Farm requisites		
Five-Year Plan period (calendar years)	Tractor supply thousand	Lorry supply thousand	Fertilizer supply million tons	Tractor park HP per 1,000 ha.	Electricity supply kwh. per ha.	Fertilizer supply kg. per ha.
Average 1961–65 (actual)	217	70	18·0	205[a]	95[a]	28·5[a]
Average 1966–70 (provisional)	293	120	36·0	285[b]	140[b]	42·0[b]
Average 1961–65 = 100	135	170	200	140[c]	147[c]	147[c]

[a] 1965.   [b] 1970.   [c] 1965 = 100.
Original Soviet statistics. Estimates.

Table 25.2 *Soviet Union. Agricultural forecasts*

Eighth Five-Year Plan (final year)	Agricultural production					
	Grains million tons	Potatoes million tons	Sugarbeet million tons	Meat million tons	Milk million tons	Eggs million tons
1970 (original)	180·0	100·0	75·0	13·0	80·0	1·9
1970 (revised)	170·0	100·0	85·0	12·0	83·5	1·9
1970 (original) = 100	94	100	113	92	104	100

Eighth Five-Year Plan (final year)	Farm requisites					
	Tractor supply thousand	Lorry supply thousand	Fertilizer supply million tons	Tractor park HP per 1,000 ha.	Electricity supply kwh. per ha.	Fertilizer supply kg. per ha.
1970 (original)	300	175	40·0	320	150	42·0
1970 (revised)	310	150	40·0	285	147	41·5
1970 (original) = 100	103	85	100	90	98	99

Eighth Five-Year Plan (final year)	Food consumption					
	Grains (as flour) kg. per head	Potatoes kg. per head	Sugar kg. per head	Meat kg. per head	Milk kg. per head	Fats and oils kg. per head
1970 (original)	150·0	130·0	35·0	40·0	125·0	16·5
1970 (revised)	150·0	130·0	40·0	40·0	125·0	16·5
1970 (original) = 100	100	100	114	100	100	100

deliver grain above the statutary quota, preventing grain retention on farms from increasing, and of the change from payment in kind to kolkhozniks to payment in cash, was clearly stronger than had been anticipated. Against this, the success of sugarbeet growers and sugar factories turned out to be greater than expected.

The average Russian diet is thus likely to give the consumer this year 3,150 calories a day (against 3,100 estimated originally), containing 100 grammes of fats, 55 grammes of plant protein and 35 grammes of animal protein. It thus resembles Mediterranean conditions rather than those of Western Europe. Although wages have risen substantially, almost half the average urban family income is still spent on purchasing this diet. All in all, this analysis confirms the conclusions reached by the latest survey of the Economic Commission for Europe, i.e. that agriculture remains the major problem sector of the Soviet economy.[1] This assessment has been confirmed by Brezhnev in his statement on agriculture, made (after the completion of this chapter) in July 1970.[2]

---

[1] *EEC*, Survey on the European Economy, part 2, chapter 1, p. 7 (Mimeographed, Geneva, 1970). A more optimistic view was expressed by H. E. Walters and R. W. Judy at the Conference on Soviet Agricultural and Peasant Affairs held at Santa Barbara, Cal. in August 1965. The two authors considered the supply of 50–5 million tons of fertilizers a realistic target, a grain acreage of 135 million hectares, a grain crop of 162–75 million tons (barn yield) and meat and milk supplies of 13–15 and 80–100 million tons respectively attainable by 1970 or thereabouts. When these projections were made, most of them seemed unlikely to come true. They seem equally improbable now (ref. J. F. Karcz, ed., *Soviet and East European Agricultures*, University of California Press, Berkeley and Los Angeles, 1967).

[2] *Pravda*, 18–21 July 1970.

26

IS THE SOVIET AGRICULTURAL
PLAN FOR 1966–70 REASONABLE?

PETER WILES, 1967

In this piece, unconnected with Dr Klatt's, I try to use Cobb–Douglas techniques to examine the feasibility of one section of a Soviet-type plan. The uninitiated should not be dazzled by the technical sophistication. For, first, it is not at all great. And secondly the usual curse of more advanced methodologies lies heavy upon this piece, for it is not really clear how in practice to apply them. Specifically, we are faced with a great range of possible weights for the inputs, and only the very bold will know which ones to choose. Thirdly, the lapse of time has brought better data, as my revision of the 1960–65 data in Table 26.1 (p. 332) shows. This happens all the time: prophecies have to be based on an accurate analysis of the recent past, and such analysis is not available until we are some way through the period about which we are prophesying.

In the past, we have too often judged the realism of a plan by using incremental capital–output ratios alone, as if capital were the sole source of value. It is however obvious that changing ratios to capital of labour, land and skill make capital quite useless as an indicator of the behaviour of output. And if this is true of the percentage increase in the stock of capital employed it is still truer of mere figures of annual gross investment. Especially in agriculture, capital is *substituted* for labour, and it might be a very fine achievement to have a zero ICOR or even a negative one. We have to use the ratio between output and *all* inputs.

The popularity of the unreliable ICOR has two principal origins. First, Keynes attributed *short*-run *general* fluctuations in an *under-employed market* economy to fluctuations in investment, which – he incorrectly said – alone activate the multiplier. But this, even if it were right, would leave us very far indeed from predicting the growth of particular sectors in a Soviet-type

331

Table 26.1

	Imputed income weights[a] 1965	% growth per annum		
		Estimate of		plan
		1968	1966	plan
		1960–65		1965–70
Labour[b]	52	−0·4	−1·1	−0·6
Land[c]	26	+0·6	+0·6	0
Capital[d]	12	+9·0	+8·0	+13·7
Current industrial inputs[e]	10	+7·0	+7·0	+8·5
Total inputs	100	+1·73	+1·24	+2·18
Total outputs, net of duplication within agriculture[f]		+2·9	+2·9	+5·0

[a] These are imputed income weights from D. G. Johnson. In ed. A. Bergson and S. Kuznets, *Economic Trends in the Soviet Union* (Harvard, 1963), p. 217, he gives 58, 30, 7, 6 for 1955. Cf. also Abraham Becker, in Rand Memorandum RM–4881–PR (Santa Monica, 1966), pp. 112–17, and *New Directions in the Soviet Economy* (Joint Economic Committee of Congress, 1966), Part IIB, pp. 376–9 for a more extended discussion. The figures I have chosen are simply a reasonable and approximate updating of Johnson to 1965 as follows: the quantity of labour has fallen by 1% p.a. and its average income has risen by 2% p.a., so for 57 write 62; the virgin lands, making allowance for quality, have added 3% to the land area, so for 30 write 31; capital and current inputs have grown by 8 and 7% p.a. respectively, so for 7 and 6 write 15 and 12. Then reduce to percentages.

[b] *1966 estimate:* The agricultural labour force decreased from 27·8 million in 1960 to 26·3 million in 1965 (derived from *SSSR v Tsifrakh v 1965 godu*, pp. 91 and 93; Nimitz, *Farm Employment in the Soviet Union*, Rand Memorandum RM–4623–PR, p. 112; *Narkhoz 1960*, p. 513). During the period 1966–70, agricultural productivity is scheduled to rise by 40–45% in the social sector, whereas the gross product of all sectors is set to rise by 32%. Assume – gratuitously – that the private sector is to increase output by 20%, and has an initial weight of $\frac{1}{4}$. Then 'social' output is to rise by 35%; so the 'social' labour force will decline by 5·5%. Now (including grain elevators, RTS, etc.) the 'social' labour force was 27 million in 1965, so the implied fall is 1·5 million. As to the private labour force, it is given as 4 million in 1964 (*N.Kh. '64*, p. 419). Private plots are to be allowed to flourish, and a great many babushki will be replaced by machinery and permitted to retire. So guess an increase of 0·5 million in 1966–70. This makes a net fall of 1·0 million in the total agricultural labour force, which was 26·3 million in 1965. Note that for the purpose of predicting output we need the total numbers of people available, not the far smaller numbers of man-years actually worked. For these cf. *New Directions in Soviet Economy* (Joint Economic Committee of Congress, 1966), Part IIB, p. 373.

1968 estimate: the same rate of decrease emerges from two very different series. *Strana Sovetov za 50 Let*, p. 163, gives labour in agriculture, excluding those exclusively in private plots, as 26·1 million in 1960, 25·6 million in 1965. John W. dePauw, in *Measures of Agricultural Employment in the USSR* (Bureau of the Census, Washington, 1968), p. 5, has 37·4 million and 36·7 million, *including all work on private plots*.

[c] The area under cultivation rose from 203·0 million hectares in 1960 to 209·1

economy. Secondly, figures for gross investment allocations (though not for capital stock) are easily come by. Leaders quarrel about them, finance ministers publish them. Mere availability, however, is not a scientific criterion.

On the other hand labour figures are quite difficult to obtain. In USSR they must normally be inferred – as here – by dividing productivity into output. The Soviet authorities are understandably reluctant to publish their labour plan *totidem verbis*, because labour is, quite unlike capital, subject almost only to market forces. So the plan is seldom fulfilled. Yet it must, of course, exist, and predictions that neglect it are worth very little.

One may say that ICORs – based, of course, on changes in capital stock – are useful only when investment is purely extensive: i.e. when technique is constant and the labour supply infinitely elastic. These are not common conditions in modern Soviet-type economies.

Next, how big is the agricultural output target in 1965–70? It happens to be a lengthy and tedious process to extract an average annual rate of growth of net agricultural output from the plan figures before us. Let me simply say that I make it 5% p.a., and am ready to submit my reasoning to any interested enquirer. It is, then, against the figure of 5% p.a. that we must judge the sufficiency of the inputs. But according to the draft plan, total inputs into agriculture appear to be scheduled to rise by 2% p.a.

The Cobb–Douglas residual for 1965–70 is thus about 3.8 per cent p.a., or over twice the value other such calculations throw up. Technical progress, qualitative improvements in the labour force, better organization (such as the zveno) and the more rational use of resources – all of which account for the

---

million hectares in 1965 (*Narkhoz* 1960, p. 387 and *SSSR v Tsifrakh v 1965 godu*, p. 71). During the period 1966–70, the new land brought under cultivation will probably be more than matched by the abandonment of those extremely marginal areas which were included in Khrushchev's grand plough-up of the virgin lands.

[d] *1966 estimate*: includes livestock, machinery, construction, irrigation, land improvement, etc. Calculation based on growth in productive capital stock. Stock of current assets, 1951–62, in Becker, RM–4881–PR, p. 190.

1968 estimate: revised data from same official sources.

[e] Fertilizers, electricity, petrol, spare parts, etc. The weight of each input is taken from the 1959 input–output table, and its rate of growth has too often had to be simply projected.

[f] *New Directions* ... , p. 352; and the unpublished workings referred to above.

residual – must do over twice as much as usual, and twice as much as in 1961–65.[1] In 1928–39 the residual in agriculture was about minus 1% p.a., and in 1940–55 about zero, according to Jerzy Karcz.[2] Mr Andrew Frank (*Journal of Political Economy*, December 1958) found a zero residual for agriculture in the Ukraine alone during the period 1937–55, after one of minus 2% p.a. in the period 1928–37.

Of the various elements in the residual, it would be bold to say that any one of them will be more operative in 1966–70 than in 1961–65, for the virgin lands and corn follies date back to 1954–58, so rationality began already in Khrushchev's latter years. The wheat irrigation scheme does not persuade me that the new government has really learned the lesson, not to impose political preconceptions upon science and nature. Nor is there much sign that the only truly effective new organization, the mechanized 'link', will be officially encouraged. We conclude, then, using the methods of calculations considered orthodox hitherto, that the plan target of 5% p.a. is not realistic.

However it is very doubtful in principle whether Johnson's or Becker's 'imputed income' weights are usable in this context. No doubt Johnson and Becker have corrected properly for the various irrationalities of Soviet pricing, to show us *how income would have been distributed* among the factors of production if Soviet agriculture had been capitalist! But we have to deal here with an irrationality of pricing that covers many other than Soviet-type economies. Wherever there is a Malthusian situation, *marginal* farm labour has far less than average productivity, though it is paid but little less than average income. In other words marginal productivity has no relation to income shares, and must be separately calculated. But when we want to predict the physical success, as opposed to the profitability in money, of the plan we must deal precisely with the marginal productivities of inputs, not their income shares. Moreover, this point applies to all countries with unemployed or (as in USSR) virtually unemployed population.

---

[1] *New Directions* had a slight negative residual for 1960–64, using slightly different weights and input series.

[2] *The Record of Soviet Agriculture at Mid-Century Point* (privately circulated, 1966), Tables 2 and 3.

For those whom words cannot convince when algebra is available, the mathematical argument is as follows.[1] The Cobb–Douglas function is of the form:

$$Q = aK^m L^{1-m} \qquad (1)$$

where Q, K and L are output, capital stock and labour employed, a is not the 'residual' (to which we come later) but a meaningless constant, and m and $1-m$ are two exponents. Now

$$m = R/Q \qquad (2)$$

where R is the net national return to capital and R/Q the income-share of capital. For

$$R = \frac{\partial Q}{\partial K}.K = amK^{m-1}L^{1-m}K = mQ \qquad (3)$$

Moreover the exponents are also partial elasticities of production. Thus from (3) we get:

$$m = \frac{\partial Q}{\partial K}.\frac{K}{Q} \qquad (4)$$

Further, since W (the national wage-bill) $= (1-m)Q$ by parity of reasoning with (2),

$$\frac{R}{W} = \frac{m}{1-m} \qquad (5)$$

Then if we take logarithms or index numbers of Q, K and L the exponents become ordinary weights. So the easy-to-calculate income-share weight is as good as the elasticity-of-production exponent.

This conclusion rests on two assumptions relevant for our purposes. First the production function must be linear and homogeneous, so that the exponents add to unity (equation 1). Secondly the factors must be paid their marginal productivities (equation 3). The first condition, it seems, often holds approximately in the real world, where there is no reason at all why actual *ex post* series for Q, K and L covering periods of technical change should yield a linear and homogeneous function. However it can at least hardly surprise us that if the

---

[1] Compare, for instance, E. H. Phelps Brown in *Quarterly Journal of Economics* (November 1957); L. R. Klein, *An Introduction to Econometrics* (1962), ch. 3; R. M. Solow in *Review of Economics and Statistics* (August 1957).

sum of the exponents is set *a priori* equal to one some pair of values for them will be reasonably satisfactory. For capital nearly always grows more, and labour less, rapidly than output: so a mere weighted average of the two inputs is certain to add up to the output – and the exponents are, as we have seen, only weights under another name. But it is, as we have seen, the second condition that over-population falsifies. We can only now derive elasticity-of-production weights from series for Q, K and L; the income-share short cut, used by Johnson, Becker and *New Directions* ... and repeated above, will not do.

Now in the Soviet case elasticities of production are highly 'Malthusian'. Thus taking Q as the national income, B. I. Iskakov *et al.*[1] arrive at

$$Q = 1 \cdot 03 \, K^{0.9} \, L^{0.1},$$

for 1951–60, where $1 \cdot 03$ is, like a above, not a rate of technical progress or a residual but a simple adjustive constant. A. Tolkachev gets a similar answer.[2] It would appear, in particular, that the notorious Soviet practice of wishing unwanted labour upon *factories* has shown up in Mr Iskakov's figures. Amazing as these results are, then, I find them entirely plausible on deeper consideration.

But before we re-do our agricultural calculations we need to re-examine the 'residual'. This represents, of course, whatever factors have not been included in L and K: organization, 'disembodied' technical progress, perhaps even education and 'embodied' technical progress, etc. For if labour and capital are both assumed to be of constant quality, as Euler's theorem demands, education and 'embodied' technical progress must be otherwise accounted for.

Now if we use the income-shares of a particular date our weights always add up to one, though we have not necessarily assumed constant returns; for Euler's theorem is not needed to make the sum of income-shares equal to one. A residual then emerges automatically, as the difference between output and inputs thus weighted; and this residual may or may not be

[1] *Problemy Optimalnogo Planirovania, Proyektirovania i Upravlenia Proizvodstvom* (Moscow, 1961), p. 131.

[2] *Planovoye Khozyaistvo*, 6/1966, p. 3: $Q = 1186L^{0.155}K^{0.845}$, where Q is net industrial production, 1950–64.

attributed to 'time'. This income-shares procedure has been used by nearly everyone hitherto except Francis Seton,[1] to whose pioneering work I owe much. With elasticities of production, on the other hand, time must be made an explicit input; otherwise the calculation will always come up with such weights for the other inputs as will most nearly 'explain' or 'exhaust' the output. As we saw, it is very easy to eliminate the residual so long as one of the inputs grows more rapidly than the output; we simply give it a high weight.

There is no reason to expect the relation between the capital and labour exponents to change much owing to the intrusion of this new factor; much experimental work gives us confidence here. Seton's formula including time is

$$Q = a \, K^m \, L^{1-m} \, e^{ct},$$

where e is the base of Napierian logarithms, t the number of years and c the annual rate of 'technical progress'.

But where Seton's techniques arouse admiration his results—very low capital exponents, very high labour exponents, and technical progress of over 6% p.a. (for Soviet industry, 1950–55, by areas) – can only cause consternation. There is, perhaps, this to be said in their defence, that if the technical progress in agriculture is low or negative it must be very high in industry in order to yield a reasonable figure for the national income.

There is no need to make such weights add up to one, whether or not they include the time 'input'; but it is necessary to assume that the residual is a function of time. Since the large majority of known residuals is positive, and since technique and education do accumulate over time, this assumption is plausible. I insert this here to indicate that I do not hold it to be proven.

I shall not here attempt to fit a production function to our agricultural data, for they are too few and inaccurate. Moreover Stalin's production function must have been entirely different from Khrushchev's. Instead I simply transfer the exponents found for industry or national income by the two Soviet statisticians. One might think it obvious that capital is even more and labour even less important in agriculture than in industry: so to use these figures would be to understate the case. But labour is so very scarce at peak harvest periods, and the

---

[1] In *American Economic Review* (May 1959), Table 4.

kind of labour that agriculture loses is very important to it. Put the marginal productivity of land at zero. We then get very arbitrary percentage weights like these:[1] labour 10, land 0, capital 49, current industrial inputs 41. Total inputs in 1961–65, then, measured by their elasticity of production in the whole of the economy, grew by 7% p.a., (6·8% by the recalculation of 1968) and will do so in 1966–70 by 10% p.a. A residual of −4·1% (−3·9%) will yield to one of −5%: a gloomy prophecy that sounds realistic enough to be fulfilled.

Such numbers are, furthermore, not absolutely absurd. There is every reason to believe that with the virgin lands scheme physical returns diminished sharply. In a market economy such inputs would not be made unless product prices rose fast enough to make them profitable. In the Soviet economy there is no necessary connection between product prices and inputs. The rises in food prices that our results justify have probably not been paralleled by the actual rises of recent years; for these were mostly made to correct social injustice between peasants and workers. Further rises are now indicated, but may not occur. Nor may the switch to food imports that is also indicated.

[1] Accepting Iskakov's 9 to 1 ratio for capital and labour, and – very arbitrarily – allotting current industrial inputs the proportion of the total weight of capital indicated by Table 26.1 here.

27

AN ECONOMETRIC ANALYSIS AND FORECAST OF SOVIET ECONOMIC GROWTH

HARUKI NIWA, 1967[1]

I   AN OUTLINE OF THE SIMPLIFIED ECONOMETRIC MODEL
NO. 4 OF THE SOVIET ECONOMIC GROWTH

It is hardly necessary to remark that what has characterized the past growth of the Soviet economy is its imbalance between the levels of production and of real wages. The industrial output of the Soviet Union increased approximately ten times during the interval between 1928 when the first Five-Year Plan was started and 1961 (in accordance with the net output index generally used in Western countries).

However, the level of real wages of urban workers in the Soviet Union showed a drastic drop during the first half of the 1930s, long before the war, and it was only between the latter half of the 1950s and 1960 that the level of immediately before the commencement of the first Five-Year Plan in 1928 was recovered and surpassed for the first time. This fact is, at first sight, almost unbelievable, but it has been confirmed by repeated calculations which many Western researchers have performed. The writer of this article has also tried to calculate the index of real wages in the Soviet Union, by employing the 'usual method' (dividing the nominal wage index by that of consumer goods prices), as well as the 'real terms method' (commodity-flow method), which extracts the real supply of goods per worker with the aid of production statistics on consumer goods. Similar results have been obtained by both methods (see Table 27.1, p. 340).

[1] The writer is deeply grateful for the earlier stages of this research to the Russian Research Center at Harvard University, Cambridge and the Institute of Asian Economic Affairs, Tokyo. He is also thankful to Abram Bergson, Holland Hunter, and Morris Bornstein for their kind advice. At the later stages, he was much indebted to Peter Wiles and Shinichi Ichimura for their helpful comments.

Table 27.1 *Estimated index numbers of real wages in the USSR, 1928-60*

	Employment in non-agricultural sector[a]	Relative share of consumer goods supply of urban area[b]	Index of the figures in col. (2)	Consumer goods production[a]	Real wage of urban worker computed by the 'real commodity flow method'. Consumer goods supply per urban worker $\left(\frac{(4)\times(3)}{(1)}\times100\right)$	Real wage index of urban worker computed by the 'usual method'[e] $\left(\frac{\text{nominal wage index}}{\text{retail price index}^f}\right)\times100$	
						Based on Laspeyres index of retail prices (using 1928 weights)	Based on Paasche index of retail prices[f]
	(1)	(2)	(3)	(4)	(5)	(6)	(7)
	1928 = 100	%	(1928 = 1.00)	1928 = 100	1928 = 100	1928 = 100	1928 = 100
1928	100	70.0[c]	1.000	100	100	100.0	100.0
1932	155	68.2	0.974	108	68	35.9	80.0
1937	210	68.9	0.984	162	76	63.4	75.9
1940	264	70.2	1.003	175	66	43.7	68.3
1950	277	76.0	1.086	174	68	57.0	80.7
1955	346	73.5	1.050	290	88	77.6	120.1
1959	361	75.3	1.076	378	112	93.4	141.2
1960	377	76.0	1.086	390	112	—	148.0

[a] Includes armed forces, house-servants, and 'discrepancies' (distributed between agricultural and non-agricultural categories). Data for this column are primarily based on the W. Eason's estimates. See W. W. Eason, 'Labor Force', in A. Bergson and S. Kuznets (eds.) *Economic Trends in the Soviet Union* (Cambridge, Mass., 1963), pp. 38-95.

[b] This series is related to the percentage share of urban trade in the total retail sales (state and co-operative stores only). Refer *Narodnoe Khoziaistvo SSSR* for the years concerned.

[c] Includes retail sales by the private stores. Cf. *Sotsialisticheskoe stroitel'stvo SSSR – statisticheskii ezhegodnik* (Moscow, 1934).

[d] Exclusive of unprocessed foods. The figures used here are related to the series for o_c (below). See H. Niwa, 'An Analysis and Forecast of the Economic Growth in the Soviet Union, *Statistical Paper Series No. 15* (Tokyo: The Institute of Asian Economic Affairs, 1966), pp. 68-76.

[e] See H. Niwa, 'Retail Prices and Real Wages in the USSR, 1928-59', *The Journal of Economic Behavior* (Tokyo), vol. I, no. 2 (October 1961).

[f] Includes collective farm market prices.

It may appear at the first glance that the sharp imbalance between the levels of production and consumption in the Soviet economy is unaccountable. But this is not so. In short, the movement of *urban* workers' real wages is decided by the race between the supply of consumer goods to cities and the *urban* labor population. If the urban share of the total supply of consumer goods is almost constant, as in the Soviet Union (where for the past 37 years it has not changed much, wavering between 70% and 76%), and if the weight of foreign trade is small, the movement of real wages is decided, in fact, by the rapidity of the growth of consumer goods production on the one hand and of the urban labor population on the other.

If a rapid increase in urban labor population should be arrested in order to speed up the rise of real wages, labor productivity should be raised by increasing the capital–labor ratio among the workers already in industry, that is, output should be increased by labor-saving devices. But if the production of capital goods should be speeded up in order to increase the capital stock, this necessitates a large input of labor into industry. In order to avoid this, investment should be concentrated on industry at the expense of other sectors. In the Soviet Union, however, the production of consumer goods depends largely upon the supply of raw materials of agricultural origin from rural districts. As agricultural production depends upon the input of capital stock and labor into agriculture, the policy to give priority to input into industry at the expense of agriculture makes it possible that the production of consumer goods will have to be curtailed owing to a lack of raw materials.

Conversely, would it be advisable to concentrate capital and labor in agriculture, and think exclusively of largely increased agricultural production, and marketable shares of agricultural products? The answer must be in the negative, for the result of such policy would be a neglect of capital investment and labor input in industry, and a possible stagnation of the entire industrial activity. Even in the present case, an increased investment in agriculture has originally been planned, and for this very reason, the production of capital goods cannot be allowed to slow down too much. If owing to the general shortage of labor force and capital stock the output of industry cannot grow enough, but capital goods production is maintained, this is possible only at the expense of the production of consumer goods. In this case, the output of such goods will naturally decrease.

All the multivarious factors are entangled in a complicated manner and simultaneously, defying any written description. There is no other recourse but an analysis with an econometric multi-equation model. During several years before writing this article, we established multi-equation models (i.e. the *Simplified Econometric Models of Soviet Economic Growth* nos. 1–3), based on the considerations described above, and we have tried out various analyses with them (see Haruki Niwa, *Soren Keikaku Keizai no Kenkyu* (Tokyo, 1966), pp. 185–216). Happily, all the 'predicted figures' for the endogenous variables estimated by means of *Models nos. 1–3* agreed marvellously well with the actual figures for the period 1935–60. Although there is not enough space to describe them in detail, one can consider that the basic frameworks of *Models nos. 1–3* reflected very well the characteristics of Soviet economic growth in 1935–60. Nevertheless, in *Models nos. 1–3* all the equations are calculated as a simple linear, or logarithmic linear, function. But it is true that Soviet economic growth from the beginning of the sixties has in certain respects not corresponded well to this 'linear model'. However, as we shall show below, this defect will be more or less corrected if the 'agricultural production function' and the 'function of the proportion of effective employment in agriculture' are made non-linear.

Bearing this in mind, the writer has attempted the construction of a new *Simplified Econometric Model no. 4 of the Soviet Economic Growth*. As described below in detail, we have considered, in *Model no. 4*, two different causal types, *Case I* and *Case II*. In *Case I* the total flow of capital goods to the sector of final demand, i.e. the level of total investment, is treated as an exogenous variable. On the other hand in *Case II* the level of investment is treated as an endogenous variable. The author believes, as we shall see below, that the comparative consideration of these two cases of the causal type of model is very useful for the analysis of the retardation of Soviet economic growth after 1960. This *Model no. 4* is an extremely concise recursive model. Naturally, all the estimates of the structural parameters have been performed by the 'successive least square method'. The observational period of statistical data for the structural estimates is 1934–63. As for the sources of the actually observed data, see the writer's paper 'An Analysis and Forecast of the Economic Growth in the Soviet Union', *Statistical Paper Series, no. 15* (Tokyo: The Institute of Asian Economic Affairs, 1966), pp. 67–79. Below are presented the equations which form the *Model no. 4* of the Soviet economic growth. The numerals for the equations are put for convenience sake, without reference to any causal relationships.

Exogenous variables (8 in each case)

$N_{c,t}$	Employment in non-agricultural sector (*Case II*)
$O_{i,t}$ and $O_{i,t-1}$	Flow of capital goods to final demand sector (*Case I*)
$O_{m,t}$	Production of munitions
$P_{,t-\frac{1}{2}}$	Total population (*Case II – $P_{,t+\frac{1}{2}}$*)
$R_{a,t-1}$	Relative share of agricultural investment in total investment (*Case II – $R_{a,t}$*)
$R_{d,t}$	Relative share of housing investment in total investment
$R_{i,t-1}$	Relative share of industrial investment in total investment (*Case II – $R_{i,t}$*)
$S_{a,t-\frac{1}{2}}$	Land (sown-area) (*Case II – $S_{a,t+\frac{1}{2}}$*)
$T_{,t-1}$	Time (year) (*Case II – $T_{,t}$*)

Endogenous variables (20 in each case)

$K_{a,t-\frac{1}{2}}$	Volume of agricultural fixed capital stock (amount at the end of the year $t-1$) (*Case II – $K_{a,t+\frac{1}{2}}$*)
$\Delta K_{a,t-\frac{1}{2}}$	Change in K_a from $t-1\frac{1}{2}$ to $t-\frac{1}{2}$ (change from the previous years, estimated at the end of each year) (*Case II – $K_{a,t+\frac{1}{2}}$*)
$K_{d,t}$	Volume of residential fixed capital stock
$\Delta K_{d,t}$	Change in K_d (change from the previous year)
$K_{i,t}$	Volume of industrial fixed capital stock (*Case II – $K_{i,t+1}$*)

HARUKI NIWA

$\Delta K_{i,t}$	Change in K_i (change from the previous year) (*Case II* – $K_{i,t+1}$)
$M_{,t}$	Supply of raw materials of agricultural origin to consumer goods industry (*Case II* – $M_{,t+1}$)
$N_{a,t-\frac{1}{2}}$	Effective employment in agricultural sector (converted into full-time employment) (*Case II* – $N_{a,t+\frac{1}{2}}$)
$N_{c,t}$	Employment in non-agricultural sector (*Case I*)
$N_{i,t}$	Employment in industry
$O_{,t}$	Industrial production
$O_{a,t}$	Agricultural production (*Case II* – $O_{a,t+1}$)
$O_{c,t}$	Consumer goods production (*Case II* – $O_{c,t+1}$)
$O_{i,t}$	Flow of capital goods to final demand sector (*Case II*)
$O_{p,t}$	Production of intermediate producer goods (including raw materials of mining origin)
$P_{r,t-\frac{1}{2}}$	Rural population (*Case II* – $P_{r,t+\frac{1}{2}}$)
$P_{u,t-\frac{1}{2}}$	Urban population (*Case II* – $P_{u,t+\frac{1}{2}}$)
$Q_{,t-\frac{1}{2}}$	Ratio between $P_{r,t-\frac{1}{2}}$ and $N_{a,t-\frac{1}{2}}$ ($P_{r,t-\frac{1}{2}}/N_{a,t-\frac{1}{2}}$) (*Case II* – $Q_{,t+\frac{1}{2}}$)
$S_{r,t}$	Relative share of consumer goods supply to rural area (*Case II* – $S_{r,t+1}$)
$W_{,t}$	Real wages (urban workers) (*Case II* – $W_{,t+1}$)
X	Input of factors of production into agriculture

Predetermined endogenous variables (4 in each case)

$K_{a,t-1\frac{1}{2}}$	(*Case II* – $K_{a,t-\frac{1}{2}}$)
$K_{d,t-1}$	
$K_{i,t-1}$	(*Case II* – $K_{i,t}$)
$N_{a,t-\frac{1}{2}}$	
$N_{c,t-1}$	
$N_{i,t-1}$	(*Case I* – any one of these)
$O_{,t-1}$	
$P_{r,t-\frac{1}{2}}$	
$P_{u,t-\frac{1}{2}}$	
$O_{c,t}$	(*Case II*)

Note: all the statistical data are compiled in the form of index number (1955 = 1·0 in the cases of R_i, R_a, and R_d and Q, and 1955 = 100 in the cases of the other variables).

In the series of T, 1934 is the first year. The observational period for the structural estimates is 1935–63 (excluding 1941–49).

The system of equations (Case I)
(Behavioral-technical equations)

(1) *Demand for intermediate producer goods* (inclusive of raw materials of mining origin)

$$\log O_{p,t} = 0.85432(0.361 . \log O_{i,t} + 0.365 . \log O_{c,t}$$
$$(0.03339)$$

$$+ 0.274 . \log O_{m,t}) + 0.29042$$
$$(0.06296)$$

$$S = 0.03123 \qquad R = 0.9888 \qquad d = 0.92683$$

As the final demand index, a series of weighted geometric means of O_m, O_i, and O_c is used. The aggregation weights used here are the '1950 weights' of the Kaplan–Moorsteen index.[1]

(2) *Industrial fixed capital formation*

$$\Delta K_{i,t} = 0.1144(O_{i,t-1} \times R_{i,t-1}) + 0.1373$$
$$(0.00765) \qquad\qquad (0.64978)$$

$$S = 1.2931 \qquad R = 0.9681 \qquad d = 2.1008$$

(3) *Agricultural fixed capital formation*

$$\Delta K_{a,t-\frac{1}{2}} = 0.1088(O_{i,t-1} \times R_{a,t-1}) - 0.0276$$
$$(0.01139) \qquad\qquad (0.97775)$$

$$S = 2.059 \qquad R = 0.9267 \qquad d = 1.3197$$

(4) *Residential capital formation*

$$\Delta K_{d,t} = 0.03875(R_{d,t} \times O_{i,t}) + 1.77582$$
$$(0.00473) \qquad\qquad (0.65075)$$

$$S = 0.7356 \qquad R = 0.9390 \qquad d = 1.5955$$

(5) *Industrial production*

$$\log O_{,t} = 1.3835(0.289 . \log K_{i,t} + 0.711 . \log N_{i,t}) - 0.7594$$
$$(0.0201) \qquad\qquad\qquad\qquad (0.0390)$$

$$S = 0.0145 \qquad R = 0.9983 \qquad d = 1.1962$$

[1] See N. M. Kaplan and R. H. Moorsteen, *Indexes of Soviet Industrial Output* (Rand RM–2495), vol. II, p. 219.

It is generally said that a rate of interest between 15% and 30% is considered, in effect, in the discussions of investment efficiency in the Soviet Russia. Here, a hypothetical rate of interest of 20% is used for the net fixed capital, and a rate of 15% and a depreciation rate of 10% for the fixed capital measured in replacement costs. Now, the net fixed capital in industry in 1950 was 272 billion roubles.[1] In terms of the flow concept, this is 54·4 billion old roubles at the interest rate of 20%. The total wage payment in industry in 1950 is calculated to have been 134 billion old roubles, assuming that the average monthly wage was 700 roubles.[2] Thus, the sum of capital and labor inputs in Soviet industry in 1950 is estimated at 188·4 billion old roubles. Then, the percentage shares of 28·9% and 71·1% have been estimated for the fixed capital and the labor force, respectively.

(6) *Agricultural production*

$$\log O_{a,t} = 2.50694 - 0.73166(0.97693)^x$$
$$S = 0.02212$$

The non-linear equation is used as the agricultural production function to represent one of the outstanding characteristics of the Soviet economy in the 'retardation period' of the first half of the 1960s. For x see Equation no. 19.

(7) *Employment in the non-agricultural sector*

$$\log N_{c,t} = 1.11053 . \log N_{i,t} - 0.20718$$
$$(0.02415) \qquad (0.04725)$$
$$S = 0.01168 \qquad R = 0.9954 \qquad d = 1.6572$$

(8) *Supply of raw materials of agricultural origin to consumer goods industry*

$$\log M_{,t} = 0.71956(2 . \log O_{a,t} - \log P_{r,t-1}) + 0.58452$$
$$(0.01808) \qquad (0.03512)$$
$$S = 0.01956 \qquad R = 0.9947 \qquad d = 2.2252$$

The form of this function is based on the following assumption. It is assumed that farmers keep some stock of agricultural

[1] Cf. R. P. Powell, 'Industrial Production', in A. Bergson and S. Kuznets (eds.), *Economic Trends in the Soviet Union* (Cambridge, Mass., 1963), pp. 150–202.
[2] Cf. N. M. Kaplan and R. H. Moorsteen, *Indexes of Soviet Industrial Output* (Rand RM–2495), vol. II, p. 219.

products and that the consumed part of such stock in the preceding year has to be rebuilt out of the produce of the current year. Then, so long as P_r is assumed to be the primary determinant of 'the consumption of farm income in kind', that is the amount of agricultural produce to be consumed by the agricultural sector, the current 'marketable share' of agricultural products is expected to depend on $O_{a,t}/P_{r,t-1}$. M, which represents the supply of raw materials of agricultural origin to consumer goods industry, depends on O_a and the 'marketable share'. So $M_{,t}$ depends on

$$O_{a,t}\frac{O_{a,t}}{P_{r,t-1}}.$$

Thus, logarithmically $\log M_{,t}$ depends on the value of $2.\log O_{a,t} - \log P_{r,t-1}$.

(9) *Consumer goods production*
$$\log O_{c,t} = 0.86250.\log M_{,t} + 0.2525$$
$$(0.02084) \qquad (0.04123)$$

$$S = 0.01622 \qquad R = 0.9954 \qquad d = 1.85834$$

In the Soviet Union, the production of consumer goods depends very largely upon the supply of raw materials of agricultural origin.

(10) *Effective agricultural employment ratio*
$$\log Q = -0.04643 + 0.18502(0.966)^t$$
$$S = 0.0202$$

It is admitted that Q, that is, the reciprocal of the effective employment ratio in agriculture, becomes lowered with the passage of time, but there must be a certain limit to this trend. (This is quite understandable, if Q is taken as the reciprocal of the effective participation ratio in the agricultural sector.) Properly speaking, a 'Q function' should be so devised to be able to set the contraction limit like the Gompertz Curve.

(11) *Urban population*
$$\log P_{u,t-\frac{1}{2}} = 1.02519.\log N_{c,t-1} - 0.05696$$
$$(0.02507) \qquad (0.04895)$$

$$S = 0.0148 \qquad R = 0.9944 \qquad d = 1.1337$$

(12) *Relative share of consumer goods supply to rural areas*

$$\log S_{r,t} = 1\cdot04861\cdot\log (100\ P_{r,t-\frac{1}{2}}/P_{,t-\frac{1}{2}}) - 0\cdot09679$$

$$R = 0\cdot9870$$

The equation is estimated by direct least square method. Observational period is 1955–63.

Note: 'S' is standard error of estimated dependent variables.

'R' is correlation co-efficient.

'd' is Durbin–Watson's Ratio.

The figures in parentheses cited under the equations are standard errors of the regression coefficients.

Definitions

(13) *Industrial production*

$$\log O_{,t} = 0\cdot162\cdot\log O_{m,t} + 0\cdot216\cdot\log O_{c,t}$$
$$+ 0\cdot214\cdot\log O_{i,t} + 0\cdot408\cdot\log O_{p,t}$$

Here , O is defined as the weighted geometric mean of O_p, O_m, O_i and O_c, for the sake of logarithmic computation. The weights used here are the '1950 weights' used in the Kaplan–Moorsteen index.

(14) *Effective employment in agricultural sector*

$$\log N_{a,t-\frac{1}{2}} = \log P_{r,t-\frac{1}{2}} - \log Q_{,t-\frac{1}{2}}$$

(15) *Total population*

$$P_{,t-\frac{1}{2}} = 0\cdot45\cdot P_{u,t-\frac{1}{2}} + 0\cdot55 P_{r,t-\frac{1}{2}}$$

The aggregation weights are derived from the 1955 urban and rural percentages.

(16) *Volume of industrial fixed capital stock*

$$K_{i,t} = K_{i,t-1} + \Delta K_{i,t}$$

(17) *Volume of agricultural fixed capital stock*

$$K_{a,t-\frac{1}{2}} = K_{a,t-1\frac{1}{2}} + \Delta K_{a,t-\frac{1}{2}}$$

(18) *Volume of residential fixed capital stock*

$$K_{d,t} = K_{d,t-1} + \Delta K_{d,t}$$

(19) *Input of factors of production into agriculture*

$$X = \{(0\cdot30\log S_{a,t-\frac{1}{2}} + 0\cdot41\log N_{a,t-\frac{1}{2}}$$
$$+ 0\cdot29\log K_{a,t-\frac{1}{2}}) - 1\cdot79\} \times 100$$

In view of the fact that our index of O_a is computed with 1958 prices, 1958 weights have been used again for an aggregated index of inputs in agriculture. The weights are derived by estimating the total value of agricultural income in 1958 (310 billion old roubles),[1] and the annual inputs (converted flow concept) for each category of factors of production in the same year. The 1958 value of gross agricultural fixed capital is estimated to have been 355 billion roubles (exclusive of livestock). It has been converted to a flow of 89 billion old roubles by the use of the assumed 15% interest rate and 10% depreciation rate. The estimated 1958 values of gross agricultural product (Soviet concept) and agricultural total cost (Soviet concept) are 535 billion roubles and 450 billion roubles respectively.[2] And, the percentage share of labor cost in the agricultural total cost is reported to be 28·3%.[3] The 1958 value of agricultural total labor cost is calculated to be 127 billion old roubles.

Thus, the weights have been computed as follows:

$$\begin{aligned}
\text{Capital} \quad & 89 \div 310 = 0 \cdot 29 \\
\text{Labor} \quad & 127 \div 310 = 0 \cdot 41 \\
\text{Land} \quad & \text{residual} = 0 \cdot 30
\end{aligned}$$

The logarithmic values of aggregated agricultural inputs here are, for convenience, indicated with the scale as follows:

$$\begin{aligned}
1 \cdot 79 &\to 0 \\
1 \cdot 80 &\to 1 \\
1 \cdot 81 &\to 2 \\
\vdots \quad & \quad \vdots
\end{aligned}$$

The figure, 1·79, is approximately equal to the actual logarithmic value of aggregated input for 1935.

(20) *Real wages (urban workers)*

$$W_{,t} = \dfrac{O_{c,t}\left(\dfrac{100 - 0 \cdot 265 S_{r,t}}{73 \cdot 5}\right)}{N_{c,t}} \times 100$$

[1] The estimates primarily depend on the data derived from N. Nimitz, *Soviet National Income and Product, 1956–1958* (Rand RM–3112–PR, June 1962), pp. 2–4.

[2] Thus, average 'cost-price ratio' of 1·19 has been applied. The ratio has been calculated from the data provided by the Soviet source. Cf. A. G. Zverev, *Natsional'ni Dokhod i Finansy SSSR* (Moscow, 1961), p. 306.

[3] Cf. A. M. Birman, *Finansy Predpriiatii i Otraslei Narodnogo Khoziaistva* (Moscow, 1960), pp. 222–43.

As the coverage of N_c is exclusive of the armed forces, house-servants and the like, in the calculation of the trend of real wages it is important to adjust it (see Table 27.8 below, p. 366).

According to the official retail trade statistics, the relative shares of consumer goods supply to urban area and rural area for 1955 can be assumed to be 73·5% and 26·5%.

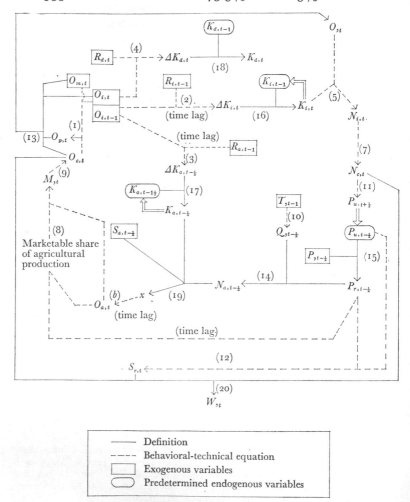

Figure 1 Graphic presentation of causal relationships in *The Simplified Econometric Model No. 4 of the Soviet Economic Growth (1935–63).*

Figures 1, 2 and 3 (pp. 350–3), are the diagrammatical presentation of *Model No. 4.*

In the theoretical structure of Figure 1, M and O_c are determined by some predetermined-exogenous variables, and then, O, N_i, and N_c by O_c and the exogenous O_i and O_m. Furthermore, this N_c determines O_c for the following period, together with the effects of some other exogenous variables. This is the causal pattern described in Figure 1 and named *Case I*, which is diagrammatically presented below in abbreviated form:

Case I

In other words, *Case I* is the one in which the levels of employment and production for agriculture and industry, or the 'service industries', and the level of real wages are decided, directly or indirectly, by the level of the production of capital goods, which will be 'exogenously' decided by the will of the government. The writer believes this model has proved to be very effective for the analysis of Soviet economic growth from the period of the pre-war Five-Year Plans under the principle of 'priority to capital goods production' until about 1960.[1]

But a different causal series can be conceived. Suppose now a time lag is introduced into the industrial capital formation function (Equation no. 2), so that the level of K_i for the present period is determined by the investment activity of the previous period. Further suppose that N_a, a hitherto endogenous variable, is in fact exogenously determined so as to secure the agricultural labor supply, and thus N_c is also provided exogenously as a direct result of the fixing of N_a. Then so long as

[1] As for the results of the simulation analysis by the use of the causal pattern of *Case I*, see the graphic presentations in the 'Appendix II' to the writer's paper, 'An Analysis and Forecast', op. cit., pp. 61–6.

O_c is determined by some predetermined-exogenous variables, O_i will be determined as an endogenous variable. Then O_i together with exogenous R_i will determine the level of K_i for the following period. Also, so long as $\mathcal{N}_c$ and other exogenous variables are provided, this endogenously determined O_i, together with the exogenous R_a, will determine the level of O_a

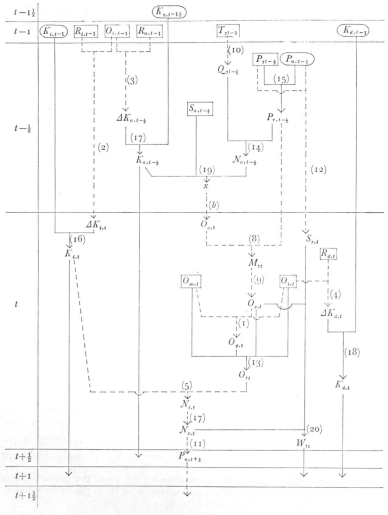

Figure 2   Causal links and time lags in the Model (*Case I*).

and consequently that of O_c through agricultural capital formation (see the abbreviated graph below, p. 354). The construction of such a causal pattern is named *Case II*.

What seems here a little illogical in *Case II*, is that we present
in this graph the relation of inverse lag: $N_{a,t+\frac{1}{2}} \to N_{c,t}$. But

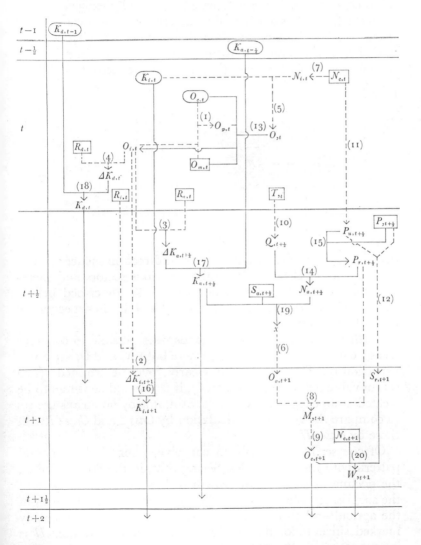

Figure 3   Causal links and time lags in the Model (*Case II*).

this can be explained by the fact that $N_{c,t}$ is in form an exogenous variable while $N_{a,t+\frac{1}{2}}$ is endogenous (see Figure 3). In other words we suppose here a situation where the official planner determines $N_{c,t}$ under the condition of Equation nos. 10 and 11, trying to maintain $N_{a,t+\frac{1}{2}}$ at a certain figure. Thus conceived, N_a can be treated as virtually exogenous.

In brief, *Case II* is one in which, as a result of the government's 'exogenous' decision of the allocation of labor force between the agricultural and non-agricultural sectors, the level of the production of capital goods (i.e. investment activity) will be

Case II

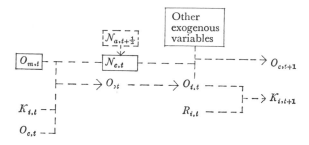

decided, and under the direct or indirect influence of this decision the level of production for various sectors and therefore that of real wages will be decided. As described below, this model is more suitable for the analysis of the Soviet economy of the first half of the 1960s.

Furthermore, if occasion demands, it is possible to conceive a case, called *Case III* hereafter, where both N_c and O_i are given exogenously. This *Case III* is clearly 'over-determined' (two sets of value for O_c are calculated), if O_m should continue to be treated as an exogenous variable. Still, it is by no means useless to compare the results of calculation by *Case I* and *Case II* with those by *Case III*.

Of course, it is possible to conceive other kinds of causal pattern with these variables. Seeing that, in the Soviet Union, the decline in the rate of growth of investment activity, and the surprisingly slow mobilization of working population from the agricultural to the non-agricultural sector, are noticeably marked since 1960, it is clear that an analysis by *Case II* is important.

As is shown in Table 27.3 below (p. 361), N_a and P_r have almost completely ceased to diminish since the beginning of the 1960s. In the same period, the percentage share of agricultural investment in the total investment, R_a, has also clearly shown an upward trend at the expense of industry and housing (see Figure 4, p. 359). This, in the writer's hypothetical view, means that the 'Stalinist Principle' which aimed at a high rate of economic growth and which was realized in the past by means of a large mobilization of labor force into industry out of agriculture, and of extreme concentration of investment on industry at the expense of agriculture, is not practised at present and is not provided with the conditions favorable for its enforcement, as the need for more agricultural production is pressing hard.[1] The decline of the rate of industrial growth in the period 1960–63 can be mainly explained, on the writer's hypothesis, in this light. In order to test this hypothesis, the analysis by 'Case II causal pattern' should be given more weight than any other.

As is clear from what we have said, Model no. 4 serves to explain 20 endogenous variables by the aid of 8 exogenous variables. It is important to know that R_i, R_a and R_d, i.e. the allocation of investment to each sector, are very strategic exogenous variables; without doubt they are entirely under governmental control. In this sense Model no. 4 is a typical model for a planned economy. Of course, it can easily calculate and predict many other important economic indicators utilizing those estimated variables. Such indexes as the trends of capital–output ratio, labor productivity, capital–labor ratio, the demographic structure between urban and rural areas, etc., are examples. The trends and structure of national income also can be readily computed (see Table 27.9, p. 367 below).

In USSR the importance of foreign trade in total economic

---

[1] The allocation of investments does not necessarily mean the depletion agricultural capital as under the direction of Stalin. As P. J. D. Wiles has shown, Stalin allotted to agriculture a constant proportion of the rapid increase in investment (see his *The Political Economy of Communism* (Harvard University Press, 1962), pp. 269–70). However, considering that this proportion was 16–17% in 1950–54 while it was 20% in 1964–65, and that the industrial investment proportion fell, on the contrary, from 44–50% in 1950–54 to 41–42% in the period after 1960, it is impossible to deny the 'relative sacrifice' of agricultural investment made by Stalin. See Figure 4 and the writer's paper, 'An Analysis and Forecast', loc. cit., pp. 67–76.

activity is small. In 1964 the percentage of total importation
to GNP was only 2·6.[1] So, to simplify things, foreign trade has
been excluded from the model. It also goes without saying that
the construction of our models has been mostly based on the
'method of real commodity flows'. Consequently the monetary
aspects of the economy have been entirely excluded; so in
Model no. 4 it is assumed that aggregate demand is invariably
assured.

In Equation no. 1, the output of intermediate producer
goods is determined by final demand. Only in this sense is the
model similar to the usual input–output system. However,
the coverages of O_p and O_i are clearly separated (and not
duplicated) from each other. At the same time, the model has
assumed the substitutability of factors of production (see
Equation nos. 5 and 19). Thus, the theoretical structure of
Model no. 4 is largely different from the Leontief's input–output
system.

As is very widely known, multicollinearity is frequently
encountered in an econometric time-series analysis. In our
Soviet case, it may be expected that there would be high inter-
correlation between capital input and labor input in the
estimation of production functions. After due consideration,
the multiple regression method has not been used, in the
estimation of Equation nos. 1, 5 and 6. Even without this
method, a very good fit has been observed. Since this *Model
no. 4* is a logarithmic model, the influence of time lag is little
reflected in it, and inventory changes are not considered either;
therefore, undulatory fluctuations cannot be ascertained. In
other words, as a typical long-term model, the primary object
of this model is to trace and to forecast the 'general trend of
growth' of various variables.

The characteristic features of the Soviet economy in the
slump period of the first half of the 1960s cannot be said to
have perfectly been grasped by this *Model no. 4*, for it is a
long-range model formed on the premise of the Soviet economic
structure observed during the past thirty years. It may not be

[1] This figure was calculated, on the one hand from the dollar value of the GNP
estimated by S. H. Cohn, 'Soviet Growth Retardation: Trends in Resource
Availability and Efficiency', *New Directions of the Soviet Economy*, by the Joint
Economic Committee of US Congress (USGPO, 1966), p. 108; and on the other
from the official Soviet figure for foreign trade.

amiss, however, to expect that to a certain extent the characteristics of the Soviet economic growth in the slump period can
be estimated, now that the 'non-linear equation' (Equation
no. 6) can be used as the 'production function' of agriculture
and that analysis with *Case II* is possible.

II THE FUTURE OF THE SOVIET ECONOMIC GROWTH

The extent to which this *Simplified Econometric Model no. 4 of the
Soviet Economic Growth (1935–63)* has succeeded in simulating
the indexes of the endogenous variables made in the past
period 1935–63, is quantitatively expressed by the R coefficient
values of each behavioral–technical equation (cited in the
preceding section). Fortunately, the goodness-of-fit has been
measured.[1]

For the purpose of getting a proper perspective of the
'future' (1964–70) of the Soviet economic growth, the writer
has made the forecasting estimates described below by *Model
no. 4* in the following two cases (which have already been
theoretically explained in the preceding section):

Case I, presuming that the production of capital goods will
grow at the annual average rate of 8·5% for the 1966–70
period.

Case II, presuming that agricultural employment (converted
into full-time employment) will maintain the 1963 level until
1970.

Concerning the allocation of total investment to agriculture,
industry, and housing, it was presumed, in order to forecast
values of variables by the use of causal links, that in *Case IA* and
Case IIA the pattern of investment allocation in 1965 would be
maintained constantly throughout the 1965–70 period. As for
the years 1964 and 1965, the actual pattern of investment for
each year respectively has been applied. For forecasting with
Case IB and *Case IIB*, the allocation pattern of investment in
1962 was assumed to remain un-changed throughout the period
1963–70.

The details of assumed figures of exogenous variables for the

---

[1] What is more, the calculated values of S, d, and 'standard errors of the regression coefficients' are also satisfactory. The 'successive least square method'
gives us the *unbiased* values of estimates. As for the result of the 'final test' of our
Model no. 4, see the writer's paper, 'An Analysis and Forecast', op. cit., pp. 61–6.

forecast with *Case I* and *Case II* are presented in Table 27.2. The forecast values according to the *Case IA* and *Case IIA* assumptions have been calculated for the period 1963–70 (see Table 27.3, p. 361).

Case IA forecasting work is, indeed, rather 'simple extrapolations', while *Case IB* and *Case IIB* computations are the 'experimental analyses'. As is demonstrated in Figure 4 of the trends of R_i, R_a, and R_d, the uniqueness of the allocation pattern of

Table 27.2 *Assumptions on the exogenous variables for forecasting* (Case I *and* Case II)

(1) S_a: the 1964 value of S_a is assumed to be unchanged during the 1965–70 period.[a]

(2) R_i, R_a, and R_d
   Case IA and *Case IIA*
      It is assumed that the 1965 values of R_i, R_a, and R_d will be maintained constantly throughout the 1965–70 period.[a]
   Case IB and *Case IIB*
      It is assumed that the 1962 values of R_i, R_a, and R_d will remain unchanged throughout the period 1962–70.

(3) O_m: for the 1963–70 period, the assumed annual rate of growth of O_m is 9·3% (the average annual rate of growth of the 1955–63 period).

(4) P: the forecasted trend of P is as follows:[a,b]

year	1955 (end of year) = 100
1966	118·7
1967	120·2
1968	121·6
1969	123·0
1970	124·5

(5) O_i: (*Case I*). For the 1966–70 period, the assumed annual rate of growth of O_i is 8·5% (average annual rate of growth of the 1961–65 period).[a]

(6) N_a: (*Case II*). As for the period of 1963–70, the level of N_a is assumed to be unchanged.[c,d]

---

[a] As for the years of 1964 and 1965, the actual figure for each year has been respectively applied.

[b] The growth trend of the total population forecasted with 'Census Bureau's Model 1 (B)' has been linked to the 1963 actual figure of P. Cf. J. W. Brackett, 'Demographic Trends and Population Policy in the Soviet Union', *Hearings: Dimensions of Soviet Economic Power*, by the Joint Economic Committee, Congress of the US (Washington, 1962), pp. 487–589.

[c] The 1963 value of N_a is 91·5 (1955 end-of-year = 100), that is the actual value.

[d] Strictly speaking, N_a is not an exogenous variable but an endogenous variable. However, as cited in the preceding section, within the framework of the '*Case II* causal pattern', N_a can be virtually determined exogenously.

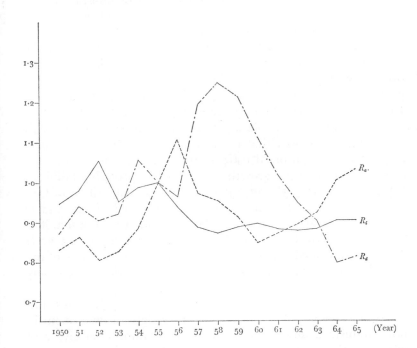

Figure 4   Trends of R_i, R_a and R_d, 1950–65 (1955 = 1·0)

The figures of R_i, R_a, and R_d refer to fixed capital investment only. They include the collective farms' investments and the investments from the decentralized sources. But they exclude the expenditures on capital repairs. 'Unproductive' investments like investment in housing are included in the total investment but excluded from the investment in agriculture and industry. In the calculations of R_i and R_a, dwelling constructions by citizens at their own expense (and with the aid of state loans) have not been included in the total investment. And, in the calculation of R_a all the collective farms' investments have been treated as 'productive' (thus, strictly speaking, there are some 'unproductive' investments included). However, in the derivation of R_d, private housing investment by individuals has been included in both the 'total investment' and the 'housing investment in 1962 was that a little more stress than in the two preceding years was laid on agricultural investment at the expense of industrial investment, and not at such a large sacrifice (as has been the case in 1963–66) of housing investment. And, as concerns the labor input in agriculture, N_a and P_r have almost completely ceased to diminish during the period 1960–65 (see Table 27.3). In view of these facts, the applicability of our hypothesis (as has been explained in the preceding section) to the declining growth of Soviet industrial production in the first half of the 1960s (especially in the period 1960–63) could be tested by these 'experimental analyses'.

As presented in Table 27.3, in the figures forecast with *Case IIA*, it is evident that the growth rate of O_i will diminish from about 9·3% around 1964 to so low a figure as about 6·8% around 1970, and the growth rate of O will probably fall from 6·4% in 1964 to 5·5% in 1970. Compared with those of *Case IIA*, however, the forecast figures with *Case IA* for O_i and O indicate that their rates of growth do not show such a manifest sign of decline in the post-1964 period. The analysis of *Case II* seems to show a correct survey of the declining tendency of the growth rate which had begun to set in in the Soviet economy around the first three years of the 1960s.

To glance over the data provided in Figure 4, it seems that the recent Soviet policy to push up the weight of investment in both industrial and agricultural sectors simultaneously, and greatly at the expense of housing, could be the quickest remedy for such a grave growth retardation as that which occurred in the early 1960s. However, as are shown in Table 27.4 the results of the comparative analysis of 'A computation' (*Case IA* and *Case IIA*) and 'B computation' (*Case IB* and *Case IIB*) are disappointing. If we substitute for the 1962 pattern of investment the 1965 pattern, we find rather small improvements in the growth trends of the variables. Probably the unforeseen

investment'. Cf. H. Niwa, 'An Analysis and Forecast of the Economic Growth in the Soviet Union', *Statistical Paper Series, no. 15* (Tokyo: The Institute of Asian Economic Affairs, 1966), pp. 75–9.

The official series for investment was revised in the *Narodnoe khoziaistvo SSSR v. 1965 g.* The sectoral breakdown of total investment for 1965 (in terms of the old series) has been estimated here by applying the sectoral percentage increases in 1965 given in the new series to the original 1964 figures reported in the previous statistical yearbook.

Table 27.3 *Some forecasted figures of Soviet economic growth*[a] (indices 1955 actual = 100)

		O	O_i	O_p	O_a	M	O_c	P_u	P_r	N_a	N_i	N_c	K_i	K_a	K_d
							Case IA								
1960	(Actual)	145·6	173·0	144·1	125·0	154·5	134·4	122·8	98·3	88·7	115·5	123·8	166·3	170·0	140·5
	(Forecasted)	142·9	—	138·0	126·8	148·9	134·2	119·8	100·5	94·6	114·8	121·0	166·1	165·3	139·9
1963	(Actual)	182·7	226·2	173·6	123·9	164·6	150·5	134·4	98·2	91·1	130·0	140·2	—	—	165·6
	(Forecasted)	184·1	—	173·8	138·2	176·5	155·0	139·1	94·2	92·2	131·6	140·0	224·3	226·0	168·2
1964	(Actual)	195·7	242·4	186·3	137·7	190·5	157·4	137·9	98·0	—	134·5	145·8	—	—	173·2
	(Forecasted)	194·9	—	183·1	142·2	182·8	159·8	142·0	94·5	90·9	134·0	142·9	247·3	252·5	177·5
1965	(Actual)	211·0	260·6	199·6	138·5	182·0	170·6	141·4	97·6	92·6	140·0	152·6	—	—	181·4
	(Forecasted)	206·3	—	192·8	145·3	188·7	164·2	145·0	94·6	91·5	136·5	145·9	272·4	281·7	187·5
1966	(Forecasted)	219·0	282·8	203·6	149·0	195·1	169·0	148·8	94·1	91·4	139·6	149·5	299·5	313·4	198·2
1968	(Forecasted)	247·7	332·9	227·6	155·8	210·1	180·1	157·4	92·3	90·5	146·7	158·0	360·8	385·1	221·8
1970	(Forecasted)	279·9	391·1	254·4	161·8	225·6	191·6	166·7	90·0	88·9	154·2	167·0	432·7	469·4	249·0
							Case IIA								
1963	(Forecasted)	182·0	218·4	172·0	138·2	176·5	155·0	137·2	95·7	91·5	130·0	138·2	224·3	203·3	168·0
1964	(Forecasted)	193·6	238·8	182·0	142·8	182·1	159·1	141·1	95·3	91·5	133·3	142·0	246·5	225·2	177·1
1965	(Forecasted)	205·7	259·2	192·3	145·8	188·1	163·7	144·8	94·8	91·5	136·3	145·7	271·3	251·3	187·1
1966	(Forecasted)	218·3	280·2	202·9	148·9	194·7	168·7	148·5	94·3	91·5	139·3	148·4	298·2	280·4	197·6
1968	(Forecasted)	244·8	321·9	225·2	155·9	209·4	179·6	156·0	93·5	91·5	145·2	156·2	358·7	345·6	220·8
1970	(Forecasted)	273·6	368·9	249·2	162·3	223·2	189·8	163·2	92·7	91·5	151·4	163·6	428·0	420·4	246·8

[a] For the sources of the actually observed data for the pre-1963 period, see the writer's paper 'An Analysis and Forecast', op. cit., pp. 67–79. The actual figures of the post-1963 period are derived from the data reported in *Narodnoe khoziaistvo SSSR v. 1965 g.*, and Joint Economic Committee, Congress of the United States, *New Directions in the Soviet Economy* (USGPO, 1966).

result stems, to some extent, from the substitutability of the factors of production assumed by our production functions (it would be better to apply a CES production function). But it is very important that, although the bad housing conditions in Soviet Russia have often been pointed out, such a cut of R_d does not mean a decline in the level of residential capital stock per head.[1] Partly for this reason, it was in a position to be 'one

Table 27.4 *Comparison of major forecasted figures in four cases for 1970* (1960 actual = 100)

	Case IA	Case IB	Case IIA	Case IIB
O_i	226·1	226·1	213·2	213·9
O	192·3	191·2	187·9	187·1
O_a	129·4	127·8	129·8	128·2
W	117·3	115·4	117·8	116·0
K_d/P_u	115·2	121·0	116·6	122·3
National income	158·1	156·2	155·8	154·1

of the quick remedies' for the Soviet economic plight in the early 1960s. The applicability of our 'hypothesis' cited in the preceding section seems to be not fairly proved by these analyses, but only one half of it.

As shown in Table 27.5 (p. 363), in the 1965–67 period, the forecast values of N_c and N_i are considerably lower than the actual values, while in the forecast values of P_u such a downward error of estimation is not evident. This is nothing but that the 'participation ratio' in the urban labor force has been pushed up more than usual. Compared with those of the original *Case IIA*, when the adjustments have been performed for such a rise of the 'participation ratio' (the adjusted case is called *Case IIA adjusted* hereafter), the forecast values of many variables indicate higher growth rates (see Table 27.6, p. 364). No doubt, the relatively good rate of growth of the Soviet industrial

---

[1] The floor space per head of urban inhabitants was greatly reduced before and after the second World War, and in 1960 the level of 1928 had not yet been recovered. The construction of dwellings was energetically accelerated in the latter half of the 1950s but the tempo slackened after 1960 when a peak was reached. Housing construction in 1963–65 was 4–9% less than in 1960. See *Narodnoe khoziaistvo SSSR* for the years concerned.

Table 27.5 *Comparison of actual and forecasted figures for P_u, N_i and N_c, 1964–67 (Case IA)* (end of year)

| | Index numbers (1955 actual = 100) | | | | | | Percentage discrepancy from actual figures | | |
| | P_u | | N_i | | N_c | | P_u | N_i | N_c |
	Actual	Forecasted	Actual	Forecasted	Actual	Forecasted	Forecasted	Forecasted	Forecasted
1964	137·9	142·0	134·5	134·0	145·8	142·9	3·0	−0·4	−2·0
1965	141·4	145·0	140·0	136·5	152·6	145·9	2·5	−2·5	−4·4
1966	144·8	148·8	144·5[b]	139·6	158·4[a]	149·5	2·8	−3·4	−5·6
1967	—	153·1	148·5[b]	143·1	—	153·8	—	−3·6	—

[a] The actual values of P_u and N_c for 1966 have been estimated by the use of the official data reported in *Vestnik statistiki*, no. 2 (1967), p. 91, no. 4 (1967), p. 93, no. 7 (1967), p. 95, no. 12 (1967), p. 3, and *Ekonomicheskaya gazeta*, no. 5 (February 1967), p. 5.
[b] The figures are indirectly derived by the aid of the official data for industrial production and labor productivity. **See** *Ekonomicheskaya gazeta*, no. 5 (1967), p. 3, and no. 4 (1968), p. 3.

production in the period 1965–67 can be partly explained in this light.

In either *Case I* or *Case II, Model no. 4* gives the forecast value of the annual rate of growth of O_a at 2·5–2·8% for the period 1960–70 (see Tables 27.3, 4, and 6). Needless to say, these

Table 27.6   *Trends of major variables forecasted with 'Case IIA adjusted'*[a]

	Index numbers (1960 actual = 100)			Average annual Growth rate (%)		
	1966	1968	1970	1960–66	1960–68	1960–70
O_i	182	216	252	10·5	10·1	9·7
O	156	177	200	7·7	7·4	7·2
O_a	119	126	131	2·9	2·9	2·7
W	111	114	117	1·8	1·7	1·6
National income	135	147	160	5·1	4·9	4·8

[a] Within the causal links of *Case IIA*, the original forecasted figures of N_i are inflated by 0·4% for 1964, 2·5% for 1965, 3·4% for 1966, and 3·8% for 1967–70.

pessimistic figures are due to the use of the agricultural production function of 'non-linear type'. But when one thinks of the stagnation of Soviet agriculture in the 1959–65 period, even these forecasted values may not be too pessimistic a picture. But M, the supply of raw materials of agricultural origin to the consumer goods industry, is expected to increase to a much greater extent than O_a, making it possible to forecast assuredly that the future rise in the marketable share of agricultural products will be an important offset to the stagnation in the Soviet agricultural production.[1]

In Tables 27.7–9 (pp. 365–7) are presented the forecasted figures for the changes of the future 'demographic structure'

[1] The average percentage share of 'State purchases and procurements' in O_a is forecast as follows:

	1955 (actual)	1966	1968	1970
Case IA	52·7	69·0	71·1	73·5
Case IIA	—	68·9	70·8	72·5

In view of the dissimilarity of coverage between M and O_a, the forecasted figures of 'marketable share' are to be considered as a rather rough approximation.

Table 27.7 *Forecasted figures of demographic structure* (end of year)

	P (in millions) (total population)		P_u (in millions) (urban population)		P_r (in millions) (rural population)		P (%)	P_u (%)	P_r (%)
Case IA									
1965	Actual	231·9	Actual	125·1	Actual	106·8	100	53·95	46·05
	Forecasted	232·1	Forecasted	128·1	Forecasted	104·0	100	55·19	44·81
1968	Forecasted	240·6	Forecasted	139·1	Forecasted	101·5	100	57·81	42·19
1970	Forecasted	246·2	Forecasted	147·3	Forecasted	98·9	100	59·83	40·17
Case IIA									
1965	Forecasted	232·1	Forecasted	127·9	Forecasted	104·2	100	55·11	44·89
1968	Forecasted	240·6	Forecasted	137·9	Forecasted	102·7	100	57·32	42·68
1970	Forecasted	246·2	Forecasted	144·2	Forecasted	102·0	100	58·57	41·43

Table 27.8 *Forecasted levels of Soviet real wages and residential capital stock per head* (1960 actual = 100)

		Case IA			Case IIA		
		1966	1968	1970	1966	1968	1970
Consumer goods production	O_e	125·8	134·0	142·5	125·5	133·6	141·2
Employment in non-agricultural sector (excluding armed forces, house-servants, etc.)	N_e	120·8	127·6	134·9	119·8	126·1	132·1
Employment in non-agricultural sector (including armed forces, house-servants, etc.)		116·5	122·6	129·1	115·6	121·3	126·6
Relative share of consumer goods supply to rural area (%)[a]	S_u	21·1	20·3	19·3	21·2	20·5	19·8
Relative share of consumer goods supply to urban area (%)		78·9	79·7	80·7	78·8	79·5	80·2
Level of real wages (urban worker)	W	112·1	114·7	117·3	112·6	115·3	117·8
Level of per head residential capital stock (urban area)	K_d/P_u	102·7	108·7	115·2	102·6	109·1	116·6

[a] This series is related to the percentage share of rural trade in the total retail sales (state and co-operative shops only).

Table 27.9 Forecasted growth of National Income (1955 actual = 100)[a]

	(actual)		Case IA (forecasted)			Case IIA (forecasted)			Case IIA Adjusted (forecasted)		
	1955	1960	1966	1968	1970	1966	1968	1970	1966	1968	1970
Industry	100·0	145·6	219·0	247·7	279·9	218·3	244·8	273·6	227·0	258·0	290·7
	(31·3)	(32·3)	(36·6)	(37·9)	(39·3)	(36·6)	(37·7)	(39·0)	(37·5)	(38·9)	(40·4)
Agriculture	100·0	125·0	149·0	155·8	161·8	148·9	155·9	162·3	149·3	157·0	164·2
	(27·1)	(24·1)	(21·6)	(20·6)	(19·7)	(21·6)	(20·8)	(20·0)	(21·4)	(20·5)	(19·8)
Services	100·0	147·7	188·8	203·5	219·4	187·6	202·4	216·0	187·6	202·3	215·6
	(41·6)	(43·6)	(41·8)	(41·5)	(41·0)	(41·8)	(41·5)	(41·0)	(41·1)	(40·6)	(39·8)
Aggregated national income	100·0	140·9	187·4	204·4	222·7	186·7	203·0	219·5	189·6	207·5	225·2
	(100·0)	(100·0)	(100·0)	(100·0)	(100·0)	(100·0)	(100·0)	(100·0)	(100·0)	(100·0)	(100·0)
Ditto, (1960 actual = 100)	71·0	100·0	133·0	145·1	158·1	132·5	144·1	155·8	134·6	147·3	159·8

( ) Percentage.

[a] As indexes of industrial and agricultural real incomes the relevant values of O and O_a have been used respectively. The index for the real income of the 'service industry' has been derived from the real wage index multiplied by the relevant index number of employment in the 'service industry' which can be easily calculated from the trends of N_e and of N_v. As for the 1955 actual structure of national income by each sector, Professor Bornstein's estimate has been used. See *The Review of Economics and Statistics*, vol. XLIV, no. 4 (1962), p. 457.

(between urban and rural areas), the 'level of real wages', the 'level of residential capital stock', and the 'national income' as revealed in *Case I* and *Case II*. Of course, it is easy to calculate and predict the trends of capital–output ratio, labor productivity, and capital–labor ratio by the numerical figures given in Table 27.3. These three important indexes related to industry are presented in Table 27.10 (p. 368). In spite of a remarkable rise in the capital–labor ratio, labor productivity increases relatively little, and there is as its corollary, a rising trend in capital–output ratio.

Table 27.10 *Forecasted trends of K_i/N_i (capital–labor ratio), O/N_i (labor productivity), and K_i/O (capital output ratio) (1955 actual = 100)*

	$(K_i/N_i) \times 100$ capital– labor ratio	$(O/N_i) \times 100$ labor productivity	$(K_i/O) \times 100$ capital– output ratio
Case IA			
1966	214·57	156·93	136·73
1968	246·03	168·93	145·64
1970	280·59	181·52	154·58
Case IIA			
1966	214·05	156·69	136·61
1968	247·04	168·56	146·56
1970	283·40	180·77	156·77

The trends of selected major forecast figures are shown in Figure 5 (p. 369). The comparative trends of major indexes of forecasted and actual values in the first half of 1960s are given in Table 27.11 (p. 370); the very good fits can be observed.

According to the forecast by Stanley H. Cohn, which is considered the most trustworthy of the sort, the average annual rate of growth of GNP is 4·5 or 5·5% in the period 1960–70.[1] The writer's forecast of the average annual growth rate in national income, however, has been 4·69% in *Case IA*, 4·5% in *Case IIA*, 4·58% in *Case IB*, 4·42% in *Case IIB* and 4·80% in *Case IIA adjusted* for the same period 1960–70. Note also that in

[1] Cf. S. H. Cohn, op. cit., p. 127.

the forecasted figures the gradual downward tendency of
average annual growth rate is dimly visible: 4·7–5·1% for
1960–66, 4·6%–5·0% for 1960–68, and 4·4–4·8% for 1960–70.

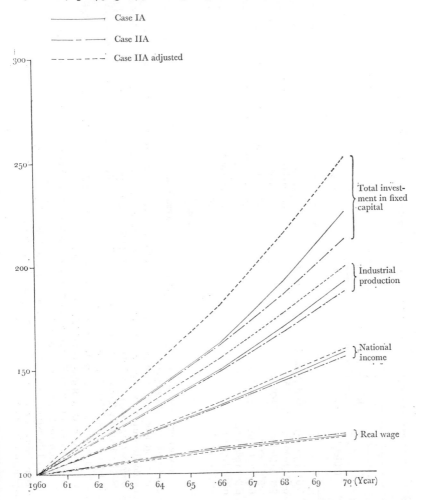

Figure 5 Some forecasted figures of major indicators (1960 actual = 100)

In short, there is no question that the industrial production
and the national income will attain a fairly high rate of growth.
But it is also almost certain that the level of real wages will rise
but slightly. It is true that the level of real wages in the Soviet

Table 27.11 *Comparison of actual and forecasted growth rates for major indicators* (average annual rate of growth, %)

	Actual			Forecasted		
	Official	Joint economic committee of the US Congress	The present study[g]	Case IA	Case IIA	Case IIA adjusted
Industrial production	8·6[a] (1960–65) 8·8[a] (1960–67)	6·9[d] (1960–65)	7·7 (1960–65)	7·3 (1960ⁱ–65) 6·7 (1960ⁱ–70)	7·1 (1960ⁱ–65) 6·5 (1960ⁱ–70)	7·7 (1960ⁱ–65) 6·8 (1960ⁱ–70)
Agricultural production	2·3[a] (1960–65) 3·5 (1960–66)	2·7[e] (1960–65)	2·7 (1960–65)	3·1 (1960ⁱ–65) 2·6 (1960ⁱ–70)	3·1 (1960ⁱ–65) 2·7 (1960ⁱ–70)	3·1 (1960ⁱ–65) 2·8 (1960ⁱ–70)
National income	6·7[a] (1960–65) 6·8[a] (1960–67)	4·9[f] (1960–65)	5·3 (1960–65)	4·9 (1960ⁱ–66) 4·7 (1960ⁱ–70)	4·8 (1960ⁱ–66) 4·5 (1960ⁱ–70)	5·1 (1960ⁱ–66) 4·8 (1960ⁱ–70)
Real wages	0·98[b] (1960–64) 2·35[c] (1960–66)	—	1·6[h] (1960–65)	1·9 (1960ⁱ–66) 1·6 (1960ⁱ–70)	2·0 (1960ⁱ–66) 1·6 (1960ⁱ–70)	1·8 (1960ⁱ–66) 1·6 (1960ⁱ–70)

^a The figures have been taken from *Narodnoye Khoziatsvo SSSR* for the years concerned, and *Ekonomicheskaya Gazeta*, no. 4 (January 1968).

^b See *Narodnoye Khoziaistvo SSSR v. 1964 g.*, p. 590.

^c As for the years of 1965 and 1966, the rate of increase of real wages has been computed with the official data of the nominal wages, state retail prices, and collective-farm market prices. See *Narodnoye Khoziaistvo SSSR v. 1965 g.*, p. 652 and p. 667, *Vestnik statistiki*, no 12, (1967). pp. 77–89, *Ekonomicheskaya gazeta*, no. 5 (February 1967), and UN, ECE, *Economic Survey of Europe in 1965*, part 1, p. 40.

^d James H. Noren; 'Soviet Industry Trends in Output, Inputs, and Productivity', *New Directions in the Soviet Economy*, by the Joint Economic Committee of US Congress (USGPO, 1966), p. 280.

^e Douglas B. Diamond; 'Trends in output, inputs, and Factor productivity in Soviet Agriculture', *New Directions in the Soviet Economy*, by the Joint Economic Committee of US Congress (USGPO, 1966), p. 346.

^f Stanley H. Cohn, 'Soviet Growth Retardation: Trends in Resource Availability and Efficiency', *New Directions in the Soviet Economy*, by the Joint Economic Committee of US Congress (USGPO, 1966), p. 126.

^g See Table 27.3 above, and the writer's paper 'An Analysis and Forecast', loc. cit., pp. 51–79.

^h Computed by the 'commodity flow method' cited in the preceding section.

ⁱ The figure for base-year 1960 is actual.

Union in 1950s nearly doubled (1·7–1·8 times). Considered in the light of such past accomplishments, the forecasted 17–18% increase of real wages for the 1960–70 may be taken as too pessimistic a view (see Table 27.8). Of course, this very low rate of increase is partly due to the fact that the coverage of O_c in our source excludes the large part of consumer durables and services. But even the official figures now available indicate that the annual average rate of increase of real wages was as low as 0·98% in 1960–64, and approximately 2·4% in 1960–66 (see Table 27.11). The writer's forecast with his model, which might be taken as too pessimistic, has already proved its validity through what has actually happened in the first half of the 1960s.

If any policy were to be enforced to maintain the annual growth rate of O_i at 8·5% up until 1970, and at the same time, to keep the level of N_a unaltered (*Case III*), the model would then be over-determined, with two sets of figures calculated for O_c. Yet it is significant to know that the O_c value calculated directly from the industrial production function (Equation no. 5), instead of coming around through the supply function of raw materials of agricultural origin (Equation no. 8), shows a rate of growth lower than that of P_u or N_c.[1] In other words, it is implied that in *Case III* the level of real wages is lowered at the onslaught of the enhanced capital goods production.

[1] The forecast figures of P_u and O_c as revealed in *Case III* are shown as follows: (1965 forecasted = 100)

	1965	1968	1970
P_u	100·0	107·7	112·7
O_c (calculated through the causal channel of Equation no. 8)	100·0	109·7	116·2
O_c (calculated directly from Equation no. 5 and Equation no. 1)	100·0	106·9	111·0

As cited in the text, the assumptions pertaining to O_i and N_a are the same as in *Case I* and *Case II* respectively. As for the investment allocation, the assumptions pertaining to R_i and R_a are similar to the case of the computation based on *Case IA* and *Case IIA*.

The writer's estimation work presupposes that the production of arms (including space rockets, artificial satellites, and the like) will be continued into the future at the past growth rate. If disarmament were realized to the extent of stopping the growth of arms production, the annual average rate of real wage increase might be raised by about 0·5%.[1]

In the Communist Party Program of the Soviet Union adopted by the resolution at the 22nd Party Congress in October 1961, the goal is set to raise the level of real wages twofold during the ten years up to 1970. The actual situation appears to be far wide of this mark. In the Five-Year Plan as it now stands, a 20% rise of the real wage level is expected for 1966–70. Although the new goal is more plausible than the original Party Program, it also seems difficult to attain.

[1] We assume the rate of growth in the output of munitions (O_m) after 1964 to be zero, and treat the other exogenous variables in the same way as in computations based on *Case IA* and *Case IIA*. The computed results are as follows:

(1960 actual = 100)

| | Real wages (urban worker) | |
	Case IA	*Case IIA*
1966	117	113
1968	121	117
1970	122	122

Compared with the figures of 'simple extrapolation' computed by *Case IA* (see Table 27.8), the effect on the level of urban real wages, when we assume that the growth of munitions output is zero, seems to be rather large.

APPENDIX:
COMPARATIVE STATISTICAL TABLE

PETER WILES

ECONOMIC PERFORMANCE OF THE COMMUNIST
COUNTRIES IN THE RECENT PAST AND THE NEAR
FUTURE

*Predictions of November 1967; only factual errors have been
corrected
(Annual rates of growth unless otherwise stated).*

	Albania 1960–65	Albania 1965–70	Bulgaria 1960–65	Bulgaria 1965–70	China 1957–65	China 1965–70	Czechoslovakia 1960–65	Czechoslovakia 1965–70[a]	D.D.R. 1960–65	D.D.R. 1965–70
1. Global production, all industry	6·8	8·6 (7·0)[b]	9	11	5[a]	7[a]	4·6	5·6	6·0	(6)
2. Producer goods		11·0	14				6·0			(7)
3. Consumer goods		6·8[a]	9				4·5			(5)
4. Volume of construction			7				−0·7		5·0[e]	(6)
5. Global production, all agriculture	6·4	12·0 (6·0)[b]	3	5·5	0[a]	2[a]	−0·5	4·1	3·0[c]	(4·5)
6. Crops		16·7	2				−3·0			
7. Livestock products		10·0	5				2·0			
8. Global industrial productivity			6·8				4·0		7·0	
9. Number of workers and employees			4·4		1·8[b]	2[c]	1·1		0·2	
10. Population	3·0	4·5[a]	0·8		3[d]	5·5[d]	0·7	(0·7)	0·1	(0·1)
11. NMP	5·8 (8·0)[c]	3·0	7·2	7	3	9	2·0	4·4	3·7	(5)
12. Fixed investment	8·8[c]	8·0 (6·0)[b]	9		1	3	0·2		4·7[a]	(10)[a]
13. Total consumption		4·0	7·0	7	2	3	2·0[c]	2·8	2·1[b]	(4)[b]
14. Visible exports	8·9	6·4	16				7·0	6·4	7·5	

15. Relation of all exports (incl. invisibles) to national income, in %, 1965	13	?	4[c]	19[b]	21·5[d]
16. Purchasing power of the currency in US cents with respect to GNP at market prices, 1965	(c 7·85)[d]	c. 87[a]	(c. 51)[e]	10·6[f]	25·0[h]
17. Population, mid-1965, millions	1·85	8·21	681[b]	14·16	17·03
18. GNP, milliards of local currency units, 1965	(7·30)[d]	c. 8·00[e]	130	224[d]	111[f]
19. GNP per head, dollars at market prices, 1965	(c. 310)[d]	84·8[a]	(c. 95)[e]	1,629[f]	1,629[h]
20. Lag of GNP, calculated in the West, on official NMP (indices)					
1950–55	—	133/179[a]	—	119/147[e]	141/185[g]
1955–60		142/159		137/141	127/147
1960–64		118/129		106/106	111/110
21. Expectation of life at birth, 1960–61	64·9	69·6	?	70 (1964)	68·3 (1955–58)
22. Students entering higher education, as percentage of the population aged 19 in 1964	8·8	15[b]	?	12·4 (1965–66)	12·3

	Hungary		N. Korea	Poland		Rumania		USSR	
	1960-65	1965-70	1960-64	1960-65	1965-70	1959-65	1965-70	1960-65	1965-70
1. Global production, all industry	8·0	6·0 (6·5)	14·5 (5·7)[c]	8·0	7·5 (7·5)[f]	14·0	11·0	8·6	8·2
2. Producer goods	8·6	6·7	12·8	9·9		15·0	11·5	9·6	8·5
3. Consumer goods	6·6	4·1	16·6	6·6		10·0	10·2	8·5	7·6
4. Volume of construction			13·4[a]	7·0	5·0[b] (3·0)[b]	12·6		4·2	
5. Global production, all agriculture	1·9[b]	2·7[b]	6·2[a]	3·0	3·3 (3·3)	2·0	5·3	2·5	
6. Crops	1·2[b]	2·3[b]	5·7[a]	3·2	3·5 (3·5)			2·0	(3)
7. Livestock products	2·5[b]	3·0[b]	7·0[a]	2·5	3·0 (3·0)			3·0	
8. Global industrial productivity	3·0[e]	5·0 (3·7)[d]	—	3·8	4·6 (4·0)	7·7		4·7	6·1 (5·2)
9. Number of workers and employees	0·3	1·3[e]	8·4	4·0[e]	2·9 (3·5)			4·4	3·6 (4·2)
10. Population		(0·3)[a]	2·4[a]	1·0	1·0	0·7	0·6	1·7	(1·7)[c]
11. NMP	4·6	3·7 (4·0)	9·9	6·0	6·0 (6·0)	9·0		6·3[b]	7·0
12. Fixed investment	11·0[b,c]	4·6[b,c]	7·8[b]	7·0	7·0 (7·0)	13·0		6·1	9·3
13. Total consumption	3·4	(2·5)	—	3·6[d]	4·0 (3·5)			2·7[e]	
14. Visible exports	11·6	7·9	6·2	10	5·0 (4·0)		8·9	8·0[d]	
15. Relation of all exports (incl. invisibles) to national income, in %, 1965	c. 38[a]		c. 12·3[d]	28[c]		18		3·5[c]	

16. Purchasing power of the currency in US cents with respect to GNP at market prices, 1965	5.6^t	$c.\ 60^d$	$4.85^t\ (5.68)^a$	$c.\ 7.7^a$	$135^g\ (121)^a$
17. Population, mid-1965, millions	10·15	$c.\ 12.29^d$	31·45	19·03	230·5
18. GNP, milliards of local currency units, 1965	206^g	$c.\ 6.23^d$	655^g	$c.\ 202^e$	241^f
19. GNP per head, dollars at market prices, 1965	$1,140^i$	$c.\ 353^d$	$1,010^i\ (1,182)^a$	814^d	$1,410^g\ (1,290)^a$
20. Lag of GNP, calculated in the West, on official NMP (indices)					
1950–55	$132/135^h$	—	$126/152^h$	$152/192^b$	$144/172^b$
1955–60	123/138	—	127/137	119/140	138/155
1960–64	120/122	—	122/126	121/140	123/126
21. Expectation of life at birth, 1960–61	69·4	—	67·8	68·3 (1965)	70
22. Students entering higher education, as percentage of the population aged 19 in 1964	$c.\ 11.3^f$	—	11 (1965)	$c.\ 11.2^a$ (1965–66)	14

NOTES TO THE APPENDIX

General

(1) Unless otherwise stated, figures in brackets are the estimates of the author of the corresponding article in November 1967.

(2) Row 22: evening and correspondence students are counted 0.5 each. The percentage given is that of freshmen of all ages per person aged 19.

(3) Rows 16 and 19: see the longer note below (pp. 380 ff.).

Albania

a Including craftsmen.

b Guess by Wiles.

c As financed by state only; i.e. collective farm investment omitted.

d Albanian statistical yearbooks furnish neither a breakdown of net material product by accumulation and consumption nor indices whereby a constant-price consumption series could be built (e.g. retail sales in constant prices, cost-of-living, real wages or real farmers' incomes). The two sources cited in Kaser, *Comecon* (London, 1967), pp. 206–7 show Albania as 18% of DDR in 1960 for NMP and personal consumption. Indexes of net material product cited in *Statistisches Jahrbuch der DDR 1968* appendix I, p. 3 for both Albania and DDR suggest a 1965 NMP per head ratio of 21%. Constant-priced investment outlays 1960 to 1964 (no data being available for 1965 for Albania) in the same source show that gross outlays by the state on investment rose 25% in Albania and all gross outlays on investment except repair-work rose 16% in the DDR. By deduction, and impressionistically, consumption per head in Albania is set at 19% of the DDR in 1965. The GNP at current prices is guessed to be 15% less than the 1967 GNP, given as 8.40 milliard lek at 1966 prices above.

Bulgaria

Unlike all the other countries, the Bulgarian predictions were made in 1968.

a First figure: GNP according to Morris Ernst in *New Directions in the Soviet Economy* (Joint Economic Committee of Congress, Washington, 1966).

b But it seems that only half complete the course.

c NMP plus 20% (15% in 1956, according to Wynnyczuk, unpublished).

d Ernst, *New Directions in the Soviet Economy*. See separate Note below (pp. 380 ff.).

China

Apart from *c* and *a*, all figures are Klatt's.

a Net, not global.

b Starting at *c.* 550 million in 1953.

c Guesstimate by Wiles.

d National income.

e See separate note below (pp. 380 ff.).

Czechoslovakia

a This is the now abandoned Five-Year Plan.

[1] Wiles, *Communist International Economics* (Oxford, 1969), p. 443.

c Individual consumption.

d NMP+23%: see Kaser, *Comecon* (London, 1967), p. 135.

e See Bulgaria *a*.

f See Bulgaria *d*.

DDR

[a] Including stocks.

[b] Individual consumption.

[c] Not so given: the figure for global production has been adjusted by utilizing the index of sales prices.

[d] See Czechoslovakia [b].

[e] Excluding construction by authorities other than specialized builders.

[f] NMP+33%: see Czechoslovakia [d].

[g] See Bulgaria [a].

[h] See Bulgaria [d].

Hungary

[a] See Czechoslovakia [b].

[b] Average growth over previous five-year's average.

[c] All investments.

[d] Assuming that agriculture will lose 200,000 workers more than the plan foresees, and dividing them equally between industry and other agricultural activities. The industrial labour force will thus grow from 1,527,000 to 1,734,000, or at 2.8% p.a.

[e] Excluding agricultural workers and employees.

[f] In the absence of figures for first-year students we have used the Polish or Albanian ratio between the first year and the total.

[g] NMP+23%: see Czechoslovakia [d].

[h] See Bulgaria [a].

[i] See Bulgaria [d].

North Korea

These figures are from Dr Pong S. Lee of the State University of NY in Albany. They appear to be the most recent available.

[a] 1960–63.

[b] Average (1961–64) ÷ average (1959–63).

[c] Dr Lee's own estimate for 1960–63, between which years the official index rose by 15.4% p.a. It so happens that in no other years does his index, which weights the actually published quantities by net value added, fall anything like so far short of the official, global index. He suspects re-armament, which his selected commodities would not reflect.

[d] Very approximate: 500 won of n.m.p. in 1966, at 1 won = 64 cents. Workings available on request from Dr Lee.

Poland

[a] Estimate by Wiles: see separate note below (pp. 380 ff.).

[b] Urban housing only.

[c] See Czechoslovakia [b].

[d] Individual.

[e] C. 2% of workers work for private enterprise.

[f] Including an estimate of 4.5% for seasonal industries.

[g] NMP+23%: see Czechoslovakia [d].

[h] See Bulgaria [a].

[i] See Bulgaria [d].

Rumania

[a] See Hungary [f].

[b] See Bulgaria [a]; but in this case Mr Ernst's figure is not well based.

[c] NMP = 168.2 (Kaser's estimate)+20% (see Czechoslovakia [d]).

[d] See Bulgaria [d].

USSR

[a] See separate note below (pp. 380 ff.).

[b] GNP according to Cohn in Joint Economic Committee of Congress, *Dimensions of Soviet Economic Power* (1962), p. 75, and *New Directions in the Soviet Economy* (1966), p. 104; the second figure is the official NMP.

[c] Cf. Wiles, *Political Economy of Communism* (1969), p. 438.

[d] Current prices.

[e] Individual and social material consumption: official figures in current prices, deflated by the retail price index (which is about 107%).

[f] NMP+25%: see Czechoslovakia [d].

[g] See Bulgaria [d].

Note on the purchasing power of Communist currencies (lines 16 and 19)
A rather lengthy justification is needed for rows 16 and 19. The most accurate method of comparing income levels is the 'Gilbert–Kravis': deflation of monetary magnitudes by 'Purchasing Power Parities' (PPPs) suitably weighted. But for these PPPs the most astonishingly different figures circulate, and I must apologize for repeating them uncritically in the first version of this piece, in *Analyse et Prévision*, Nov. 1967. The study of Communist PPPs is in a deplorably rudimentary state. The quality discounts that should apply to nominally similar goods are simply not known. The differences between the Paasche and the Laspeyres formula are very great, and commonly neglected. The most often quoted rates seem to rest on very little basis.[1]

Some students take refuge in the 'Tarn and Campbell' method: comparisons of physical outputs, weighted by values added or as near as may be. Where data are complete this method is identical to the deflation of a global monetary sum by a PPP. In particular it yields a Paasche and a Laspeyres formula. But it neglects perforce services, and the more complicated goods. Moreover neither price nor output data are ever anything like complete, and in this case output data are inherently less reliable, since physical output ratios differ very much more than price ratios;[2] a point especially important where international trade bulks large or where governments decide what to produce. The effect of this is that one can extrapolate from known to unknown prices (incomplete PPP), but not from known to unknown quantities. The most arbitrary price systems are nothing like so arbitrary as the quantity patterns that go with them, and I find this point wholly decisive in favouring the use of the PPP where it is at all possible. There exist however

[1] For a general account of the unsatisfactory state of this subject, cf. my contribution to ed. J. Degras and A. Nove, *Soviet Planning* (Oxford, 1964).
[2] Wiles, op. cit.(1964), p. 113.

valiant and not wholly unconvincing attempts to use many quantity comparisons.[1]

Then there is the Jánossy method. He and Novozamsky and Beckerman–Bacon[2] are most sophisticated statisticians but – as so often – less good economists. They regress a very few Communist output statistics on the relation between capitalist output statistics and capitalist national income. These regressions are purely empirical and obliterate the Paasche–Laspeyres distinction. They arrive, too, for whatever reason, at figures which appear strongly biased against Communist countries. Who, for instance, would believe that Soviet income per head was 40% of West German, or Hungarian and Polish 25%? The shortfall of this method from the PPP method runs at about 40%. Nevertheless its inter-Communist comparisons seem reasonable. We therefore revert to the PPP.

To begin with the *consumption rouble*, the most quoted figure is Morris Bornstein's, for 1955.[3] He bases himself on Norman Kaplan and Eleanor Wainstein.[4] Their studies are from printed lists, though they do take account of quality as far as they can. With many adjustments he does not spell out, Bornstein arrives at R.15 = $1 and R.8 = $1 with US and Soviet weights respectively. These figures give an unprecedently large Paasche–Laspeyres spread for the rouble (1·83:1). However the Paasche–Laspeyres spread for dollar versus lira in 1950 was 1·75:1,[5] so perhaps this is acceptable.

Then the Statistisches Bundesamt[6] has two calculations for x roubles = 1 DM, including rents:

---

[1] A. Tarn and R. W. Campbell in *AER* (September 1962) (for Soviet and US industry); F. Pryor and G. J. Staller in *Economics of Planning* (Oslo) 1/1966 (many comparisons for many Communist countries).

[2] F. Jánossy, *A Gazdasági Fejlettség Mérhetősége és uj Mérési Módszere* (The Measurability of Economic Development and a Way of Measuring It) (Budapest, 1963); J. Novozamsky in *Politicka Ekonomie*, 8/1966; W. Beckerman, *International Comparisons of Real Income* (OECD, 1966); W. Beckerman and R. Bacon in *Economic Journal* (September 1966). The latter seem to use in no case more than three commodities! I find the logic of this impossible to grasp, in view of the arbitrariness of Communist outputs. The figures are conveniently collected in M. Kaser, *Comecon*, (2nd ed., London, 1967), pp. 135–6. This method was previously used for intertemporal comparisons in Soviet industry by F. Seton, in *Manchester Statistical Society* (1957) and *Soviet Studies* (1960).

[3] In *Comparisons of the US and Soviet Economies* (Joint Economic Committee of Congress, 1959), pp. 385–6.

[4] RAND RM–1692–1 of 1956 and RM–1906 of 1957.

[5] Cf. Milton Gilbert and Irving Kravis, *An International Comparison of National Products and the Purchasing Power of Currencies* (OEEC, 1954), Tables 27–30.

[6] *Preise Löhne Wirtschaftsrechnungen, Reihe 10, Internationaler Vergleich der Preise für die Lebenshaltung* (Kohlhammer, Wiesbaden, 1967).

	number of *goods and services*	*West German* *weights*	*Soviet* *weights*
1954	98	5·26	3·84
1958	137	4·16	3·23

Both reckonings however are from printed lists. Using the $/DM
PPP from the same source, the implied $/R. PPP in 1955 is R.
12·5 = $1 by West German weights.

The comparison shopper has the advantage of not basing himself
on printed lists. The first serious comparison shopper is Alec Nove.[1]
He admits, however, to having made insufficient quality discounts

Table 1   *Cost of living* (1955 = 100)

	USSR (Soviet weights)		USA (US weights)	UK (British weights)
State shops (official)	101	78·0		
Kolkhoz market (official)	112	12·0		
Services: monthly wage index less an arbitrary 10% for productivity increase	121	4·6		
Rents and public utilities	101[a]	5·4		
	c. 103·3			
Add 5% for concealed price increases specified by Hanson (p. 214)	*c.* 108 (1965)		117·5 (1965) 90·0 (1950)	114·9 (1965) 76·2 (1950)

[a] My guess.

against the rouble (p. 246). He arrives at old R. 35 = £1 for
consumption including rents in 1955, Soviet weights only. The
second serious comparison shopper is Philip Hanson,[2] who gets new
R. 4·74 = £1 in 1965, on about the same Soviet weights as Nove
(see his p. 226). His figure with British weights is actually lower:
R. 3·48 = £1. However he seems not to have used the ordinary

[1] In *Was Stalin Really Necessary?* (London, 1964).
[2] *Oxford Institute of Economics and Statistics Bulletin*, 3 (1965).

Paasche formula in the case of Soviet weights. Applying this, we [1] arrive at R. 3·42 by Soviet, and R. 4·25 by British, weights; so R. 3·80 by Fisher's Ideal.

To use British results we need a plausible $/£ ratio. Gilbert and Kravis (op. cit.) arrive at $3·3 = £1, by US weights in 1950 (consumption only), and $4·4 = £1,[2] by British weights. The movement of the costs of living has been as shown in Table 1 (1955 = 100). Accordingly we may sum up for the consumption PPP in Table 2 (old roubles).

Table 2 *Consumption PPPs for the rouble*

1955	R. 15 = $1	US weights (Bornstein, i.e. mainly Kaplan/Wainstein)
1955	R. 8 = $1	Soviet weights (Bornstein, i.e. mainly Kaplan/Wainstein)
1955	R. 12.5 = $1	West German weights (Stat. Bundesamt)
1955	R. 38.5 = £1	Soviet weights (Nove)[a]
1965	R. 47.4 = £1	Soviet weights (Hanson)[b]
1965	R. 34.8 = £1	British weights (Hanson)[b]
1955	£1 = $3.25	Fisher's Ideal (Gilbert and Kravis)
1955	R. 11.8 = $1	(Nove, Soviet weights, divided by 3.25)
1955	R. 9.9 = $1	(Hanson, Soviet weights, corrected for cost of living and divided by 3.25)
1955	R. 12.2 = $1	(Ditto, UK weights)

[a] Applying an arbitrary 10% quality discount to the rouble (see text).
[b] As recomputed by Mrs Arnoll, and converted into old roubles.

This is rather satisfactory. Hanson's Fisher's Ideal agrees to within 1% with Kaplan/Wainstein's, and everyone else seems to be 'in the same ball park'. I shall therefore posit *R. 9 = $1*, for consumption in 1955, including rents, by Soviet weights, and *R. 13 = $1* by US weights (averaging Hanson and Kaplan/Wainstein).

Bornstein's PPPs for other sectors are hard to criticize or defend, partly because his own treatment (q.v.) is so summary (see Table 3). This yields a PPP of *new R. 0·83 = $1* for the GNP in 1965, by

[1] These recomputations were done by my research assistant Mrs Helen Arnoll. She has also recomputed the PPP by the Laspeyres formula (British weights) and arrives at a somewhat different answer in this case too, as shown.
[2] The Statistisches Bundesamt (op. cit.) has $4.94 = £1 in 1955, consumption only, West German weights.

Fisher's Ideal formula; and on this are based the figures in parentheses, rows 16 and 19.

Turning now to the zloty, as usual we have more data for consumption, but they are very poor. My own estimate[1] in 1964 was 13·0 zlotys = $1 (Fisher's Ideal, including rents). Also for that year a very careful analysis by the Polish central statistical office yielded a PPP of 102 zlotys = 100 schillings, excluding rent,[2] by Fisher's

Table 3

| | Expenditures in GNP | | PPPs with | | (Soviet price |
	USSR (R. md.)	USA ($ md.)	Soviet/US weights (old R. = $1)		indices, 1955–65)
Consumption	840·8	269·7	9	13	108[c]
Investment	263·5	77·2	5[a]	7[a]	89[d]
Defence	144·6	38·4	4[a]	5[a]	102[e]
Government administration	36·9	12·1	3[b]	3[b]	121[f]
GNP 1955	1,285·8	397·5	9·41	10·05	104
Deflator 1955–65, and PPP 1965	1·04	1·22	8·04	8·56	

[a] Bornstein's original PPPs.

[b] Bornstein has 2, which is the rouble/dollar salary equivalent. It seems at least less arbitrary to assume that Soviet civil servants are 50% less efficient than their US counterparts. The efficiency gap is greater elsewhere.

[c] See previous text.

[d] Average of official construction and machinery indices.

[e] Average of official machinery index and my index for government administration.

[f] My service cost index, as in Table 1.

Ideal. This may be converted into DM(W): 100 schillings were worth 17·64 DM(W) (Fisher's Ideal) excluding rent.[3] So by this indirect reckoning 1 DM(W) = 5·78 zlotys. But by direct reckoning the Statistisches Bundesamt arrives at 1 DM(W) = 7·55 zlotys (West German weights only, excluding rent). Applying the Amt's dollar –DM(W) PPP of 3·58 (Fisher's Ideal, excluding rent), we arrive at 21·8 and 28·5 zlotys = $1, without rents, or about 20 and 26·1 zlotys including rents. Then the price changes in 1965 in Poland

[1] Wiles, *Communist International Economics* (New York, 1969), p. 431.

[2] Privately communicated.

[3] Statistisches Bundesamt, op. cit.

APPENDIX 385

and USA mean a relative depreciation of the dollar by 1%. More-over there are two very fair zloty–rouble comparisons. Ya. Kot-kovski[1] has 16·2 zlotys = 1 new rouble by Soviet weights and 15·9 by Polish weights for 'consumer goods' in 1959–60. Secondly the non-commercial rate with the rouble (below) was fixed at 15·26 zlotys = 1 new rouble in April 1963. Rouble and zloty consumption prices have been rising at about the same rate since then, so it is enough to use a rouble/$ PPP for 1965. At R. 1 = $0·91 (allowing for price changes from 1955, see above), this implies 16·8 zlotys = $1. Although my own calculation is the only direct one, I am alarmed by the hostility it has incurred in Polish and Polonological circles, so shall compromise at 16·0 zlotys = $1.

The rest of the calculation follows in Table 4.

Table 4   *Zloty–dollar PPP*

		Polish[c] weights	US[f] weights
		(%, 1955)	
Consumption, including rents, unweighted	16·0[a]	61·1	65·5
Machinery for investment, unweighted	34·5[g]		
Construction services	10·0[b]		
Investment	22·7[d]	24·3	20·5
Defence	22·2[e]	4·5	11·3
Government administration	10·0[b]	10·3	2·9
PPPs for GNP, zlotys per dollar		(17·3)	(17·9)

[a] See text above.
[b] Very much a guess; since this is largely pure labour I use my PPP for haircuts (Wiles, loc. cit.).
[c] Thad Alton et al., *Polish National Income and Product* (Columbia, 1965), p. 62.
[d] The weight of machinery in fixed investment was 36%: *Rocznik Statystyczny* (1966), p. 62. But stockpiling was 25% of all gross investment (Alton, loc. cit.). I have valued this at 34·5 zlotys.
[e] 49·5% went on direct labour (Alton op. cit., p. 178), and is valued at 10·0 zlotys. The rest is valued at 34·5 zlotys.
[f] Table 3.
[g] Wiles, loc. cit.

Other PPPs for the zloty have been very different. The Poles themselves use actual or shadow rates of exchange of about 50 zlotys = $1 that *imply* a gross underestimate of the purchasing

[1] In *Voprosy Ekonomiki* 8 (1966), p. 87.

power of the zloty (Wiles, op. cit. (1969), pp. 431–3); but this is not the same as an actual underestimate, since the rates are deliberately fixed low to make a large volume of exports possible (they do not govern imports, the volume of which is fixed at a very high level by the plan *a priori*).[1]

For the rest, this Polish section is shorter for one reason only: Poland is a less important country and fewer people have written about the zloty. I arrive, very hesitantly, at a PPP for the GNP in 1965 of *17·6 zlotys* = $1. It would be a travesty to describe the formula as Fisher's Ideal: let us rather say 'neutral weights'. This rate yields the figures in parentheses in rows 16 and 19 of the table.

There is also a serious PPP for the yuan: *1·97 yuan* = $1 in 1955 by Fisher's Ideal formula.[2] In this case however Chinese weights give 1·04 yuan and US weights 3·46 yuan: results so divergent as to make any average meaningless. We must therefore neglect the yuan for purposes of comparison with third currencies, though I have duly entered the 'appropriate' yuan–dollar figures in the table (US and Chinese prices have both risen gently since 1955).

As to the other countries, there exist at least official consumption PPPs, agreed between the governments. These are the 'non-commercial' rates of exchange. In units of currency per one rouble, they were fixed in April 1963, and may be compared with various private Communist estimates (see Table 5).

The Tuzex shops in Czechoslovakia sell luxury and hard-currency goods in 'Tuzex crowns'. Any tourist may buy such crowns at a certain rate against his own currency. This applies also to natives, who must pay 100 kčs for 31·2 Tuzex crowns. The rates quoted here are those for the rouble divided by those for other currencies. I have no knowledge at what dates or on what basis these rates were fixed, so they are unusable. But it is perhaps not altogether insignificant that they confirm the private Communist estimates: the official non-commercial rates appear systematically to undervalue the rouble.

Nevertheless my colleague Dr Machowski, to whom I owe much good criticism and many new references,[3] prefers the non-commercial rates to virtually all other possible PPPs, since they are the product of serious negotiation by responsible people, not mere economists. They are based on a single basket, suitable to a four-member family, of 33 food, drink and tobacco items, 22 manu-

---

[1] Wiles, op. cit. (1969), pp. 431–3. It follows that the shadow rates for exports can *never* be used – for other Communist countries are not all that different.

[2] W. W. Hollister, *China's Gross National Product* (MIT, 1958), pp. 142–7; cf. Wiles, op. cit. (1969), p. 145.

[3] Cf. E. Klinkmüller and H. Machowski in *Ost Europa Wirtschaft* 2 (1966).

factured goods and 14 services, of which rent is probably not one.
The prices appear to be those of early 1963.[1] Using these rates to
convert the whole national income, and not merely consumption
less rents, Machowski and Klinkmüller put USSR below Bulgaria
and on a level with Rumania! Their figure for 1965 is $773 per head,
whereas Ernst's is $1,410 (see row 19).

Table 5   *Miscellaneous Consumption PPPs*

	Official non-commercial[a]	Private estimates		Tuzex[c]
Albania (old lek)	84			
Bulgaria (new leva)	0·78			0·88
China (yuan)	1·29			
Czechoslovakia (kčs)	9·6	14·5/10·7[d]	10·0[b]	11·9
DDR (DM(O))	3·2			3·84
Hungary (forint)	13·1		16·0[b,c]	14·7
Rumania (leu)	8·3			11·4
Poland (zloty)	15·26	16·2/15·9[d]	18·7[b]	16·2

[a] *Polish Economic Survey*, II (1963).
[b] West German weights, from Statistisches Bundesamt, op. cit.
[c] For 1963: M. Brdek and J. Holeček in *Planovane Hospodarstvi* 2 (1965).
[d] Kotkovski, loc. cit., Soviet–Czechoslovak and Soviet–Polish weights, 1959/60.
[e] Given without rents only. I appreciate it above by 7%, which is the difference
due to including rents in the zloty and the kčs.

Now it is undeniable that the non-commercial rates may be right,
and possible that 'everyone else is out of step'. But, first, they are
contradicted by the various private Communist calculations shown.
Secondly when we contrast consumption with the rest of the
national income, Communist price structures differ among themselves. Consumption PPPs are no substitute for properly worked
out national-income PPPs.
   Thus the Chinese structure is quite different from the Soviet
structure. In 1952 the dollar bought 1·8 yuan of consumer goods and
2·68 yuan of investment goods;[2] while in 1955 it bought R. 11 of
consumption goods versus R. 6 of investment goods (Table 3).
Thus the rouble price pattern is much more 'pro-investment' than

[1] Culled by Dr Machowski from Willi Ehlert and Klaus Kolloch's *Habilitations-
schrift* for the Hochschule für Oekonomie in Berlin-Karlshorst (1965).
[2] Hollister, op. cit. Fisher's Ideal is used, but the Paasche–Laspeyres spread is
extremely wide.

the dollar price pattern, and the latter is much more 'pro-invest-ment' than that of the yuan. Again in Poland in 1965 the dollar bought 16 zlotys' worth of consumption goods, but perhaps 22·4 zlotys' worth of investment goods (Table 4). So the zloty price pattern inclines to the Chinese, not the Soviet, side of the dollar price pattern. Now consumption goods are traditional and invest-ment goods new in China and Poland. So their price patterns need not surprise us. But the rouble *might* seem paradoxical. However, as Hanson has shown,[1] USSR has for a very long time concentrated her R and D, her best current labour, her economies of scale and most of her capital in the output of machinery, raw materials, weapons and industrial buildings. While the factory prices of these things have risen *pari passu* with retail prices in USA, they have risen much more slowly in USSR ever since 1928 at least. So Soviet efficiency is lop-sided by American standards, *and still more lop-sided by Chinese and Polish ones.*

There is nothing paradoxical about this. We have every reason to suppose that the young, inexperienced, subsidized and un-specialized Polish heavy industry should be peculiarly inefficient by Polish standards, and the choice of a shadow rate of exchange for exports of 1 zloty = $0·02 confirms this: Polish exports are extremely expensive, and a 'shadow devaluation', out of all proportion to the real purchasing power of the zloty, has taken place in order to make it financially possible to sell them at world prices. So with similar indirect tax structures Poland and USSR *should* show the difference of price pattern that we find;[2] and this is a very strong argument against using consumption PPPs to make comparisons between Communist national incomes.

As to per capita outputs in other countries, we have the figures below (Table 6). Originally for various years, these results have all been brought to the year 1965 by means of the GNP growth figures in our table or in other good sources.[3]

This table can only be described as 'all over the place'. The only

---

[1] Philip Hanson, *The Consumer in the Soviet Economy* (London, 1968), pp. 88–9, 131.

[2] The US indirect tax structure is surprisingly similar. Such taxes are 13% of consumption at market prices, as opposed to 20% in USSR.

[3] I have used Ernst and Cohn as in the table. Note that I have, in cases H and I, corrected comparisons of the international level of consumption by means of GNP growth rates. Most of these references are from M. Kaser, *Comecon* (2nd ed., London, 1967), p. 206. I have omitted J. Smilek in *Hospodarske Noviny*, 29 (1966), and A. Karpinski and B. Zielinska in *Gospodarka Planowa* 6 (1962), as they explain their methods too little; and the national income estimates of Kotkovski himself, op. cit., p. 88, as his methods are obviously too crude. However Kotkovski explains his consumption estimates re-assuringly, and he gives (op. cit., p. 83) a good bibliography of Communist sources.

Table 6 *National Income per capita, 1965* (DDR = 100)

Method	Czechoslovakia	Hungary	Poland	Rumania	Bulgaria	USA	USSR	West Germany	original year
NMP or GNP									
(J) A	87	80	76	50	51	—	—	—	1958
(TC) B	92	69	62	43	48	164	78	—	1955
(J) C	93	59	58	49	56	—	70	—	1964
(GK) D	97	—	61	—	67	—	72	—	1959–60
(J) E	89	68	56	38	48	—	66	—	1960
(GK, TC) F	100	70	62	50	52	227	86	—	1965
(TC, GK) G	102	73	63	49	50	233	—	140	1964
(J) H	85	59	55	44	52	280	68	134	1965
Consumption									
(J) I	105	56	59	61	48	363	95	228	1960

Note: (J) means Jánossy, (TC) Tarn–Campbell, (GK) Gilbert–Kravis.

Sources: (A) J. Novozamsky, *Vyrovnavani ekonomicke urovne zemi RVHP* (Prague, 1965), pp. 22–23 (Jánossy method); (B) Pryor and Staller, op. cit. (Tarn–Campbell method, variously weighted); (C) Novozamsky, *Politicka Ekonomie*, no. 8 (1966), p. 731 (Jánossy method); (D) Kotkovski, op. cit., combining his consumption figures on p. 88 with his accumulation figures on p. 89. Both are by Gilbert–Kravis methods, and I have weighted them by the official proportions between accumulation and consumption in the current yearbooks; (E) F. Jánossy, op. cit. (Jánossy method); (F) *Soviet Economic Performance: 1966–67* (Joint Economic Committee of Congress, May, 1968), pp. 12, 16, 119. I have added the US figure myself. (G) M. Ernst in *New Directions in the Soviet Economy* (Joint Economic Committee of Congress, 1966), p. 877 (Tarn–Campbell and Gilbert–Kravis methods). I have added the US figure myself; (H) Eva Ehrlich, *Nemzetközi Elemzesek a Magyar Tavlati Tervezeshez*, vol. A (Hungarian National Planning Office, 1968), p. 50 (Jánossy method); (I) W. Beckerman and R. Bacon, *Economic Journal* (September 1966), p. 533 (Jánossy method).

rows that contain no evident absurdity are F and G. Their weighting is disputable, they embody too many subordinate calculations such as the conversion of DM(W) into dollars, and these calculations have nowhere been published. But they are for a recent date and have been recently revised. It is reassuring that these 'prize' rows are on the Gilbert–Kravis and the Tarn–Campbell methods. By comparison the Jánossy method shows up badly. A has implausibly high figures for Hungary and Poland; C for Bulgaria; E puts Rumania too low; G is absurdly favourable to Rumania, USA, USSR and West Germany. H is too low for Hungary, too high for USA. But other methods too can err: B is too low for USA, and D too high for Bulgaria.

In this unsatisfactory situation I have simply accepted F (the revised version of G), and based all results on the US figure of $3,501 per head p.a. in 1965.